ISSUES OF
WAR AND PEACE

ISSUES OF WAR AND PEACE

Nancy Gentile Ford

Major Issues in American History
Randall M. Miller, Series Editor

GREENWOOD PRESS
Westport, Connecticut • London

Library of Congress Cataloging-in-Publication Data

Ford, Nancy Gentile, 1954–
    Issues of war and peace / Nancy Gentile Ford.
      p. cm.—(Major issues in American history, ISSN 1535–3192)
    Includes bibliographical references and index.
    ISBN 0–313–31196–X
    1. United States—History, Military—Case studies. 2. United States—History,
Military—Sources. 3. War and society—United States—History—Case studies.
4. War and society—United States—History—Sources. I. Title. II. Series.
E181.F675 2002
355'.00973—dc21   2001019986

British Library Cataloguing in Publication Data is available.

Library of Congress Catalog Card Number: 2001019986
ISBN: 0–313–31196–X
ISSN: 1535–3192

First published in 2002

Greenwood Press, 88 Post Road West, Westport, CT 06881
An imprint of Greenwood Publishing Group, Inc.
www.greenwood.com

Printed in the United States of America

The paper used in this book complies with the
Permanent Paper Standard issued by the National
Information Standards Organization (Z39.48–1984).

10 9 8 7 6 5 4 3 2 1

Copyright Acknowledgments

The author and publisher gratefully acknowledge permission to reprint the following material.

"A Whig," originally republished in Frank Moore, ed., *Diary of the American Revolution* (New York: Charles Scribner, 1860). Reprinted with permission from William Dudley, ed., *The American Revolution: Opposing Viewpoints* (Greenhaven Press, 1992), pp. 184–187.

"Aedanus Burke's Address to the Freemen of the State of South Carolina, 1783." Reprinted with permission from William Dudley, ed., *The American Revolution: Opposing Viewpoints* (Greenhaven Press, 1992), pp. 184–187.

"The Federalist Position on Militias at the Hartford Convention, 1814." From *The Proceedings of a Convention of Delegates* (Boston: Wells and Lilly, 1815), pp. 6–11. Reprinted by permission of the John Hay Library, Brown University, Providence, Rhode Island.

"Resolutions of the Hartford Convention, 1814." From *The Proceedings of a Convention of Delegates* (Boston: Wells and Lilly, 1815), pp. 21–22. Reprinted by permission of the John Hay Library, Brown University, Providence, Rhode Island.

"Eyewitness Account of the New York City Draft Riot." From By Eye Witnesses, *The Bloody Week! Riot, Murder & Arson, Containing a Full Account of This Wholesale Outrage on Life and Property* (New York: Coutant & Baker, Publishers, 1863). Reprinted by permission of the John Hay Library, Brown University, Providence, Rhode Island.

"A Popular Song Laments the Draft." From "When This Cruel Draft Is Over," Broadside, c. 1863. Reprinted by permission of the New York Historical Society.

"The Hiroshima Diary of Doctor Michihiko Hachiya, August 6, 1945." From *Hiroshima Diary: The Journal of a Japanese Physician, August 6–September 30, 1945* by Michihiko Hachiya, translated by Warner Wells, M.D. Copyright © 1955 by the University of North Carolina Press. Used by permission of the publisher.

"Harold L. Ickes Compares Nathan Hale and Douglas MacArthur, May 7, 1951." From "Harold L. Ickes: Nathan Hale and MacArthur," *The New Republic*, May 7, 1951, p. 15.

"The Stars and Stripes Criticizes the Firing of MacArthur, April 19, 1951." From "Fired the Wrong Man," *The Stars and Stripes*, April 19, 1951, p. 1.

Dedicated to
my husband, David

Contents

Series Foreword

This series of books presents major issues in American history as they have developed since the Republic's inception to their present incarnation. The issues range across the spectrum of American experience and encompass political, economic, social, and cultural concerns. By focusing on the major issues in American history, the series emphasizes the importance of an issues-centered approach to teaching and thinking about America's past. Major Issues in American History thus reframes historical inquiry in terms of themes and problems, rather than as mere chronology. In so doing, the series addresses the current, pressing need among educators and policymakers for case studies charting the development of major issues over time so as to make it possible to approach such issues intelligently in our time.

The series is premised on the belief that understanding America demands grasping the contentious nature of its past and applying that understanding to current issues in politics, law, government, society, and culture. If "America" was born as, and remains, an idea and an experiment, as many thinkers and observers have argued, issues inevitably have shaped whatever that America was and is. In 1801, in his presidential inaugural address, Thomas Jefferson reminded Americans that the great strength of the new nation resided in the broad consensus citizens shared as to the rightness and necessity of republican government and the Constitution. That consensus, Jefferson continued, made dissent possible and tolerable and, we might add, encouraged dissent and debate about critical issues thereafter. Every generation of Americans has wrestled with such issues as defining and defending freedom(s), determining America's place in the world, waging war and making peace, receiving and assimilating new peoples, balancing church and state, forming a "more perfect union," and pursuing "happiness." American identity (identities) and interest(s) are not fixed. A nation of many peoples on the move across space and up and down the socioeconomic ladder cannot have it so. A nation charged with ensuring that, in Abraham Lincoln's words, "government of the people, by the people, for the people, shall not perish from the earth" cannot have it so. A nation whose heroes are not only soldiers and statesmen but also ex-slaves, women reformers, inventors, thinkers, and cowboys and Indians cannot have it so. Americans have never rested content with being locked into set molds in thinking and doing—not as long as dissent and difference are built into the character of a people that dates its birth to the American Revolution and annually celebrates that lineage. As such, Americans have been, and are, by heritage and habit an issues-oriented people.

We are also a political people. Issues as varied as race relations, labor organizing, women's place in the workforce, the practice of religious beliefs, immigration, westward movement, and environmental protection have been, and remain, matters of public concern and debate and readily intrude into politics. A people committed to "rights" invariably argues for them, low voter turnout in recent elections notwithstanding. All the major issues in American history have involved political controversies as to their meaning and application, but the extent to which issues assume a political cast varies.

As the public interest spread to virtually every aspect of life during the twentieth century—into boardrooms, ballparks, and even bedrooms— the political compass enlarged with it. In time, every economic, social, and cultural issue of consequence in the United States has entered the public realm of debate and political engagement. Questions of rights— for example, freedom of speech, freedom of religion, and equality before the law—and authority are political by nature. So, too, are questions about war and society, foreign policy, law and order, the delivery of public services, the control of the nation's borders, and access to and the uses of public land and resources. The books in Major Issues in American History take up just these issues. Thus all the books in this series build political and public policy concerns into their basic framework.

The format for the series speaks directly to the issues-centered character of the American people and the democratic polity and to the teaching of issues-centered history. The issues-centered approach to history views the past thematically. Such a history respects chronology but does not attempt to recite a single narrative or simple historical chronology of "facts." Rather, issues-centered history is problem-solving history. It organizes historical inquiry around a series of questions central to understanding the character and functions of American life, culture, ideas, politics, and institutions. Such questions invariably derive from current concerns that demand historical perspective. Whether they are determining the role of women and minorities in shaping public policy, or considering the "proper" relationship between church and state, or thinking about U.S. military obligations in the global context, to name several persistent issues, the teacher and the student—indeed, responsible citizens everywhere—must ask such questions as "how and why did the present circumstance and interests come to be as they are?" and "what other choices as to policy and practice have there been?" so as to measure the dimensions and point the direction of the issue. History matters in that regard.

Each book in the series focuses on a particular issue with an eye to encouraging readers and users to consider how Americans at different times have engaged the issue based on the particular values, interests, and political and social structures of the day. As such, each book is also necessarily events based in that the key event that triggered public concern and debate about a major issue at a particular moment serves as the case study for the issue as it was understood and presented during that historical period. Each book offers a historical narrative overview of a major issue as it evolved; the narrative provides both the context for understanding the issue's place in the larger American experience and the touchstone for considering the ways Americans encountered and engaged the issue at different times. A chronology of events further establishes the place of the issue in American history. The core of each book is the series of between ten and fifteen case studies of watershed events that defined the issue, arranged chronologically to make it possible to track the development of the issue closely over time. Each case study stands as a separate chapter that opens with a historical overview of the event and a discussion of the significant contemporary opposing views of the issue as occasioned by the event. A selection of five to eight critical primary documents (printed whole or in excerpts and introduced with brief headnotes) from the period under review presents differing points of view on the issue. Each chapter also includes an annotated research guide of print and nonprint sources to guide further research and reflection on the event and the issue. Each volume in the series concludes with a general bibliography that provides ready reference to the key works on the subject at issue.

Such an arrangement ensures that readers and users—students and teachers alike—will approach the major issues within a problem-solving framework. Indeed, the design of the series and each book in it demands that students and teachers understand that the crucial issues of American history have histories and that the significance of these issues might best be discovered and recovered by understanding how Americans at different times addressed them, shaped them, and bequeathed them to the next generation. Such a dialectic for each issue encourages a comparative perspective not only in seeing America's past but also, and perhaps even more so, in thinking about its present. Individually and collectively, the books in the Major Issues in American History series thereby demonstrate anew William Faulkner's dictum that the past is never past.

Randall M. Miller
Series Editor

Preface

I was very excited when Randall Miller, the series editor, asked me to write this book. "War and Society" is my favorite class to teach, since it gives me an opportunity to combine social, cultural, political, religious, economic, and diplomatic history with military history. In this book, I have chosen eleven case studies that reflect key debates on war and society in U.S. history from the American Revolution through the Persian Gulf War. Each debate is followed by a selection of primary sources contemporary to the time that express a variety of viewpoints on the issue. Sources include excerpts from speeches, diaries, pamphlets, broadsides, songs, newspaper articles, congressional debates, and government reports. The debates and documents help bring to light the complexities of American military conflicts and allow us to better understand crucial issues in the study of war and peace.

Many of the documents came from historical archives, including the U.S. Army Military History Institute (MHI), Carlisle Barracks, Carlisle, Pennsylvania; the Swarthmore College Peace Library, Swarthmore, Pennsylvania; the John Hay Library, Brown University, Providence, Rhode Island; the New York Historical Society, New York, New York; the National Archives, Mid Atlantic Region, Philadelphia, Pennsylvania; the National Archives, College Park, Maryland; and the Historical Society of Pennsylvania, Philadelphia, Pennsylvania. Special thanks to all the dedicated archivists and librarians who make the historians' job much easier. A number of newspapers, news magazines, and academic presses gave me permission to reprint documents, including *Time*, the *New Re-*

public, the *New York Times*, the *Stars and Stripes*, University of North Carolina Press, and W.W. Norton & Company. Thanks also to Orville Schell and Jonathan Schell for allowing me to reprint their "Letter to the Editor" in the *New York Times*.

For sparking my interest in the study of war and society, I am grateful to Kenneth L. Kusmer, Russell F. Weigley, and Randall Miller. Their commitment to history and their impressive scholarship continue to inspire me. I am grateful to Bloomsburg University of Pennsylvania for giving me a Research and Development Grant, reassignment time, and a sabbatical in order to complete this book. Thanks also to Barbara Radar and Betty Pessagno at Greenwood Press for their important assistance.

I also am indebted to friends and family who helped me with this project. First, I must thank my friend and colleague Doug Karsner for reading the entire manuscript and giving me important feedback. His guidance was invaluable. I am very grateful to Sandy Yule, who typed most of the primary source documents in this book. Thanks also to Jen Albertson, Heather Yoder, and Jamie Hunsinger who finished the typing project; Annie Barnhard and Kara Schultz, who helped to proofread the documents (a very tedious job at best); and Woody Holton, Jennifer Keene, Bill Hudon, and Jeff Davis, who offered advice. Thanks also to all my friends at *Mail Room Etc.*

Much-needed moral support came from my family: Sam, Jackie, Frank, Lorrie, Kristi, Julie, Jim, Denise, Jessica, Nikki, Corrina, and Jake Gentile; Bob, Pat, Robin, Mickey, Daisy, and Daphne Ford; Sherilyn Glass; Cindy O'Connell; Dale and Esther Franklin; Lee and Annie Barnhardt; Dave, Sandy, Corey, and Katie Yule; Ron, Kara, and Noah Shultz; and John, Janet, and Elizabeth Bodenman. Trying to finish much of this book during a sabbatical led to many all-nighters and a neglected house, husband, and child. Thanks to Miranda, my wonderful stepdaughter, for being patient with me as I struggled to finish this book. Above all else, I am appreciative of my husband, David, who took care of our house, daughter, pets, and me while starting a new job and also reading this entire manuscript. His love and support gave me the needed energy to complete the task. David, I dedicate this book to you with all my love.

Chronology of Events

1775	Fighting begins in Lexington and Concord; the Continental army is created.
1776	Declaration of Independence is signed.
1777	Battle of Saratoga takes place.
1778	French and American military alliance is concluded.
1780	Battle of Kings Mountain is fought.
1781	British forces surrender at Yorktown; American Revolution ends.
1789	French Revolution begins.
1792	Militia Act of 1792 is passed.
1793	England and France go to war.
1794	Whiskey Rebellion in Pennsylvania occurs.
1795	Jay Treaty with British is ratified.
1798	XYZ Affair is announced to the public; United States and France enter Quasi-War; Alien and Sedition acts are passed.
1802	West Point Military Academy is founded.
1803–1804	American campaign against Tripoli takes place.

1807   Embargo Act is passed.

1809   Non-Intercourse Act is passed; Embargo Act is repealed.

1810   Macon's Bill No. 2 is enacted.

1811   Battle of Tippecanoe takes place.

1812   Congress declares war against Britain.

1814–1815   Hartford Convention of New England Federalists is held; Battle of Horseshoe Bend takes place; Treaty of Ghent ends War of 1812.

1815   Battle of New Orleans is fought.

1821   Mexico gains independence from Spain; Stephen F. Austin settles the first American community in Texas.

1823   Monroe Doctrine is announced.

1830   Indian Removal Act is passed; Mexico closes Texas to further American settlement.

1836   Texas declares independence from Mexico.

1838   Cherokee Removal—Trail of Tears occurs.

1845   Texas annexed by joint resolution of Congress.

1846   Congress declares war upon Mexico; Wilmot Proviso passes in the House.

1847   Wilmot Proviso is reintroduced but fails to pass in the Senate.

1848   Treaty of Guadalupe Hidalgo formally ends Mexican War.

1850   Compromise of 1850 is formulated.

1854   Kansas-Nebraska Act is passed.

1857   Dred Scott Supreme Court decision is announced.

1858   Lincoln-Douglas debates are held.

1860   South Carolina secedes from the Union.

1861   Confederate States of America is established; Civil War begins as Confederates fire on Fort Sumter; the First Battle of Bull Run takes place.

1862   Battles of Shiloh, Bull Run (second), and Antietam are staged.

1863   Emancipation Proclamation is issued; battles of Gettysburg and Vicksburg take place; New York City draft riot begins.

1864   Sherman marches through Georgia.

1865   Civil War ends; Lincoln is assassinated.

1865–1867   Great Sioux War takes place.

1867   Reconstruction Act of 1867 is passed.

1869   Board of Indian Commissioners is created.

1874–1875   Sioux fight to keep the Black Hills of Dakotas.

1876   Battle of Little Big Horn, "Custer's Last Stand," takes place.

1877   Chief Joseph and the Nez Perce are defeated.

1884   Naval War College is created.

1887   Dawes Severalty Act is passed.

1890   Sioux Ghost Dance Movement is formed; Wounded Knee takes place; Indian Wars end; Alfred Thayer Mahan's *The Influence of Sea Power upon History* is published.

1898   Spanish-American War begins; Anti-Imperialist League is formed.

1899   Senate ratifies treaty acquiring the Philippines; guerrilla war in the Philippines begins.

1900   Army War College is created.

1903   The General Staff is developed.

1914   United States sends military to Veracruz, Mexico; First World War begins in Europe; United States begins debate over Preparedness Movement.

1917   United States enters World War I; Espionage Act is passed; Bolshevik Revolution erupts.

1918   Sedition Act is passed; World War I ends.

1928   Kellogg-Briand Pact (renouncing war) is concluded; American isolation continues.

1933   New Deal begins.

1939   World War II begins in Europe.

1941   Atlantic Charter is established; Pearl Harbor is attacked; the
            United States enters World War II against Japan and Ger-
            many.

1942   War Labor Board is formed; Emergency Price Control Act is
            passed; Japanese Americans are interned through Executive
            Order 9066.

1944   D-Day—the Allies invade Normandy to liberate France.

1945   Yalta and Potsdam conventions are held; atomic bombs are
            dropped on Hiroshima and Nagasaki; World War II ends.

1947   Truman Doctrine and Marshall Plan are announced; House
            Un-American Activities Committee holds hearings; National
            Security Act of 1947 is enacted.

1948   Berlin blockade begins; U.S. armed forces are desegregated.

1949   NATO is created; Berlin blockade ends; Soviet Union ex-
            plodes atomic bomb; China falls to the Communists.

1950   NSC-68 is created; Korean War begins; Senator McCarthy's
            anti-Communist crusade begins.

1951   Truman removes MacArthur from command in South Ko-
            rea.

1953   Korean War ends.

1954   Army-McCarthy hearings are held; French surrender to Viet-
            minh at Dienbienphu; CIA stages coups in Iran and Guate-
            mala.

1955   Warsaw Pact is created.

1956   Hungarian Revolt—Communist forces overrun Hungary.

1960   American U-2 plane is shot down by Soviets; the Green Be-
            rets are organized.

1961   President Eisenhower warns against the dangers of the
            military-industrial complex; Bay of Pigs invasion of Cuba
            takes place.

1962   Cuban Missile Crisis occurs.

1964   Gulf of Tonkin Resolution is announced.

1965   North Vietnam is bombed with Operation Rolling Thunder;
            antiwar march on Washington takes place.

1967   Vietnam Veterans Against the War is formed.

1968	Tet Offensive in Vietnam occurs; My Lai Massacre takes place.
1972	North Vietnam is bombed on Christmas Day.
1973	Vietnam cease-fire is concluded.
1975	South Vietnam falls to North Vietnamese Communists.
1979	SALT II Treaty is signed in Vienna but stalls in the Senate; Iranian fundamentalists seize U.S. embassy in Tehran and take hostages.
1982	U.S. peacekeeping troops are sent to Lebanon.
1983	U.S. sends troops to Grenada; Marines are killed by car bomb in Lebanon.
1983	President Reagan announces Strategic Defense Initiative; Beirut terrorist bombing kills 241 marines; marines attack anti-American regime on Grenada.
1985	Mikhail Gorbachev initiates reforms in the Soviet Union.
1986	U.S. air attack on Libya takes place; Iran-Contra Affair comes to light.
1987	Iran-Contra hearings are held.
1989	Berlin Wall is torn down.
1990	Iraq invades Kuwait.
1991	Persian Gulf War begins; Iraq is bombed; Persian Gulf War ends.
1992	U.S. troops sent to Somalia.
1994	United Nations launches air attack on Serbian strongholds in Bosnia.
1999	Americans troops join NATO's Kosovo mission to stop Serbian "ethnic cleansing."

Introduction

In the words of British war correspondent Colonel Charles à Court Repington, "the history of mankind is the history of war." War has always been central to American identity. With more than a dozen military conflicts, including a Revolutionary War, a Civil War, two World Wars, and a protracted Cold War fought since the birth of the United States, war is an intricate part of American society. Each war propelled the nation toward key changes during and after each conflict as it transformed the political, economic, social, and cultural characteristics of the home front. Likewise, these same characteristics directly affected the formation and design of the U.S. armed forces and helped direct its military strategy. In addition, many military men used their victories on the battlefield to win public office and became an important part of the American political scene.

Recently, scholars have embarked on a new and exciting approach to military history that extends beyond the "top-down" writings of traditional historians preoccupied with the actions of generals and the older "drum and bugle" interpretations of combat. The conventional approach almost exclusively focused on the role of military leaders and provided specific details of skirmishes and battles. "New military" historians now incorporate the experiences of the "common soldier" and look at broader issues of class, race, ethnicity, gender, and citizenship in war. In addition, these scholars link military history with cultural and social issues and explore the interconnections of political, economic, religious, diplomatic, and cultural aspects that affect both war and society. Historians investigate how these aspects altered the structure, power, and strategy of the U.S. military and continually redefined civil-military relationships. Historians also study the significant transformation that occurred in both the military and civilian communities due to the long geopolitical struggle between the Soviet Union and the United States. This new approach, often called social-military history, represents the advance guard of the field, and it results in a complex examination of war and society in America. This book utilizes the new military history to understand the American way of war.

The United States was born in war. Military conflicts shaped and reshaped the nation throughout its history. The legacy of American military traditions grew out of its colonial experience, when the settlers began to depend on militia forces for protection from Indians and belligerent European nations. Creating a professional army was out of the question, since colonists could not dedicate the manpower or afford the cost of such organizations, nor did they have the authority to create a permanent army. In addition, some settlers, such as German pacifists, came to America to escape compulsory military service. By the mid-eighteenth century, American colonists who knew of the writings of European philosophers that warned against standing armies as a threat to liberty were leery of any effort to maintain a large professional force. Colonists only had to look to the past—to the Roman Empire or the English Civil War—for examples of military oppression, and as historian Russell Weigley noted, subsequently they "guarded jealously the principle of civilian control of the military."[1] But settlers were hardly opposed to a military. While pacifist rulers of Quaker Pennsylvania rejected the militia system, all other colonies supported it and mandated universal white adult male military service. Citizens trained to be soldiers in order to take up arms and answer the call in a crisis. Colonists also expected the British army and navy to protect them from Indians on the frontier and rival European powers and pirates elsewhere. However, beginning in the eighteenth century, the American experience with the British army during the imperial wars made them suspicious and resentful of the military of the mother country.

The American Revolution revealed both the intrinsic problems with the militia system and the complexities of fighting a war in an atmosphere of widespread apathy and political dissent. Training citizens to be part-time soldiers did not come without problems. In a largely agricultural society, many could not commit to long-term engagements that went beyond the defense of their own communities, and most were not trained or equipped to go up against England's professional soldiers. Therefore, in 1775, the Continental Congress sanctioned the development of the Continental army and selected Colonel (soon to be General) George Washington to lead the troops. Many American military leaders, especially General Washington, preferred the more disciplined, trained Continental army to the militia when engaged in a conflict with the "redcoats." But the Continental Congress remained suspicious of a "national army" and, lacking many resources and any taxing power, jealously meted out their support. The Patriots fought the war with a core from the Continental army and the assistance of French soldiers, along with a large number of "irregulars" (militia, partisans) who rallied to defend their home areas when British or Loyalist forces threatened. The new nation's victory against the British in 1781 demonstrated that despite problems with the militias, many of these groups played a critical part in helping the Continental army defeat the enemy. Their success, though limited, created the legendary image of citizen-soldiers as heroes of the War of Independence. Indeed, the picture of the gallant Patriot militiamen made up of citizen-soldiers and bands of partisan frontiersmen doing battle with skilled British regulars is ingrained in the American national consciousness.

The Revolution also reflected the harsh divisions caused by popular dissent in war. The idea of a cohesive group of Americans taking up arms against the oppressive British monarchy represents the popular image of America's rebel forces, but, in truth, the new nation was far from unified. American Loyalists and Patriots engaged in heated debates over the political, economic, and ideological pros and cons of independence in newspapers and pamphlets, and such differences sometimes burst into deadly violence. The War of Independence also became a civil war. Many American Loyalists took up arms with the British troops or formed their own militias under British command. American Patriot militiamen clashed with American Loyalist militiamen in battle, particularly in the southern campaign. At the same time, slaves ran to British lines seeking freedom, dissenters prowled the countryside, and mutineers in the American army threatened military order. War seemed to be tearing the fledgling "United" States apart.

When the conflict against the British ended, it became increasingly clear that the United States needed a stronger federal government. Popular uprisings against the new government, such as the 1786 Shays' Rebellion, and democratic dissent led some political leaders to fear that the republican experiment would unravel before it got started. Delegates to the Constitutional Convention of 1787 addressed questions concerning the power of the states versus the federal government and the need for a strong standing army. The provision in the Constitution for creating an army reflected the concern of leaders, such as Washington, that without such power the United States would gain neither respect nor the ability to protect their vital interests. The decision, however, was directly tied to deeply held ideological beliefs concerning the obligation of citizens to defend their new nation, and the fear that a standing army could prove, in Samuel Adams's words, "dangerous to the liberties of the people."[2] Eventually, the Founding Fathers settled on a two-army tradition—state militias and a small regular army, initially of 1,216 men. Although supporters of militia reform failed to place state militias under federal supervision, the Militia Act of 1792 required all free, white, "able-bodied" male citizens (between the ages of 18 and 45) to serve in the militia. Fearing the possibility of excessive power in the Executive Branch, leaders agreed that Congress should hold the power to declare war.[3]

The ratification of the Constitution in 1788 and the Bill of Rights in 1791 did not end the tensions among many Americans over the direction of the new nation during the late eighteenth century. Moreover, developments in Europe affected military thinking in the United States. The French Revolution forced Americans' hand as war spread over the Atlantic world. Disagreements regarding federal power, economic principles, and foreign policy intensified within the United States as the war between Great Britain and France threatened to envelop the young republic. Angry over raids on merchant ships and Europe's lack of respect for America's rights of neutrality, the United States endeavored to negotiate. Diplomatic attempts, such as the Jay Treaty with England and the XYZ Affair with France, did not get the intended results. Therefore, President John Adams (elected in 1796) successfully pressed Congress for revival of the American navy, while Alexander Hamilton (leader of the Federalist party) argued for a substantial increase in the regular army. Congress created the Department of the Navy in April 1798 and approved a "new army" of up to 10,000 men. (The "old army" remained on the frontier.) Prior to this, the U.S. government used a smaller military force to put down the Pennsylvania Whiskey Rebellion in 1794, and to open and defend the West to early expansion. Congress also allowed for the president to call another 30,000 men into service in the event of war. Under the stress of a looming conflict, the Federalist-dominated Congress passed the Alien and Sedition acts (1798). The Federalists expected the Alien Act to keep immigrants, especially radical Frenchmen, at bay by making it more difficult for aliens to participate in American political life, and the Sedition Act to shut down the voice of Federalist opponents, the Jeffersonian Democratic-Republicans. America had failed its first test of preserving civil liberties under the strains of an approaching war. Although President Thomas Jefferson (Democratic-Republican, elected in 1800) suspended the Alien and Sedition acts and began to dismantle the new army upon taking office, he understood the importance of educating army officers, and he supported the establishment of the United States Military Academy at West Point. As America continued to be pulled into the European conflict, Jefferson and his successor, James Madison (elected 1808), tried but failed to solve the problems with trade embargoes, and both presidents began slowly to rebuild America's military strength. During the early years of the nineteenth century, the strains between Britain and the United States mounted.

Anglo-American and Indian-settler tensions deteriorated further with events in the American West. Although the British finally removed their troops from the Northwest as promised years before, American settlers remained convinced the British were continuing to cause problems by turning the Indians against them on the frontier. The friction between Indians and American settlers broke into military conflict when American leaders, such as Indiana governor William Henry Harrison, demanded that tribes give up their land. Harrison's fame from the 1811 Battle of Tippecanoe helped win him the presidency thirty years later.

By June 1812, just three decades after the American Revolution, the United States was once again at war with Great Britain. The fierce contentions between Federalists and Republicans did not end with the declaration of war. Instead, a critical debate arose over the Republican-dominated government's right to use the state militias in Federalist-dominated New England. The War of 1812 brought to a head the long and heated debate over states' rights versus federal power, especially as it related to the federalization of state armies. At the Hartford Convention (December 15, 1814 to January 5, 1815), New England Federalists stood strong in protest of federal military policies, but the war ended before the issue could be fully tested.

Ironically, the most famous battle, that at New Orleans, took place after peace was declared. This victory for General Andrew Jackson along with the Kentucky Long Rifles and Tennessee Volunteers not only perpetuated the myth of the moral and military superiority of the citizen-soldier, but also allowed the general to use his popularity as a national hero to gain the presidency. Riding the wave of postwar nationalism, supporters of military reform applauded the establishment of a postwar American army of 12,000 men and the commitment to build up, incrementally, the American navy to improve its coastal defense.

The Mexican-American War, which began in 1846, brought new challenges as fierce debates over the possible acquisition of western lands exacerbated sectionalism and intense arguments over slavery and military policy. The debate started with the Wilmot Proviso in August 1846. As part of the Two Million Bill, Congressman David Wilmot sought to prevent the expansion of slavery into any new territory acquired in the war against Mexico. When the bill failed to pass the Senate, it was reintroduced with the Three Million Bill in February 1847. Like the Two Million Bill, this latter bill would give President James K. Polk funds to bring a quick end to the war. In reality, Polk intended to use the money to secure vast Mexican lands spreading from New Mexico to California.

Once again, Wilmot tried but failed to get the Wilmot Proviso through Congress.

Debates over the bill came at a time when the spirit of Manifest Destiny gripped the nation, causing expansionists to declare that it was America's God-given right and duty to spread its "superior" institutions to the California shores. They also maintained that opening up the Pacific trade would boost the American economy. Although the Mexican War commenced with a sense of political party unity—Democrats supported the war, Whigs opposed it—the debate over expansionism helped to reshape the political scene. Arguments over the Three Million Bill and the attached proviso pushed the movement toward sectionalism as northern Whigs began to side with northern Democrats in an adamant protest against military policy and the spread of slavery. The Mexican War had a profound impact on the nation. It advanced the expansionist fever, reinstated the slavery debate to the floors of Congress, destroyed the Second Party system (Democrats vs. Whigs), created a schism between North and South, and pushed the nation on a path toward civil war.

When the Civil War came, it brought with it much confusion and chaos. It represented the nation's most tragic war, setting American against American, brother against brother. At the start of the conflict, the Union attempted to create a fighting force of state militias and volunteer forces to expand the regular army. At first, thousands of men motivated by patriotism, economic opportunity, and the thrill of war joined the cause. But as the realities of the war—widespread devastation and mounting deaths—became clear, the United States faced serious manpower shortages. By August 1862, President Abraham Lincoln and Congress turned to a federalized system of conscription.

Conscription also became one of the most controversial arguments of the time as many Americans questioned the right of the United States to institute a draft in a democracy. The system allowed for a draftee to pay a commutation fee of $300 to be excused from service or pay for a substitute. Heated debates arose over the increase of federal power and the inequity of the draft. Republicans supported national conscription, hoping this military necessity would bring more power to the federal government and expedite a shift from localism to nationalism. Northern Democrats (now a small party due to sectionalism) strongly disagreed. They protested against the inequity of the draft system, which clearly discriminated against the lower classes since the upper classes could afford to pay their way out of military service.

Although draft resistance was much in evidence in Illinois, Indiana, Iowa, Massachusetts, Michigan, Minnesota, New Hampshire, Ohio, Vermont, and Wisconsin, the New York City draft riots were the worst. They grew out of the stress and strain of a divided country engaged in a bloody civil war. But like many other issues that faced the nation, the violent five-day riots also developed from mounting tensions over political, ethnic, racial, religious, and economic issues, and a disagreement over state versus federal power. The riots helped to reform conscription policy into a more equitable system—one that disallowed commutation fees or substitutions—when the nation faced its next attempt at a national conscription during World War I.

The Civil War also ushered in a new era for the federal government since the burden of war caused the size and power of the government to expand rapidly as the Union attempted to handle the financial, logistical, and manpower needs of the war. While the South struggled for supplies and transport, the federal government's investment in the railroad system helped the Union army to achieve success and eventually transform the rails into a transcontinental system. As the southern home front faced economic hardship made worse with the Union blockade, war fueled a thriving economy in the North. The situation in the South was made worse by the Emancipation Proclamation of January 1, 1863, which served as a military strategy as well as a political statement. It not only promised to free enslaved blacks, but also to take away the agricultural and industrial labor supply of the Confederacy, and create a situation in which African Americans would run to the advancing northern army for freedom and protection. Similarly, the northern recruitment of blacks into the Union army added to the demise of the Confederacy. The Civil War also affected the role of women. Manpower shortages allowed many women to transcend gender barriers, enabling them to work as teachers, clerks, nurses, and, in some cases, doctors.[4]

The attempt to reunify the North and the South at the conclusion of the Civil War created a new role for the U.S. military, that of an occupational force. When the defeated southern leaders sought to reimpose their will on the postwar South by thwarting efforts at true freedom for black Americans, the Republican party conceded that it would need to assert federal authority to gain respect and ensure order in the former Confederacy. Congress passed the first Reconstruction Act in 1867, which divided the South into five military districts, with each district headed by a military general. In the words of historians Allan R. Millett and Peter Maslowski, "the Army became a political instrument, a role that it did not relish but undertook as a means of self-preservation." Now the U.S. military held the power to "remove and appoint officials, register voters, hold elections, regulate court proceedings, and approve state constitutions."[5] The War Department's Freedmen's Bureau attempted to protect and assist freed blacks and represented yet another new role for the American military. But the federal military in the postwar South was undermanned and short-lived. The relatively small numbers of soldiers located there were largely stationed in towns and were unable either to prevent or punish violence in the countryside. By the late 1870s, conservative white Southerners had regained control of the state governments, and the military's role had almost ended.

The end of the Civil War also brought with it a renewed expansionist spirit. But as settlers headed toward the trans-Mississippi West, they threatened the Native American "ways of life." When the government attempted to force Indians onto reservations, brutal armed conflicts erupted. For many white Americans, events like Custer's Last Stand became rallying symbols. As with previous Indian Wars over eastern lands, intense fighting lasted for years. Finally, American military prowess, the destruction of the buffalo, and the disruption of native life led to U.S. "victory" over the Plains Indians. The defeat brought to an end most organized Indian armed resistance to white encroachment by 1890, encroachment that had begun in the early 1600s and periodically manifested itself in prolonged and bloody skirmishes and battles that came in and out of focus for over three centuries.

With the end of the Indian Wars in the late nineteenth century, civilian and military leaders played an important role in the Indian Americanization Movement. Although traditional historians often portray military officers as isolated from civilian society, in actuality, many played key roles in the American political and social scene before and after their retirement from service. As in the past, many military leaders (veterans of the Civil War and/or the Indian Wars) traded wartime popularity for political and social positions. Military leaders also joined the debate over the "Indian Question." Many officers saw their reform mission as a benevolent way of helping Native Americans adjust to the modern world. Specifically, they publicly supported policies that would turn "nomadic" Indians into "sedentary agriculturists" and "uplift" and "civilize" them through the Americanization process. Brigadier General Richard H. Pratt spearheaded the Indian School Movement, which took children from their tribes, taught them English, introduced them to industrial vocations, and Christianized them. Although many tribes gave into what they saw was the inevitable, other Native Americans fought back. Many refused to send their children to Indian schools or to take land allotments. They also sent petitions to Congress protesting policies that destroyed customs "as old as the history and traditions" of their tribes. The Indian Wars marked the defeat of the trans-Mississippi tribes and began a new conquest for the soul of the Native American peoples.

During the late nineteenth century, industrialization, urbanization, and massive immigration were quickly changing the American landscape. Widespread oppression associated with unregulated capitalism—low wages, long hours, dangerous and abusive working conditions—led to widespread labor strife and frequent strikes. As with previous situations of political dissent starting in the late eighteenth century, the federal government relied on the state militias (now a volunteer group called the National Guard) and the regular army as a "national police force" to regain order. Socialized in the middle-class value system, American military officers accepted the American economic system based on capitalism. Unable to identify with the plight of the working class, officers were troubled by labor strife and worked with the government to maintain social order.[6]

By the close of the nineteenth century, Manifest Destiny, nationalism, Protestant mission, economic expansionism, and Americanization, entwined with Anglo-Saxonism and Social Darwinism, led to the quest for American empire overseas. As the imperialist spirit swelled, many reformers pushed for modernization of the U.S. military, which had fallen to an army of less than 30,000 men after the close of the Civil War and a small navy of mostly obsolete sailing vessels. Although the Indian Wars engaged the American army, the navy played a secondary role until the excitement of overseas expansion gripped the nation. In 1890 navy officer Alfred Thayer Mahan encouraged Americans to look beyond the continent and linked national economic and political success with navalism in *The Influence of Sea Power upon History*. Mahan's work confirmed the beliefs of many naval personnel and inspired others to accelerate the modernization of the U.S. Navy, especially in light of the growing technological changes in shipbuilding and steam power. Officers studied naval strategy in context with overseas expansion at the new Naval War College. During the 1898 Spanish-American War, the new U.S. Navy proved its worth by smashing the Spanish Navy in actions off the Philippine and Cuban coasts, and by the turn of the century, its size and strength fell in line with that of the European powers.[7]

Victory in the Spanish-American War catapulted the United States into a formal empire with the acquisition of Guam, Puerto Rico, and the Philippines. Although America now joined the ranks of global colonial powers, this new status did not come without resistance. Imperialists and anti-imperialists began an intensive debate over the annexation of the Philippines in 1900. The growing expansionist drive, combined with new social philosophies (Social Darwinism and Anglo-Saxonism), convinced imperialists that America, as a "superior nation," had the duty to "uplift" and "civilize" people judged "unfit" to survive on their own, such as the Filipinos. Anti-imperialists, such as Mark Twain and Jane Addams, opposed annexation. Many argued that denying the self-determination of any people undermined the virtuous principles of the Declaration of Independence and the Constitution. Other anti-imperialists, influenced by the prevalent atmosphere of the day, fought against the incorporation of "darker" peoples they deemed inferior.

The decision to annex the Philippines and the subsequent insurrection of the Filipino people challenged the nation as it stood at the crossroads of overseas expansion. The American foreign policy elite chose empire. The lessons learned from this experience helped accelerate the modernization of the U.S. Army and Navy and to bring the country closer to the status of a world power.

The overseas conflicts made it abundantly clear that much like the old navy, the army was in desperate need of improvement, too. Acute supply and logistical problems, combined with outdated equipment, wool uniforms, "embalmed" meat, and a general state of chaos, made fighting the Spanish-American War and Philippine Insurrection difficult. In the early years of the twentieth century, with both wars behind the United States, Secretary of War Elihu Root led a group of army reformers to professionalize and modernize the army. Reformers convinced Congress to establish the General Staff in February 1903, with "supervisory authority" over the War Department and the military branches. A chief of staff now advised the president and the secretary of war. Congress increased the size of the regular army to 3,820 officers and 84,799 men, and the federal government expanded its power to include more of a "dual control" over the state National Guard units. Federal funding paid for training and new equipment, and Congress set standards for commissioning officers and recruiting citizen-soldiers. Other reforms included the army educational reforms, the establishment of the Army War College, and the joint cooperation of the army and navy branches.[8]

With the dawn of a new century, the United States began to embrace its new role as a recognized world power. But would it be ready to fight when needed? At the turn of the century, American military and political leaders began an intense debate over universal military training and service. Advocates argued that America needed to train an army of citizen reservists to be ready for possible war and considered the militia and volunteer army antiquated at best. Mandatory military training would allow a regular force of 100,000 men to be quickly and efficiently expanded into a mass army. But others deemed obligatory military service undemocratic. As Europe once again tumbled into war in 1914, the debate over preparedness continued. But now it became complicated by a new argument over whether the United States should join the conflict. By the spring of 1917, the United States entered World War I, and young Americans found themselves drafted to fight and die in trench warfare and in confrontations on the high seas. Mass conscription replaced the old volunteer army because of the manpower demands of modern industrial wars.

The nation was not unified behind the war. Class, ethnic, and ideological diversity, along with the unpopular nature of the conflict, convinced U.S. leaders to mobilize public opinion. In carefully constructed propaganda designed to "sell" the war to the American people, the U.S. government demanded undying loyalty and total conformity. The Espionage and Sedition acts (1917 and 1918, respectively) exacerbated the growing atmosphere of mistrust and led to censorship of both the spoken and written word. Fueled by the alarming jingoistic fever, hysteria soon gripped the nation, as super-patriots attacked the peace community and radicals who opposed U.S. involvement in the European war. Members of various ethnic groups, especially German-Americans, also became targets. Freedom of speech and press were trampled in the rush for unity of purpose, and arguments between dissenters and government propagandists exploded over civil rights and democracy. Dissenters fought back through speeches, pamphlets, public demonstrations, and the legal system. They argued that the Espionage and Sedition acts directly violated the First Amendment, they questioned the constitutionality of drafting pacifists against their will, they noted the hypocrisy of "fighting for democracy" in Europe while shutting down civil liberties at home, and they worked to bring a peaceful conclusion to the war. Loss of civil liberties in the war led to the creation of the American Civil Liberties Union.

World War I created a tremendous strain on society, as the nation struggled to balance its democratic principles with its need for a united home front. The failure to do so further divided the country and created a postwar atmosphere that made radicalism, ethnic pride, and pacifism difficult and even unacceptable. The postwar years also served once again to transform the military. American society, now determined to remain isolated from world affairs, established neutrality acts at home and international peace agreements abroad. America also began to reduce its army and navy. The National Defense Act of 1920 established an alternative to a strong standing army by relying on the National Guard that could reach up to 435,000 troops. This federal reserve force would supplement the regular army of 280,000 officers and men. If needed, the government could also rely on World War I veterans.[9]

Soon, the army and navy scrambled to keep an effective fighting force under the constraints of dwindling military budgets, and the branches fiercely competed for limited funds. This development became even more pronounced when new air warriors began to demand "a piece of the pie." The industrial revolution introduced new and deadly weapons to the World War I arsenal, including machine guns, submarines, and airplanes. In the postwar years, a debate over the use of the airplane took center stage, when a number of military officers, led by Brigadier General William "Billy" Mitchell, argued that the next war would be an air war. Mitchell appealed to military leaders and Congress to support the development of an independent air force, but he had to settle for the Army Air Service. Mitchell's outspoken support of Giulio Douchet's strategic bombing doctrine caused him to fall out of favor with many of his superiors. Douchet, a European military theorist, argued for extending bombing raids beyond military installations to the enemy's industrial areas and cities. By attacking the "vital center," Douchet contended that the morale and will of the enemy people would be broken. To a world struggling to maintain the international law of noncombatant immunity—the belief that war is fought between soldiers, not civilians—Douchet's strategic bombing doctrines were rejected on moral grounds. Arguments between Congress and military leaders took their toll in 1926, when Mitchell was court-martialed for insubordination, and he retired from the army. The moral indignation over bombing civilians lost its fervency when Great Britain and Germany resorted to strategic bombing during World War II. When the United States entered the war, it reluctantly joined in the bombing raids.[10]

Wartime mobilizing in World War II resulted in the increase of government powers, already expanded from New Deal reforms. With 15 million men and women in uniform, the nation turned to its war economy to equip, clothe, and feed the troops. Laborers worked steadily and even drew overtime pay in war industries. The workforce included 19 million women. Some 14 million traded traditional domestic, waitress, and clerical jobs to build planes, ships, and other war materials. Others, some 5 million women, were employed for the first time, drawn to war work by popular patriotic images of Rosie the Riveter promoted by the government. Despite improvement in the wage system, females generally received less pay then their male counterparts, as they made temporary inroads into male-dominated positions. Many African Americans also found industrial employment during the war. Over a million blacks migrated from the South to the North and West to take jobs in war production or in the expanding federal government during World War II. This migration began prior to World War I when African Americans began to flee to the North to escape political disenfranchisement and economic discrimination. Despite economic advancement during the war, the United States continued to fight with a segregated army, and de facto discrimination greeted blacks in both the North and West.

For the United States, the bombing of Pearl Harbor and events in Europe forced America to fight a two-front war in the Atlantic and Pacific theaters. By 1945, with the European war coming to a close, American leaders still faced a major challenge to win the war against Japan. The answer soon came in the form of a new and deadly weapon. World War II saw the development of, in Secretary of War Henry L. Stimson's words, "the most terrible weapon ever known in human history"—the atomic bomb. Debates over use of the bomb against Japan erupted between scientists and American political and military leaders. Supporters of the atomic weapon argued that it would end the war quickly and save American lives. Many also saw this as a natural extension of strategic bombing campaigns, which catapulted the civilian death toll to reach into the millions. But a number of key scientists worried about releasing such a destructive force and feared that a resulting arms race could lead to the annihilation of humankind. They argued for an alternative show of strength to demonstrate the destructive power of the new weapon. Debates raged for months until atomic bombs were finally dropped on Hiroshima and Nagasaki in 1945, killing hundreds of thousands. With the end of World War II, came the release of some 110,000 Japanese Americans (mostly American citizens) interned in Relocation Camps in the United States.

Although historians continue to argue over the decision to drop the bomb, the unleashing of atomic weapons and the subsequent nuclear arms race that developed between the United States and the Soviet Union had an extraordinary impact on the future of the world. Nuclear weapons escalated the Cold War, damaged the economy, and pitted the superpowers against each other in a deadly game over Third World loyalties. President Harry S. Truman's Containment Policy gave the U.S. military new responsibilities to stop the spread of communism. Events like the Berlin blockade and airlift in 1948 further accelerated the animosity between the United States and the Soviet Union. Two opposing alliance systems, the North Atlantic Treaty Organization (NATO) and the Warsaw Pact, also divided the world. In America, the Cold War fanned the fires of a new Red Scare, led to the creation of the military-industrial complex, and brought forth a new crisis in civil defense. Many fell victim to McCarthyism as the House Un-American Activities Committee attempted to stamp out perceived "radicalism" in the government, universities, the entertainment industry, and even the U.S. Army. Cold War hysteria expanded in 1949, when the Soviets developed their own atomic bomb and China "fell" to the Chinese communist leadership. The Cold War also fueled the April 1950 National Security Council landmark recommendation known as NSC-68, which dramatically reshaped the civil-military relationship and expanded American armed forces into unprecedented numbers. The deep-rooted fear of the inherent dangers of a strong standing army disappeared under the stress and strain of the Cold War. Now millions of American men and women served in the U.S. military (finally desegregated in 1948) throughout the world. The military defense budget reached into the billions of dollars as the United States assumed the military leadership of the free world. New and deadlier nuclear weapons replaced the outdated atomic bomb, dramatically changing the nature of warfare. Fearful that global conflicts could lead to possible nuclear annihilation, future wars would be fought for limited objectives—for "balance, not victory."

America's first limited conflict took place in Korea. It began with a war to push advancing North Korean troops back across the thirty-eighth parallel that separated the communist North from the southern Republic—a division that grew out of World War II and the Cold War conflict. But as the war progressed, sharp disagreements developed between General Douglas MacArthur, who insisted that the United States throw back communism in North Korea and carry the war to "Red China," and President Harry S. Truman, who wanted to fight a limited war to contain communism without triggering an all-out war in Asia. As the two argued over military strategy and whether to escalate the conflict to unify Korea, public criticism of U.S. involvement in the "police action" rose amid frustrations over the cost in American lives for a vague concept of "containment." When MacArthur took his position to the public, many political leaders accused the general of insubordination. After Truman relieved MacArthur of command, an intense debate ensued in the public forum. Soon it reached the floor of the United States Congress. The debate over civil-military authority challenged important democratic principles that placed civilian authority above military power and led to emotional arguments over U.S. military policy—a policy now hampered by Cold War restraints and nuclear weapons. Limited war left the public endeavoring to understand this crisis of command, and their confusion rose as the Korean War continued in a stalemate that took the lives of some 54,200 young Americans.

President Dwight Eisenhower faced a new challenge when he sought to balance the federal budget, cut taxes, and reduce military expenditures. Still dedicated to containment, Eisenhower offered a "New Look" to foreign policy, which relied on nuclear superiority and the threat of massive retaliation to give "more bang for the buck." Since the Soviet Union now had the capability of responding with nuclear weapons, the dangerous standoff became known as "mutually assured destruction," or MAD. Instead of using conventional forces, the president also preferred the use of covert operations, carried out by the Central Intelligence Agency (CIA), in places like Iran and Guatemala. He argued that using the CIA saved soldiers' lives and money. During the 1950s Cold War, government military related contracts continued to entwine the American economy with a war economy as the military-industrial complex became even more incorporated into the structure of the country.

The "cold warrior" days of President John F. Kennedy shifted the focus of American foreign policy to the Third World in an attempt to build pro-Western nations. Kennedy and Secretary of Defense Robert McNamara objected to Eisenhower's "neglect" of the U.S. military and began rebuilding the conventional forces. But Kennedy's "flexible response" to world problems also included the use of the CIA and the buildup of nuclear weapons to include intercontinental ballistic missiles (ICBMs), Polaris, and submarines. Cold War tensions reached perilous levels in 1961 and 1962, when the U.S. military and the Soviet military stood in a dangerous standoff in Berlin and during the Cuban Missile Crisis, respectively. As with his predecessor, Kennedy also used American military leaders as advisors in Vietnam. There, they tried to shore up the corrupt and decaying government of Ngo Dinh Diem as South Vietnam plunged into a bloody civil war.

During the 1960s, military advisors in Vietnam turned into hundreds of thousands of American combat troops. The conflict was unlike any war in recent memory. Outgunned, the Viet Cong, as the pro-Communist South Vietnamese rebels were called, resorted to guerrilla warfare, sniper fire, booby traps, and land mines to fight their American enemy. The villager by day could easily become the enemy by night. The war was even more complex since the Viet Cong received support from Communist North Vietnam. Unable to measure success in territories gained as with past wars, the Johnson administration calculated it in body counts and attrition rates. Strategic objectives seemed unfocused as decades of involvement blurred into a quarter century. Although many American soldiers entered the Vietnam War believing they were fighting communism, they soon learned the only real goal was simply to stay alive.

The Vietnam War continued the legacy of the Cold War, as Americans fought another limited war that left the country sharply divided. Since the end of World War II, animosity between the Soviet Union and the United States—between communism and capitalism—had been played out in Third World nations in a deadly game of global power. Much like the Korean War, the conflict in Vietnam put new strains on society, caused by the confusion and chaos of the war. Antiwar protests gripped the nation, and television coverage gave Americans a steady diet of war's horrors to soldiers and civilians in South Vietnam. More and more Americans ended their support of the war. Soldiers returning on an individual rotation found themselves at home just days after leaving Vietnam. No parades, no celebration greeted them. The new president, Richard Nixon, adopted a strategy of "Vietnamization" in 1969, shifting military responsibility to South Vietnamese troops, while increasing American air strikes and withdrawing American soldiers—all to make American withdrawal orderly and seemingly policy rather than defeat. When Americans learned Nixon had "escalated" the war by bombing North Vietnamese bases in Cambodia, antiwar protests erupted across America. The killing of college students demonstrating against the war at Kent State University and Jackson State College sobered the nation. Now, Americans were killing each other over the Vietnam War. Nixon retreated and private peace talks continued. In the end, though, President Richard Nixon's "peace with honor" was just a platitude for defeat. America had lost its first war.

As the Berlin Wall fell in 1989, the United States claimed victory in the Cold War with the Soviet Union and focused on its role as the world's main peacekeeping force. When Iran invaded Kuwait in 1990, NATO forces looked to America to lead the war against Saddam Hussein. With the onset of the Persian Gulf War, the cry of "No More Vietnams" could be heard echoing throughout American society. Clearly, a protracted conflict that ended in the death of America's youth on the battlefield in the Middle East would not be acceptable.

During the Persian Gulf War, politicians, defense analysts, and military leaders argued over the nation's growing dependency on high-tech weaponry, especially its reliance on air power to win wars. This war was fought primarily with American air power in a stunning performance of technological superiority. During the conflict, many analysts even argued that the war could be won, with a nominal cost of lives, through air power alone. But others cautioned not to let the flash of new technology blind Americans into believing ground troops would be unnecessary in the Persian Gulf, and many noted it was too soon to test the effectiveness of computer-driven weaponry.

The victory in the Persian Gulf helped the nation lay the ghosts of the Vietnam War to rest by avoiding a prolonged ground war with unclear objectives. But the postwar debate over the success of the new technology continued on the floor of Congress in an intense dispute over the true effectiveness of air power. Many politicians and military analysts continue to warn the nation that future wars may not bring quick victories with minimal American losses via high-tech weaponry. This would be particularly true in fighting the unseen enemy—terrorists.

When citizen-soldiers and Continental troops took up arms against the powerful forces of the British Empire over two centuries ago, the future of the young republic was unsure. Yet, despite its tenuous beginnings, the U.S. government grew into a global power by the mid-twentieth century. During that time, America's armed forces were transformed from bands of citizen-soldiers in local militias to the largest professional military in the world. America's military expanded in both size and strength to match and then exceed its old European rivals. By the mid-twentieth century, Americans' fear of a strong standing army gave way under the pressure of intense geopolitical turmoil and modern weapons of mass destruction. As events unfolded throughout its history, the American people accepted the demise of laissez-faire government and came to permit and even expect federal intervention. Close civil-military relations became an intrinsic part of American society. Today, it is commonplace for military leaders to play a key role in advising the president and Congress in official national security positions. The American economy remains connected to military production, though much reduced from the Cold War days. As with its intervention in places like Somalia and Kosovo, the United States continues its role as a world police force, now equipped with a large standing professional and technologically adept military.

From its revolutionary past to the dawn of the twenty-first century, Americans have not always agreed on the direction of the country. The stress and strain of military conflict brought to bear passionate arguments and intense debates, as each major war served to reshape both the nation and its armed forces. Military history can be clearly understood only if war is studied in context with its relationship to social, cultural, political, religious, economic, diplomatic, and technological issues. This relationship is complex and cannot be separated. Exploring military history in any other way would be like viewing a Monet picture at close range—one would only see a multitude of colored patches. But if one steps back and takes the time to reflect on the larger picture, images emerge, connections are made, and the story becomes complete. Thus is the portrait of war and peace in America.

NOTES

1. Russell F. Weigley, *History of the United States Army* (New York: Macmillan, 1967), p. 6.

2. Ibid., p. 75; Allan R. Millett, "The Constitution and the Citizen-Solder," in Richard H. Kohn, ed., *The United States Military under the Constitution of the United States 1789–1989* (New York: New York University Press, 1991), pp. 97–119.

3. John Whiteclay Chambers II, *To Raise an Army: The Draft Comes to Modern America* (New York: Free Press, 1987), pp. 28–29.

4. Russell F. Weigley, *The American Way of War: A History of United States Military Strategy and Policy* (New York: Macmillan, 1977), p. 138.

5. Allan R. Millett and Peter Maslowski, *For the Common Defense: A Military History of the United States of America* (New York: Free Press, 1984), p. 243.

6. Ibid., p. 247.

7. Ibid., pp. 233–234; Weigley, *The American Way of War*, pp. 173–84.

8. Weigley, *History of the United States Army*, pp. 318–22; Millett and Maslowski, *For the Common Defense*, pp. 311–15.

9. Millett and Maslowski, *For the Common Defense*, p. 366; Weigley, *The American Way of War*, p. 208.

10. Weigley, *The American Way of War*, p. 226.

1

The Battle of Kings Mountain: Patriots versus Loyalists in the American Revolution

In the fall of 1780, British major Patrick Ferguson warned Carolinians in the Blue Ridge Mountains to "desist from their opposition to the British arms, and take protection under his standard [or he would] march his army over the mountains, hang their leaders, and lay their country waste with fire and sword."[1] If Ferguson thought that his threat would intimidate the frontiersmen, he was wrong. Instead, it worked to rally together previously neutral backcountry settlers who took up arms with local "Patriots" and American frontier militiamen from North Carolina and Virginia. Together, they attacked the British force at Kings Mountain, South Carolina. But this was no ordinary battle, for the ranks of Ferguson's troops were filled with Americans—all loyal to the British Crown. As fighting unfolded on a crisp October afternoon in 1780, American Patriots faced American Loyalists in a bloody battle that proved to be a decisive turning point in the American Revolution. In the words of Sir Henry Clinton, commander of the British forces, Kings Mountain "unhappily proved the first Link of a Chain of Evils that followed each other in regular Succession until they at last ended in the total loss of America."[2]

While it is heartening to portray a cohesive America unified in its conflict against Great Britain, this simply was not the reality. Colonists faced somber and complicated challenges in the years before and during their War of Independence—including the issue of loyalty. The new nation's quest for freedom eventually resulted in two conflicts—a revolution against Britain and an internal civil war pitting Americans against

Americans. Furthermore, while many military leaders debated the effectiveness of American militia forces in the Revolution, the drama in the Carolinas ultimately concluded with a key victory for the southern militia units—a victory framed by a dramatic partisan struggle. The Battle of Kings Mountain also helped perpetuate the popular image of the "virtuous" citizen-soldiers' gallant struggle as Americans took up arms to free their homeland from British tyranny—a picturesque image later ingrained in our national psyche.

PATRIOTS VERSUS LOYALISTS

In 1776, economic, political, and religious tensions between the British North American colonies and their mother country, Great Britain, led to a declaration of independence and subsequently an all-out war. Historians continue to debate the particular causes of the American Revolution. Some emphasize the British economic clampdown in the colonies, while others focus on ideological struggles over political rights. In 1765, shortly after the conclusion of the French and Indian War, the British government attempted to reduce its rising debt by imposing taxation and trade restrictions on the American colonies. Many Americans resented the growing number of British "redcoats" ever present in their cities and objected to "taxation without representation" in the British Parliament. As Americans resisted the Sugar Act, the Stamp Act, the Navigation Acts, the curtailment of western expansion, and other British policies, thirteen colonies began to unify in a common cause. Patriots also embraced republican ideology, blossoming from the American Enlightenment, which called for individual liberty and the right of the people to form their own government. Resistance—petitions, economic boycotts, demonstrations, and riots—turned to a call for independence after the attempts to seek change failed. Revolutionary leaders argued that war against the mother country was now justified and necessary.

Thomas Paine's *Common Sense* and other patriotic literature inspired nationalism and increased the growing numbers of Patriots. However, not everyone supported independence. During the Revolutionary War, Americans divided roughly into two camps, Patriots and Loyalists, and many Americans allied with neither, trying to stay neutral and out of the way of the war. To the revolutionary Patriots, "the struggle for independence was the greatest test of the chosen people. In it they bore the weight of both their heritage and God's promise for the future."[3] But not everyone agreed, and more than 20 percent of the white population—some half a million people—remained openly loyal to the British monarchy.

Loyalists could be found throughout the American colonies, but their strongholds included New York, New Jersey, and the southern colonies, especially the eastern parts of Maryland and the western areas of the Carolinas. Whatever their disagreements with British colonial policies might be, Loyalists looked with favor on America's economic, political, and cultural ties with Great Britain and did not want to sever the colonial relationship. Some among them argued that "independence" from the cosmopolitan and tempering Old World would unmoor the colonies' social order. The anti-British violence of the 1760s and 1770s led many to contend that independence would mean political chaos and civil war, perhaps even barbarism. Other Loyalists simply resisted change, while still others remained "loyal" because the "patriots" represented their old political enemies. Although many opposed British taxation and other economic restrictions, they maintained that these issues were not worthy of a revolution.

While thousands of American Loyalists fled to England during and immediately after the war, most remained behind. A number of well-known colonists from the elite classes stayed loyal to the Crown, including the governor of Massachusetts, Thomas Hutchinson; the chief justice of Massachusetts, Peter Oliver; the royal governor of New Jersey, William Franklin (son of Benjamin Franklin); and the Speaker of the Pennsylvania Assembly, Joseph Galloway. Loyalists could also be found in great numbers among older, conservative Americans who were both wealthy and educated. Many Loyalists held royal posts as customs officials or judges, while others had lucrative mercantile connections to the British economy. Clergy of the Anglican church could be found among the pro-British, as could upper-class conservative lawyers whose work tied into the British colonial bureaucracy.

In some cases, Loyalists came from the lower classes, such as many New York and New Jersey farmers, who stood in opposition to wealthy Patriot landowners. Similarly, struggling farmers living along Maryland's eastern shores and facing the burden of economic hardship turned against the elite Patriots who held wealth and political power. Many immigrant groups, such as Scots Highlanders, Scots-Irish, Germans, and French, also chose either Loyalist or Patriot sides. The Scots Highlands immigrants tended to support the Loyalists, while the Scots-Irish often became Patriots. A small number of Germans, Dutch, and French, convinced that religious freedom would be better assured under the British, became Loyalists. But many others from these same groups joined the Patriot efforts. Germans in Pennsylvania, Maryland, and Virginia, for instance, supported the Revolution in great numbers, and a large percentage of the Continental army consisted of Scots-Irish, German, and to a lesser extent, Irish soldiers. British general Henry Clinton expressed concern about the "Irish element" who fought with the Continental forces. He called them, seasoned by British oppression in their homeland and ready to fight for freedom, his "most serious Antagonists."[4]

Patriots argued that Loyalists were nothing more than traitors who betrayed the cause of American independence, and referred to them as "Tories"—a negative term taken from a conservative party in England that traditionally supported the king over Parliament. American Patriots named themselves Whigs after the English opposition party and sarcastically defined a Tory as "a thing whose head is in England and its body in America" with a neck that "ought to be stretched." In Patriot-dominated areas, Whigs intimidated, attacked, and sometimes hung Loyalists, and many Tories lost their lands, which were confiscated and sold to help pay for the rebellion. In the political "theater" of the Revolution, a few Loyalists were tarred and feathered or received the "grand Tory ride" through the streets, balancing perilously over a sharp fence rail. Such public humiliation and punishment served to remind "neutrals" and Loyalists that the Patriots would tolerate no opposition. One must choose sides. Perhaps not surprisingly, about 80,000 Loyalists fled the country for the safety of England or its other colonies.

Perhaps the situation was most complex for freed African Americans, black slaves, and Indians. As British forces overran the southern colonies/states, they recruited thousands of slaves with the promise of freedom, and many slaves living near British troops fled to serve as laborers, soldiers, and spies. Everywhere above the Carolinas, Patriots worked to rally free blacks in support of the Revolution. In some cases, enslaved African Americans received freedom in exchange for military service with the Patriots, and some 5,000 African Americans served in the American forces. Both the British and American Patriots also sought the support of the Indians. Many tribes resented the encroachment of American settlers as they expanded west, while others were tied to the American economy through trade and treaties. Eventually, Indian tribes fought on both sides, while others stayed neutral.

CITIZEN-SOLDIERS VERSUS PROFESSIONAL SOLDIERS

The American Revolution introduced the two-army tradition to the United States—the colonial/state militias and the regular army. The militia system drew together local men—"citizen-soldiers"—who organized to protect their communities. It grew out of the colonists' need for defense against Indians and European antagonists, but it also represented an inherent fear of a strong standing army. During the American Revolution, local militias made up of citizen-soldiers—farmers, frontiersmen, and townspeople—played an important role in the War of Independence. In an effort to organize a military force capable of fighting a "conventional war," the Continental Congress also agreed to form the Continental army under the leadership of George Washington in June 1775. Washington, Colonel Henry Knox (the army's senior artillerist), and other military leaders preferred to rely on the more professionally trained men in the Continental army. They argued that the militia system too often proved ineffective. Desertion was high, and untrained men frequently failed in their attempt to go up against the British army. Many militiamen also refused to leave the communities they vowed to protect. Therefore, Washington campaigned for an expanded national force.

But the notion of a strong military made some Americans uncomfortable. Many colonists had fled their homelands to escape the tyranny of monocracies and objected to obligatory military service in a national army. They argued that a strong standing army would undermine local and regional autonomy by centralizing and increasing the power of the federal government. In addition, the maintenance of such an army would be a costly burden on a people already angry over taxation. Opponents contended that a large armed force of professional soldiers could represent a threat to freedom and become an easy weapon for possible despotic leaders to use against the people. "As men whose education was heavily classical, the members [of the Continental Congress] were thoroughly aware of the military autocracies of the ancient world."[5] They pointed to Oliver Cromwell, who had established political power in Britain a century earlier after securing control of the military. But the need for additional soldiers, compounded by problems associated with short enlistments, led military leaders to speak out. In a September 24, 1776, letter to Congress, General Washington addressed the problems with the militia system and asked for expansion and improvements in the Continental army: "To place any dependence upon Militia, is, assuredly, resting upon a broken staff. Men just dragged from the tender Scenes of domestick [sic] life; unaccustomed to the din of Arms; totally unacquainted with every kind of Military skill, which being followed by a want of confidence in themselves, when opposed to Troops regularly train'd [sic], disciplined, and appointed, superior in knowledge, and superior in Arms, makes them timid, and ready to fly from their own shadows."[6] Washington also argued that militiamen were not used to "the sudden change in their manner of living" and often got sick. They also grew impatient and began to resent their loss of "unbounded freedom" as the war progressed. The general maintained that it would be "cheaper to keep 50, or 100,000 Men in constant pay" than to rely on half the number "and supply the other half occasionally by Militia." He dismissed the dangers to freedom associated with a national army, contending that "the Evils to be apprehended from one, are remote."[7] Therefore, Washington joined Knox, Alexander Hamilton, and other leaders to push for improvements in and the expansion of the Continental army.

To keep soldiers from drifting in and out of the Continental army, especially during planting and harvest seasons, Congress offered bounty money and free land as recruitment incentives to attract long-term enlistees. States also filled quotas for the army through conscription, but allowed drafted men to avoid service by paying fines or hiring substitutes. Many long-term Continental soldiers who answered the call came from the poorer classes and from the newly arrived ethnic groups. Despite the progress of the Continental army, the militias continued to play an essential part in the Revolution. Of the more than 300,000 Americans who fought in the war, approximately half served in the Continental army and half were militiamen. Partisan bands of backcountry men who took up arms to defend their homelands from approaching British soldiers also aided in America's quest for freedom.

But divided loyalties among Americans complicated an already-distressful situation as the nation quickly fragmented. More than 20,000 American Loyalists took up arms with the British regulars, while many others formed local Loyalist militias. As the war progressed, intense violence often erupted between partisan militias who terrorized each other on and off the battlefield.

THE SOUTHERN STRATEGY

By 1778, the British failure to defeat the American troops in the northern states and France's agreement to provide the Patriots with both military and economic assistance put England in a defensive position and forced the British military to reconsider its strategy. British leaders now looked south in hopes of taking advantage of strong Loyalist support in securing the region under pro-British colonial governments. The British were also responding to pressure from Loyalists and their American counterparts living in England, who demanded that the British military assist the Loyalist effort in the South. Although northern Loyalists "usually turned out only when the British army could support them and then in small numbers," the southern Loyalists did fight against southern Patriots, but "uprisings failed because they lacked British military support."[8] Hope for military success in the South now came with the combined effort of the British and Loyalist forces. The British also considered the South a valuable economic area, especially with its products of tobacco, rice, and indigo. Securing the southern colonies would put the British in a better position to protect its Caribbean trade from French encroachment. Once the South was put into the hands of Loyalist governments, the British planned to return north to continue to do battle with American Patriots in the middle and New England colonies.

In November 1778, careful to retain enough British forces to occupy New York City, British commander Clinton headed south. During the next year, British troops captured Savannah and Augusta, Georgia, overran the colony, and organized loyal militia units to fight with the British regulars. In May 1780, with a force 10,000 strong, the British focused their efforts on Charleston, South Carolina, America's fourth-largest city and the commercial center of the southern colonies. For five weeks, American forces tried to hold off the British, but they soon surrendered many of their Continental regiments—5,500 troops—in one of the most devastating defeats of the war. Charleston was lost.

After Clinton returned to New York in the spring of 1780, Major General Charles (Lord) Cornwallis, considered a skilled and forceful leader, took charge of the British troops in the South. Under Cornwallis, the British removed Patriots from office, neutralized militia forces, intimidated South Carolinians into taking loyalty oaths, and even threatened some with the option of jail or British service. In August 1780, General Horatio Gates attempted to turn the tide with American troops—both regular soldiers and inexperienced militiamen—and met the British forces in Camden, South Carolina, but the battle ended in a distressing defeat for the Americans. Cornwallis instructed Lieutenant Colonel Banastre Tarleton and Major Patrick Ferguson to chase the remaining Patriot soldiers north. It looked as if the British plan to secure the South would succeed. But at the northern border of the colony, at Kings Mountain, a band of American backcountry riflemen joined other American Patriot militiamen and stood ready to stop the American Loyalist troops.

ETHNIC AND CLASS DIVISIONS IN THE CAROLINAS

The Battle of Kings Mountain brought together Americans from different regions, ethnic groups, class standings, and ideological perspectives, and in many ways it reflected the true complexities of the Revolutionary War. Long-standing ethnic, regional, and class tensions that dominated the Carolinas in the early eighteenth century found their way into the American Revolution, especially when it came to choosing sides. Political tension divided the southern colonies into western and eastern factions, especially during the prewar Regulator movement. While other areas of the American colonies were focusing their energy on the issue of British taxation, western farmers in North Carolina protested against the oppression of eastern Carolina's colonial elite. Banding together and over 6,000 strong, this group of Regulators objected to their lack of participation in the colonial government, the corruption of colonial leaders, excessive taxation, high court costs, and western land speculation and demanded official title to their farms. In South Carolina, frontiersmen also objected to their limited role in the colony's politics, but in many ways the situation was reversed. The South Carolina colonial elite did little to help the backcountry, where gangs of bandits raided properties, stole livestock, and terrorized local farmers. With no law enforcement, courts, or jails to maintain order, Regulators felt compelled to take matters into their own hands, creating their own brand of vigilante justice. Although the establishment of a circuit court in 1769 helped end the need for the Regulators, tension between the west and the east continued and soon exploded with the onset of the American Revolution.

Like many other areas of the American colonies, North and South Carolina attracted immigrants from various parts of Europe. While English immigrants generally settled along the eastern shores, the Scots Highlanders and Germans lived inland, and Scots-Irish (formerly Lowlanders) dominated the Carolina frontiers. Highlanders emigrated directly from Scotland. However, Scots Lowlanders first migrated to Ireland during the seventeenth century, taking advantage of economic opportunities made possible when King James I continued the British subjugation of the Irish people. In the early eighteenth century, many Scots-Irish migrated to the New World, where they hoped to find better economic opportunities and religious freedom. Here they preferred the isolation and separation from authority that the backcountry could offer. Scottish Highlanders and Lowlanders "might have lived in different countries, for they were very dissimilar people and they hated each other," and these centuries-old tensions crossed the ocean to resurface in the east-west Carolina conflict.[9] By 1776, the frontier also served as the home for a sizable number of German immigrants.

At the outbreak of the Revolutionary War, the Carolinians, like inhabitants of other areas in the thirteen colonies, divided into Patriots, Loyalists, and neutrals. Scots Highlanders and recent English immigrants traditionally remained loyal to the Crown, and more than 2,000 joined Clinton's forces. Many of the backcountry Scots-Irish and Germans supported the rebellion, while others in the frontier initially chose a neutral path in the Revolution. Feuding families and hostility between locals added to the divisions between the Whigs and Tories throughout the colony. Whigs also worried about Carolinians who took a neutral stand, especially those who wanted to "enjoy the fruits of independence" without fighting for it. But many in the frontier, attracted to the area's isolation, simply wanted to stay out of the conflict.

A British officer noted the Patriots' revolutionary "passion" and found that in South Carolina, "the People of this Part of America, are infinitely more violent in their Resentments, and prejudices against England, and their determin'd Revolution more fixed to be separate from Us for ever." But many Loyalists were just as passionate in their support of the Crown and a hatred of the Patriots, and a brutal civil war ensued. "Revolutionaries and loyalists waged an intermittent, vicious vendetta war" in New York, New Jersey, and the Carolinas, particularly in South Carolina. Here, American general Nathanael Greene concluded, "the Whigs and Tories persecute each other, with little less than savage fury. There is nothing but murders and devastation in every quarter." One of Greene's aides also described the bloodshed as Americans attacked Americans. "The two opposite principles of whiggism and toryism have set the people of this country to cutting each other's throats, and scarce a day passes but some poor deluded Tory is put to death at his door."[10]

As the fighting moved south, many more Tories joined Loyalist militias or became scouts. But what made this division confusing was that South Carolinians sometimes "switched" sides. For instance, people forced to sign loyalty oaths by the British sometimes responded to excessive force from the British forces by joining the rebels. The brutality by local Loyalists and the threat of the approaching British army also pushed many "fence-sitters" from "apathy to rage." This was particularly true of the backcountry settlers, who, feeling threatened, now answered the Patriots' call.

THE BATTLE OF KINGS MOUNTAIN

Life in the backcountry was difficult. Frontier families resided in the western mountains of South Carolina and also along the Holston, Watauga, and Nolichucky rivers where Virginia, North Carolina, and what would become Tennessee joined together. Historian John Buchanan described "the Over Mountain" men as "hardened by the toil of pioneering [and] further hardened by Indian fighting": "His life could indeed be short, nasty, and brutal. But if he survived falling trees, fever, snake bites, drowning, disease, backbreaking labor, blood poisoning, and the scalping knife, he rode into a fight a warrior for the ages."[11]

In addition to the setbacks with the British occupation of Charleston and Gates's defeat at Camden came the treason of Benedict Arnold—all creating a series of devastating blows to the Patriot forces. Things were particularly critical in the South, where "redcoats" under Cornwallis were now successfully heading toward North Carolina. To make matters worse, word soon came that the British had hung several Carolinians who—after being forced to sign loyalty oaths—had fought instead with American militiamen. Resentment escalated as British and Loyalist troops pillaged farms and raided towns for food and other supplies.

Upon receiving word from the commander of the British troops, Major Ferguson led a force of one thousand Loyalist militiamen northward along the South Carolina frontier with instructions to protect Cornwallis's left flank. Along their path, Loyalists tore the region apart. Their "progress through the countryside inflicted excesses and sufferings on numbers of patriot citizens. There was plundering of 'cattle, horses, beds, wearing apparel, bee-gums, and vegetables of all kinds—even wresting the rings from the fingers of females.' "[12]

After Ferguson threatened the mountain region with "fire and sword," popular frontier leader Isaac Shelby, a descendant of French Huguenot settlers, organized a group of partisan backcountry fighters. Afterward, he convinced the fiery and charismatic commander of the frontier militia from the Watauga and Nolichucky rivers, John Sevier, to join forces. Most of the backcountry men were Scots-Irish settlers, who, historian Wilma Dykeman contended, "momentarily subject[ed] their cherished individualism to demands of the common good—in fact, their common survival. Their leaders exemplified much of the natural authority, unhesitating militancy, and tactical skill shown by ancient [Scottish] chieftains."[13] Shelby and Sevier united the backcountry fighters with North Carolinian militiamen under the leadership of Colonel Charles McDowell and Colonel Benjamin Cleveland. Colonel William Campbell's group of Virginia militiamen also joined the growing force.

They all met at a chosen place along the Watauga River at Sycamore Shoals and planned their attack. This coalition was "composed of patriot riflemen of the farmer, hunter, and Indian fighting class from the frontiers of the two Carolinas and Virginia."[14] Historian George C. Mackenzie described the "army" with no uniforms—one thousand men dressed in buckskins and homespun shirts, tan home-dyed breeches, and wide-brimmed hats, their "long hair tied in a queue." A Scots-Irish clergyman, the Reverend Samuel Doak, inspired the backcountry soldiers with the biblical story of Gideon's victory over the Midianites that ended with the "battle cry—'The sword of the Lord and of Gideon!' "[15]

On October 7, 1780, backcountry frontiersmen and militiamen met face-to-face with Ferguson's troops at Kings Mountain, South Carolina—Patriots against Loyalists, Americans against Americans, militiamen against militiamen. While the Loyalists " 'depended on their discipline, their manhood, and the bayonet,' the mountain men relied upon their skill as marksmen."[16] After a short, but deadly battle that took several hundred lives—including those of British leader Major Ferguson and South Carolina Patriot leader and guide Colonel James William—the Loyalists surrendered.

Lieutenant Anthony Allaire, one of Ferguson's men, recorded the fate of some of the men taken prisoners after the battle. In his diary, he described the backcountry trial that condemned thirty Loyalists. "In the evening they began to execute Lieut. Col. Mills, Capt. Wilson, Capt. Chitwood, and six others, who unfortunately fell a sacrifice to their infamous mock jury. Mills, Wilson, and Chitwood died like Romans—the others were reprieved."[17] However, Colonel Shelby's account was quite different. He claimed that two magistrates complete with a jury presided over the trial of thirty-six Loyalists under North Carolina law. Nine were hung before Shelby called a stop to the executions. The colonel also noted that prior to the Kings Mountain engagement, Loyalists hung "eleven patriots . . . for being Rebels."[18]

Historians who study the battle agree with British commander Clinton that Kings Mountain represented a key turning point of the American Revolution. After losing the protection of his left flank, Cornwallis was forced to abandon his plans to overrun North Carolina. His mission to subdue revolutionary forces in the South under Loyalist control suddenly failed—at what seemed to be the height of British success. Kings Mountain reinvigorated Patriots and encouraged other backcountry men to join the cause. Many joined Daniel Morgan's men who fought at Cowpens, South Carolina, another critical event of the American Revolution when British and Loyalist troops met American Patriots. Until the war's end, the South continued in the grips of a savage battle between Patriots and Loyalists.

With skilled military leaders like Daniel Morgan, Francis Marion, and Nathanael Greene, southern revolutionaries found success against overwhelming odds with their own version of backcountry warfare with the help of militiamen and Continentals. The American alliance with France also helped move the Revolution toward victory, particularly in the southern campaign when the French fleet overpowered the British navy in the Chesapeake. A combined force of French and American troops soon proved victorious against the British. In October 1781, just one year after the Battle of Kings Mountain, Lord Cornwallis faced the final humiliation of defeat when the British surrendered at Yorktown, Virginia.

NEW DEBATES—PATRIOTS VERSUS LOYALISTS

At the successful conclusion of the Revolutionary War, Americans engaged in a new debate—over the punishment of Tories. In many states, former Loyalists were stripped of their lands without trial, were refused voting rights, and were shunned, while others faced the threat of deportation. Americans remained sharply divided on this issue, some harshly attacking the Tories, accusing them of every injustice found in the war and calling for their banishment. One Whig dramatically contended: "Drive far from you every baneful wretch who wished to see you fettered with the chains of tyranny. Send them where they may enjoy their beloved slavery to perfection—send them to the island of Britain; there let them drink the cup of slavery and eat the bread of bitterness all the days of their existence."[19] Other Patriots called for reconciliation and argued against the confiscation of Tories' lands from former Loyalist soldiers or their widows and children. Chief Justice Aedanus Burke of South Carolina pleaded with his countrymen to prove that "we mean that the word *Republic* should signify something more than mere *sound*." The Constitution would eventually make the confiscation of Tory lands illegal, but for many, the stigma of being a Loyalist continued for generations.

CONCLUSION

As historians continue to study the American Revolution, many focus on the inadequacies of the militia system and note the important role played by the Continental army in the conflict. Others argue that the contributions of the American militias should not be overlooked. Scholars also engage in a debate over what motivated men to fight in the Revolution. Many agree with historian Mark E. Lender's conclusion that economic opportunities, not idealism, motivated enlistment in the Continental army, which was primarily made up of the poor and the working class. They downplay the image of the virtuous and patriotic citizen-soldier fighting for the freedom of his homeland. Other historians, led by Charles Royster, challenge this conclusion and maintain that patriotism and self-sacrifice drove men to serve in both Washington's forces and militia units. Devoted to the principles of their new nation, men continued to fight despite increasing adversity and growing impoverishment. But to truly understand the American Revolution, scholars cannot overlook its complexities. Many join with Gregory T. Knouff to contend that "men were most likely to volunteer when their felt their communities were endangered. They also fought out of commitment to ideals that were particular to their class, regional, ethnic, and racial status."[20]

In many ways, the Battle of Kings Mountain exemplified the complexities of the American Revolution. It demonstrated how deep the bitterness ran between the American Patriots and the American Loyalists. It helped explain the conviction of citizen-soldiers—motivated by regional conflict, ethnic tension, class disputes, and political ideology—as each chose a side in the struggle between Britain and its American colonies. It showed that despite clear problems with the American militia system, these groups, along with backcountry partisan bands, played a crucial role in defeating the enemy, especially in the South. The success at Kings Mountain also bolstered the popular legend that the American Revolution was fought and won by yeoman farmers who replaced their plows with rifles and by backcountry riflemen who used their skills as marksmen to become masters of irregular warfare. In the end, George Washington congratulated the men who fought in the Battle of Kings Mountain and concluded that their victory would "in all probability have a very happy influence upon the successive operation in that quarter." The general called the success of the backcountry citizen-soldiers "proof of the spirit and resources of the country."[21]

NOTES

1. Wilma Dykeman, *With Fire and Sword* (Washington, D.C.: U.S. Government Printing Office, 1991), unnumbered, but found on p. 2 of the prologue.

2. George C. Mackenzie, *Kings Mountain* (Washington, DC: U.S. Department of the Interior, 1961 reprint), p. 1.

3. Charles Royster, *A Revolutionary People at War: The Continental Army and American Character, 1775–1783* (New York: W.W. Norton, 1981), p. 9.

4. Charles Patrick Neimeyer, *America Goes to War: A Social History of the Continental Army* (New York: New York University Press, 1996), p. 40.

5. Russell F. Weigley, *History of the United States Army* (New York: Macmillan, 1967), p. 30.

6. "George Washington to Continental Congress," September 24, 1776, *The Writings of George Washington*, vol. 6, the George Washington Papers at the Library of Congress, 1741–1799, online source from Library of Congress, American Memory Web Site, http://rs6.loc.gov/ammen/gwhtml/gwhome.html, p. 3.

7. Ibid.

8. Lawrence E. Babits, *A Devil of a Whipping: The Battle of Cowpens* (Chapel Hill: University of North Carolina Press, 1998), p. 1.

9. John Buchanan, *The Road to Guilford Courthouse: The American Revolution in the Carolinas* (New York: John Wiley & Sons, 1997), pp. 86–87.

10. The British officer is quoted in Royster, *A Revolutionary People at War*, pp. 278–79; Greene's aide and Greene are quoted on p. 277; the Royster quote is found on p. 277.

11. Buchanan, *The Road to Guilford Courthouse*, p. 207.

12. Dykeman, *With Fire and Sword*, unnumbered, but quote appears on p. 6 of chapter 5, "Britain's Tenacious Bull Dog."

13. Ibid., unnumbered, but taken from p. 1 of chapter 6, "The Over-Mountain Men."

14. Ibid., p. 7.

15. Mackenzie, *Kings Mountain*, pp. 11–12.

16. Ibid., p. 20.

17. Anthony Allaire, *Diary of Lieut. Anthony Allaire* (New York: The New York Times and Arno Press, 1968), p. 32. Excerpts of Allaire's Diary first published in 1881 in Lyman Copeland Draper, *King's Mountain and Its Heroes: History of the Battle of King's Mountain, October 7th, 1780, and the Events Which Led to It* (Cincinnati: P.G. Thomson, 1881). *Note*: Most sources cite James Williams's rank as Colonel; however, Allaire called Williams as Brigadier General.

18. "King's Mountain—By Col. Issaac Shelby," reprinted in Draper, *King's Mountain and Its Heroes.*

19. "A Whig," originally published in *Pennsylvania Packet*, August 5, 1779, reprinted in Frank Moore, *Diary of the American Revolution* (New York: Charles Scribner, 1860). This excerpt from William Dudley, ed., *The American Revolution: Opposing Viewpoints* (San Diego: Greenhaven Press, 1992), pp. 184–187 (reprinted with permission).

20. Mark E. Lender, "Enlistment: Economic Opportunities for the Poor and Working Classes," in John Whiteclay Chambers II and G. Kurt Piehler, eds., *Major Problems in American Military History* (Boston: Houghton Mifflin Co., 1999), pp. 75–83; Charles Royster, "Enlistment: Patriotic Belief in the Cause of Freedom," in Chambers and Piehler, eds., *Major Problems*, pp. 83–87; and Gregory T. Knouff, "Enlistment: The Complexity of Motivations," in Chambers and Piehler, eds., *Major Problems*, p. 92.

21. "George Washington, General Orders, October 27, 1780," *The Writings of George Washington*, vol. 20, the George Washington Papers at the Library of Congress, 1741–1799, online source from the Library of Congress, American Memory Website, http://lcweb.2.loc.gov/amhome.html.

DOCUMENTS

1.1. George Washington Argues against Dependence upon Militia,
September 24, 1776

---

*As the enlistment terms for most of the Continental forces were
about to expire, General George Washington appealed to Congress for an expanded and improved army. In his letter to the
Continental Congress, he questioned the effectiveness of the militia system and dismissed fears associated with a strong standing
army. While many historians agree with Washington's critical
assessment of the militia, others argue that despite problems, militiamen played a key role in the American Revolution.*

"To congress"

Sir: From the hours allotted to Sleep, I will borrow a few Moments to
convey my thoughts on sundry important matters to Congress. I shall
offer them, with the sincerity which ought to characterize a man of can-
dour; and with the freedom which may be used in giving useful information, without incurring the imputation of presumption. . . .

To place any dependence upon Militia, is, assuredly, resting upon a
broken staff. Men just dragged from the tender Scenes of domestick [*sic*]
life; unaccustomed to the din of Arms; totally unacquainted with every
kind of Military skill, which being followed by a want of confidence in
themselves, when opposed to Troops regularly train'd [*sic*], disciplined,
and appointed, superior in knowledge, and superior in Arms, makes
them timid, and ready to fly from their own shadows. Besides, the sudden change in their manner of living, (particularly in the lodging) brings
on sickness in many; impatience in all, and such an unconquerable desire
of returning to their respective homes that it not only produces shameful,
and scandalous Desertions among themselves, but infuses the like spirit
in others. Again, Men accustomed to unbounded freedom, and no con-
troul [*sic*], cannot brook the Restraint which is indispensably necessary
to the good order and Government of an Army; without which, licen-
tiousness, and every kind of disorder triumphantly reign. To bring Men
to a proper degree of Subordination, is not the work of a day, a Month
or even a year; and unhappily for us, the cause we are Engaged in, the
little discipline I have been labouring [*sic*] to establish in the Army under
my immediate Command, is in a manner done away by having such a

mixture of Troops as have been called together within these few Months. . . .

These Sir, Congress may be assured, are but a small part of the Inconveniences which might be enumerated and attributed to Militia; but there is one that merits particular attention, and that is the expence [*sic*]. Certain I am that it would be cheaper to keep 50, or 100,000 Men in constant pay than to depend upon half the number, and supply the other half occasionally by Militia. . . .

The Jealousies of a standing Army, and the Evils to be apprehended from one, are remote; and in my judgment, situated and circumstanced as we are, not at all to be dreaded; but the consequence of wanting one, according to my Ideas, formed from the present view of things, is certain, and inevitable Ruin; for if I was called upon to declare upon Oath, whether the Militia have been most serviceable or hurtful upon the whole; I should subscribe to the latter.

Source: "George Washington to Continental Congress," September 24, 1776, the Writings of George Washington, vol. 6, the George Washington Papers at the Library of Congress, 1741–1799, on-line source from the Library of Congress, American Memory Website, http://lcweb.2.loc.gov/amhome.html, p. 3.

1.2.   A Whig, 1779

Written by an anonymous author, this fiery newspaper editorial claims that the new nation is being too lenient on Loyalists and demands that they be banished from the United States. The author calls Tories traitors who are "undermining" liberties and ruining the country.

Among the many errors America has been guilty of during her contest with Great Britain, few have been greater, or attended with more fatal consequences to these States, than her lenity to the Tories. At first it might have been right, or perhaps political; but is it not surprising that, after repeated proofs of the same evils resulting therefrom, it should still be continued? We are all crying out against the depreciation of our money, and entering into measures to restore it to its value; while the Tories, who are one principal cause of the depreciation, are taken no notice of, but suffered to live quietly among us. We can no longer be silent on this subject, and see the independence of the country, after standing every shock from without, endangered by internal enemies. Rouse, America! Your danger is great—great from a quarter where you least expect it. The Tories, the Tories will yet be the ruin of you! 'Tis high time they were separated from among you. They are now busy engaged in undermining your liberties. They have a thousand ways of doing it, and they make use of them all. Who were the occasions of this war? The Tories! Who persuaded the tyrant of Britain to prosecute it in a manner before unknown to civilized nations and shocking even to barbarians? The Tories! Who prevailed on the savages of the wilderness to join the standard of the enemy? The Tories! Who have assisted the Indians in taking the scalp from the aged matron, the blooming fair one, the helpless infant, and the dying hero? The Tories! Who advised and who assisted in burning your towns, ravaging your country, and violating the chastity of your women? The Tories! Who are the occasion that thousands of you now mourn the loss of your dearest connections? The Tories! Who have always counteracted the endeavors of Congress to secure the liberties of this country? The Tories! Who refused their money when as good as specie, though stamped with the image of his most sacred Majesty? The Tories! Who continue to refuse it? The Tories! Who do all in their power to depreciate it? The Tories! Who propagate lies among us to discourage the Whigs? The Tories! Who corrupt the minds of the good people of these States by every species of insidious counsel? The Tories! Who hold a traitorous correspondence with the enemy? The Tories! Who daily sends them intelligence? The Tories! Who take the oaths of allegiance to the States one day, and break them the next? The Tories! Who prevent your battalions from being filled? The Tories! Who dissuade men from entering the army? The Tories! Who persuade those who have enlisted to desert? The Tories! Who harbor those who do desert? The Tories! In short, who wish to see us conquered, to see us slaves, to see us hewers of wood and drawers of water? The Tories! . . .

'Tis time to rid ourselves of these bosom vipers. An immediate separation is necessary. I dread to think of the evils every moment is big with, while a single Tory remains among us. May we not soon expect to hear of plots, assassinations, and every species of wickedness their malice and rancor can suggest? For what can restrain those who have already imbrued their hands in their country's blood? . . . Awake, Americans, to sense of your danger. No time to be lost. Instantly banish every Tory from among you. Let America be sacred alone to freemen. Drive far from you every baneful wretch who wished to see you fettered with the chains of tyranny. Send them where they may enjoy their beloved slavery to perfection—send them to the island of Britain; there let them drink the cup of slavery and eat the bread of bitterness all the days of their existence—there let them drag out a painful life, despised and accursed by those very men whose cause they have had the wickedness to espouse. Never let them return to this happy land—never let them taste the sweets of that independence which they strove to prevent. Banishment, perpetual banishment, should be their lot.

Source: "A Whig," originally published in *Pennsylvania Packet*, August 5, 1779, reprinted in Frank Moore, ed. *Diary of the American Revolution* (New York: Charles Scribner, 1860). This excerpt from William Dudley, ed., *The American Revolution: Opposing Viewpoints* (San Diego: Greenhaven Press, 1992), pp. 184–187 (reprinted with permission).

1.3.   Diary of Lieutenant Anthony Allaire of Ferguson's Corps: Memorandum of Occurrences during the Campaign of 1780

Lieutenant Anthony Allaire served with Ferguson's corps during the Battle of Kings Mountain. His diary not only reveals what happened at the battle, but also helps us understand the tension that existed between American Loyalists and American Patriots. In the following excerpt, Allaire, looking at events from the British and Loyalists' point of view, discusses the execution of Loyalist soldiers, the treatment of Loyalist prisoners, and his disdain for republican philosophy.

Friday, [October] 6th. Got in motion at four o'clock in the morning, and marched sixteen miles to Little King's Mountain, where we took up our ground.

Saturday, 7th. About two o'clock in the afternoon twenty-five hundred Rebels, under the command of Brig.-Gen. Williams, and ten Colonels, attacked us. Maj. Ferguson had eight hundred men. The action continued an hour and five minutes; but their numbers enabled them to surround us. The North Carolina regiment seeing this, and numbers being out of ammunition, gave way, which naturally threw the rest of the militia into confusion. Our poor little detachment, which consisted of only seventy men when we marched to the field of action, were all killed and wounded but twenty; and those brave fellows were soon crowded as close as possible by the militia. Capt. DePeyster, on whom the command devolved, saw it impossible to form six men together; thought it necessary to surrender to save the lives of the brave men who were left. We lost in this action, Maj. Ferguson, of the Seventy-first regiment, a man much attached to his King and country, well informed in the art of war; he was brave and humane, and an agreeable companion; in short, he was universally esteemed in the army, and I have every reason to regret his unhappy fate. We had eighteen men killed on the spot; Capt. Ryerson and thirty-two privates wounded of Maj. Ferguson's detachment; Lieut. McGinnis, of Allen's regiment of Skinner's Brigade, killed. Taken prisoners, Two Captains, four Lieutenants, three Ensigns, and one Surgeon, and fifty-four sergeants rank and file, including the mounted men under the command of Lieut. Taylor. Of the militia, one hundred were killed, including officers; wounded, ninety; taken prisoners, about six hundred. Our baggage all taken, of course. Rebels lost Brig.-Gen. Williams, one hundred and thirty-five, including officers, killed; wounded, equal to ours. . . .

Thursday, 12th. Those villains divided our baggage, although they had promised on their word we should have it all. . . .

Saturday, 14th. Twelve field officers were chosen to try the militia prisoners—particularly those who had the most influence in the country. They condemned thirty—in the evening they began to execute Lieut. Col. Mills, Capt. Wilson, Capt. Chitwood, and six others, who unfortunately fell a sacrifice to their infamous mock jury. Mills, Wilson, and Chitwood died like Romans—the others were reprieved.

Sunday, 15th. Moved at five o'clock in the morning. Marched all day through the rain—a very disagreeable road. We got to Catawba, and forded it at Island Ford, about ten o'clock at night. Our march was thirty-two miles. All the men were worn out with fatigue and fasting—the prisoners having no bread or meat for two days before. We officers were allowed to go to Col. McDowell's, where we lodged comfortably. About one hundred prisoners made their escape on this march. . . .

Saturday, 21st. Several Tory women brought us butter, milk, honey and many other necessaries of life. Moved at ten o'clock in the morning, and marched fourteen miles to Mr. Headpeth's plantation, a great Tory, who is at present with Lord Cornwallis. We lodged at Mr. Edward Clinton's, who is likewise with Lord Cornwallis. . . .

Wednesday, 25th. The men of our detachment, on Capt. DePeyster passing his word for their good behavior, were permitted to go into houses in the town without a guard. . . .

Sunday, 29th. Col. Cleveland waited on Capt. DePeyster and the rest of the officers, and asked us if we, with our men, would come and hear a sermon at ten o'clock. He marched the militia prisoners from their encampment to the town, and halted them; and sent an officer to our quarters to acquaint us they were waiting for us. We then ordered our men to fall in; marched to the front of the prisoners; the whole then proceeded on to a height about half a mile from the town. Here we heard a Presbyterian sermon, truly adapted to their principles and the times; or, rather, stuffed as full of Republicanism as their camp is of horse thieves.

Monday, 30th. A number of the inhabitants assembled at Bethabara to see a poor Tory prisoner executed for a crime of the following nature, viz: A Rebel soldier was passing the guard where the prisoners were confined, and like a brute addressed himself to those poor unhappy people in this style: "ah, d——n you, you'll all be hanged." This man, with the spirit of a British subject, answered, "Never mind that, it will be your turn next." But Col. Cleveland's goodness extended so far as to reprieve him.

Source: Anthony Allaire, *Diary of Lieut. Anthony Allaire* (New York: The New York Times and Arno Press, 1968.), pp. 1–33. Excerpts of Allaire's Diary first published in 1881 in Lyman Copeland Draper, *King's Mountain and Its Heroes: History of the Battle of King's Mountain, October 7th, 1780, and the Events Which Led to It* (Cincinnati: P.G. Thomson, 1881). *Note*: Most sources cite James Williams's rank as Colonel; however, Allaire called Williams as Brigadier General.

1.4.   Colonel Isaac Shelby's Account of Kings Mountain, 1780

Colonel Isaac Shelby, one of the leaders of the backcountry men, provides an account of the Battle of Kings Mountain from the perspective of the Patriots. Shelby condemns the "cruel and un-justifiable" execution of eleven Patriots by Loyalists before arguing that the trial and execution of nine Loyalist prisoners after the Kings Mountain battle was fair and just.

In September, 1780, Maj. Ferguson, who was one of the best and most enterprising of the British officers in America, had succeeded in raising a large body of Tories, who, with his own corps of regulars, constituted an effective force of eleven hundred and twenty-five men [one thousand were Loyalists]. With a view of cutting off Col. Clarke, of Georgia, who had recently made a demonstration against Augusta, which was then in the hands of the British, Ferguson had marched near the Blue Ridge, and had taken post at Gilbert Town, which is situated but a few miles from the mountains. Whilst there he discharged a patriot, who had been taken prisoner, on his parole, and directed him to tell Col. Shelby, (who had become obnoxious to the British and Tories from the affair at Musgrove's Mill,) that if Shelby did not surrender, he (Ferguson) would come over the mountains, and put him to death, and burn his whole County.

It required no further taunt to rouse the patriotic indignation of Col. Shelby. He determined to make an effort to raise a force, in connection with other officers which should surprise and defeat Ferguson. . . .

Ferguson, finding he could not elude the rapid pursuit of the mounted mountaineers, had marched to King's Mountain, which he considered a strong post, and which he had reached the night previous. The mountain or ridge, was a quarter of a mile long, and so confident was Ferguson in the strength of his position, that he declared, "the Almighty could not drive him from it."

Ferguson did all that an officer could do under the circumstances. His men too fought bravely. But his position, which he thought impregnable against any force the patriots could raise, was really a disadvantage to him. . . .

The slaughter of the enemy was great, and it was evident that further resistance would be unavailing; still Ferguson's proud heart could not think of surrender. He swore "he never would yield to such a d——d banditti," and rushed out from his men, sword in hand, and cut away until he broke his sword, and was shot down. . . .

Owing to the number of wounded, and the destitution of the army of all conveyances, they traveled slowly, and in one week had only marched about forty miles. When they reached Gilbert Town, a week after the battle, they were informed by a paroled officer, that he had seen eleven patriots hung at Ninety Six a few days before, for being Rebels. Similar cruel and unjustifiable acts had been committed before. In the opinion of the patriots, it required retaliatory measures to put a stop to these atrocities. A copy of the law of North Carolina was obtained, which authorized two magistrates to summon a jury, and forthwith to try, and if found guilty, to execute persons who had violated its precepts. Under this law, thirty-six men were tried, and found guilty of breaking open houses, killing the men, and turning the women and the children out of doors, and burning the houses. The trial was concluded late at night. The execution of the law was as summary as the trial. Three men were hung at a time, until nine were hung. Three more were tied ready to be swung off. Shelby interfered, and proposed to stop it. The other officers agreed, and the three men who supposed they had seen their last hour, were untied. . . .

At the time Shelby and his co-patriots raised their force, Cornwallis, supposing he would meet no further serious resistance in North or South Carolina, had projected the invasion of Virginia in three columns. He was to advance in the centre, a second detachment was to march on his right, and Ferguson was to command the left wing. The time for the invasion was fixed, officers were out through the country collecting the Tories, and a few days more would have made them very strong. The defeat of Ferguson prevented this invasion, and so intimidated the Tories, that most of them declined joining the British, generally preferring to make a profession of faith to King George rather than take up arms in his behalf. . . .

It is impossible for those who have not lived in its midst, to conceive of the exasperation which prevails in a civil war. The execution, therefore, of the nine Tories at Gilbert Town, will by many persons be considered an act of retaliation unnecessarily cruel. It was believed by those who were on the ground, to be both necessary and proper, for the purpose of putting a stop to the execution of the patriots in the Carolinas by the Tories and the British. The event proved the justice of the expectation of the patriots. The execution of the Tories did stop the execution of the Whigs. And it may be remarked of this cruel and lamentable mode of retaliation, that whatever excuses and pretences the Tories may have had for their atrocities, the British officers, who often ordered the execution of Whigs, had none. Their training to arms and military education, should have prevented them from violating the rules of civilized warfare in so essential a point.

Those patriots who desired to continue in the service after the battle at King's Mountain, especially the refugees, wished to be formed into a corps and to be under the command of Gen. Morgan. To effect this Col. Shelby went to head-quarters and saw Morgan, who said they were just the men he wanted. Gen. Gates consented, and the Board of War of North Carolina ordered out these militia, who marched up and joined Morgan; most of them were with him the next campaign, and proved the stuff they were made of at the nobly-won battle of the Cowpens.

Source: "King's Mountain—by Col. Issaac Shelby" reprinted in Lyman Copeland Draper, *King's Mountain and Its Heroes: History of the Battle of King's Mountain, October 7th, 1780, and the Events Which Led to It* (Cincinnati: P.G. Thomson, 1881), pp. 540–546.

1.5.   Aedanus Burke's Address to the Freemen of the State of South Carolina, 1783

Chief Justice Aedanus Burke of South Carolina who served with a revolutionary militia and later became a member of the U.S. Congress, wrote an appeal for a fair treatment of Loyalists. Burke condemned laws that stripped Loyalists of their property without trial, forced Loyalists to pay heavy fines, and excluded them from voting or holding office. In the following excerpt, Burke reminded readers that American liberty should be extended to all.

Friends and fellow citizens,

The proceedings of the late Assembly held at Jackson borough have already excited the attention not only of this but of other States; and some of the laws then enacted are of so serious a nature; that the memory of them will last, and their consequences operate, when the authors of the measures shall be no more. By one of those laws, upwards of two hundred men who have been citizens of this State before the reduction of Charlestown, have been stripped of all their property; innocent wives and children involved in the calamity of husbands and fathers, their widows are deprived of the right of dower, their children disinherited, and themselves banished forever from this country. And this without process, trial, examination, or hearing; and without allowing them the sacred right of proving their innocence on a future day. Under other acts of that assembly, a number of the inhabitants are subjected to heavy fines, some near one third, others to one eighth and some to a tenth part of their estate, real and personal, without better proof of crime than report and suggestions. Another act excludes from the freedom of voting or being elected to a seat in the legislature, almost a majority of our citizens. The crimes of all consist in the part which they were said to have taken after the reduction of South Carolina by the British army. . . .

Every country of which we have any account from history, has had its day of woe and affliction, by foreign invasion, or civil discord, as we have had. But in every one of them as soon as the troubles were over, and the country regained; the government returned to its antient form, and the subjects were reinstated in the participation of their rights and privileges. And this is not only agreeable to justice, but the freedom and liberty of the country would be destroyed if it were otherwise. If in a republic a few could set up pretensions to superior political merit, over the whole aggregate body of the people, and deprive the latter of their rights and privileges, this would be nothing more nor less than over-throwing the constitution, seizing on the liberties of the people, and set-ting up an arbitrary government of the *few*. The laws of nations as well as the rights of nature therefore dictate, that when a country oppressed by a foreign power regains its liberty, the citizens should be restored to all the rights and liberties they before enjoyed. . . .

It is impossible not to feel distress when we reflect on the miseries that each party in a civil war, inflict on the other as they become up-permost. The cruel oppressions of the British, particularly the personal insults and outrage we suffered from their officers, after the fall of the country, is enough to make a man shudder. . . .

The experience of all countries has shewn, that where a community splits into a faction, and has recourse to arms, and one finally gets the better, a law to bury in *oblivion* past transactions is absolutely necessary to restore tranquility. For if after a civil war, and one party vanquished, persecution was to go on; if the fury of laws and the fierce rage of pas-sions prevailed, while the minds of men were yet fired by deadly re-venge against their fallen adversaries; this would be worse than keeping up the war: It would be carrying on hostility under the shape of justice, which is the most oppressive, and of all other injustice, excites the greatest detestation, in the most violent factions and division. . . .

It is a maxim in politics, that if a breach be made in the constitution of a government, and it be not healed, it will prove as fatal to its freedom, as a wound that is neglected and suffered to mortify, would be to the life of a man. I proved clearly that ours received a mortal one; and should the present assembly leave it *to inflame* without applying a cure, we cease to be a free people. The remedy I speak of is lenient, all healing. *Repeal at once the late election act, the amercement law, and the confiscation act, as far as it affects those who were our citizens.*—And in order that such proceedings may not be drawn into precedent hereafter, let there be a clause, *to obliterate those three acts* from the journals of both houses. *Pass an act of amnesty and oblivion, with as few exceptions as possible*; allowing such as may be excluded, a day to come in and be heard, either before the court of sessions, on a fair and public trial; or should they be men whose inveteracy, power or influence may be dangerous to the State, and are not liable to punishment by our laws; let them have a hearing before the legislature on articles of impeachment.—Provided that we mean that the word *Republic* should signify something more than mere *sound, pass an Act for dissolving the present Assembly.*

If every citizen cannot enjoy the rights of *election and representation* according to the constitution, I hope no body will be so idle as to talk of *Liberty. This, and the reversal of the three acts above mentioned*, is the measure, *and the only one* that can reconcile us to the friendship of each other; it will put an end to silly distinctions and faction: leave us at liberty to shake hands as brethren, whose fate it is to live together; and it will stand as a more lasting monument of our national wisdom, justice and magnanimity, than statues of brass or marble.

Source: Aedanus Burke, *An Address to the Freemen of the State of South-Carolina,* 1783. This excerpt from William Dudley, ed., *The American Revolution: Opposing Viewpoints* (San Diego: Greenhaven Press, 1992), pp. 184–187 (reprinted with permission).

1.6.   Ballad of King's Mountain from a Patriot's Perspective, 1780

Written shortly after the Battle of Kings Mountain, this ballad describes the defeat of the Tory soldiers and celebrates the Patriots' victory.

'Twas on a pleasant mountain the Tory heathens lay,
With a doughty Major at their head, one Ferguson, they say,
Cornwallis had detach'd him a thieving for to go,
And catch the Carolina men, or lay the Rebels low,
The scamp had rang'd the country in search of Royal aid,
And with his owls perch'd on high, he taught them all his trade.

But, ah! That fatal morning, when Shelby brave drew near,
'Tis certainly a warning that Government should hear,
And Campbell brave, and Cleveland, and Colonel John Sevier,
Each with a band of gallant men to Ferguson appear.

Just as the sun was setting behind the western hills,
Just then our trusty rifles sent a dose of leaden pills;
Up—up the steep together brave Williams led his troop,
And join'd by Winston, bold and true, disturb'd the Tory coop.

The Royal slaves—the Royal owls, flew high on every hand,
But soon they settled—gave a howl, and quarter'd to Cleveland;
I would not tell the number of Tories slain that day,
But surely it is certain that none did run away.

For all that we're a living we're happy to give up,
So let us make thanksgiving, and pass the bright tin cup;
To all our brave regiment, let's toast 'em for their health,
And may our glorious country have joy, and peace, and wealth.

Source: "King's Mountain—1780," reprinted in Lyman Copeland Draper, *King's Mountain and Its Heroes: History of the Battle of King's Mountain, October 7th, 1780, and the Events Which Led to It* (Cincinnati: P.G. Thomson, 1881), pp. 592–593.

1.7.   Supposed Loyalist Song by Gen. J. W. DePeyster

Written by General J.W. DePeyster, this ballad describes the hardship of war and the suffering of Loyalist prisoners at the hands of the "rebels." Perhaps DePeyster was related to Captain Abraham DePeyster, who served in Ferguson's corps during the Battle of Kings Mountain and raised the white flag of surrender after Ferguson was killed.

They caught us on a mountain bald, 'twas no place for a stand,
For woods and thickets, dense and close, the summit did
    command,
But those who led us on that day, of "Crackers" had no fear,
And when we charg'd the varments ran—did quickly disappear.

But vain was pluck, and vain each charge, for from each tree
    there came,

A deadly rifle bullet, and a little spurt of flame;
The men who fired we could not see—they pick'd us off like
   game,
To call such work fair fighting seems a misuse of the name.

So ev'ry shot told one by one, till of the reg'lar few,
Most lay stark dead, just where they fell, like beasts in a battue,
Then the militia cried "enough," and loud for quarter bawl'd,
And huddled in a bunch, and whipp'd, upon that mountain bald.

Alas! Alas! Our Gen'ral fell, quite early in the fight,
Eight bullets in him—each enough to kill a man outright,
Our second he got plump'd also, and then the game was up,
When fell the Bull-dog Ferguson, and next the Bull-dog's pup.

D——n 'em, we kill'd as many "Rebs" as they had kill'd of us.
But then as pris'ners we were bound, some suffer'd ten times
   worse,
And some had better far been shot than stripp'd, starv'd, and
   froze,
And see those hung, our comrades dear, a struttin' in their
   clothes.

Source: Gen. J.W. DePeyster, "Supposed Loyalist Song," reprinted in Lyman Copeland Draper, *King's Mountain and Its Heroes: History of the Battle of King's Mountain, October 7th, 1780, and the Events Which Led to It* (Cincinnati: P.G. Thomson, 1881), p. 593.

ANNOTATED RESEARCH GUIDE

Books and Articles

Babits, Lawrence E. *A Devil of a Whipping: The Battle of Cowpens*. Chapel Hill: University of North Carolina Press, 1998. Examines events that led up to the Battle of Cowpens, a decisive engagement that followed Kings Mountain. Includes a brief discussion of the Battle of Kings Mountain. Many of the backcountry men who served at Kings Mountain also fought with Patriot military leader Daniel Morgan at Cowpens.

Buchanan, John. *The Road to Guilford Courthouse: The American Revolution in the Carolinas*. New York: John Wiley & Sons, 1997. Detailed account of the War of Independence in the Carolinas that traces the development of the Loyalist-Whig conflict, discusses the skirmishes and battles of the South, and includes a chapter on Kings Mountain.

Coffman, Edward M. "The Duality of the American Military Tradition: A Commentary." *Journal of Military History* 64, no. 4 (2000): 967–980. Examines the struggle between the state militias and the regular standing army throughout the history of the United States. Traces Americans' fear of a national army and the transformation of "citizen armies" (militias) into the National Guard.

Dykeman, Wilma. *With Fire and Sword*. Washington, D.C.: U.S. Government Printing Office, 1991. Overview of the Battle of Kings Mountain, written for the National Park Service.

Higginbotham, Don. *Daniel Morgan: Revolutionary Rifleman*. Chapel Hill: University of North Carolina Press, 1961. Examines Morgan's military tactics—hit-and-run, guerrilla warfare—used to help defeat the British and Loyalist forces in the South. Includes a brief discussion of Kings Mountain.

———. *War and Society in Revolutionary America: The Wider Dimension of Conflict*. Columbia, S.C.: University of South Carolina Press, 1988. Higginbotham connects the American Revolution with broader social issues.

Messick, Hank. *King's Mountain: The Epic of the Blue Ridge "Mountain Men" in the American Revolution*. Boston: Little, Brown, 1976. Tells the story of the backcountry men who fought against Ferguson's Loyalist troops at Kings Mountain. The book is not footnoted, but it includes reprints and excerpts from primary sources throughout its narrative.

Royster, Charles. *A Revolutionary People at War: The Continental Army and American Character, 1775–1783*. New York: W.W. Norton, 1979; reprinted by University of North Carolina Press, 1996. Examines the complexities of the American Revolution, including origins of the war, motivations for fighting and the tension between Loyalists and Patriots.

Shy, John. *A People Numerous and Armed: Reflections on the Military Struggle for American Independence*. Ann Arbor: University of Michigan Press, 1990. A collection of essays captures the social and military issues of the American Revolution.

Web Site

http://www.army.mil/cmh-pg/books/revwar/km-cpns/awc-kml.htm. U.S. Army Center of Military History. Online book collection that includes a detailed discussion of the Battle of Kings Mountain.

2

The Hartford Convention: Federalists versus Republicans in the War of 1812

The American Revolution brought together thirteen distinct colonies into one country. However, at the war's end, key differences threatened to divide the new nation even before it could create a unified republic as Americans clashed over issues of federal power, military strength, economic principles, and foreign policy. The debates became fierce at times and reached a crescendo with the Hartford Convention during the War of 1812. One key issue was the dispute over the federal government's use of New England militia forces, which reflected long-standing debates over state versus federal power and over the organization of the U.S. military forces. The War of 1812 was one of the most unpopular conflicts in American history, perhaps surpassed only by the Vietnam War, and the deep divisions that crystallized during this conflict affected the nation for decades to come.

After the Revolutionary War, it became clear to many Americans that the Articles of Confederation, America's first frame of government, were inadequate. Although the Articles served their purpose to help unite the colonies into a single cause, they did not provide for the needs of the young republic in crucial areas of the economy and security. Agreeing to a new constitution was difficult, and the critical differences, somewhat veiled by the exigencies of fighting the British, soon became abundantly evident. Debates ensued between small states and large states over representation and, although muted, between the northern and the southern states over slavery. The biggest debate developed between the Federalists and the Antifederalists.

The Federalists advocated a strong central government, a standing army of professional soldiers, and a commercial economy that could compete with European standards. Federalists believed that a system of checks and balances built into the frame of government would guard against despotism. Antifederalists did not agree. They feared that the creation of a strong national government would concentrate power in the hands of a few and would only lead to the oppression of the American people. They pointed to America's own history with England and to the tyranny of other European monarchies. For the Antifederalists, significant power had to remain in the hands of individual states.

MILITIA VERSUS REGULAR ARMY

Debate also continued regarding the defense of the new nation. During the Constitutional Convention, "it was conceded that a national [military] force could be maintained, but the country would rely chiefly on the militia for defense." To make militias readily available for national use, the framers agreed that the federal government "must be able to use state militias or else it would have to rely on a standing army."[1] Although the Constitution's framers agreed to a two-army system—state militias and a small national force—the debate over the size of the army continued even after Americans ratified the Constitution, in 1789. Many, pointing to militia problems that occurred during the American Revolution, questioned whether state militia forces would be able to make the grade against enemies with professional armies. Nevertheless, "in regard to the militia, Congress foiled nationalist aspirations" to change the system. President George "Washington and [Secretary of War Henry] Knox urged Congress to reorganize the militia into an effective force under national control, but militia legislation was a touchy political question." Antifederalists continued to see a regular army of professional soldiers as a possible threat to the young republic, and "it struck at the root of state vs. federal power and had a direct impact on every citizen."[2] Indeed, it was an article of faith among most Americans, who had learned about the perennial dangers of standing armies during their own revolutionary awakening of the 1760s and 1770s, that the presence of a standing army meant that tyranny already was afoot.

In the spring of 1792, Congress did address proposals to reform the militia system, looking for a way to create well-armed, well-trained, and disciplined state militias that could be called up for federal use when necessary. Reformers pushed for preparedness and standardization when they called for militia reform. What was needed was a way to ensure national defense without relying on a large regular army and yet to give the federal government needed access to state troops when necessary. The 1792 Call Forth Act gave the president the right to "call forth" the militia in case of invasion, while the Uniform Militia Act set up a system of universal military service for all able-bodied white men between the ages of eighteen and forty-five. Despite various efforts at military reform, problems with the militia systems were never really ironed out, and the debate over the training and use of the state militias continued to haunt the nation until it turned into a deeply divisive crisis during the War of 1812.

THE NEW NATION

The new nation began with a Federalist-dominated government under the leadership of President George Washington. Secretary of the Treasury Alexander Hamilton took center stage in the next chapter of the drama between the two opposing political factions, and Hamilton's name became synonymous with Federalist policy. In particular, Hamilton focused on improving the domestic economy and pulling the nation out of its large war debt through an excise tax, a national bank, and a tariff (tax) on foreign goods. Hamilton equated a strong domestic economy with a powerful world position—a position that could help the United States hold its own in possible future wars with Britain, France, or Spain. Secretary of State Thomas Jefferson led the opposition's fight against the bank, excise taxes, and protective tariffs, but Federalists ruled the day in Washington's administration.

During the 1790s, events in Europe and in the American West forced the United States to reexamine its foreign policy. Interference in the western territories by England, which claimed large tracts of land and formed alliances with powerful Native American tribes, did not go unnoticed by the new nation. The French Revolution, which began in 1789, was met with division in the United States as Federalists and Antifederalists (many of whom became the Democratic-Republicans) argued over America's responsibility to aid its old ally. Federalists saw the revolution as a brutal mob attack on the upper class, while Democratic-Republicans (commonly referred to as Republicans) hoped that the bloodshed would bring forth a new republican government in France. The decision by the United States to remain neutral became more and more difficult as the conflict eventually transformed into a war between England and France in 1793 that engulfed the Atlantic world and then into the Napoleonic Wars in 1799. Republicans tended to be sympathetic to France, particularly because of the "special relationship" the United States had with the European nation that had developed when the French helped Americans win their independence. The Federalists' growing economic relationship with England led many to express pro-British sentiment. Still, the British provoked widespread American criticism when they began replacing their depleted British navy by pressing (forcing) American merchant seamen into British service on the high seas. American tempers rose when Britain increased its fortifications in the American West, laid claim to land north of the Ohio River, and urged Indians to resist the advancement of American settlers.

Choked by a British blockade in the French Caribbean, the French asked for aid from the United States, citing the Franco-American alliance. Not sure of America's response, the British seized some three hundred American merchant ships in the West Indies and forced scores of American seamen into service on their naval vessels. American merchant ships also faced attack from both of these belligerent countries.

In an attempt to curb the escalating wave of antagonism, President Washington sent Chief Justice John Jay to London in 1794 to seek harmony between the two nations. Although Jay had some success with securing limited commercial trade rights in British colonies and a vague agreement to vacate western posts, the British refused to give in to most of the American demands. This included the young nation's definitions regarding the rights of neutrality that would protect American trade and merchant sailors. Desperate to avoid war with England, which Washington feared would undo the American republican experiment, he accepted British terms in the Jay Treaty. Many, especially the Republicans, saw the treaty as a failure, but it did usher in a decade of relative peace with the British, who relaxed their impressment of American seamen and "protected" American vessels from French marauders in an effort to keep open British trade with the Caribbean. The French, angered by America's abrogation of a treaty with their country and thinking that the Washington administration had "allied" with the British, now stepped up their own assault on American merchant ships. An undeclared "quasi-war" with France followed. When President John Adams took office in 1797, he directed his peacekeeping efforts at the French when he sent an envoy to Paris. But American efforts failed again, this time because the U.S. negotiators, unable to muster funds necessary to satisfy French demands, refused to pay bribe money to meet with the French foreign minister.

TOWARD WAR

With two failed treaties and American merchant sailors and ships at risk, Adams took action. Following George Washington's adage "The best way to preserve peace is to prepare for war," the Federalist-dominated Congress established the Department of the Navy and created the U.S. Marine Corps.[3] Congress also authorized the formation of an army of 10,000 men. Although the Republicans were irritated by the Europeans' lack of respect for American rights, they objected to an increase in the national military, preferring instead to rely on state militias made up of citizen-soldiers. New alien laws and the Sedition Act also outraged Republicans when they were passed in 1798 by the Federalist-dominated Congress. The Alien Act (directed primarily at French immigration to keep "radical" ideas and revolutionaries out of America) increased the residency requirements from five to fourteen years for aliens who wanted to become citizens. Since many of America's new immigrants identified with and tended to vote for Republican candidates instead of the more "aristocratic" Federalists, the Republicans saw the act as a direct attack on their party—which in many ways it was. The Sedition Act made it a crime, punishable by imprisonment and heavy fines, to defame falsely U.S. government officials—except, significantly, the vice president, who then was Thomas Jefferson—or hamper the policies of the government. Republicans asserted that authorities used the act to shut down their newspapers when they protested Federalist policy, which was, to Republicans, a clear violation of the Bill of Rights. In disgust, Vice President Jefferson and James Madison anonymously penned the Virginia and Kentucky Resolutions, which claimed that individual states had the right to "null and void" any federal law that violated the Constitution. Republicans also criticized increased taxes from the new military expenditures and the Federalists' pro-British foreign policy. Upset with the direction of the country, Republicans vowed to fight back.

Their opportunity came with the election of 1800, which sharply pitted Republicans against Federalists. This time, the Republicans triumphed. The new Republican-controlled Congress of 1801 refused to reenact Federalist policies, including the Alien and Sedition acts and the excise tax. It also decreased the army to some three thousand men, now mostly scattered in the frontier, and reduced the size of the navy.

A respite in the European wars from 1801 to 1803 gave the new Jefferson administration a time to heal party divisions, to acquire the vast Louisiana Territory from France, to remove a dangerous European threat from the path of westward movement and commerce, and to put the navy in use to fight "pirates" in the Mediterranean. Any hope for a quiet and peaceful Republican administration disappeared when European conflict resumed in 1803. Once again, the British blockaded French harbors, apprehended American cargo as contraband, impressed American merchant sailors into the British navy, and stirred up Indian resistance in the western frontier. Merchant sea captains watched helplessly as British commanders blatantly ignored protection papers (similar to a passport) issued to American seamen as proof of their citizenship. The Royal Navy also targeted American ships transporting products from the French West Indies to France—a voyage the British claimed violated the rules of neutrality, since this was not an established American trade route before the outbreak of the European war. Americans answered the charge with a solution of "broken voyages"—simply bringing West Indies cargo to the United States before reexporting it to France—something that did not escape the fiery disapproval of the British. Although many sailors on American merchant ships were undoubtedly deserters from the Royal Navy and thus not "protected" even by America's understanding of international law, the British kidnapped some 6,000 innocent Americans. To make matters worse, a number of British assaults took place close to America's eastern shores, and in 1807 the British stopped and boarded an American warship, the *Chesapeake*, and took off apparent deserters from the British navy.

Foreign relations had progressively deteriorated since 1806, when Parliament issued a series of orders in council that demanded that all ships heading to France must first stop at British ports and required all neutral ships entering the British blockade to secure special trading licenses. The French fired back with the Berlin and Milan decrees threatening to confiscate ships heading to or leaving British ports or following the British orders in council. Trapped between two enemy forces determined to destroy the other, the United States could not escape becoming entangled in the European war.

The proud republic groped for a way out that would preserve "republican" honor and principles and protect American interests. A large chorus of condemnation led by Republicans called for an embargo of European goods. Although appalled by the events unfolding on the seas, the Federalists, whose livelihood depended upon overseas trade, argued for continued negotiations. But by December 1807, after failed attempts at peace and amid calls for some reprisal for the *Chesapeake* affair, Jefferson pushed through the Embargo Act, which forbade American ships to sail to any foreign shores. The Republicans contended that Europe so needed American trade that the embargo would bring concessions from Britain and France and avoid the expense and dangers of expanding American military and naval power. But the act proved fatal, for, with little hope for a quick settlement, America soon fell into a prolonged economic depression.

Republican President James Madison, elected in 1808, recognized that abolishing overseas trade hurt America more than its adversaries, and that the unpopular act created an unbearable political burden for the ideology of Republicanism. In 1809, the Non-intercourse Act reopened global imports and exports, except for trade with the British and the French. In 1810 Congress passed Macon's Bill No. 2, which resumed trade with England and France, but dangled a carrot in front of the two antagonists. The bill announced that whichever nation repealed its decrees first, America would stop trade with the other country. Napoleon, in a skilled strategic game, saw this as an opportunity to pit the United States against the British. He quickly jumped at the offer and announced that France had revoked the Berlin and Milan decrees. In reality, the emperor never intended to respect America's international trading rights, but, just as Napoleon had planned, the British retaliated, confiscating American cargo, seizing ships, impressing merchant sailors, and inciting Indian attacks on the American frontier.

REPUBLICAN "WAR HAWKS"

Public protest poured forth from Republican strongholds in the West and the South. Dominating this group were the war hawks led by Henry Clay of Kentucky and John C. Calhoun of South Carolina. This group argued that war was a matter of national honor—to defend the principles of republican government. They also wanted to demonstrate that the Republicans had the will and strength to defend America. Both principles and party were on trial. Many war hawks also hoped that a war against England would open up the continent for American expansion. These ardent expansionists sought a way to end British meddling in the frontier in order to defeat the Indians and expedite western movement. Some treasured the hope of taking Canada, thereby removing the British from the continent. Some southern members of the party saw the taking of western lands as a way of expanding slavery. Slaveholders also sought to incorporate Spanish-controlled Florida, thus cutting off an escape path for runaway slaves.

Another major point of contention was the lack of respect that England showed to the new nation on the open seas. Angry Republicans challenged Federalists to take up arms, citing the solidarity of the American Revolution, when "like a band of thirteen brothers" they fought together for the "common defense."[4] Republican newspapers often adapted the rhetoric of the War of Independence to their cause and harkened back to the days when virtuous citizens took up arms to defeat their common enemy. They asked their political opponents, "Was it for this the patriots of *seventy-six* fought—was it for this the sires of those *brave tars* bled and died?"[5] For months before the war, they continued to report British violations of neutrality. On January 9, 1812, Philadelphia's *General Aurora Advertiser* detailed the "notorious" British commander Captain James R. Dacres's kidnapping of Nathaniel Snow of Philadelphia. When Snow objected to his impressment by showing Dacres his protection paper (proving his American citizenship), the British captain shot back, "You may light your pipe with the protection!!—I will put you in the first watch."[6] In protest, the Republican paper cried out, "Can these things be borne by a free people—if so, why not renounce our independence and become colonists of a tyrant at once?"[7] Northern Republicans equated the impressment of American sailors with slavery and bondage and called Americans slaves to British exploitation.

Can freemen debate long whether their sons shall be slaves or not; better would it have been to have continued slaves; then we had not known the blessing of liberty, or the disgrace of free men being held in bondage; suffering privations and wants, enduring the writhing under the pains of cruel and inhuman floggings—degenerated beings, unworthy to be called my brothers, cannot their groans, their cries nor their affecting petitions, reach your hearts, cannot your shame or my tears rouse your indignation—turn to our sacred constitution—does not that make it your duty to rescue them—does not principle—does not honor call for war?[8]

By spring, tension on the high seas and in the western frontier brought the dark clouds of war to the horizon. On June 18, 1812, unaware that Parliament had finally revoked its orders in council, Madison requested and received a declaration of war against the "United Kingdom of Great Britain and Ireland and the dependencies thereof."[9] Just thirty-one years after the surrender of Cornwallis at Yorktown, America and Great Britain found themselves once again at war—a war that created a great chasm between Republicans and Federalists, eventually culminating in the downfall of the Federalists and a remaking of the Republicans.

When Republicans called for war in early 1812, some predicted that Great Britain would never invade the United States. In an April 14, 1812, editorial in the *Washington National Intelligencer*, Republicans called the idea "absurd," contending that England's forces were too busy all over the world to "assail" the United States. "Can anyone believe that, under such circumstances, the British government could be so infatuated as to send troops here for the purpose of invasion?"[10] The editor was dead wrong. British troops challenged American forces in such places as Canada, the Great Lakes area, the Chesapeake Bay, Washington, D.C., Baltimore and New Orleans and on the high seas. The War of 1812 raged on for almost three years.

THE FEDERALISTS

The traditionally pro-British Federalists reacted to the news of war with great fury. Although they were fervent advocates of a strong military presence, they looked at the development of a powerful national army and navy more as a deterrent than as a provoker of war. They contended that despite the British assault on American merchant ships, businessmen engaged in neutral trade had made good profits. War, they argued, would have a devastating effect on the farming and commercial economy of the United States. Not surprisingly, the Federalists were strongest in the commercial and manufacturing areas of the North, with the greatest numbers found in New England. Federalist newspapers there carefully outlined their objections to war. Typical of the Federalist view was the plea from Federalists gathered in New Jersey, who in 1812 called for a repeal of the declaration of war: "We were not invaded—no power even threatened [us]; we still enjoyed a tenfold greater portion of internal and even external happiness and prosperity than any other nation in the world. Our agriculture, commerce and manufactures, the great products of our fields, forests and fisheries, growing out of the industry and enterprise of seven millions of free and virtuous citizens, were yet but little impaired."[11]

Federalists also claimed that the United States was totally unprepared for war. In the words of Connecticut's General Assembly, America was "without fleets, without armies, with an improvised treasury, [and] with a frontier by sea and land extending many hundred miles, feebly defended."[12] As the nation prepared for war, Federalists predicted that high taxation would follow. Furthermore, if the war broke up the alliance between the British and the Indians, it would facilitate western expansion and result in an even more decentralized nation—something the Federalists strongly opposed because they thought that this would undermine the central government.

Federalists' protests incorporated rhetoric from old revolutionaries when they warned that an invasion of Canada could bring American federal troops into the area, resulting in "large bodies of armed troops quartered among" New Englanders and ushering in a "reign of Terror and the Bayonet."[13] Perhaps ironically, Federalists also used the philosophy of Republicans Jefferson and Madison and cited their nullification doctrine calling for states' rights to supersede federal policy when such policy was deemed unconstitutional—and Federalists questioned the constitutionality of the War of 1812.

THE HARTFORD CONVENTION

The unpopular nature of the War of 1812 severely divided the nation along ideological, economic, and even geographic lines. Federalists pounded away at Republican "tyranny" and even the mismanagement of the war as Federalist newspapers, speeches, and resolutions kept up a constant drumbeat of criticism and foreboding. A number of states also held conventions where war opponents discussed their plans of action or composed official protests. The apex of the Federalist antiwar stance came on December 15, 1814, when New Englanders, fuming over the prolonged war, met at a convention in Hartford, Connecticut. Twenty-six delegates deliberated until January 5, 1815. At first, the more radical Federalists called for New England to secede from the Union and form its own country if the Republicans did not end the war. However, the moderates took control and carefully spelled out their grievances with the Republican-dominated national government.

Key to the convention was the debate over the federal use of state militias, as the long-standing argument had resurfaced with the War of 1812. One major concern was the attempt by the federal government to have more control over state militia forces. In particular, Congress wanted to send New England's militias, the best in the nation, to the western frontier. The New England Federalists adamantly opposed this for three reasons. First, sending the militias to help secure or open up the frontier would only feed Republican expansionists' hopes, which the Federalists thought dangerous. Second, Federalists considered the federal transfer of the militias without state approval to be a direct violation of states' rights. "Under the Constitution the militia could be called into national service only for specific purposes. The [New England] governors insisted they, not the President, had the right to determine when these exigencies existed, and they denied their existence."[14] Ironically, this came from the same political party that had formerly advocated the federal government's supremacy over the states. Third, the use of the militia would leave New England "exposed and vulnerable" to British attack, since "the main body of the regular army has been marched to the frontier.—The navy has been stripped of a great part of its sailors for the service of the Lakes. Meanwhile the enemy scours the sea-coast, blockades our ports, ascends our bays and rivers, makes actual descents in various and distant places, holds some by force and threatens all that are assailable with fire and sword."[15]

The Hartford conventioneers also strongly protested the secretary of war's call "compelling the militia and other citizens of the United States by a forcible draft or conscription to serve in the regular armies."[16] In their convention resolution, the Federalists equated drafting with "impressment" and contended: "The armies of the United States have always been raised by contract, never by conscription, and nothing more can be wanting to a Government, possessing the power thus claimed, to enable it to usurp the entire control of the militia, in derogation of the authority of the State, and to convert it by impressment into a standing army."[17]

New England Federalists further objected to the high taxes caused by raising state military expenditures. "The militia have been constantly kept on the alert, and harassed by garrison duties, and other hardships, while the expenses, of which the National Government decline the reimbursement, threaten to absorb all the resources of the States."[18] The Hartford delegates asked for compensation from the federal government for revenues lost in overseas trade, contending that "commerce, the vital spring of New-England's prosperity, was annihilated."[19]

The New Englanders also demanded additional constitutional amend-

ments related to incorporation of new states, trade embargoes, and declarations of war. These important decisions, they argued, should only be
passed with a two-thirds congressional vote. In addition, the Federalists
advocated the restriction of naturalized citizens from holding public office and concluded the "same person" should "not be elected president
of the United States a second time" with the proviso that presidents
could not be elected from the same state two terms in succession.[20] In
January 1815, armed with their resolutions, representatives from the
Hartford Convention headed to Washington, D.C., to make their demands in person. But the Federalists' arrival there coincided with the
announcement of the Ghent peace treaty and the exciting news of a stunning American victory by General Andrew Jackson in New Orleans.
Communication delays helped Americans confuse the chronology of
events and convince themselves that Jackson's triumph at New Orleans
preceded and caused the Treaty of Ghent, although in fact the treaty
already had been negotiated before the battle. More important, the mythology that rapidly emerged about American military superiority—as-
suring victory—of the Kentucky "long rifles" and other "farmer"
volunteers under Jackson's command defeating the finest British soldiers
on the plains outside New Orleans—reaffirmed the American belief that
"virtue" triumphed over professionalism and that reliance on "citizen-
soldiers" was America's best defense. As the nation celebrated the defeat
of its old adversary, many began to construe the Hartford resolutions as
angry words from traitors of a patriotic war.

CONCLUSION

The War of 1812 dealt a deathblow to the Federalists, but the Republicans did not escape their own tribulations. With the demise of the Federalists, "everyone" became "Republicans." Growing far too diverse for
any effective cooperation, the party imploded during the following decade, leading to the Second Party system (Democrats vs. Whigs) of the
Jacksonian Era.

At the war's end, military and political leaders called for reform. They
acknowledged that the war had consisted of too many "humiliating defeats, including the loss and destruction by fire of the Capital itself."
Many also recognized the superiority of America's regular army over the
militia forces but still recognized the need for reform. "Amidst the re-
verses and chaos . . . the training program of a few exceptional Regular
Army officers, combined with the fortunes of war and the valor of a
small body of American infantrymen, permitted a few Regular Army
regiments to win uncommon distinction for themselves and to bestow
upon the whole Regular Army an unaccustomed luster."[21] Although debates over the military continued at the conclusion of the war, there was

a general acceptance that professionalization of the armed forces and improvements in the militia system were definitely necessary. This awareness allowed Secretary of War John C. Calhoun to propose military reforms in 1820 that would begin to place the militia in a secondary role behind the regular army.

The War of 1812 brought to the forefront a cavernous debate over political, economic, military, and diplomatic policy and skewed the already-confusing argument over states' rights versus federal power. It also highlighted the intense battle over western expansion. Many of these issues did not disappear with the Treaty of Ghent, but instead grew into a fiery flame that eventually exploded in two new conflicts—the Mexican-American War and the American Civil War.

NOTES

1. C. Edward Skeen, *Citizen Soldiers in the War of 1812* (Lexington: University Press of Kentucky, 1999), p. 5.

2. Allan R. Millett and Peter Maslowski, *For the Common Defense: A Military History of the United States of America* (New York: Free Press, 1984), p. 89.

3. Donald R. Hickey, *The War of 1812: A Forgotten Conflict* (Urbana: University of Illinois Press, 1989), p. 5.

4. "Honor Calls for War," *General Aurora Advertiser*, June 19, 1812, p. 2.

5. Ibid.

6. "Impressment," *General Aurora Advertiser*, January 9, 1812, p. 2.

7. Ibid.

8. Ibid.

9. "An Act Declaring War between the United Kingdom of Great Britain and Ireland and the Dependencies Thereof and the United States of America and Their Territories," *United States Statutes at Large*, June 18, 1812; "An Act," *Pennsylvania Gazette*, June 24, 1812, p. 2.

10. "Washington City," *Washington National Intelligencer*, April 14, 1812, p. 1.

11. "Convention of New-Jersey," *Pennsylvania Gazette*, July 29, 1812, p. 1.

12. Quoted from Lawrence Delbert Cress, " 'Cool and Serious Reflections': Federalist Attitudes toward War in 1812," *Journal of the Early Republic* 7 (Summer 1987): 132.

13. Ibid., p. 135.

14. Millett and Maslowski, *For the Common Defense*, p. 103.

15. *The Proceedings of a Convention of Delegates, From the States of Massachusetts, Connecticut, and Rhode-Island; the Counties of Cheshire and Grafton, in the State of New-Hampshire; and the County of Windham in the State of Vermont;—Convened at Hartford, in the State of Connecticut, December 15, 1814* (Boston: Wells and Lilly, 1815), p. 11.

16. Ibid., p. 7.

17. Ibid.

    18. Ibid., p. 11.
    19. Ibid.
    20. Ibid., p. 21
    21. Russell F. Weigley, *History of the United States Army* (New York: Macmillan, 1967), p. 117.

DOCUMENTS

2.1.   An Antifederalist Protests a Standing Army, January 24, 1788

Federalists and Antifederalists battled over political, economic, military, and foreign policy issues in speeches, pamphlets, and newspapers throughout the young nation. One of their major debates centered on the size, strength, and duties of a standing army. Federalists thought that a professional trained army was necessary for the protection of the nation. Antifederalists feared that a standing army posed a threat to the Republic and to the individual rights of the people. They preferred to rely on citizen-soldiers in state militias whenever possible. The following is an excerpt from an article published in the New York Journal *on January 24, 1788, that explains the Antifederalists' position. Although it is signed "Brutus" after the Roman republican who played a role in the assassination of Julius Caesar in Rome, historians believe it was written by Antifederalist Robert Yates. Yates was a state judge and served as New York's delegate to the Constitutional Convention.*

The liberties of a people are in danger from a large standing army, not only because the rulers may employ them for the purposes of supporting themselves in any usurpations of power, which they may see proper to exercise, but there is great hazard, that an army will subvert the forms of the government, under whose authority, they are raised, and establish one, according to the pleasure of their leader.

We are informed, in the faithful pages of history, of such events frequently happening.—Two instances have been mentioned in a former paper. They are so remarkable, that they are worthy of the most careful attention of every lover of freedom.—They are taken from the history of the two most powerful nations that have ever existed in the world; and who are the most renowned, for the freedom they enjoyed, and the excellency of their constitutions:—I mean Rome and Britain.

In the first, the liberty of the commonwealth was destroyed, and the constitution overturned, by an army, led by Julius Caesar, who was appointed to the command, by the constitutional authority of that commonwealth. He changed it from a free republic, whose fame had sounded, and is still celebrated by all the world, into that of the most absolute despotism. A standing army effected this change, and a standing army supported it through a succession of ages, which are marked in the annals of history, with the most horrid cruelties, bloodshed, and carnage;—The most devilish, beastly, and unnatural vices, that ever punished or disgraced human nature.

The same army, that in Britain, vindicated the liberties of that people from the encroachments and despotism of a tyrant king, assisted Cromwell, their General, in wrestling from the people, that liberty they had so dearly earned.

You may be told, these instances will not apply to our case:—But those who would persuade you to believe this, either mean to deceive you, or have not themselves considered the subject. . . .

It will probably be necessary to keep up a small body of troops to garrison a few posts, which it will be necessary to maintain, in order to guard against the sudden encroachments of the Indians, or of the Spaniards and British; and therefore, the general government ought to be invested with power to raise and keep up a standing army in time of peace, without restraint; at their discretion. . . .

It is also admitted that an absolute prohibition against raising troops, except in cases of actual war, would be improper; because it will be requisite to raise and support a small number of troops to garrison the important frontier posts, and to guard arsenals; and it may happen, that the danger of an attack from a foreign power may be so imminent, as to render it highly proper we should raise an army, in order to be prepared to resist them. But to raise and keep up forces for such purposes and on such occasions, is not included in the idea, of keeping up standing armies in times of peace.

It is a thing very practicable to give the government sufficient authority to provide for these cases, and at the same time to provide a reasonable and competent security against the evil of a standing army—a clause to the following purpose would answer the end:

As standing armies in time of peace are dangerous to liberty, and have often been the means of overturning the best constitutions of governments, no standing army, or troops of any description whatsoever, shall be raised or kept up by the legislature, except so many as shall be necessary for guards to the arsenals of the United States, or for garrisons to such posts on the frontiers, as it shall be deemed absolutely necessary to hold, to secure the inhabitants, and facilitate the trade with the Indians: unless when the United States are threatened with an attack or invasion from some foreign power, in which case the legislature shall be authorized to raise an army to be prepared to repel the attack; provided that no troops whatsoever shall be raised in time of peace, without the assent of two thirds of the members, composing both houses of the legislature.

A clause similar to this would afford sufficient latitude to the legislature to raise troops in all cases that were really necessary, and at the same time competent security against the establishment of that dangerous engine of despotism a standing army.

Brutus

Source: Brutus, "To the People of the State of New-York," *New York Journal*, January 24, 1788, p. 1.

2.2.   A Republican's Call for War, April 14, 1812

During the early months of 1812, many Republicans contended that the United States should declare war on Great Britain. The anonymous author of the following newspaper article argued that war was inevitable, so why delay the decision? Furthermore, the writer was convinced that Great Britain would not invade the United States. He was wrong.

The public attention has been drawn to the approaching arrival of the *Hornet*. . . . We are among those who have attached to this event a high degree of importance, and have, therefore, looked to it with the utmost solicitude.

But, if the reports, which we now hear are true, that with England all hope of honorable accommodation is at an end, and that with France our negotiations are in a forwardness encouraging expectations of a favorable result, where is the motive for longer delay? The final step ought to be taken, and that step is WAR. By what course of measures we have reached the present crisis, is not now a question for patriots and freemen to discuss. It exists: and it is by open and manly war only that we can get through it with honor and advantage to the country. Our wrongs have been great; our cause is just; and if we are decided and firm, success is inevitable.

Let war therefore be forthwith proclaimed against England. With her there can be no motive for delay. Any further discussion, any new attempt at negotiation, would be as fruitless as it would be dishonorable. With France we shall be at liberty to pursue the course which circumstances may require. The advance she has already made by a repeal of her decrees; the manner of its reception by the government, and the prospect which exists of an amicable accommodation, entitle her to this preference. If she acquits herself to the just claims of the United States, we shall have good cause to applaud our conduct in it, and if she fails we shall always be in time to place her on the ground of her adversary.

But it is said that we are not prepared for war, and ought therefore not to declare it. This is an idle objection, which can have weight with the timid and pusillanimous only. The fact is otherwise. Our preparations are adequate to every essential object. Do we apprehend danger to ourselves? From what quarter will it assail us? From England, and by invasion? The idea is too absurd to merit a moment's consideration. Where are her troops? But lately she dreaded an invasion of her own dominions from her powerful and menacing neighbor. That danger, it is true, has diminished, but it has not entirely and forever disappeared. The war in the Peninsula, which lingers, requires strong armies to support it. She maintains an army in Sicily; another in India; and a strong force in Ireland, and along her own coast, and in the West Indies. Can anyone believe that, under such circumstances, the British government could be so infatuated as to send troops here for the purpose of invasion? The experience and the fortune of our Revolution, when we were comparatively in an infant state, have doubtless taught her a useful lesson that she cannot have forgotten. Since that period our population has increased threefold, whilst hers has remained almost stationary. The condition of the civilized world, too, has changed. Although Great Britain has nothing to fear as to her independence, and her military operations are extensive and distant, the contest is evidently maintained by her rather for safety than for conquest. Have we cause to dread an attack from her neighboring provinces? That apprehension is still more groundless. Seven or eight millions of people have nothing to dread from 300,000. From the moment that war is declared, the British colonies will be put on the defensive, and soon after we get in motion, must sink under the pressure. . . . The great question to which the 13 United States have to decide; is, whether they will relinquish the ground which they now hold, or maintain it with the firmness and vigor becoming freemen.

Source: "Washington City," *Washington National Intelligencer*, April 14, 1812, p. 3. Punctuation and grammar have been reprinted directly from the original source.

2.3.   Republicans Call for War, June 19, 1812

In the following "Call for War," Republicans challenged Federalists once again to fight against British "lawlessness, cruelty and inhumanity," especially the "enslaving" of American sailors by British sea captains. Republicans also utilized patriotic rhetoric in their efforts to gain support for the war with England and often made references to the American Revolution.

At the close of the revolution and previous to the formation of the constitution, the citizens of the United States were like a band of thirteen brothers about to associate for common defense, each had a right to debate on the articles of association, each had a right to be heard, each had contributed his treasure, each had spilt his blood or risked his life to gain *freedom for all*—the association was completed and each brother went his way; one to "plough the ocean," one to plough his farm, and one to subdue the wilderness. In short, all betook themselves to whatever employment or occupation suited their fortunes, their inclinations, or their habits best—A few years glided away in peace; success attended all their undertakings, and prosperity crowned their industry. At length "news" arrived, that the children of their brother who had gone to "subdue the wilderness," had been murdered by the savages; his houses laid in ashes, his crops destroyed, his horses stolen, and himself carried off into captivity. All assembled agreeably to their articles of association, completely *equipt* [*sic*] for *war*. They marched to the wilderness, chastised the savages, rescued their brother, and restored peace and good order.

Soon after, tidings came that the insidious nation they first had conquered, had taken captive one of the sons of him that followed the sea—he had been taken whilst about his lawful business, and was now obliged to serve on board their ships of war.—The father appealed to his brothers, and begged them to assist him in rescuing his son—but, alas! their honor slumbered—they advised "negociation [*sic*]."—While they were negociating [*sic*], another son was *kidnapped* and stolen; and, moreover, he was obliged to assist in *kidnapping* his brethren—to aggravate the matter, they claimed these sons as their subjects—because (as was supposed) they were white people and spoke the English language—the captives, however, disdained to belong to a nation so destitute of feeling, of humanity or of honor, and wrote to their father for proof of their legitimacy, and begged to be rescued from bondage—on this occasion the father and patriot addressed his brethren: "While you continue," said he, "in fruitless negociation [*sic*], my sons are in bondage; while year after year you consent to discuss the principle of 'stealing' them, you admit it is possible they have a right to take them. Was it to make my children slaves, that I joined you in throwing off the *British yoke*—was it for this, that I endured the fatigue, the toil, and the peril of 'a seven years war'—was it for this, that I sacrificed my treasure, and received the wounds that caused these scars—was it for this, that I marched to avenge the wrongs committed on my brother by the savages. What were his wrongs to mine, his sons are dead and died by savage hands, but their deaths are nobly revenged; nor were they or we dishonored by their fated end; my sons die a living death,' or live an eternal shame and disgrace to you and to me. Can freemen debate long whether their sons shall be slaves or not; better would it have been to have continued slaves; then we had not known the blessings of liberty, or the disgrace of freemen being held in bondage; suffering privations and wants, enduring and writhing under the pains of cruel and inhuman floggings—degenerate beings, unworthy to be called my brothers, cannot their groans, their cries nor their affecting petitions, reach your hearts, cannot your shame or my tears rouse your indignation—turn to our sacred constitution—does not that make it your duty to rescue them—does not principle—does not honor call for war?"

Is not this a picture of the conduct of our government with regard to their sons of liberty? Letters, supplications and petitions have been received from our impressed seamen and their friends—fathers have stated their disgrace and implored their protection—mothers have bewailed their suffering and want, and prayed their rescue—brothers have seen their agonizing pains, and sworn to avenge them—they have waited with more than human patience for the result of "negociation" [sic]—their hearts sicken at a retrospect. Years have been wasted, and every year has added hundreds of our fellow citizens to the list of victims of British lawlessness, cruelty and inhumanity. Was it for this the patriots of *seventy-six* fought—was it for this the sires of those *brave tars* bled and died? There was but one way to discuss the right of impressing American seamen—a prompt demand should have been made to deliver them up; a refusal or hesitation, followed by immediate war. But let us delay no longer—delay is always dangerous—but now it is death; while the remedy is preparing, the patient dies; and while a certain secretary spends eight months to organize an army which might have been organized in three months thousands of our fellow citizens are suffering more than the horrors of hell, or the torments of the inquisition. Had this army been sent into Canada three months ago, those provinces had now been twice in our possession. . . . The moment has arrived, when energy and decisions are indispensably necessary—prompt and vigorous measures are looked for by the nation—an immediate execution of the laws passed by congress is expected.

The crisis has arrived, that the U. States must take up their arms, and show to the world they are a brave, and when their rights are invaded, a warlike people—that they are great and magnanimous, and deserve and will be respected.

QUINTIUS

Source: "Honor Calls for War," *General Aurora Advertiser*, June 19, 1812, p. 2. Italics, punctuation, and grammar have been reprinted directly from the original source.

2.4.   The Federalist Position of the Convention of New Jersey, July 4, 1812

Federalists, who opposed the War of 1812, gathered together at various conventions to discuss their course of action. At the New Jersey Conference, Federalists acknowledged the need for a strong military for defense purposes but objected to its use in the current war. They also questioned the motives for the war, since Great Britain had not invaded the United States. Subsequently, the Federalists sought to repeal the declaration of war.

FELLOW-CITIZENS,

A crisis has at length arrived in the administration of the public affairs of this country, in which every one of us has a deep and solemn concern. It is not our purpose to review the various acts and proceedings of those to whom the people for twelve years past have entrusted the management of these affairs. Unhappily they seem to have left us to reflect upon our divisions and misfortunes. Most unequivocally, however, do we declare our confidence in the great body of citizens, whatever may have been our distrust or dissatisfaction in regard to many men in office, and the measures they have pursued.

We believe the people, to whatever set of men and measures they have attached their confidence and support, could only mean, and did mean, the good, the peace, and prosperity of a country rendered dear to them by so many privileges and blessings. It is to this people, so enlightened, so independent and patriotic, (and may we trust, so candid as to confide in our sincerity) that we now address ourselves.

On the 18th of June, a small majority of congress did by a law declare war on the part of the United States, against the united kingdom of G. Britain and Ireland, and its dependencies. . . .

We address you then, fellow-citizens, at this awful crisis, produced by the war law, in the language of freemen and free agents—in the consciousness of pure motives, and penetrated by the profoundest feelings of patriotic regard for our dear country. . . .

A law, debated and passed in secret, has placed this extensive country and all its great interests of peace—commerce—agriculture—union—and future prosperity, on the fate of war.

Defense, within our own borders, and even arming our own vessels for defense on the seas, against both French and English aggression, was a practicable and not a hazardous expedient.—But without preparation, and without trial of the means of defense, dissention in our country, and general opposition to war, to become the attacking power, and to declare open, general, and offensive war, against one of the great contending states of Europe—we repeat it fellow citizens, is an event in the history, even of these times, which fills us, and we believe the great body of the people, with grief and amazement.

We were not invaded—no power even threatened it; we still enjoyed a tenfold greater portion of internal and even external happiness and prosperity than any nation in the world. Our agriculture, commerce and manufactures, the great products of our fields, forests and fisheries, growing out of the industry and enterprise of seven millions of free and virtuous citizens, were yet but little impaired, except by our own internal restrictions, which could at any time be suspended or removed. . . .

How unfortunate, when men prefer the honour [*sic*] of persevering in error to the honour of retracting it; and when their country too is at stake. Beside the decay of agriculture, commerce and revenue, war will vitiate the morals of our people, particularly the rising generation. Is it nothing to bring on a general decline of virtue, order and regard for life, property, and private rights? Will not war necessarily produce this, with a decline also of industry and the evils of a widespreading insolvency? . . .

We cease, fellow citizens, to reflect on these direful but certain *consequences*, of a *protracted* WAR. Your own cool reflections will go far beyond the reach of these remarks to open to you its certain miseries—its doubtful issue, and multiplied horrors.—Those of us, and of you, who have witnessed its scenes of distress, in the revolution, which is past, can want no dissuasive. We address ourselves more especially to those who may be strangers as yet to the calamities of war. In the sincerity of our hearts, and what but motives of love to our country can influence us, we intreat our fellow citizens, if any of them could lend an ear to this war, to PAUSE, before they give it their APPROBATION, or by stimulating it forward, make too wide the breach to be healed.

Those of our rulers who imprudently have pledged themselves, step by step, to *war*—*those*, who consult their passions, or profit from commissions, army employments, and public offices—men in the southern and western states, who will suffer little; all, indeed, who will thrive and grow great upon its length and devastation—nay, even many sincere friends of their country, may unthinkingly, or rashly, *advise* you to *War*. But in a matter of importance, let each citizen calmly judge for himself . . . whether they expect that a long and deadly warfare, for such causes as have been mentioned, will be better than continued Peace, Commerce, Agriculture, Security and Union, among ourselves?

Is it not evidently better to *regain* Peace, and all its certain advantages, than to proceed in the dangerous path of *War?* Surely we may anticipate that a People, so enlightened and thoughtful of consequences, will not decide to carry on this war, so declared, longer than the time necessary to procure its constitutional REPEAL. We trust that most of our citizens will see the policy and the benefits of Neutrality, and of going back to the ground of *Negociation* [*sic*].

Source: "Convention of New-Jersey," *Pennsylvania Gazette*, July 29, 1812, p. 1. In reprinting this primary source, "Old English" letters were changed when necessary for easier reading. Italics, punctuation, and grammar have been reprinted directly from the original source.

2.5.   The Federalist Position on Militias at the Hartford Convention, 1814

In December 1814, delegates from the New England states met in Hartford, Connecticut, to discuss their opposition to the war and to draft a resolution of their objectives. In particular, Federalists rejected the congressional proposal to institute a draft and to transfer New England's militia forces to the western frontier. The conventioneers argued that moving the military would leave the New England states vulnerable to attack. In the following excerpts from the Convention Proceedings, Federalists spell out the relationship between the militia and the federal government as defined by the Constitution and expressed deep concerns about any other use of these state forces.

The authority of the National Government over the militia is derived from those clauses in the Constitution which give power to Congress "to provide for calling forth the militia, to execute the laws of the Union, suppress insurrections and repel invasions"—Also, "to provide for organizing, arming and disciplining the militia, and for governing such parts of them as may be employed in the service of the United States, reserving to the States respectively the appointment of the officers, and the authority of training the militia according to the discipline prescribed by Congress." Again, "The President shall be Commander in Chief of the army and navy of the United States, and of the militia of the several States, *when called into the actual service of the United States.*" In these specified cases only, has the National Government any power over the militia; and it follows conclusively, that for all general and ordinary purposes, this power belongs to the States respectively, and to them alone. It is not only with regret, but with astonishment, the Convention perceive that under colour [*sic*] of an authority conferred with such plain and precise limitations, a power is arrogated by the executive government, and in some instances sanctioned by the two Houses of Congress, of control over the militia, which if conceded, will render nugatory the rightful authority of the individual States over that class of men, and by placing at the disposal of the National Government the lives and services of the great body of the people, enable it at pleasure to destroy their liberties, and erect a military despotism on the ruins.

The power of compelling the militia and other citizens of the United States by a forcible draft or conscription to serve in the regular armies, as proposed in a late official letter of the Secretary of War, is not delegated to Congress by the Constitution, and the exercise of it would be not less dangerous to their liberties, than hostile to the sovereignty of the States. . . . The armies of the United States have always been raised by contract, never by conscription, and nothing more can be wanting to a Government, possessing the power thus claimed, to enable it to usurp the entire control of the militia, in derogation of the authority of the States, and to convert it by impressment into a standing army. . . .

In the prosecution of this favourite [*sic*] warfare, Administration have left the exposed and vulnerable parts of the country destitute of all efficient means of defence [*sic*]. The main body of the regular army has been marched to the frontier.—The navy has been stripped of a great part of its sailors for the service of the Lakes. Meanwhile the enemy scours the sea-coast, blockades our ports, ascends our bays and rivers, makes actual descents in various and distant place, holds some by force and threatens all that are assailable with fire and sword. The sea-board of four of the New-England States, following its curvatures, presents an extent of more than seven hundred miles, generally occupied by a compact population, and accessible by a naval force, exposing a mass of people and property to the devastation of the enemy, which bears a great proportion to the residue of the maritime frontier of the United States. This extensive shore has been exposed to frequent attacks, repeated contributions, and constant alarms. The regular forces detached by the national Government for its defence, are mere pretexts for placing officers of high rank in command. They are besides confined to a few places, and are too insignificant in number to be included in any computation.

These States have thus been left to adopt measures for their own defence [*sic*]. The militia have been constantly kept on the alert, and harassed by garrison duties, and other hardships, while the expenses, of which the National Government decline the reimbursement, threaten to absorb all the resources of the States. The President of the United States has refused to consider the expense of the militia detached by state authority, for the indispensable defence [*sic*] of the State, as chargeable to the Union, on the ground of a refusal by the Executive of the State, to place them under the command of officers of the regular army. Detachments of militia placed at the disposal of the General Government have been dismissed either without pay, or with depreciated paper. The prospect of the ensuing campaign is not enlivened by the promise of any alleviation of these grievances. . . .

If the war be continued, there appears no room for reliance upon the national government for the supply of those means of defence [sic], which must become indispensable to secure these States from desolation and ruin. Nor is it possible that the States can discharge this sacred duty from their own resources, and continue to sustain the burden of the national taxes. The Administration, after a long perseverance in plans to baffle every effort of commercial enterprise, had fatally succeeded in their attempts at the epoch of the war. Commerce, the vital spring of New-England's prosperity, was annihilated. Embargoes, restrictions, and the rapacity of revenue officers had completed its destruction. The various objects for the employment of productive labour [sic], in the branches of business dependent on commerce, have disappeared. The fisheries have shared its fate. Manufactures, which Government has professed an intention to favour [sic] and to cherish, as an indemnity for the failure of these branches of business, are doomed to struggle in their infancy with taxes and obstructions, which cannot fail most seriously to affect their growth. The specie is withdrawn from circulation.

From these facts, it is almost superfluous to state the irresistible inference, that these States have no capacity of defraying the expense requisite for their own protection, and, at the same time, of discharging the demands of the national treasury.

Source: The Proceedings of a Convention of Delegates, From the States of Massachusetts, Connecticut, and Rhode-Island; the Counties of Cheshire and Grafton, in the State of New-Hampshire; and the County of Windham in the State of Vermont;—Convened at Hartford, in the State of Connecticut, December 15, 1814 (Boston: Wells and Lilly, 1815), pp. 6–11. Italics, punctuation, and grammar have been reprinted directly from the original source.

2.6.   Resolutions of the Hartford Convention, 1814

At the conclusion of the Hartford Convention in January 1815, New England Federalists agreed to a series of resolutions concerning the war and future policies of the United States government. Shortly afterward, representatives went to Washington,

D.C., to present their resolutions to Congress. Excerpts from their political demands about war in America are presented here.

Our nation may yet be great, our union durable. But should this prospect be utterly hopeless, the time will not have been lost, which shall have ripened a general sentiment of the necessity of more mighty efforts to rescue from ruin, at least some portion of our beloved Country.

THEREFORE RESOLVED—

That it be and hereby is recommended to the Legislatures of the several States represented in this Convention, to adopt all such measures as may be necessary effectually to protect the citizens of said States from the operation and effects of all acts which have been or may be passed by the Congress of the United States, which shall contain provisions, subjecting the militia or other citizens to forcible drafts, conscription, or impressments, not authorized by the Constitution of the United States.

Resolved, That it be and hereby is recommended to the said Legislatures, to authorize an immediate and earnest application to be made to the Government of the United States, requesting their consent to some arrangement, whereby the said States may, separately or in concert, be empowered to assume upon themselves the defence of their territory against the enemy; and a reasonable portion of the taxes, collected within said States, may be paid into the respective treasuries thereof, and appropriated to the payment of the balance due said States, and to the future defence of the same. The amount so paid into the said treasuries to be credited, and the disbursements made as aforesaid to be charged to the United States.

Resolved, That it be, and it hereby is, recommended to the Legislatures of the aforesaid States, to pass laws (where it has not already been done) authorizing the Governours [*sic*] or Commanders in Chief of their militia to make detachments from the same, or to form voluntary corps, as shall be most convenient and conformable to their Constitutions, and to cause the same to be well armed, equipped and disciplined, and held in readiness for service; and upon the request of the Governour [*sic*] of either of the other States, to employ the whole of such detachment or corps, as well as the regular forces of the State, or such part thereof as may be required and can be spared consistently with the safety of the State, in assisting the State, making such request to repel any invasion thereof which shall be made or attempted by the publick [*sic*] enemy.

Resolved, That the following amendments of the Constitution of the United States, be recommended to the States represented as aforesaid, to be proposed by them for adoption by the State Legislatures, and, in such cases as may be deemed expedient, by a Convention chosen by the people of each State.

And it is further recommended that the said States shall persevere in their efforts to obtain such amendments, until the same shall be effected.

First. Representatives and direct taxes shall be apportioned among the several States which may be included within this union, according to their respective numbers of free persons, including those bound to serve for a term of years, and excluding Indians not taxed, and all other persons.

Second. No new State shall be admitted into the union by Congress in virtue of the power granted by the Constitution, without the concurrence of two thirds of both Houses.

Third. Congress shall not have power to lay any embargo on the ships or vessels of the citizens of the United States, in the ports or harbours [*sic*] thereof, for more than sixty days.

Fourth. Congress shall not have power, without the concurrence of two thirds of both Houses, to interdict the commercial intercourse between the United States and any foreign nation or the dependencies thereof.

Fifth. Congress shall not make or declare war, or authorize acts of hostility against any foreign nation, without the concurrence of two thirds of both Houses, except such acts of hostility be in defence [*sic*] of the territories of the United States when actually invaded.

Sixth. No person who shall hereafter be naturalized, shall be eligible as a member of the Senate or House of Representatives of the United States, nor capable of holding any civil office under the authority of the United States.

Seventh. The same person shall not be elected President of the United States a second time; nor shall the President be elected from the same state two terms in succession.

Resolved, That if the application of these States to the government of the United States, recommended in a foregoing Resolution, should be unsuccessful, and peace should not be concluded, and the defence [*sic*] of these States should be neglected, as it has been since the commencement of the war, it will in the opinion of this Convention be expedient for the Legislatures of the several States to appoint Delegates to another Convention, to meet at Boston, in the State of Massachusetts, on the third Thursday of June next, with such powers and instructions as the exigency of a crisis so momentous may require.

Resolved, That the Hon. George Cabot, the Hon. Chauncey Goodrich, and the Hon. Daniel Lyman, or any two of them, be authorized to call another meeting of this Convention, to be holden in Boston, at any time before new Delegates shall be chosen, as recommended in the above Resolution, if in their judgement the situation of the Country shall urgently require it.

HARTFORD . . .

GEORGE CABOT,	JAMES HILLHOUSE,
NATHAN DANE,	JOHN TREADWELL,
WILLIAM PRESCOTT,	ZEPHANIAH SWIFT,
HARRISON G. OTIS,	NATHANIEL SMITH,
TIMOTHY BIGELOW,	CALVIN GODDARD,
JOSHUA THOMAS,	ROGER M. SHERMAN,
SAMUEL S. WILDE,	DANIEL LYMAN,
JOSEPH LYMAN,	SAMUEL WARD,
STEPHEN LONGFELLOW, JR.	EDWARD MANTON,
DANIEL WALDO,	BENJAMIN HAZARD,
HODIJAH BAYLIES,	BENJAMIN WEST,
GEORGE BLISS,	MILLS OLCOTT,
CHAUNCEY GOODRICH,	WILLIAM HALL, JR.

Source: The Proceedings of a Convention of Delegates, From the States of Massachusetts, Connecticut, and Rhode-Island; the Counties of Cheshire and Grafton, in the State of New-Hampshire; and the County of Windham in the State of Vermont;—Convened at Hartford, in the State of Connecticut, December 15, 1814 (Boston: Wells and Lilly, 1815), pp. 21–22. In the collection of the John Hay Library, Brown University, Providence, Rhode Island. Italics, punctuation, and grammar have been reprinted directly from the original source.

ANNOTATED RESEARCH GUIDE

Books and Articles

Banner, James M., Jr. "A Shadow of Secession? The Hartford Convention, 1814." *History Today* 38 (September 1988): 24–30. Discusses the tension between the Federalists and Democratic-Republicans prior to the War of 1812 and focuses on the position of New England's Federalist leaders during the Hartford Convention. Banner argues that the convention set a precedent for resistance during the Civil War.

———. *To the Hartford Convention: The Federalists and the Origins of Party Politics in Massachusetts, 1789–1815*. New York: Alfred A. Knopf, 1970. Traces the origins of the New England Federalist party from the birth of the new nation through the Hartford Convention.

Hickey, Donald R. *The War of 1812: A Forgotten Conflict*. Urbana: University of Illinois Press, 1989. Tracks the diplomatic path to the War of 1812 and details the military conflict that followed. Provides a comprehensive chapter on the Hartford Convention, especially noting the significance of Federalists' resistance to the new national military policies.

Pitcavage, Mark. " 'Burthened in Defence of Our Rights': Opposition to Military Service in the War of 1812." *Ohio History* 104 (Summer–Autumn 1995): 142–162. Examines Ohio's opposition to the War of 1812, particularly to military policies that left the state vulnerable to Indian attacks with the absence of fighting-age men, and also explores Ohio's difficulties in maintaining an effective state militia.

Skeen, C. Edward. *Citizen Soldiers in the War of 1812.* Lexington: University Press of Kentucky, 1999. Analyzes the heated debate over the federal government's use of state militias (which laid the foundation for the Hartford Convention) and examines the experience of the militias, their successes and failures, throughout the War of 1812.

Stagg, J.C.A. *Mr. Madison's War: Politics, Diplomacy, and Warfare in the Early American Republic, 1783–1830.* Princeton, NJ: Princeton University Press, 1983. Provides detailed information on the foreign policy conflicts that led to the War of 1812 and gives political and military details of the conflict. One chapter focuses on "The Final Crises" and analyzes the significance of the Hartford Convention.

———. "New York Federalists and Opposition to the War of 1812." *World Affairs* 142, no. 3 (1980): 169–187. Explains the role of New York's antiwar Federalists during the War of 1812.

Web Sites

http://www.mtholyoke.edu/acad/intrel/feros-pg.htm. Professor of International Politics Vincent Ferraro of Mount Holyoke College provides reprints of government documents and newspaper articles on the War of 1812, as well as links to other foreign policy sites.

http://www.yale.edu/lawweb/avalon/diplomacy/br1814m.htm. Yale Law School's Avalon Project provides primary sources from the War of 1812, focusing principally on diplomatic issues.

3

The Three Million Bill and the Wilmot Proviso: The Debate over Westward Expansion during the Mexican War

The Mexican War (1846–1848) is often overlooked or understudied, yet this war radically reshaped American politics, distinctly changed the geography and economics of the country, and ultimately set the stage for perhaps the most significant war in American history—the Civil War. At first, the Whig party stood unified against "Mr. Polk's War," accusing President James K. Polk, a Democrat, of pushing the nation into an unnecessary military engagement. However, as the war progressed and political strain intensified between the North and the South, a realliance of the political parties began to take shape. Many northern Whigs joined forces with northern Democrats who opposed the expansion of slavery to face off against congressmen from the South and West. They quarreled over military policy in the Mexican War and over the issue of permitting slavery in any new territory secured in the conflict. But partisan politics was by no means totally supplanted by sectionalism, and many—now representing minority voices within their party—spoke out. The only things that could be counted on in the debate over the Mexican conflict were anger and chaos.

The arguments over the Mexican War came at a time when America was in the process of redefining itself. In an optimistic attitude shaped by growing nationalism, a belief in progress, and a spirit of boundlessness, America looked westward. The country saw itself as a model republic, ordained by God, with the self-imposed responsibility of spreading its "superior" cultural, political, and economic institutions from sea to shining sea. Economic expansionists with commercial ambitions were drawn like a beacon to the Pacific trade. Newspaper editor John L. O'Sullivan best captured the reform spirit of the day when he coined the term "Manifest Destiny." When war came with Mexico, the possibility of a vast territorial acquisition—the spoils for the American victors—was too much to resist for many political leaders.

The slave issue complicated Manifest Destiny. Many antislavery advocates warned that once slavery moved into the territories, it would corrupt free labor everywhere by closing off the West to free-soil principles. It would also strengthen slavery's interest in Congress and hitch America's fortunes ever more to the yoke of "the slave power." Western expansion thus threatened to accelerate the growing tension between the North and the South, a tension that Congress was trying desperately to suppress through compromise or silence.

One of the most controversial arguments in Congress came with the February 1847 Three Million Bill, which asked for an unrestricted sum of up to three million dollars to be given to President James Polk to bring a quick end to the war. The bill sparked heated debates over the government's military strategy, which instead of placing maximum military force at the area of contention—the Rio Grande—it called for the U.S. military to secure Mexican lands throughout the Southwest. The bill gave many U.S. congressmen and senators the opportunity to express their support or disapproval of military strategy in the Mexican War. Irate voices charged President Polk with turning a simple boundary dispute into an all-out war for conquest of Mexican lands. When Congressman David Wilmot, a Democrat from Pennsylvania, asked to attach his proviso outlawing slavery in any territory acquired as a result of the Mexican War, a feverish debate arose on the floor of both the House and the Senate.

Many predicted that the angry sparring over western expansion would only bring ruin to the nation and create a cavernous divide that could never be repaired. Senator Reverdy Johnson, a Whig from Maryland, solemnly declared that only two things could come out of the Three Million Bill, "civil war with all its inconceivable evils, or the disruption of the Union."[1] Others, like Senator Lewis Cass, a Michigan Democrat and a devoted advocate of expansion, scoffed at their worried colleagues. Cass concluded, "In the distant horizon, not a cloud as big as the prophet's hand, is to be seen, which is to overspread the heavens, and to burst in thunder and in tempest upon us."[2] Cass was wrong, for the heavens did open up, and thunder and lightning fell like sharpened swords on the nation in a storm that brewed for over thirteen years before it finally tore the Union apart.

THE MEXICAN WAR

In 1820, Americans began to move into Texas at the invitation of the Mexican government, but they never fully accepted Mexican authority.

Tension between the American settlers and the leaders of Mexico turned into a crisis when the Mexican government attempted to reassert its authority over the region by, among several measures, insisting that the "Texans" honor Mexico's ban on slavery. In 1835, Texans rebelled and, after a year of fighting, declared themselves an independent republic. Shortly afterward, Texas requested admission into the United States. But the possibility of annexation came at a crisis point in American history as the nation struggled to maintain a delicate balance of power between free and slave states. Antislavery forces led by Quaker abolitionist Benjamin Lundy warned that annexing Texas would forever give slavery the advantage in Congress and the nation, and that this huge area might be divided into as many as fifteen slave states. Congress decided to keep Texas statehood at a distance since slavery had long been part of its political and economic fiber. Mexico never officially acknowledged the independence of Texas and grew angrier at renewed efforts to make it an American state. As more Americans moved westward, many ended up settling in various areas of Mexican territory, and too many disdained Mexican authority as they looked to the United States for protection.

In the presidential election of 1844, James Polk and the Democrats played on the general American urge for "Manifest Destiny" by promising to assert American claims to the Pacific Northwest region and to "reannex" Texas, a phrase based on the popular myth that Texas was America's by right of the Louisiana Purchase. The Polk victory led lame-duck President John Tyler to push for the annexation of Texas. When Congress finally annexed Texas in 1845, Mexico cut off diplomatic ties with the United States, and President Polk zealously prepared for war. Polk sent the U.S. Navy to the Gulf of Mexico, put the Pacific fleet on alert, and dispatched the American army into Mexican territory.

A boundary dispute represented the most significant disagreement between Texas and Mexico, and the United States dispatched a diplomat to negotiate a settlement. Texans maintained that the Rio Grande represented their southern boundary—a river that extended about two thousand miles into the Southwest. Mexico contended that the Texas border ended with the Nueces River, located a hundred miles to the north of the Rio Grande. One possibility was for Texas to give up its claims (in the millions) for losses incurred during Mexican control of the region if Mexico would acknowledge the Rio Grande boundary. But Polk really wanted more. Already challenging the British over the Oregon Territory, Polk envisioned the California and New Mexico territories—vast lands stretching over half a million acres—as part of America's destiny as well. The president was anxious to obtain lands in the Southwest that would expand the country to the Pacific Ocean, and he began lobbying Congress to declare war on Mexico. Before long, Mexican and U.S. troops stood face-to-face along the Rio Grande. When Mexican troops crossed the river to engage in a skirmish with two American companies, Polk moved quickly to seek a declaration of war. In a dramatic statement, the president told the nation that Mexico had invaded American territory and "American blood" had been shed on "American soil." By May 1846, the United States was at war with its southern neighbor.

Not everyone agreed with the decision to go to war. Henry David Thoreau penned his famous essay "Civil Disobedience" in his opposition to the conflict, arguing that it was the duty of American citizens to stand against any "immoral" act by the government. The Massachusetts legislature issued a resolution calling the war unconstitutional, and abolitionists asked for a moratorium on any expansion of slavery westward. The Mexican War helped to expand the Free-Soil party, a rather successful third party with roots in abolitionism. Although free-soilers did not contest slavery in the South, they adamantly opposed its expansion westward. They argued that northern settlers would be unable to compete with the "free" labor of slaves in western territories and thus would face economic disadvantages. They painted a picture of southern aristocrats growing richer by the hard toil of "degraded slaves" as honest white workers faced economic ruin. While the party consisted of many abolitionists who spoke out for black rights, some free-soilers held racist attitudes and wanted to exclude all African Americans from the western territories to keep the area open for white settlers only.

As the Mexican War progressed, General Zachary Taylor successfully fought his way southward toward Mexico City; Colonel Stephen Kearny moved quickly to secure New Mexico and California (the latter with the help of the U.S. Navy); and General Winfield Scott attacked and captured the coastal city of Veracruz. The bloody and brutal war was culminating in American victory. Every success by the U.S. military drove the expansion issue further into the spotlight.

THE WILMOT PROVISO

On August 8, 1846, President Polk asked Congress to appropriate two million dollars to expedite an end of the U.S. war with Mexico and settle the boundary dispute between the two nations. While his views were not directly expressed in the "Two Million Bill," many congressmen knew that Polk desired to go well beyond a boundary settlement to acquire Mexican lands in the Southwest. Although most congressmen supported any effort to end the war quickly, many, especially in the North, feared that the procurement of Mexican lands would lead to the spread of slavery and exacerbate the growing tension between the slave and free states. Some congressmen angrily accused Polk of purposely engineering the Mexican War in order to increase American territory and create a continental empire.

In August 1846, Congressman David Wilmot presented the Wilmot

Proviso as an attachment to the Two Million Bill to stop the spread of slavery into any lands secured by a peace treaty with Mexico. Wilmot, a Democrat from Pennsylvania, was serving his first term in the Twenty-ninth Congress. In his proviso, the senator stated:

> Provided, that as an expressed and fundamental condition to the acquisition of any territory from the Republic of Mexico by the United States, by virtue of any treaty which may be negotiated with them, and to the use by the Executive of the moneys herein appropriated, neither slavery nor involuntary servitude shall exist in any part of said territory, except for crime whereof the party shall first be duly convicted.[3]

After some discussion and counterproposals, the proviso passed rather quietly in the House by a vote of 87 to 64 under the pressure to pass the Two Million Bill and complete business by the end of the session in late 1846. The Senate's discussion of the Two Million Bill and the attached Wilmot Proviso was stalled, and the session ended without the bill being passed.

However, in early 1847, a sudden and remarkable storm erupted when Congress reconvened. One single motion, made on February 1, 1847, ignited one of the most heated debates in the history of the U.S. Congress, a debate over the conduct and outcome of the Mexican War and the destiny of the nation. It began when Congressman Charles J. Ingersoll proposed to approve a Three Million Bill, put forth essentially to replace the Two Million Bill. The bill increased the unrestricted funds for President Polk to "bring the existing war with Mexico to a speedy and honorable conclusion."[4] When David Wilmot spoke up to reintroduce his proviso as an amendment to the new bill, opponents tried to silence him by using parliamentary procedure. The Pennsylvania congressman was eventually able to reintroduce the proviso, and once Wilmot had the attention of the House, he did "not intend to surrender, or be deprived of the floor." In a speech on February 8, 1847, he spoke out against the expansion of slavery into the Southwest and demanded "that this Government preserve the integrity of *free territory* against the aggressions of slavery—against its wrongful usurpations."[5] Debate over the Three Million Bill and the attached Wilmot Proviso raged in the House for two weeks. This bill also created a fiery discourse in the Senate when Senator Ambrose H. Sevier, a Democrat from Arkansas, called the Three Million Bill up for special order.

DEBATING THE THREE MILLION BILL

The Three Million Bill created a debate over the use of the U.S. military in the Mexican conflict. While the war began with a sense of political-party unity—Democrats supported it, Whigs opposed it—a dramatic conflict erupted over American military policy and western expansion. Increasingly, southern and western leaders joined forces to rationalize American military policy that had quickly transformed from a conflict over a boundary dispute in Texas to a war for western lands. They argued that territory gained was a universal by-product of war and a natural fulfillment of America's Manifest Destiny.

In introducing the Three Million Bill in the Senate, A.H. Sevier reminded his fellow politicians that the country was fighting a costly war in lives and money. The Arkansas Democrat argued that if three million dollars would bring about peace, Congress should not hesitate to act. Although he maintained that the acquisition of California and New Mexico was never the original intent of the conflict with Mexico, America now "expected to receive indemnity . . . for the expenses of the war . . . and this indemnity was expected in the shape of territory."[6] (Sevier later served as the minister to Mexico and helped to negotiate a peace treaty between the two countries, which included the acquisition of lands.)

In the House, Congressman Alexander D. Sims, a Democrat from South Carolina, was one of the first to justify America's "military occupation" of Mexican lands. He argued that the original purpose of the war was not to "conquer" Mexican territory. However, "according to the laws of war, [the United States had] a right to make conquests . . . to occupy the country, to establish provisional governments, and to seize upon even more than is necessary to indemnify [America] for the injuries we complain of and the expenses of the war."[7] Furthermore, he reminded congressmen that it was their legislature's job to declare war, not to secure peace. Sims contended that according to the Constitution, the president, as commander-in-chief, was responsible for the conduct of the war and the negotiation of peace, and Congress must respect Polk's judgment in both the use of the military and the formation of a peace treaty.

Senator Lewis Cass maintained that the Constitution was in "no danger" and the nation in "no crisis" despite the growing opposition to military policies in the Mexican War. Cass had served in the U.S. Army during the War of 1812 and had risen to the rank of brigadier general. After the war, he became the governor of the Michigan Territory before being appointed as the secretary of war under Andrew Jackson. Later, Cass unsuccessfully ran for president, returned to the Senate, and served as the secretary of state under President James Buchanan. On the eve of the Civil War, Cass became well known for his "popular-sovereignty" stance when he argued that the slave issue in western territories should be decided by the popular vote of the local people.

During the 1847 debate over the Three Million Bill, Senator Cass allied himself with President Polk and the southern branch of the Democratic party. He joyously embraced Manifest Destiny and celebrated the possibility of gaining new western lands that would open up the nation to the "magnificent bay of St. Francisco, one of the noblest anchorages in the world." Expansion, the senator contended, would also provide the nation with the economic advantages of the Pacific trade. Lastly, he argued that acquiring new western lands would save America from the stagnation and "social evils" found in Europe due to the confines of limited land. The Michigan senator saw western expansion in terms of intellectual stimulation, economic progress, and American destiny: "The mightiest intellects which when compressed in thronged cities, and hopeless of their future, are ready to break the barriers around them the moment they enter the new world of the West, feel their freedom, and turn their energies to contend with the works of creation, converting the woods and the forests into towns, and villages, and cultivated fields, and extending the dominion of civilization and improvement over the domain of nature."[8]

Many others used the debate over the Three Million Bill to speak out against American military policy. Some critics went so far as to claim that Polk conspired to make war with Mexico in order to expand the institution of slavery into western lands. Congressman Solomon Foot, a Vermont Whig, described the war as an "invasion and conquest." He concluded that it was "not only unjust to Mexico but fraught with evil, strife and contention to ourselves."[9] Senator Jacob W. Miller, a Whig from New Jersey, joined forces with other northern Democrats to dispute the logic of the bill, especially its proposed purpose—to bring a "speedy and honorable" end to the war. Miller asked, if the U.S. military really wanted a quick victory, why then were the American troops scattered throughout Mexican territory? Furthermore, why were American soldiers on the "road to the city of Mexico—to the 'Halls of the Montezumas' " instead of near the source of conflict, the Rio Grande? The New Jersey senator questioned the supposed object of the defensive war—to settle a boundary dispute between Texas and Mexico—and asked why this was not the primary focus of the peace effort. Miller noted that instead, some 80,000 American soldiers had been called into service, and "the armies of this republic had already spread themselves at the direction of the President, from Tampico, on the Gulf, to the Pacific Ocean, a distance of several thousand miles." Miller expressed outrage that as part of their mission to conquer, President Polk had sent the U.S. military around Cape Horn with the "purpose of invading and taking possession of California."[10]

Despite growing sectionalism, some western Whigs continued to speak out against the war. Senator James Morehead, a Kentucky Whig, contended that expansion went against the ideal of the American Republic and dishonored the Constitution. The senator pointed out that Mexico was a "weak and powerless" enemy that could have been defeated at the start of the conflict with a "few troops." He criticized the president for placing his "party men"—southern Democrats—"to take charge of this war." While Morehead acknowledged the president's role as commander-in-chief, he warned that giving Polk such a large sum of unrestricted money was unprecedented and possibly dangerous, especially since the president was conducting the conflict as a "war of conquest." Furthermore, he argued that securing Mexican territory and setting up civil governments in foreign lands went against the Constitution. He questioned whether the United States should follow the path of European governments with the "dismemberment of a neighboring nation" that would surely result in an extraordinary division among its own people in America: "What sort of policy is it that will lead us into the pursuit of territorial acquisitions at the expense of our own domestic peace and concord? What sort of policy is that which will lead us on step by step in the pursuit of conquest, while at home there is such formidable opposition to a policy of this sort as to endanger the very institutions of the Government?"[11]

While western expansion captured the imagination of many people who embraced the spirit of Manifest Destiny as a righteous cause to spread democracy and the superiority of the American "Anglo-Saxon Race," others looked with disfavor at the process. Morehead could not escape prevailing racist views when he questioned the value of incorporating Mexican lands into the United States. Morehead warned that if Polk succeeded in his plan to expand the United States from sea to sea, America will have "acquired a large number of the population of Mexico, an ignorant, a fanatic, a disorderly people—a population having none of the elements of character in common with the people of this country— a population sprung from a different origin, having none of the blood of the Anglo-Saxons running in their veins—a people differing from you in origin, in character, in feelings, and in principles."[12] Furthermore, Morehead asked if the supporters of expansion intended to turn the Mexican people into slaves or serfs, or give them the rights and privileges enjoyed by American citizens.

Senator John C. Calhoun, a South Carolina Democrat, surprised many of his fellow southerners when he harshly criticized the direction of the Mexican War. Although Calhoun was an ardent defender of the slavery system and would later lead the charge to expand it, the South Carolinian nevertheless spoke out in opposition to the war. In February 1847, with the Mexican War still raging, he argued that the U.S. military should engage in a defensive, not an offensive, campaign. Previously, Calhoun had served as a congressman in the House and as the secretary of war during President James Monroe's administration. He became the vice president for both John Quincy Adams and Andrew Jackson and the secretary of state for President John Tyler. During the debate over the Three Million Bill, Calhoun countered President Polk's recommendation "that the war be prosecuted in order to obtain indemnity for the expenses of the war itself" and asked how "this war be best conducted in order to bring it most advantageously to a successful termination." Like Morehead, Calhoun accepted racist views of the Mexican people and warned against incorporating "colored and mix-breed Mexicans" into the United States. He further warned that the continued dispute over the Mexican War was creating "a domestic question of the most irritating and dangerous character."[13]

THE DEBATE OVER SLAVERY

One of the most controversial aspects of the Three Million Bill was the debate over slavery and its possible expansion into any western territory secured by a future peace treaty with Mexico. In fact, the Wilmot Proviso, when it was attached to the Three Million Bill, triggered furious arguments in Congress and in the press that reflected the supercharged emotionalism of the day. As in the debate over military policy, the slavery debate helped to manifest sectionalism. But not everyone argued on sectional lines. Widespread racist attitudes lay as the undercurrent in much of the discourse. The tension became so heightened that some went so far as to predict that the acquisition of Mexican lands would accelerate the debate over slavery to dangerous levels until it destroyed the nation.

In a passionate speech to restrict slavery in any Mexican territory acquired in the war, David Wilmot declared, "Sir, as a friend of the Union, as a lover of my country, and in no spirit of hostility to the South, I offer my amendment. Viewing slavery as I do, I must resist its further extension and propagation on the North American continent. It is an evil, the magnitude and the end of which no man can see."[14] In his support of the Wilmot Proviso, Congressman Bradford R. Wood of New York joined with other northern Democrats to call slavery an "aristocratic institution" that went against Christianity.

Opponents of the Wilmot Proviso strongly disagreed. Congressman Seaborn Jones, a Democrat from Georgia, took exception to Wood's contention and expressed "bitterness" against the New Yorker who "was filled with holy indignation in contemplating the damning sin of the Southern States."[15] Jones claimed that in fact the Bible supported slavery. Like many of his southern counterparts, Congressman A.D. Sims of South Carolina substantiated his support for territorial accession with his desire to spread slavery and the power of the "Slave States" westward. He also used religion to justify the institution and argued that throughout history slavery had existed. He concluded, "No man, who is a Christian, can denounce slavery as immoral. In the laws of Moses, slavery is introduced and provided for: slavery is recognised [sic] throughout the Bible. . . . I believe in the abiding good sense and Christianity of the American people; that they will not rise—in the face of Providence and in contempt of the laws of the Bible."[16]

Southern Democrat Howell Cobb of Georgia took a different approach when he claimed that the Constitution provided for two different areas of the country, one slave and one free, "to grow in parallel." Cobb "opposed any restriction such as that contemplated in the Proviso—permitting the North to extend her territory, her government, her power, strength and influence, while the South stood 'her limits fixed, bound hand and foot.' "[17] Although Senator Calhoun was very critical of Polk's aspirations for Mexican lands, he nevertheless attacked the Wilmot Proviso as a violation of southerners' right to reside with "their property" (slaves) in any and all American territory.

Racism also played a key role in the debate. In a speech before Congress, Congressman John S. Chipman of Michigan broke from other western Democrats when he challenged the slavery issue and asked if the Wilmot Proviso was worth the dangerous road the nation would face if it should pass. Chipman said that he "regretted to hear gentlemen avow upon that floor their readiness to see the federal Union shattered to ten thousand atoms. . . . As he heard the sentiments which had been uttered in that Hall, his blood curdled around his heart." The nation was at stake with every argument over the expansion of slavery in lands acquired in a peace treaty with Mexico. Chipman criticized abolitionists' efforts to liberate slaves and argued that before the institution was ended, slaves needed to be "morally and intellectually" elevated to "improve [their] condition." Furthermore, he expressed outrage that philanthropists put the future of their country in danger to protest against the expansion of slavery. In Chipman's "humble opinion, the preservation of the Union was worth a million times more than the pitiful consideration of a handful of degraded Africans."[18]

Congressman A.D. Sims strongly disagreed that the congressional debate over slavery would lead to the destruction of the United States. He put his faith in the common sense of the people to come to some agreement. "When difficulty arises, though it may look startling and dangerous, I have no doubt that the difficulty will be overcome." Sims put his trust in the "good sense and the patriotism" of Americans and predicted, "The child is not born who shall witness a dissolution of the union."[19] He was wrong.

As the possibility of expanding slavery westward continued to be a hotly debated topic in Congress, the war helped to strengthen the antislavery movement because it brought more attention to the cause. Fiery debates over the war with Mexico occurred in the public forum as reports of the conflict, sent to newspapers by the new telegraph system, quickly reached the masses. Soon the debates over slavery were reordering political priorities, disturbing (even disrupting) party alignments, and favoring those who insisted on a "slave power" or "abolitionist conspiracy" argument, thus giving credence to extremists.

The Treaty of Guadalupe Hidalgo formally ended the war in 1848, when the United States "purchased" half a million acres of Mexican land stretching from western Texas to California. (Critics called the $15-million purchase "guilt-money" for "stealing" this vast area.) The treaty forced Mexico to give up its California and New Mexico territories, lands that include present-day Arizona, California, Nevada, New Mexico, Utah, and parts of Colorado.

CONCLUSION

The Mexican War had a profound impact on antebellum American politics. A border dispute between Texas and Mexico, fed by expansionists' visions and a quest to perpetuate slavery, created turmoil and conflict in the halls of Congress. Although both the House and the Senate preferred to avoid the slavery issue whenever possible, the Three Million Bill and the accompanying Wilmot Proviso opened the door for a heated debate over the westward expansion of slavery. The war also served as a watershed for an intense debate over the use of the military in the Mexican War and accelerated the transformation of partisan politics into sectionalism. The notion of Manifest Destiny helped to motivate expansionism and justify the annexation of western lands. However, after much intense discussion, Congress decided that it was in the nation's best interest to separate the Three Million Bill from the Wilmot Proviso. Although the military appropriations bill passed both the House and the Senate in early 1847, Congress agreed to postpone the question of slavery in lands acquired through the Mexican War until these lands were actually annexed.

The Second American Party system (Democrats vs. Whigs) met its demise shortly before the end of the conflict, since the war helped to bolster the Free-Soil party and subsequently undermine the Whigs. The dark clouds of sectionalism became even stormier with the emerging Third Party system that pitted southern Democrats against northern Republicans. The war escalated Generals Zachary Taylor and Winfield Scott to hero status, and both were soon cast as presidential candidates. By 1850 President Taylor faced a new crisis as the acquisition of the Mexican lands drove opponents back into a fiery debate over the future of these new American territories, especially when California asked for statehood. The antagonism and rage prevalent during the war resurfaced and lasted for more than a decade. By December 1860, shortly after the election of Abraham Lincoln, the Republican candidate committed to no further extension of slavery into the territories, the nation lost its struggle for unity and compromise. Within a few short months, eleven southern states seceded from the Union rather than submit to Republican rule, which secessionists regarded as the advance guard of abolitionism. Civil war followed.

Even with the carnage of the Civil War still fresh in the minds of Americans, the nation did not stop looking westward. As the nation rallied to recapture its nationalistic spirit previously brought on by the success of the Mexican War, it once again hailed "Manifest Destiny" as an American mantra. With visions of a continental empire and their belief in Manifest Destiny firmly in hand, Americans surged forward as they professed their God-given right to spread their "superior" institutions throughout the United States and beyond. But expansion came with further consequences, and new wars came quickly on the heels of Manifest Destiny.

NOTES

1. Senator Reverdy Johnson, quoted in Charles Buxton Going, *David Wilmot, Free-Soiler: A Biography of the Great Advocate of the Wilmot Proviso* (D. Appleton and Company, 1924; reprint, Gloucester, MA: Peter Smith, 1966), p. 206. Going's book includes detailed excerpts of the congressional debates over the Wilmot Proviso.

2. "In Senate, Three Million Bill," Senator Lewis Cass, *Congressional Globe*, 29th Cong., 2nd sess., February 10, 1847, p. 367.

3. Congressman David Wilmot, quoted in Going, *David Wilmot, Free-Soiler*, p. 98.

4. "The Three Million Loan," Senator A.H. Sevier, *Congressional Globe*, 29th Cong., 2nd sess., February 2, 1847, p. 306.

5. "Restriction of Slavery Speech of Mr. D. Wilmot, of Pennsylvania, in the House of Representatives," *Congressional Globe*, 29th Cong., 2nd sess., February 8, 1847, p. 314.

6. "The Three Million Loan," Senator A.H. Sevier, *Congressional Globe*, 29th Cong., 2nd sess., February 2, 1847, pp. 306–307.

7. "Naval Appropriation Bill," Congressman A.D. Sims, *Congressional Globe*, 29th Cong., 2nd sess., January 29, 1847, pp. 290–291.

8. "In Senate, Three Million Bill," Senator Lewis Cass, *Congressional Globe*, 29th Cong., 2nd sess., February 10, 1847, p. 367.

9. Solomon Foot, quoted in Going, *David Wilmot, Free-Soiler*, p. 188.

10. "Three Million Loan," Senator Jacob W. Miller, *Congressional Globe*, 29th Cong., 2nd sess., February 2, 1847, p. 306.

11. "In Senate, Three Million Bill," Senator James Morehead, *Congressional Globe*, 29th Cong., 2nd sess., February 8, 1847, p. 345.

12. Ibid.

13. "Three Million Bill," Senator John C. Calhoun, *Congressional Globe*, 29th Cong., 2nd sess., February 9, 1847, p. 356.

14. "Restriction of Slavery Speech of Mr. D. Wilmot, of Pennsylvania, in the

House of Representatives," *Appendix to the Congressional Globe*, 29th Cong., 2nd sess., February 8, 1847, p. 314.

15. Seaborn Jones, quoted in Going, *David Wilmot, Free-Soiler*, p. 193.

16. "Naval Appropriation Bill," Congressman A.D. Sims, *Congressional Globe*, 29th Cong., 2nd sess., January 29, 1847, p. 291.

17. Howell Cobb, quoted in Going, *David Wilmot, Free-Soiler*, p. 184.

18. "The Wilmot Proviso: Remarks of Mr. J.S. Chipman, of Michigan, in the House of Representatives," *Appendix to the Congressional Globe*, 29th Cong., 2nd sess., February 8, 1847, pp. 322–323.

19. "Naval Appropriation Bill," Congressman A.D. Sims, *Congressional Globe*, 29th Cong., 2nd sess., January 29, 1847, p. 291.

DOCUMENTS

3.1. Senator Jacob W. Miller Opposes the Three Million Bill, February 2, 1847

Senator Jacob W. Miller, a New Jersey Whig, spoke out against the Three Million Bill and opposed President Polk's military policy, which positioned American troops throughout Mexico's territory. Miller argued that if Polk really wanted to end the war quickly, he should have concentrated American troops directly against the enemy forces and focused the peace negotiations on the boundary dispute between Texas and Mexico. In the following excerpt from the Congressional Globe's *summary of Miller's February 2, 1847 speech, the senator criticized the war and offered solutions to end it quickly without new land acquisitions.*

If [Mr. Miller] thought that an end could be put to this unfortunate war by passing this bill, and placing three millions of dollars in the hands of the President, he would willingly vote for it; but he must be permitted to say that he did not see how the placing of this money in the hands of the President could restore to this country an honorable and permanent peace. . . .

He understood the chairman of the committee to say that peace might be made, or at least that the President of the United States would consent on his part to conclude this war, if Mexico would consent to cede to the United States the whole of New Mexico and the whole of Upper California.

They had now for the first time, from an official source, the information which the country had long desired to obtain, viz.: to what extent, and for what purpose, this war was to be further prosecuted. They were now told that it was for the purpose of acquiring, by force of arms, or what he considered to be the same thing, driving Mexico by force of arms, or the people of Mexico, to consent to surrender to the United States, New Mexico and California. This war, then, according to the information which they had now received, was converted into a war of conquest. . . .

But he would candidly say that if he believed an end could be put to this war in an honorable manner, by withholding the appropriations for it, he would withhold his vote from any supplies of men and money for the purpose of prosecuting the war any longer. . . .

This little war, commenced, whether by the act of Mexico or the President of the United States, he would not stop to inquire, had been growing larger and larger as time had elapsed; and, as the army had advanced into Mexican territory, the enemy had fallen before it; but every victory that we had gained seemed to add strength to our adversaries. . . . The road to the city of Mexico—to the "Halls of the Montezumas"—seemed to grow longer and longer, and the revels which many gentlemen anticipated at the close of this war in the "Halls of the Montezumas" had been preceded by many a carnival of blood. . . .

Mr. Miller continued. If this war was to be continued another year, it would require all the energies of this nation, both physical and pecuniary, to sustain it. . . . The armies of this republic had already spread themselves at the direction of the President, from Tampico, on the Gulf, to the Pacific Ocean, a distance of several thousand miles; and if this war was to be carried on with vigor, this army must be sustained in a foreign country. All its munitions of war, all the provisions necessary to supply it, would have to be transported at an immense expense. One part of the army of this republic had just passed round Cape Horn, for the purpose of invading and taking possession of California—going by water a distance of some fifteen thousand miles; and an army of this kind must and will require an expenditure of money which will be an oppressive burden on the people of this country. . . .

Well, and what had been the great scheme to conquer Mexico, or to "conquer a peace?" Why, as far as could be seen, they had invested Mexico with our armies, as the waters surround the continent. One portion of our army was on the Rio Grande; another was penetrating Mexico some hundred miles up; a third was penetrating the center by Santa Fe; a fourth was sent round Cape Horn to take possession of California; and the navy of the United States occupied the Gulf of Mexico and the Pacific Ocean; so that the republic of Mexico was completely surrounded by our arms. They desired, it was said, to conquer a peace, and the way to do it was to take possession of the Halls of the Montezumas; and to do that, they had stationed their armies at the extreme points—in remote provinces. They commenced as far from the point of attack as they could get. They sent their armies into the provinces of Mexico to fight with the elements in the wilderness. They sent their navy into the Gulf and the Pacific. And for what purpose? . . .

But if the plan were to conquer a peace, why was it that the troops were not concentrated at some point and marched to that point where an effectual blow could be struck, and then make known that we were ready to make peace on the settlement of the boundary line between Mexico and Texas, and the payment of the indemnities due to our citizens? If that object had been made known, they would have had peace long ago. But instead of that, an army had been sent round Cape Horn to California, to attack that province, and to establish a civil government there. This had been published to all the world, and it was well understood that this Government was grasping after territory. . . .

Suppose they got New Mexico and California by a treaty of peace, what were they to do with them? . . . Why, there were people there; there are citizens of Mexico there. What was proposed to be done with them? He doubted very much whether, under our form of government, they could bring into the United States, by means of conquest, a foreign people and territory. . . . Could they by conquest compel the people of another republic to become citizens of the United States? Why, we have proclaimed to the world that no man can be compelled by force of arms to owe allegiance to any country; and that he has the right to throw off his allegiance to any sovereign on earth. . . . Did they by force of arms intend to compel an entire people to become citizens with us?

But what do we want with New Mexico? Why should we surrender the claims of our citizens to the two millions of indemnities, and take pay in land? Do we want land? Are we so cramped that we cannot live without enlarging the area of the country? Is the valley of the Mississippi worn out? Is the rich and fertile soil there to be forsaken, and are our people to go to Mexico to seek new homes? And what do we want with California? Is it that on the Pacific Ocean we want a secure harbor? . . . Would they never stop in their acquisitions? When they got New Mexico and California, would they not push their acquisitions further? Was not the temptation great?

Mr. Miller had (he said) honestly believed this war with Mexico could be settled, and settled in two or three months, if the Senate would, by resolution, advise the President to settle the differences between the two countries, by an adjustment of the original causes of the war. If we will say that our object is not acquisition; if we will say that we will be willing to make peace, on a settlement of the boundary line of Texas and the payment of the indemnities, we will have peace. . . .

If we had gone to war because the blood of American citizens had been shed on American soil—and that was the word which went forth through the country, and struck every ear and heart—if for that our armies had been marched to and across the Rio Grande, to right ourselves before the world, and to defend our rights and honor, how were we to be satisfied by taking pay in land—by the cession of California and New Mexico, and by subjugating the people of New Mexico to our Government? He [Miller] discarded such a settlement as that, as dishonorable to the country. All we had to do was to compel Mexico to settle the original causes of war.

Source: "Three Million Loan," Senator Jacob W. Miller, *Congressional Globe*, 29th Cong., 2nd sess., February 2, 1847, pp. 307–308.

3.2.   Speech of David Wilmot in the House of Representatives in Favor of the Restriction of Slavery, February 8, 1847

Congressman David Wilmot, a Pennsylvania Democrat, spoke out against the expansion of slavery and reintroduced the Wilmot Proviso as an attachment to the Three Million Bill. The proviso called for the restriction of slavery in any territory acquired in the war between the United States and Mexico. Its introduction in 1846 and reintroduction in 1847 ignited a furious debate on slavery and expansion that finally exploded in civil war in 1861. The following is an excerpt from Wilmot's February 8, 1847 speech against slavery summarized in the Congressional Globe.

The House being in Committee of the Whole on the state of the Union upon the Three Million Bill—Mr. Wilmot addressed the committee as follows: Mr. Chairman, I suppose it will be proper for me to notify the Committee that I intend to move to amend the bill now under consideration, by the additional section which has been read, without designating the particular place in the bill where I desire it to stand. I do not wish to deprive the gentleman from Virginia (Mr. Dromgoole), or any one else, of the opportunity to move any amendment to this bill; but I am embarrassed by the rules of the House (with which I am but little acquainted) and I do not intend to surrender, or be deprived of the floor. I wish to be heard upon this question, and I cannot consent to yield to the gentleman from Virginia, and thereby be deprived, by the operation of some Parliamentary rule, of an opportunity of vindicating this amendment, and the position I occupy before the House and the country. . . .

Sir, it will be recollected by all present that at the last session of Congress an amendment was moved by me to a bill of the same character as this, in the form of a proviso, by which slavery should be excluded from any territory that might subsequently be acquired by the United States from the Republic of Mexico.

Sir, on that occasion, that proviso was sustained by a very decided majority of this House. Nay, sir, more, it was sustained, if I mistake not, by a majority of the Republican party on this floor. I am prepared, I think, to show that the entire South were then willing to acquiesce in what appeared to be, and, in so far as the action of this House was concerned, what was, the legislative will and declaration of the Union on this subject. It passed this House. Sir, there were no threats of disunion sounded in our ears. It passed here and went to the Senate, and it was the judgment of the public, and of men well informed, that, had it not been defeated there for want of time, it would have passed that body and become the established law of the land. . . .

But, sir, the issue now presented is not whether slavery shall exist unmolested where it now is, but whether it shall be carried to new and distant regions where the footprint of a slave cannot be found. This, sir, is the issue. Upon it I take my stand, and from it I cannot be frightened or driven by idle charges of Abolitionism. I ask not that slavery be abolished. I demand that this Government preserve the integrity of *free territory* against the aggressions of slavery—against its wrongful usurpations. Sir, I was in favor of the annexation of Texas. I supported it with my whole influence and strength. I was willing to take Texas as she was. I sought not to change the character of her institutions. Slavery existed in Texas—planted there, it is true, in defiance of law; still, it existed. It gave character to the country. True, it was held out to the North that at least two of the five States to be formed out of Texas would be free. Yet, sir, the whole of Texas has been given up to slavery. The Democracy of the North, almost to a man, went for annexation. Yes, sir, here was an empire larger than France given up to slavery. Shall further concessions be made by the North? Shall we give up free territory, the inheritance of free labor? Must we yield this, also? Never, sir, never, until we ourselves are fit to be slaves. The North may be betrayed by her representatives, but upon this great question she will be true to herself—true to posterity. Defeat! Sir, there can be no defeat. Defeat to-day will but arouse the teeming millions of the North, and lead to a more decisive and triumphant victory to-morrow.

But, sir, we are told, that the joint blood and treasure of the whole country [is] being expended in this acquisition, therefore, it should be divided, and slavery allowed to take its share. Sir, the South has her share already; the installment for slavery was paid in advance. We are fighting this war for Texas and for the South. . . .

Now, sir, we are told that California is ours; that New Mexico is ours—won by the valor of our arms. They are free. Shall they remain free? Shall these fair provinces be the inheritance and homes of the white labor of freemen or the black labor of slaves? This, sir, is the issue—this is the question. . . .

Sir, as a friend of the Union, as a lover of my country, and in no spirit of hostility to the South, I offer my amendment. Viewing slavery as I do, I must resist its further extension and propagation on the North American continent. It is an evil, the magnitude and the end of which no man can see.

Source: "Restriction of Slavery Speech of Mr. D. Wilmot, of Pennsylvania, in the House of Representatives," *Congressional Globe*, 29th Cong., 2nd sess., February 8, 1847, pp. 314–317.

3.3.   Senator James Morehead Opposes the Three Million Bill, February 8, 1847

Senator James Morehead, a Kentucky Whig, questioned the constitutionality of President Polk's military policy, claiming that Polk had turned a boundary dispute between Texas and Mexico into a war of conquest for Mexican lands. Like many of his colleagues, Morehead was unable to escape his ethnocultural upbringing when he described Mexicans as inferior to Anglo-Saxon Americans. The following is taken from a summary of Morehead's February 8, 1847 speech in the Senate.

Mr. Morehead rose to address the Senate. . . . The bill proposed to appropriate the sum of three millions, to be applied, under the direction of the President of the United States, to defray such extraordinary expenditures as might be necessary to bring the war to a speedy and honorable conclusion. . . . The bill confers on the President an unprecedented and enormous power; a measure not only unexampled in our history, but in opposition to the spirit of our institutions.

We are engaged in a war with a powerless enemy; an enemy so weak and powerless, that, at the commencement of the conflict, it was deemed only necessary to send the few troops we had into the field to insure a compliance with our demands; and now we are called on to sanction an extraordinary expenditure of three millions to bring the war to a close. The contest is not to be determined by the prowess of our arms, but by the application of money; and the bill proposes to grant this money to the President, to be expended at the will of the President, and without any other restriction than a provision that he shall account for it hereafter. . . .

When the President nominated a set of party men to take charge of this war, no opposition was made from his side of the Chamber; and when, at this session, they asked for more men and more money, they stood side by side with them in granting both. Whenever they wanted money for the purpose of carrying on the war, it was granted them. But when they came for three millions of dollars, on the assumption that the President of the United States was responsible, and that Congress had nothing to do but grant it, he, for one, was compelled to take his stand in support of the rights of the Legislative department of the Government. The proposition of gentlemen on the other side was, that it was our duty to give him the money which he asked for, without requiring any explanation of the objects or purposes to which it was to be applied. . . .

This war with Mexico was about to subject the Constitution of the United States to a still severer trial than those it had heretofore experienced. They were now occupying a new attitude in view of their constitutional powers, and in view also of the course which expediency required. Hitherto the wars in which they had been engaged were wars for human liberty, or in defense of violated rights. Now there was pending a war of conquest. What were the obligations resting upon the Government of the United States in view of such a state of things? Should they, in imitation of the Governments of Europe, prosecute a war for conquest to the dismemberment of a neighboring nation? Did the genius of our Constitution permit the adoption of such a course? He thought that the great American doctrine was a doctrine peculiarly applicable to the support and protection of our domestic institutions, totally distinct from any purpose of acquiring foreign territory by conquest. But now it seemed, in view of the attitude in which we were placed, in a war which had been brought on, as they were told by their friends on the other side, by Mexico, and merely recognized by us, that a war of this character was to be prosecuted with vigor and energy, for the purpose of acquiring territory and of setting up our own civil institutions within the territory thus acquired; thus extending, as it was said, the limits of freedom by the prosecution of this war of conquest. . . .

What sort of policy is it that will lead us into the pursuit of territorial acquisitions at the expense of our own domestic peace and concord? What sort of policy is that which will lead us on step by step in the pursuit of conquest, while at home there is such formidable opposition to a policy of this sort as to endanger the very institutions of the Government? . . .

There was a question involved in this consideration which overshadowed them like a cloud. The great question of slavery, as the conscript fathers of the Republic well knew when the Government was first established, would become the more dangerous the more it was agitated. Why, then, should they pursue a policy that would lead to such agitation? . . .

Again: suppose you make a treaty upon this basis, and it is confirmed by the Senate: what do you gain? You have additional territory; what do you propose to do with it? I suppose there is not a citizen of this country who, if the question were put to him, would not say that you have territory enough already. But you acquire additional territory. What else do you acquire? You will have acquired a large number of the population of Mexico, an ignorant, a fanatic, a disorderly people—a population having none of the elements of character in common with the people of this country—a population sprung from a different origin, having none of the blood of the Anglo-Saxons running in their veins—a people differing from you in origin, in character, in feelings, and in principles—having nothing in common with you. What are you to do with them? Are you to govern them as you do your slaves in those States which now tolerate the institution of slavery? Are you to treat them as serfs belonging to the land which you acquire, as attached to the soil? Or will you put them on a level with the people of this country? Will you give them the privileges which your people enjoy, and enable them to regulate and control the destinies of the Government? . . .

I know how apt we are to look upon the Representatives in these halls as opposed to each other upon all questions submitted to them, because they represent different portions of the country, and, to some extent, different interests; but, upon a question like this, it will be found that they represent but one people, having a common object to promote the good of the whole nation.

Source: "In Senate, Three Million Bill," Senator James Morehead, *Congressional Globe*, 29th Cong., 2nd sess., February 8, 1847, pp. 344–345.

3.4.   Congressman J.S. Chipman Opposes the Wilmot Proviso, February 8, 1847

The opposition of Congressman John S. Chipman to the Mexican War reflected a prevailing racist view toward African Americans that ran through much thinking about who belonged in the West and the proper place for blacks in the Republic. In the following excerpt from a Congressional Globe *summary of his February 8, 1847 speech before the House, Chipman, a Democrat from Michigan, argued that the disruption of the Union was not worth a fight over slavery.*

The Three Million Bill and the Wilmot Proviso being under consideration in Committee of the Whole—

Mr. Chipman addressed the committee. . . . When he resolved upon the course which he should take in reference to that great question which has been brought before them [the Wilmot Proviso], he was not aware that any other northern man had determined to vote against the proposition. He [Chipman] regretted to hear gentlemen avow upon that floor their readiness to see the federal Union shattered to ten thousand atoms.

As he heard the sentiments which had been uttered in that Hall, his blood curdled around his heart. He trembled at the thought of the dissolution of this fair Confederacy. He knew but one ground on which to stand as a patriot, in view of the circumstances in which they were placed: that was upon the ground of compromise, by which these States were united and bound together. In this humble opinion, the preservation of the Union was worth a million times more than the pitiful consideration of a handful of degraded Africans. He repeated, when gentlemen pretending to love their country would place the consideration of the nominal liberation of a handful of degraded Africans in the one scale, and this Union in the other, and make the latter kick the beam, he would not give a fig for their patriotism. Did all this pretended negro patriotism, then, spring from philanthropy or a love of country? What would these pretended philanthropists accomplish, supposing that they should succeed in liberating that handful of degraded Africans? Would they benefit the slave by liberating him, without providing for his colonization? What would they accomplish? They would drive him to a cold climate, uncongenial to his constitution, and force him to a state of degradation immensely lower than his present state—yes, to starvation. They must elevate the slave morally and intellectually first, if they would improve his condition. But, how happened it that gentlemen would prohibit slavery from all newly-acquired territory?

Source: "The Wilmot Proviso: Remarks of Mr. J.S. Chipman, of Michigan, in the House of Representatives," *Appendix to the Congressional Globe*, 29th Cong., 2nd sess., February 8, 1847, pp. 322–323.

3.5.   Senator Lewis Cass Supports the Three Million Bill, February 10, 1847

Senator Lewis Cass, a Michigan Democrat, expressed excitement over the possibility of gaining new western lands at the conclusion of the Mexican War. To Cass, it was America's Manifest Destiny to spread its "superior" cultural, political, and economic institutions throughout the continent. In the following excerpt from a summary in the Congressional Globe, *Cass celebrated westward expansion and warned that if the United States did not expand, it would face intellectual and economic stagnation similar to that of Europe.*

[Mr. Cass said:] I do not rise, sir, with the emotions so visibly felt, and so eloquently described by the distinguished Senator from South Carolina. I do not consider this country, or its institutions in the slightest danger. Never was it more free, powerful, or prosperous, than at the present moment, when untimely warnings come to assail us. The public sentinel may sleep upon his watchtower. In the distant horizon, not a cloud as big as the prophet's hand, is to be seen, which is to overspread the heavens, and to burst in thunder and in tempest upon us. We are, indeed, engaged in a foreign war, which demands the solicitude of every good citizen. But the scene of its operations is two thousand miles-distant; and, come the worst that may, we can at any time withdraw into our own country. Disgraceful, indeed, would be such a movement; but it would be still better than the evils predicted, and according to the nature of the apprehensions expressed, it would terminate the danger.

Mr. President, it gives me great pain to hear any allusions to the dissolution of this Confederacy; and of all the places in this republic, this high place is the last, in which they should be expressed. The Constitution is in no danger. It has survived many a shock, and it will survive many more. There are those now in the Senate—and I am among them—who were born before it came into being.

We have grown with our growth and strengthened with our strength, till the approach of physical infirmities, the kindly warnings of nature, bid us prepare for another and an untried world. And the Constitution, too, has grown with its growth and strengthened with its strength, till from three millions it governs twenty millions of people, and has made them the happiest community upon the face of the globe. . . .

Mr. President, I shall not touch any of the topics before us, as a sectional man. I view them, and shall present them, as an American citizen, looking to the honor and interests of his country, and of his whole country. In these great questions, of national bearing, I acknowledge no geographical claims. What is best for the United States is best for me; and in that spirit alone shall I pursue the discussion.

A strong desire pervades this country, that a region, extending west of our present possessions to the Pacific Ocean, should be acquired and become part of our Confederacy. . . . It would give to us a large territory, a great deal of it calculated for American settlement and cultivation, and it would connect us with the great western ocean, giving us a front along its shores in connexion [sic] with Oregon of, perhaps, thirteen or fourteen degrees of latitude. It would give us also the magnificent bay of St. Francisco, one of the noblest anchorages in the world, capable of holding all the navies of the earth; and from its commanding position, controlling, in some measure, the trade of the northern Pacific. But, sir, besides these advantages, commercial and geographical; there are important political considerations, which point to extension as one of the great measures of safety for our institutions.

In Europe, one of the social evils is concentration. Men are brought too much and kept too much in contact. There is not room for expansion. Minds of the highest order are pressed down by adverse circumstances, without the power of free exertion. There is no starting-point for them. Hence the struggles, that are ever going on, in our crowded communities. And hence the *emeutes*, which disturb and alarm the Governments of the Old World, and which must one day or other shake them to their center. . . .

The mightiest intellects which when compressed in thronged cities, and hopeless of their future, are ready to break the barriers around them the moment they enter the new world of the West, feel their freedom, and turn their energies to contend with the works of creation; converting the woods and the forests into towns, and villages, and cultivated fields, and extending the dominion of civilization and improvement over the domain of nature. This process has been going on since the first settlement of our country; and while it continues, whatever other evils betide us, we shall be free from the evils of a dense population, with scanty means of subsistence, and with no hope of advancement. . . .

We are at war with Mexico, brought on by her injustice. Before peace is established, we have a right to require a reasonable indemnity, either pecuniary or territorial, or both, for the injuries we have sustained. Such a compensation is just in itself, and in strict accordance with the usages of nations. . . .

It is now objected to, as an immoral proposition, a kind of bribery, either of the Government of Mexico, or of its Commanding General; and the honorable Senator from Maryland, who is not now in his seat, said emphatically and solemnly, "that this project of terminating the war by dis-'membering a sister republic, is so revolting to my 'moral sense of propriety, honor, and justice, that 'I should see my arms palsied by my side, rather 'than agree to it." [*sic*] The "dismemberment" of which the honorable member speaks is previously defined by himself. . . .

The object of the President has been distinctly stated by himself. It is to have the money ready, and if a satisfactory treaty is signed and ratified, then to make a payment into the treasury of Mexico, which will be disposed of by the Government of that country, agreeably to its own laws. . . .

As to the idea, that such an arrangement is something like bribery, it seems to me it will not bear the slightest investigation. A strange kind of bribery this! . . . This is a proposition made by one nation to another, in the face of the world. It is not to enable Mexico to carry on the war, as an honorable Senator seems to suppose, for it is not to be paid till the war is over.

Source: "In Senate, Three Million Bill," Senator Lewis Cass, *Congressional Globe*, 29th Cong., 2nd sess., February 10, 1847, pp. 367–368.

ANNOTATED RESEARCH GUIDE

Books and Articles

Bauer, Jack K., and Robert W. Johannsen. *The Mexican War, 1846–1848*. Lincoln: University of Nebraska Press, 1992. Examines the history of the Mexican War and how it helped to shape the American Civil War.

Frazier, Donald S., ed. *The United States and Mexico at War: Nineteenth-Century Expansionism and Conflict*. New York: Macmillan, 1998. Includes over six hundred encyclopedia articles and biographies detailing various aspects of the Mexican War.

Going, Charles Buxton. *David Wilmot, Free-Soiler: A Biography of the Great Advocate of the Wilmot Proviso*. D. Appleton and Company, 1924. Reprint. Gloucester, MA: Peter Smith, 1966. This biography of the life of David Wilmot includes numerous reprinted excerpts from congressional debates over the Wilmot Proviso and related arguments concerning the war between the United States and Mexico.

Johannsen, Robert W. "America's Forgotten War." *Wilson Quarterly* 20, no. 2 (1996): 96–107. Examines the political atmosphere that led up to the Mexican War and the significance of the conflict in American history.

Johannsen, Robert W., John M. Belohlavek, Thomas R. Hietala, Samuel J. Watson, Sam W. Haynes, and Robert E. May. *Manifest Destiny and Empire*. College Station: Texas A&M University Press, 1997. Includes a reprint of six lectures by leading historians who examine Manifest Destiny in antebellum America.

Morrison, Michael A. " 'New Territory versus No Territory': The Whig Party and the Politics of Western Expansion, 1846–1848." *Western Historical Quarterly* 23 (1992): 25–51. Explores Whig opposition to the Mexican War, their protest against acquiring Mexican lands, and their fight against the expansion of slavery.

———. *Slavery and the American West: The Eclipse of Manifest Destiny and the Coming of the Civil War*. Chapel Hill: University of North Carolina Press, 1997. Provides a detailed analysis of the impact of slavery as it expanded westward. Includes a chapter on Whig politics and the reaction of northern and southern Whigs to the possible accession of Mexican territory.

Ohrt, Wallace. *Defiant Peacemaker: Nicholas Trist in the Mexican War*. College Station: Texas A&M University Press, 1997. Examines the life of Nicholas Trist, particularly his role in negotiating the Treaty of Guadalupe Hidalgo, which ended the Mexican War.

Singletary, Otis A. *Mexican War*. Chicago: University of Chicago Press, 1962. Provides an overview of the Mexican War and connects the political and military aspects of the war.

Stephanson, Anders. *Manifest Destiny: American Expansionism and the Empire of Right*. New York: Hill and Wang, 1995. Analyzes the spirit of expansion prevalent in the United States from early settlement to the present.

Watkins, T.H. "The Taking of California." *American Heritage* 24, no. 2 (1973): 4–7, 81–86. Looks at the "conquest" of California in the 1840s as Manifest Destiny motivated leaders like John C. Fremont to secure California.

Winders, Richard Bruce. *Mr. Polk's Army: The American Military Experience in the Mexican War*. College Station: Texas A&M University Press, 1997. Examines the experiences of American rank-and-file soldiers and their leaders who fought in the Mexican War from a social, cultural, and political perspective.

Web Site

http://www.pbs.org/kera/usmexicanwar. Scholars from the United States and Mexico provide their analysis of the Mexican War, including a discussion of Manifest Destiny, President Polk, the war from the Mexican viewpoint, and the legacy of the Mexican War.

4

The New York City Draft Riot: Volunteers and Draft Resisters in the Civil War

On a warm and cloudy day in July 1863, a crowd of people gathered outside the Ninth District provost marshal's headquarters at the corner of Third Avenue and Forty-sixth Street in New York City. Apprehension quickly spread through the group as they waited to hear the names of the young men to be drafted into the Union army. According to one eyewitness account, as the last name was pulled from the lottery wheel, "a stone came crashing through the window," and a mob of people armed with crowbars, table legs, guns, and knives dashed into the building. After the rioters destroyed the draft wheel and "scattered" the pieces of papers bearing the names of New Yorkers, someone from the crowd doused the room with turpentine and set the provost marshal's office on fire.[1] Thus began the "bloody" New York City draft riot.

The riot lasted five days—five days of brutality, arson, lynching, and murder. A riot that began with a violent protest against conscription escalated into a fierce debate over federalism versus localism, Democrats versus Republicans, Catholics versus Protestants, and working class versus upper class. Before it was over, the riot transformed into an ethnic and racial conflict. Although draft disruptions took place in a number of areas throughout the Union, "the New York City antidraft riot . . . was the worst riot in American history."[2]

MANPOWER NEEDS

At the start of the Civil War in 1861, Congress utilized America's traditional method of recruiting soldiers through the state militias and federal volunteer forces. This method honored the country's deeply held beliefs in mustering up volunteer citizen-soldiers during wartime as opposed to maintaining a large standing army or drafting men into service. Looking back to the colonial experience, many Americans feared that an army of professional soldiers could be used to oppress the people and undermine democracy. Many also advocated the use of state militia forces over a regular army, since the latter would give too much power to the federal government. In the early days of the Civil War, President Abraham Lincoln asked the states for citizen-soldiers in the form of 75,000 three-month militiamen and 42,000 U.S. volunteers. He also enlarged the regular army from 17,000 to 40,000 men. Hundreds of thousands of young men, driven by patriotic fervor and the excitement of war, rushed to join in record numbers.

Expecting a short war and attempting to cut costs, Secretary of War Edwin Stanton stopped taking volunteers and shut down federal recruiting offices in January 1862. This miscalculation proved disastrous. Union losses in the spring of 1862 in battles at Shiloh and during the Peninsula Campaign against Confederate soldiers sent the death rate soaring and made it clear that this would not be an easy victory for the North. Unsanitary camp conditions bred malaria, typhoid, and measles. New technological changes in the development of weaponry made killing much more efficient and much more brutal. Doctors in poorly equipped and makeshift hospitals fought against all odds to keep soldiers alive. Military mismanagement, irregular pay, inadequate supplies, and long periods of inactivity and fatigue further lowered troop morale. As the war dragged on, problems continued, and casualties mounted, enlistment dropped off. The military also expected a large reduction of soldiers when one-year enlistment terms ended in the summer of 1862.

To meet its manpower needs, the U.S. government issued a proclamation in July 1862 offering a bounty of $100 to be paid to three-year enlistees ($25 when they signed up, $75 when they were discharged). Shortly afterward, Congress enacted the Militia Act. This act required all able-bodied men between the ages of eighteen and forty-five to serve in the militia and authorized the president of the United States to call the state militia forces into federal service for up to nine months. The act also made it clear that if the states could not fill their quota of required soldiers, they would need to institute a state draft.

But the bounty system did not work as planned. Bounty jumpers enlisted in more than one community in order to collect the initial bonus. Deserters left the army in droves, seasoned soldiers resented new enlistees brought in under the bounty system, and professional recruiting agents cheated naïve soldiers out of their bounty money. The Militia Act proved no easier to implement. In August 1862, President Lincoln used the act to call into service 300,000 militiamen and instructed the states to fill their quotas by initiating a state draft, if necessary. State governors loudly protested against the draft and argued that they did not have enough time to get volunteer recruits before being forced to resort to conscription. Thousands of men responded to the threat of a draft by fleeing their homes or countering with attacks on draft officials and conscription offices. In reality, the U.S. government never enforced the Militia Act, but the threat of conscription encouraged states to meet the draft quotas, especially when many communities sweetened the bounty offer with their own contributions of money, food, and clothing. But the manpower shortage was not solved for long, for extensive casualties at Antietam in September and Fredericksburg in December 1862 and epic losses through disease and desertion once again created a desperate need for soldiers.

THE DEBATE OVER THE NATIONAL DRAFT

As manpower needs increased, the U.S. government moved closer to a federalized system of drafting—a controversial system that would further splinter the North and lead to the violent New York City draft riot. The U.S. Congress knew that instituting a national draft could possibly result in political suicide in the next election, but after heated debates and compromises, it nevertheless passed the Enrollment Act in March 1863. In particular, Democratic congressmen fought to safeguard their state militias and protect the civil liberties of war dissenters. Once these issues were discussed, enough Democrats added their votes to the Republican majority to make the measure a reality. The Enrollment Act created a "Class I" and "Class II" system. Class I included all physically and mentally fit men between the ages of twenty and thirty-five and all unmarried men between thirty-five and forty-five. Naturalized aliens and immigrants who declared their intention of becoming citizens were also eligible for the draft. Exemptions included high-level federal officials, state governors, and sons of dependent widows or sons of infirm parents. Class II included all other able-bodied men, who could be drafted only after all Class I enrollees. The conscription act allowed a draftee either to pay a commutation fee of $300 to get out of service or to pay a substitute to take the draftee's place. It also provided for federal provost marshals to canvass local neighborhoods house-by-house for draft-eligible men.

The Republicans primarily consisted of upper-class businessmen and middle-class skilled workers from the East and enterprising western farmers. But Republicans could also be found in many small towns, especially in New England, western New York, and the Great Lakes area. This diverse group supported national conscription not only as a military necessity, but also as a way for the federal government to show strength

and power—something desperately needed after two years of unresol-
ved warfare. Many Republicans also maintained that the draft would
shift the focus from localism to nationalism and create the unifying spirit
needed to win the war. Others praised the commutation and substitution
provisions. Senator Henry Wilson, one of the founders of the Republican
party and chair of the congressional Military Affairs Committee, argued
that the commutation provisions made the draft more equitable, since it
kept the price of substitutes down to a reasonable cost. Republican newspapers agreed, attesting that commutation created an automatic ceiling
for the hiring of substitutes. Republican entrepreneurs maintained that
the provision would allow skilled workers to pay their way out of service
so they could continue manufacturing much-needed military equipment
and clothing. While the *New York Times* applauded business leaders who
enlisted, editors carefully warned against such a practice, claiming that
it would close down the city's economy. "Their businesses, in a large
number of instances, would come to a stand-still, and probably not less
than a hundred thousand men, who are dependent upon their daily labor
for their daily bread, would be thrown out of employment. Great warehouses, great factories, would be closed, and all their employees would
be thrown into the street. Capital would be locked up, machinery would
stand still, ships would rot, and thousands of people would be driven
to seek charity or to starve."[3]

To most Republicans, the draft represented a positive step toward creating nationalism, increasing the strength of the federal government, and
meeting manpower requirements. As historian Grace Palladino explains,
the Republican administration argued that conscription "offered an equitable, democratic, and certain means of attaining recruits." The draft
also "promised to forge nationalism necessary to pursue total war . . .
teach citizens their duty to the state . . . [and] force citizens to realize that,
in time of war, the requirements of the state superseded local, individual
interests."[4]

But not everyone saw conscription that way, and the issue further
divided the political parties in the North. When war was first declared,
Stephen A. Douglas, one of the key leaders of the northern Democratic
party, visited the president to pledge the party's support for the war.
But the early death of Douglas in 1861 and the growing disagreements
between the Republicans and the Democrats on the conduct of the war
and economic and social policies forced a split in the Democratic party.
By 1862 this party divided into the Peace Democrats (who opposed Republican military policies) and the War Democrats (who tended to side
with the Republicans on many key war-related issues). The urban working classes (immigrant and native born) in the East, western farmers, and
southerners from the border states generally made up the Peace Democrats. They joined with many Democratic newspapers to argue against

the high cost of commutation (almost a worker's yearly income) that discriminated against the lower classes and allowed the upper class to escape military service. In fiery debates, they lamented that the national draft would send the lower classes to die in the bloody battles and turn the conflict into "a rich man's war and a poor man's fight." New York governor Horatio Seymour called conscription unconstitutional and vowed to bring it to an end. Outraged by commutation, both Samuel Medary, the editor of the conservative journal *Crisis*, and Clement L. Vallandigham, a prominent leader of the Peace Democrats and a former Ohio congressman, sarcastically referred to the payment as "THREE HUNDRED DOLLARS OR YOUR LIFE."[5] A circa 1863 song expressed the anguish of the draft:

> Dearest William, they will draft you;
> They have placed your name on the list;
> If you possessed a brown stone front,
> Three hundred dollars wouldn't be miss'd.
>
> Chorus: I hope they will not draft you,
> Or put your name in the wheel;
> When this cruel draft is over,
> Oh! how contented I will feel![6]

Peace Democrats also worried that the national conscription would bring too much power to the federal government and further erode local and state control. As historian John Whiteclay Chambers II notes, "In a land where the only federal presence had been an occasional postman or customs clerk, the Enrollment Act authorized the army to assign provost marshals to be in charge of the draft in every congressional district."[7] As the war progressed, many Peace Democrats, referred to as "Copperheads" by their opponents, called for the Union to negotiate peace with the Confederacy. When Vallandigham, frustrated by his lack of success, threatened that the western states might form their own union with the South, Lincoln had him exiled to the South.

IMPLEMENTING THE DRAFT

Implementing the national conscription did not occur without substantial problems. Once the provost marshals established offices in local districts, their door-to-door search for eligible draftees sometimes proved difficult and even dangerous. Draft resisters used various methods to avoid conscription, including providing fictitious identities and using names of deceased individuals. Some simply left town. Others resorted to armed resistance and in a few cases even murder. Overworked draft officials not only collected names of enrollees and arranged for medical exams, but the government also charged them with the responsibility to arrest deserters and capture spies. Once the provost marshals collected all the names of eligible men in the district, they put them in a wheel. At a public gathering, a blindfolded man carefully pulled out the names of newly selected soldiers.[8]

Draft resistance followed in Minnesota, Wisconsin, Michigan, Illinois, Ohio, Indiana, Iowa, Vermont, New Hampshire, Massachusetts, and New York. As tension mounted, protests against conscription often enveloped other issues, such as the encroachment of federal authority on local communities and discontent with Republican legislatures. Many of the dissenters were working-class, native-born and immigrant Democrats, who often mixed their resentment over conscription with workplace frustrations and bitterness against Republican "bosses." They also expressed animosity against African Americans and feared that they would become competitors for jobs in the future after Republicans had made emancipation a war aim in 1863.

THE NEW YORK CITY DRAFT RIOT

In his examination of the New York City draft riot, Iver Bernstein explained that what began "as a demonstration against the draft soon expanded into a sweeping assault against the local institutions and personnel of President Abraham Lincoln's Republican Party, as well as a grotesque and bloody race riot."[9] The violence began early on Monday morning, July 13, 1863, when Irish Catholic, German, and native-born Protestant workers closed factories and shops, cut telegraph poles, pulled up railway tracks, and severely beat John A. Kennedy, the police superintendent, all on their way to the Ninth District draft pull. Carrying signs that said, "No Draft," the angry mob responded with vengeance after officials finished announcing the names of newly conscripted men, and soon they set the provost marshal's office on fire. As the flames began to blaze, the rioters moved on and joined others in various locations throughout the city. In particular, they protested outside places associated with Republican power or influence, and despite the fact that the officials temporarily suspended the draft, the mobs continued to vandalize and burn down conscription offices. Mobs attacked wealthy and prominent Republicans and looted and destroyed many of their homes and businesses. "The crowds on the Upper East Side avenues had now swelled into a 'concourse of over twelve thousand' that included men, women, and children of every social grade who had put down their work to discuss the Conscription Act or merely to watch the disturbance and ponder what direction it would take."[10]

While some rioters were satisfied with the day's work, others had only begun to vent their anger and frustration. Like the war raging between the states, the New York City draft riot took on a life of its own and unfolded in uncontrollable directions. For five days, the violence came in waves, like a tsunami, threatening to swallow up the city. By mid-week, Irish Americans dominated the scene. For many of these rioters, forced to work long hours for poor wages and in horrific working conditions, this was a chance to seek revenge on Republican bosses, newspaper editors, and politicians. Many directed their rage at prominent Republican businessmen by looting, vandalizing, or setting fire to their homes and offices. Irish targets included the home of Horace Greeley, an abolitionist leader and the Republican editor of the *New York Tribune*, as well as other Republican newsmen. A mob also "sacked" the mayor's home. The rioters gathered more and more workers as they marched from factory to factory, shop to shop, construction site to construction site. Along the way, they attacked city police and federal officers and continued to destroy communication and transportation lines.

Soon the main focus of the mob turned to the African American community. Tension between the Irish and blacks in the North had stemmed from the massive immigration of the Irish in the early nineteenth century, when the European immigrants seeking employment competed with the small population of blacks. Also, the Irish faced harsh anti-Catholic attitudes and blatant job discrimination by native-born whites, who tried to keep the Irish on the bottom rung of the socioeconomic ladder. The immigrants fought back. Having experienced some advancement by the eve of the Civil War, the Irish feared being pulled back down the ladder. "Many of New York's poor immigrants believed the Democratic orators who in spring and early summer 1863 predicted that emancipation would bring north low-wage black freemen to compete with white laborers for employment."[11] To make the situation worse, inflation played havoc with the city's economy, and poverty and unemployment were on the rise. In the minds of the poor immigrant workers, the draft served to pour salt in their wounds—forcing them to fight and die in the Civil War, only to be replaced by freed slaves from the South. Their response was brutal as they beat, mutilated, and murdered black men and women and vandalized, destroyed, and burned down their homes and churches. The Irish mob also attacked leading abolitionists. Their path of destruction included an orphanage for black children. "The crowd had swelled to an immense number at this locality, and went professionally to work in order to destroy the building, and, at the same time, to make appropriation of anything of value by which they might aggrandize themselves. When all was taken, the [orphanage] was then set on fire."[12]

During the riot, angry mobs hung a number of black men from trees and lampposts. An eyewitness described one incident. "Last evening about 5 o'clock, a gang of rioters entered the house of a colored man near the corner of Twenty-eight street and Seventh avenue, and commenced beating him in the most unmerciful manner. A company of soldiers passing that way caused the rioters to desist and retreat, but they returned immediately and hanged the poor unoffending negro [sic]."[13]

Unable to regain control of the city, officials sent for federal troops, who arrived from the fields of Gettysburg to help the police put down the riot. Soldiers restored order on Friday, July 17, but not before more than one hundred people lost their lives. Countless others suffered injuries, and scores lost their homes and businesses.

WHO WAS TO BLAME FOR THE RIOT?

Long before the eerie glow of the embers from the burning city died out, Republicans and Democrats began an intense debate over who was to blame for the bloody riot. Newspaper editors also went head-to-head over the draft and the causes of the fatal New York disturbances. Republicans called the Peace Democrats disloyal and accused them of working with southern traitors to disrupt the Union. The editor of the *Chicago Tribune* concluded that there was "good reason to believe" that Copperheads incited the draft resistance by working with "sneaking agents" from the Confederacy. He lamented that the "saddest thing" in the "glorious struggle" was that "there are men among us so lost to every noble impulse and patriotic feeling, that they will strike hands with traitors, and raise up and urge on mobs of outcasts and desperadoes to rob, hang and slaughter their own brethren and neighbors; and give their homes and possessions to pillage and the torch—if so doing they can help the cause of treason, and make rebellion triumphant."[14] The Chicago editor vowed that "this country will neither be given up to mobs nor to slavery. . . . King mob can no more save the rebellion than King Cotton."

Other Republican newspaper editors blamed the foreign born, "whose prejudice and passions had been wrought upon by demagogues and bad men to that degree they were led to lift sacrilegious hands against that Government which is and has been whilst on our soil, their efficient protector."[15] The authors of *The Bloody Week!*, an eyewitness account of the New York City draft riot, adamantly contended that "no matter what was the assumed cause of the outbreak, politically," there could be "no justification for murdering peaceful citizens—for pillaging and burning private dwellings—and for rendering homeless innocent babes."[16]

Peace Democrats painted a very different picture. While some called the attack on the black community inexcusable, they placed the blame for the violence on the shoulders of abolitionists. A rural Pennsylvania newspaper, the *Columbia Democrat*, published in an area known for its strong Democratic stance, called the attack on African Americans "unjustifiable," but argued that it was the legitimate consequence of the abolition policy. The editor offered a solution for preventing such violence—"get rid of the Abolition party as soon as possible."[17]

When Republicans in New York moved to censure Governor Horatio Seymour, calling him a traitor for his strong position against the draft and criticizing him for how he handled the riot, the Honorable Thomas C. Fields, senator from the Seventh District, rose to his defense. Fields blamed the drama on the Republicans who "adopted the unequal and hateful [draft] law" and praised Seymour for his struggle for class equality. The Democratic politician also expressed sympathy for the rioters.

> These poor men, filled with the same spirit, with the same blood flowing through their veins that flows through yours and mine, susceptible to the same feelings, controlled by the same excitement, assuaged by the same consolation of relief, in the hour when what they conceived to be an oppressive act of the government was about to be put in force, became frenzied, and for a moment lost the balance of reason which should ever give direction to human contact—for a moment assumed, what under a republican form of government should never take place—forcible resistance of law.[18]

CONCLUSION

The New York City riot was not the only example of draft resistance during the Civil War, nor was it the first time the working class responded with violence to oppression. Historians who study this topic do not always agree on what sparked draft dissent, but most find that "overt resistance to the federal draft occurred principally in Democratic areas among the foreign-born and working class."[19] Scholars cite a number of factors as the catalyst for draft protest, including political disagreements between the Republicans and Peace Democrats, resistance to growing federal power, working-class resentment of the upper class, and racial tension and job competition between poor immigrants and African Americans. Most historians are careful to note that workers did not object to military service as much as to the inequity of the draft. The act threatened to delegate the poor, unable to pay the $300 fee or hire a substitute, to the battlefields. In an effort to match the upper-class "exemption" from the draft, local communities scurried to try to collect enough money for workers' commutation fees, and class antagonism continued. In July 1864, Congress voted to repeal the commutation fee.

Although African Americans became one of the main targets of the New York rioters, black soldiers played an important role in the successful completion of the war, and some 200,000 blacks served in the Union army. The Emancipation Proclamation allowed the large-scale recruitment of African American soldiers, who had to work hard to overcome racist stereotypes and gain the respect of military leaders. Black soldiers also faced disturbing consequences, since African Americans captured by the Confederacy could be reenslaved or killed at the hands of angry southerners. Ironically, the glorious 54th Massachusetts Colored Infantry, commanded by abolitionist Robert Gould Shaw of Boston, valiantly scaled the battlements of Fort Wagner, South Carolina, in 1863, just a few days after the Irish attacked blacks in New York. Republican leaders in New York made much of the contrasting "patriotism."

The New York City draft riot served to change future conscription policy. With America's entrance into World War I, leaders carefully studied the Civil War draft system and concluded that draft exemptions played a key role in perpetuating the riot. To avoid another catastrophic situation, the Selective Service decided to disallow substitutions, purchase exemptions, and bounty payments. As a result, the World War I draft ensued with relative ease.

The stress and strain of war can have a detrimental impact on any country, especially a war that divides a nation—North against South, brother against brother—as with the American Civil War. This stress and strain was clearly evident in the New York City riot. Like fine grains of gunpowder, political divisions, class issues, and racial conflict all funneled their way into the national debate over conscription and exploded one quiet July morning in 1863, leaving a city spinning out of control for five long days, and a nation shocked for much longer.

NOTES

1. By Eye Witnesses, *The Bloody Week! Riot, Murder, and Arson, Containing Full Account of This Wholesale Outrage on Life and Property* (New York: Coutant & Baker, 1863). In the Collection of the John Hay Library, Brown University.

2. John Whiteclay Chambers II, *To Raise an Army: The Draft Comes to Modern America* (New York: Free Press, 1987), pp. 53–54. Ironically, the Confederate of America, which held up the banner of states' rights, was the first to institute a national draft.

3. "Business Men as Conscripts," *New York Times*, July 19, 1863, p. 4.

4. Grace Palladino, *Another Civil War: Labor, Capital, and the State in the Anthracite Regions of Pennsylvania, 1840–68* (Urbana: University of Illinois Press, 1990), pp. 95–96.

5. James W. Geary, *We Need Men: The Union Draft in the Civil War* (De Kalb: Northern Illinois University Press, 1991), p. 105.

6. *When This Cruel Draft Is Over*, broadside, c. 1863, in the collection of the New York Historical Society.

7. Chambers, *To Raise an Army*, p. 52.

8. Geary, *We Need Men*, pp. 73–74.

9. Iver Bernstein, *The New York City Draft Riots: Their Significance for American*

Society and Politics in the Age of the Civil War (New York: Oxford University Press, 1990), p. 3.

10. Ibid., p. 19.

11. Ibid., pp. 9–10.

12. By Eye Witnesses, *The Bloody Week!* p. 8.

13. Ibid., p. 26.

14. "Mobs and Rebellion," *Chicago Tribune*, July 16, 1863, p. 2.

15. "The Foreign Element in the Recent Riots," *Baltimore American*, July 20, 1863, p. 2.

16. By Eye Witnesses, *The Bloody Week!* p. 1.

17. "Editorial," *Columbia Democrat*, July 25, 1863, p. 1.

18. *Speech of Hon. Thomas C. Fields of New York, Delivered in the Senate of the State of New York, February 10th and 11th, 1864* (n.p.: Comstock & Cassidy, 1864), p. 5. In the collection of the U.S. Army Military History Institute.

19. Geary, *We Need Men*, p. 107.

DOCUMENTS

4.1.   Eyewitness Account of the New York City Draft Riot

The following excerpt is from an eyewitness account of the New York City draft riot, published in 1863, which provided details of the violent drama of July 13–17, 1863.

It is not without a shudder that we proceed to give an account of the horrors perpetrated on the citizens of the city of New York—the catalogue of a series of barbarities almost without a parallel in the dark ages, and certainly transcending anything of modern times. The bombardment of a city by a foreign foe is nothing to be compared to it. In such a case the citizens are banded together in the common cause of defence [*sic*], but when a band of men—thirsting for blood and hungry for plunder—are in our midst, led on by men maddened with drink, and utterly lost to every sense of humanity and decency—and whose only ambition is plunder and murder, language fails to express the horrors of the scene.

No matter what was the assumed cause of the outbreak, politically, that cause was no justification for murdering peaceful citizens—for pillaging and burning private dwellings—and for rendering homeless innocent babes. The mind can scarcely conceive a worse picture than this city presented during Monday, Tuesday and Wednesday. The howls of these barbarians and inhuman ruffians, as they marched from one street to another, the crackling of the flames, the crash of the falling walls, the roar of cannon and the rattling of musketry, mingled with the cries of pain and rage from the multitude. The honest citizen knew not at what moment the torch would be applied to his own dwelling, and his family obliged to take refuge in the streets. Mothers wrung their hands in agony, fathers looked pale and careworn, while the younger members of the family were terror stricken at the sights they beheld. . . .

Nine o'clock was the hour announced for the draft to commence for the day in that district, and nine o'clock brought together at these headquarters an assemblage of people numbering some two hundred.

The morning was cloudy and warm, and the darkness which surrounded the office and its inmates seemed as a precursor of the stirring events which were about to take place. As soon as the doors were opened the crowd immediately entered and the drawing commenced. It was half-past ten o'clock before the drawing actually commenced. Provost Marshal Jenkins stood upon the table, and called off the names as they were taken from the wheel.

THE ATTACK COMMENCED.

As the last name was called a stone came crashing through the window, which was undoubtedly the signal for a general attack. The crowd outside, which by this time had increased to a very large number, rushed into the room, and immediately all was confusion. The first thing the crowd did was to take hold of the wheel and break it into pieces scattering the papers all around on which were inscribed the names. The crowd was armed in all sorts of methods; some with crowbars, others with legs of tables, some with pieces of furniture, and not a few with revolvers and bowie knives.

THE BUILDING SET ON FIRE.

After destroying everything which was in the room, one of the crowd took out a large can of turpentine and scattering it around the floor, applied a light to the same, and soon the whole building was in flames. . . .

THE CONFLICT WITH THE PEOPLE.

Arriving at the corner of Forty-second street, further passage was barred by a crowd of some three thousand persons, who flourished their weapons and told the soldiers that they could proceed no further except at the expense of their lives. The soldiers at this moment were in close column, and looked as if they meant work. All the people who were there assembled seemed determined to do anything—even sacrifice their lives—rather than that the soldiers should triumph over them.

Bricks now began to fly and a general confusion prevailed. The soldiers were hemmed in so that they could hardly move. There was, however, a kind of temporary hush in the tumult; the crowd staggered hither and thither, as if from the most intense excitement; the soldiers, who had their pieces at an "order arms," brought them to a shoulder. No order seemed to be given at the same time. One piece went off, and then simultaneously. . . .

THE SOLDIERS RUN.

As soon as the soldiers poured their volley into the multitude they immediately turned and ran, being pursued in hot haste by thousands. The people seemed to follow them with untiring energy, and it is said scarcely one escaped from the clutches of those who laid hands upon them.

HORRIBLE SCENES.

The scenes which occurred after these soldiers fired into the people and commenced their rapid retreat by running down the avenue were certainly of an appalling nature. Excuse must be made for the conduct of the crowd by the glaring fact that a number of their kindred had been shot down in cold blood by their sides, while fighting in defence [sic] of the same principle. The soldiers threw away their muskets in order the better to expedite their skedaddling, and these were taken up by their pursuers and used against them. When one of them was overtaken he was beaten almost into jelly, and, fainting from loss of blood and exhaustion, the poor fellow was thrown into some alleyway, and left to take care of himself as best he might. At the corner of Thirty-ninth street and Third avenue the crowd seized hold of one of the soldiers, and after disfiguring him in a terrible manner, cutting open his cheek and back part of his head, he was fortunately rescued by a gentleman present who was more or less acquainted with the leaders. He was carried into a store on the corner, and his wounds attended to. The poor fellow was almost in a dying state—his eyes seemed fast working into the glare of death. Over him stood the man who had saved his life, attending to his every want, and contributing consolation to him in his sufferings. As the wounded soldier slowly recovered, he could only give expression to his thankfulness for the service rendered by a melancholy smile. It is thought that this man will not recover. There were hundreds of incidents of this melancholy description. . . .

ANOTHER NEGRO HANGED.

Last evening about 5 o'clock, a gang of rioters entered the house of a colored man near the corner of Twenty-eight street and Seventh avenue, and commenced beating him in the most unmerciful manner. A company of soldiers passing that way caused the rioters to desist and retreat, but they returned immediately and hanged the poor unoffending negro [sic].

WHAT CAN BE DONE FOR THE NEGROES!

Near the scene of riot, in the neighborhood of the Seventh avenue, a poor old negro [sic], who has to move about on crutches, and his poor old wife whose hair is white with age, have been turned out of house and home by the rioters, and last night they were constantly exposed to insults and outrage and death at the hands of the mob.

Source: By Eye Witnesses, *The Bloody Week! Riot, Murder and Arson, Containing a Full Account of This Wholesale Outrage on Life and Property* (New York: Coutant & Baker, 1863). In the collection of the John Hay Library, Brown University.

4.2.   The *Chicago Tribune* Editorializes against Mobs Incited by Agents of Rebellion, July 16, 1863

The editor of the Chicago Tribune *argued that Southern traitors incited the New York City draft riot and warned the rebels that the North would not tolerate mob violence or slavery.*

There is good reason to believe that this threatened resistance to the draft is incited and set going by the sneaking agents of rebellion, who are working everywhere, openly when they dare, and secretly when they must, to divide and distract the North, and so bring about that state of war here which is now the last and sole hope of Secession. It is the saddest thing we know in this glorious struggle of the free North against banded slaveholders who seek to destroy the Union and the country, that there are men among us so lost to every noble impulse and patriotic feeling, that they will strike hands with traitors, and raise up and urge on mobs of outcasts and desperadoes to rob, hang and slaughter their own brethren and neighbors; and give their homes and possessions to pillage and the torch—if so doing they can help the cause of treason, and make rebellion triumphant. But by all this, loyal and true men will neither be cast down nor disheartened; they will summon up new resolution, greater vigilance, and more unflinching courage; and carry the country and the cause safely through, in spite of both open traitors in the field, and secret traitors in their own homes and streets. This country will neither be given up to mobs nor to slavery. They cannot conquer, either when they fight separately or fight together. This new combination cannot win. King mob can no more save the rebellion than King Cotton.

Source: "Mobs and Rebellion," *Chicago Tribune*, July 16, 1863, p. 2.

4.3.   The *New York Times* Advises Business Men Not to Sign Up as Conscripts, July 19, 1863

The following editorial from the New York Times *applauded businessmen who served in the military, but warned that such a practice would put an economic strain on the city and leave "a*

*hundred thousand" workers without employment. The editor rec-
ommended that businessmen should pay the commutation fee to
get out of service unless they were willing to "forsake" their business.*

We print a note from a gentleman doing business in "William-street,"
who says he is willing to bind himself to serve in the ranks if he is
drafted under the Conscription law, and he asks the patriotic and wealth-
ier classes of citizens if they will not, following his example, also bind
themselves to serve if drafted, "without availing themselves of the obnoxious $300 clause?"

The gentleman is a member of a well-known and heavy business house
in the City, and he sends us his name and his card as an evidence of the
sincerity of his purpose.

We are glad to know that there are thousands and tens of thousands
of such instances of patriotic devotion. Thousands of men in independent
circumstances have joined the army, some as officers and others as privates. They gladly submit to all the fatigues and hardships of the campaign, and enjoy with a zest the hard-tack of the soldier. Luxury and
business have all been thrown to the winds, and families have been left
behind, that they might serve the cause of freedom and the country they
love. We are glad to know all this, and hope the time will never come
when it will be otherwise; for rich and poor are alike interested in the
upholding of our country's institutions.

But if any very large number of the great mercantile and businessmen
of the City were to enlist as soldiers, what would be the effect upon the
commerce and trade of the City, and upon our "poor men?" If even two
thousand of our large merchants, importers and manufacturers were to
go personally into the ranks when conscripted, their businesses, in a
large number of instances, would come to a stand-still, and probably not
less than a hundred thousand men, who are dependent upon their daily
labor for their daily bread, would be thrown out of employment. Great
warehouses, great factories, would be closed, and all their employees
would be thrown into the street. Capital would be locked up, machinery
would stand still, ships would rot, and thousands of people would be
driven to seek charity or to starve.

While, therefore, we would not urge a single business man, or a man
in easy circumstances, to pay his exemption fee, if he feels it consistent
with his public responsibilities to forsake his business and serve as a
conscript, we cannot see that it would aid the interest of those who are
dependent on their daily labor to have the business of the City inter-
rupted by the absence of those whose brains and capital carry it on.

Source: "Business Men as Conscripts," *New York Times*, July 19, 1863, p. 4.

4.4.   The *Baltimore American* Blames Immigrants for the Riot, July 20, 1863

An editorial in the Baltimore American *called conscription "fair" and "equitable" and placed the responsibility for the New York City draft riot on the city's immigrants.*

All accounts from the scenes of the late riots in New York concur in stating that the mob was largely represented by the foreign-born population of that city, whose prejudice and passions had been wrought upon by demagogues and bad men to that degree that they were led to lift sacrilegious hands against that Government which is and has been whilst on our soil, their efficient protector. This is the more lamentable, the more earnestly to be deplored, when we consider that we owe to the more enlightened and patriotic of *this same class* many of our most glorious triumphs in the field; that, recognizing in our National Flag the symbol of protection for the exiles and the oppressed of all nations, they have rallied with enthusiasm to defend it, and to insure its final triumph over those who would rend asunder that mighty nationality of which it is the fitting emblem. The deluded have, however, been taught a severe and timely lessen. They have learned that there is intelligence enough, courage, patriotism enough, to defend our unity, our free institutions against assaults from every quarter; and they have learned, too, that the administrators of the laws cannot stop to debate public rights, or the justice of legislation accomplished—but that the laws, once enacted by the proper authority, the duty of the citizen is submission. . . .

Let no exile from the oppressive Governments of the old world, then, consent to lift a hand against the only protection to which he can flee on this continent; but let all determine to sustain the Government to the uttermost. The conscription, fair, equitable, as it is, must be enforced; the rebellion must be put down. The Government is perfectly competent to the task, and cannot be scared or driven from its purpose by any riotous demonstrations whatever. . . .

Let the disaffected, then, the traitors of every grade, get out of its way. Its course marked out, it will aggress upon none who aggress not upon it; and if there are those yet in the land who cannot see the madness of opposing its decrees, let the consequences be upon their own heads. Sharp as have been the lessons commended to mob violence in New York and elsewhere, they are a portion of the wholesome teachings of the hour, and are in no danger now of being forgotten; and if the penalties incurred by ignorance are not less severe in certain cases than those incurred by crime, it is in the nature of events inevitable, because the one must not become the associate in deeds of blood with the other. Let us be glad that the case is no worse—let us be thankful that justice and firmness have finally triumphed.

Source: "The Foreign Element in the Recent Riots," *Baltimore American*, July 20, 1863, p. 2.

4.5.   Blaming the Abolitionists: An Editorial in the *Columbia Democrat*, July 25, 1863

In a rural Pennsylvania newspaper, the Columbia Democrat, *the editor blamed abolitionists for the New York City draft riot.*

The attacks which were made upon the poor Negroes during the recent riots were altogether unjustifiable. But they are the legitimate consequence of the Abolition policy; and the best way to "lighten the awful misery" which has been brought upon the colored race, and the white population also, is to get rid of the Abolition party as soon as possible. . . .

A Fact Easily Observed.—Whenever you find a newspaper continually denouncing Democrats as traitors and copperheads, you can set the editor down as a coward and a fool. It is a sure sign.—All honorable, high-minded men never resort to such low slang and abuse. He thinks more of his character as a patriot and a christian [*sic*] than to be caught engaged in such dirty work. He knows that Democrats and Republicans fill one common grave on the battle field, and that if ever this rebellion is put down it must be done by the united strength of both parties, and instead of attempting to inaugurate civil war between Democrats and Republicans in the North, he urges them to unite their strength, and crush out this rebellion. Fools, however, talk differently. Such men are a withering curse to the community in which they reside, and are, as it were, barriers in the way of uniting public sentiment.

Source: "Editorial," *Columbia Democrat*, July 25, 1863, p. 1.

4.6.   Thomas C. Fields, a New York State Senator, Criticizes the Inequality of the Draft, February 10th and 11th, 1864

In 1864, the New York State Senate moved to censure Governor Horatio Seymour in response to his handling of the New York City draft riot and for his antidraft position. (The conflict did not stop the governor from running for president in 1868.) The following excerpt is taken from a speech by the Honorable Thomas C. Fields, who defended the governor and criticized the inequality of the draft.

[Governor Seymour] is censured, because he pledged himself to use every effort to prevent any inequality between the rich and the poor in carrying out the provisions of the law providing for the draft. Was he in that justly liable to censure? Were there any inequalities? I do not ask the Senator from the 16th and the 22d [*sic*] to take Democratic testimony; but I ask them if they will be bound by the testimony of members of their own party? I will place upon the witness stand of Senator Wilson, of Massachusetts, the chairman of the Military Committee of the Senate; and what does he say? He says there was inequality in the draft. He told us in the Senate of the United States that the object of the draft was as much to obtain money as men. He told us that we now had more men than we knew what to do with. Then why is the Governor of the state of New York to be held up to public censure when a leading man of your own party, in the Senate of the United States speaks of the same facts—presents the same conclusion, and with a boldness and frankness which I admire, tells us that the very object of the draft was to obtain money as well as men, and that there was inequality between the rich man and the poor in its provisions? It was the unchecked and extensive knowledge that the law of Congress allowed a money commutation that provoked the hostility—that aroused the frenzy of thousands, who, conscious of their inability [to pay] the amount of commutation, keenly felt that poverty alone doomed them to the ranks and would cause great sacrifices to their families. Who was most to blame, Mr. Chairman, the Republican party which adopted the unequal and hateful law, or Governor Seymour, who merely avowed his design to co-operate with the municipal authorities in providing for the poor the same comparative immunity conferred upon the rich and prosperous? We have for years tried to impress upon our people that ours is a just and equal government—that [its] burdens rest as lightly upon the people [as] the dews of Heaven; that no particular class or conditions of men are subject to any exercise of tyranny. These poor men, filled with the same spirit, with the same blood flowing through their veins that flows through yours and mine, susceptible to the same feelings, controlled by the same excitement, assuaged by the same consolation of relief, in the hour when what they conceived to be an oppressive act of the government was about to be put in force, became frenzied, and for a moment lost the balance of reason which should ever give direction to human contact—for a moment assumed, what under a republican form of government should never take place—forcible resistance of law. But can you hold Governor Seymour responsible for that? Certainly not. He did every thing in his power to allay the riot as soon as possible. Well, sir, the riot was put down and peace restored.

Source: Speech of Hon. Thomas C. Fields of New York, Delivered in the Senate of the State of New York, on the Governor's Message, February 10th and 11th, 1864 (n.p.: Comstock & Cassidy, 1864). In the collection of the U.S. Army Military History Institute.

4.7.   A Popular Song Laments the Draft

> *This song, probably composed in response to the Enrollment Act of 1863, expressed the view of a loved one upset by the enactment of the "cruel draft."*

Dearest William, they will draft you;
They have placed your name on the list;
If you possessed a brown stone front,
Three hundred dollars wouldn't be miss'd.

Chorus: I hope they will not draft you,
Or put your name in the wheel;
When this cruel draft is over,
Oh! how contented I will feel!

They tell me that when you are drafted,
You'll be sent to the seat of war;
Then in battle you'll be wounded,
And come home with many a scar.

Chorus: I hope they will not draft you,
And take you away from me;

When this cruel draft is over,
Oh! how happy I will be!

If the Rebels they should kill you,
Then what would become of me?
I'm sure I'd die broken-hearted,
If your face I ne'er should see.

Chorus: I hope they will not draft you,
And leave me alone to mourn,
When this cruel draft is over,
And you should ne'er more return.

Source: When This Cruel Draft Is Over, broadside, c. 1863, in the collection of the New York Historical Society.

ANNOTATED RESEARCH GUIDE

Books and Articles

Bernstein, Iver. *The New York City Draft Riots: Their Significance for American Society and Politics in the Age of the Civil War*. New York: Oxford University Press, 1990. Explores the political, social, and economic complexities of the New York City draft riot.

Chambers, John Whiteclay, II. *To Raise an Army: The Draft Comes to Modern America*. New York: Free Press, 1987. Traces America's transformation in military policy from the colonial period through the late twentieth century. Includes a detailed chapter on the implementation of the Civil War draft.

Cook, Adrian. *The Armies of the Streets: The New York City Draft Riots of 1863*. Lexington: University Press of Kentucky, 1974. Provides a detailed overview and analysis of the New York City draft riot with a comprehensive appendix listing information about those killed, wounded, and arrested along with data on the known rioters.

Geary, James W. *We Need Men: The Union Draft in the Civil War*. De Kalb: Northern Illinois University Press, 1991. Provides a complete study of the Civil War draft, including the political evolution from volunteerism to conscription and the resulting impact on the nation. Includes background and analysis of the New York City draft riot.

Murdock, Eugene C. *One Million Men: The Civil War Draft in the North*. Madison: State Historical Society of Wisconsin, 1971. Examines the history of the northern draft during the Civil War.

Palladino, Grace. *Another Civil War: Labor, Capital, and the State in the Anthracite Regions of Pennsylvania, 1840–68*. Urbana: University of Illinois Press, 1990. Examines the complexities of working-class resistance in the Pennsylvania coal mines as they intersected with Civil War politics. Includes a chapter on the workers' opposition to the draft.

Web Site

http://www.nyhistory.org/draftriots.html. Site of the New York Historical Society. Contains primary documents and teacher units, including several
sources and activities related to New Yorkers' responses to the draft in
1863.

5

The Defeat of Chief Joseph and the Nez Perce: The Debate over the "Indian Question"

"Hear me, my chiefs, I am tired. My heart is sick and sad. From where the sun now stands I will fight no more forever," declared Chief Joseph of the Nez Perce Indians when he surrendered to General Nelson Miles in October 1877.[1] But the U.S. government expected the American Indians to do more than surrender their arms; it also expected them to surrender their traditions and cultures. Many civilian and military reformers in the late nineteenth century saw their mission as benevolent when they attempted to Americanize and Christianize the Indians of the trans-Mississippi West in the white man's image. While some humanitarians who had lived among the Creek, Choctaw, Cherokee, and other tribes gained a respect for the various Indian cultures, most reformers were blinded by their own ethnocentric ideology and saw the situation filtered through the lenses of the dominant Anglo-Saxon culture. These reformers failed to appreciate fully or value the Indian "ways of life" when they left tribes with two choices—assimilation or annihilation.

Military officers often transferred their war-time notorieties and skills for important positions in American politics and society after their retirement from service. A number of key military officers joined social reformers in a debate over the "Indian Question." While some military leaders preferred to see the complete extinction of Native American peoples, others became outspoken advocates for the Indians. These military reformers acknowledged atrocities and injustices committed by both sides during the wars, and many even expressed respect for Native American cultures. Yet they, like many civilian social reformers, argued that it was time for the Indian to change. Brigadier General Richard H. Pratt, who played a leading role in the Indian Americanization movement, argued that the only way to "save the man" was to "kill the Indian."[2] He was joined by General Nelson Miles in his call for Indians to learn "the English language, habits of industry, the benefits of civilization [and] the power of the white race."[3] Many reformers called for dividing the Indian reservations into land allotments in order to "smash the tribal connection [and] force Indians to work the land." They saw education as vital to "uplifting" Indian children to "quicken the process of cultural evolution."[4] But as historian David Wallace Adams noted, the Indian responded by pointedly asking, "How much change? Must hunters take up the plow? Must the sacred ways of the ancestors be thrown over for the black book of the missionary? And what of the children? Perhaps that was the most difficult question of all. What would become of the children?"[5]

When warfare ceased in the American West after several decades of conflict, many Indian leaders fought a new war of words. They challenged Americanization efforts that robbed Indian children of their cultural identities and protested against land allotments that undermined the Indians' concept of communal landownership and tribal government. Perhaps the best-known and most respected Indian leader was Chief Joseph of the Wal-lam-wat-kin band of the Nez Perce Indians. (His Indian name was In-mut-too-yah-lat-lat, or Thunder-traveling-over-the-mountain.) Through his writings, interviews, and visits to the nation's capital, Chief Joseph became a national symbol of valor in the struggle for Indian freedom.

WESTWARD HO

Since the early 1600s, European settlers who arrived on the eastern coast of North America had steadily pushed Indians westward. Although Indian cultures were not static, tribes still followed many centuries-old traditions, but contact with European cultures did change their way of life. Exchange brought horses, firearms, and new textiles to the American Indian, but it also carried diseases—measles, diphtheria, and smallpox—that devastated many tribes. Alcohol also served to undermine the Indians. Still, pre–Civil War White-Indian contact was relatively limited west of the Mississippi River, and the U.S. government attempted to "contain" tribes there.

While Mexicans, Chinese, and settlers of European descent all lived in the American West by the early nineteenth century, most of the land—approximately half of the United States—was inhabited by various migrant and indigenous Indian tribes. Tribes could be found in many areas of the western territories, including the Nez Perce in Oregon, Idaho, and

Washington; the Blackfeet in Montana; the Sioux in Minnesota and the Dakotas; the Cheyenne in Colorado and Wyoming; the Apache in Arizona, Texas, and New Mexico; and the Comanche and Kiowa in Texas.

A renewed interest in western expansion during the post–Civil War era rapidly changed the landscape of the American West and eventually led to the destruction of much of the older Indian traditions. The transformation began with the construction of railroads, which soon dotted the western scenery. Accompanying telegraph systems made communication throughout the huge country possible, and a number of federal government land acts provided free or inexpensive land. Railroads made access to the West much easier by carrying settlers, manufactured goods, and farm supplies westward and agricultural goods, cattle, and mined raw materials to eastern markets. Not surprisingly, a great migration followed as millions poured across the Mississippi River. Some settlers came because of free land or in search of gold, while others saw the vast plains as an escape from industrial America. Missionaries headed west with the goal of Christianizing Native Americans, and land speculators hoped to capitalize on cheap land they would later sell at a substantial profit. Army posts positioned throughout the western land protected the pioneers as they settled the trans-Mississippi West.

With expansion, settlers began to encroach on Indian lands and endangered their way of life, disturbing migratory hunting paths, root grounds, and agricultural areas. The buffalo represented an important resource for the Plains Indian peoples, and many Indians followed its migration and used every part of the beast for food, shelter, clothing, tools, and weapons. But railroad workers and settlers killed off tens of thousands of buffalo for food and sport, and hunters profited from killing the animal and selling its hide. The rapid destruction of the buffalo threatened the survival of the Indians. But even more devastating was the conflict that erupted in the American West after the Civil War, exacerbated by a great migration of settlers and a new gold fever. The proposed solution was to place Indians on reservations.

In the words of military historians Allan Millett and Peter Maslowski, "The reservation system combined blatant greed and misguided philanthropy." In designing the reservation policy, the U.S. government argued that if Indians were "confined to unwanted land," pioneers could settle the trans-Mississippi West unimpeded. "Denied their nomadic life style, [Indians] could be 'civilized'—taught the white man's language, turned into sedentary agriculturists and Christianized." But when Indians resisted the reservation policy, "the Army had to force compliance."[6] Federal troops attempted to push tribes onto selected, often-inferior lands, and conflicts between the American military and western Indians quickly arose. The tension between settlers and Indians led Governor of Colorado, John Evans, to issue a proclamation that authorized "all citizens of

Colorado, either individually, or in such parties as they may arrange, to go in pursuit of all hostile Indians on the Plains [and] also, to kill and destroy [Indians] as enemies of the country, wherever they may be found."[7] Military atrocities, such as the massacre of Indians at Sandy Creek, Colorado (Nov. 1864), received much press, but army officers noted examples of "Indian Behavior" that included "torturing captives and mutilating the dead." Acts of cruelty on both sides continued as armed skirmishes and all-out battles followed for three decades.

General William T. Sherman described the military's "difficult" job during the Indian Wars. "There are two classes of people, one demanding the utter extinction of the Indians, and the other full of love for their conversion to civilization and Christianity. Unfortunately the army stands between them and gets the cuff from both sides." Sherman complained that humanitarians cried "Butchery!" when the army killed "too many Indians," but frontiersmen scorned the troops as cowards "if it killed too few."[8] Army officers "despised pontificating humanitarians" as much as they "dislike rapacious frontiersmen." "Many of them . . . lamented the government's records of broken treaties . . . preferred negotiation to bloodshed and took an active interest in Indian welfare." But many officers also clearly understood why the Indians chose to resist. Although Sherman was certainly not well known for showing compassion toward Indians, he wrote, "We took away their country and their means of support, broke up their mode of living, their habits of life, introduced disease and decay among them, and it was for this and against this they made war. Could anyone expect less?"[9] Between 1866 and 1890, the Indian Wars continued as Native Americans resisted the reservation policy.

CHIEF JOSEPH AND THE NEZ PERCE

The warfare that raged between federal troops and Indians eventually affected peaceful tribes that had long engaged in harmonious relations with settlers. This included various Nez Perce Indians scattered around the Cascade and Bitterroot Mountain regions of north central Idaho, southeastern Washington, and northeastern Oregon. However, when gold was discovered in the Nez Perce area, the U.S. government attempted to force the Indians to give up a significant portion of their land. While other Nez Perce groups caved in to the pressure and signed a treaty in 1863, Chief Joseph's "nontreaty" Nez Perce of Oregon's Wallowa Valley refused to sign the treaty or move onto the Nez Perce Indian Reservation in Idaho. The nontreaty Nez Perce also turned away from Christian beliefs preached by local missionaries. By 1877, tension built beyond control as greedy settlers, land speculators, and cattle ranchers pushed too far and the young Nez Perce warriors pushed back, killing a number of pioneers. The army responded by sending General Oliver O. Howard to force the Wallowa Nez Perce onto the Idaho reservation. Howard, a Civil War hero, had served as the commissioner of the post–Civil War Freedmen's Bureau and was on the board of Howard University, a school he helped found for freed blacks in Washington, D.C. The general returned to active military service in the Indian Wars and now faced the Nez Perce. To avoid war, Chief Joseph decided to move his band to new lands in Canada. For over ten weeks, the Nez Perce warriors, women, children, and old men led army soldiers on a chase over some 1,700 miles, engaging in more than a dozen bloody skirmishes, before being stopped. When Colonel (later General) Nelson Miles intercepted the Nez Perce some forty miles from Canada, he promised Chief Joseph that his band could return home if they surrendered. In October of 1877, Chief Joseph told Miles: "I am tired of fighting. Our chiefs are killed. . . . The old men are all dead. . . . The little children are freezing to death. . . . My people—some of them—have run away to the hills and have no blankets; no food. No one knows where they are—perhaps freezing to death. I want to have time to look for my children and see how many of them I can find. Maybe I shall find them among the dead."[10] But General Sherman overrode Colonel Miles's promise, despite the pleas from both Miles and Howard to let the Nez Perce go home. Instead, the band was first sent to Fort Leavenworth, Kansas, and then into exile on Indian land in Oklahoma. Many died there from rampant diseases. Although Chief Joseph stopped fighting with weapons, he spent the rest of his life fighting with words for the freedom of his tribe and the rights of the Indian people.

THE DEBATE OVER THE "INDIAN QUESTION"

Even before the final defeat of the Native Americans in the West, the debate over the "Indian Question" began. In her 1881 book *A Century of Dishonor*, Helen Hunt Jackson joined other reformers in protest of the widespread corruption and graft found in the Bureau of Indian Affairs that filled the coffers of dishonest agents while Indians faced starvation on the reservations. Clearly, the reservation system that reduced Indians to wards of the government was not working, and something had to change.

Many social reformers spoke out against the mistreatment of the western Indians. In press releases, journal articles, books, and speeches, they highlighted the immorality of leaving Indians to die on barren lands and criticized the government for the years of broken treaties, unfulfilled promises, and lies. Some organized into such groups as the Indian Rights Association, the Boston Indian Citizenship Association, and the Women's National Indian Association. But the well-intentioned reformers could not escape the prevailing ideological and cultural consensus of their day. Many social reformers sought to solve the "Indian Question" with answers from their own Anglo-Saxon culture. Their solution was as-similation. Their resolution for the "uncivilized" Indians was to "Amer-icanize" them and groom them into "independent, industrious, and civilized" American citizens. Only a small minority of white leaders pro-tested the new direction of the government's Indian policies. Some went to live among the trans-Mississippi tribes, while others argued that the real purpose of the Indian land allotments was to steal millions of acres of land, cleverly labeled excess, from Native American reservations.

Many military leaders joined the debate over the "Indian Question" in public addresses and writings in leading journals. Military officers were often held in high esteem in late-nineteenth-century America, and many filled key positions in the business and political sectors upon re-tirement from military service. In the early 1880s, General Miles, well known for his military endeavors against the American Indians, joined the debate with speeches and writings. Miles contended that both the white man and the Indian must take responsibility for the conflict and the brutal way each side fought. But to him, the real issue was how to proceed. In a public address in 1881, he asked whether the country should continue its "vacillating and expensive policy that has marred our fair name as a nation and a Christian people." Or should the nation "devise some practical and judicious system by which we can govern one quarter of a million of our population, securing and maintaining their loyalty, raising them from the darkness of barbarism to the light of civilization, and put an end to these interminable and expensive Indian wars"?[11] To Miles, the answer was simple: use unoccupied military posts as schools to educate the Indians in the American language and culture and teach them a vocational trade. The final goal, Miles concluded, was that "the white man and the Indian should be taught to live side by side, each respecting the rights of the other, and both living under wholesome laws, enforced with ample authority and exact justice."[12] In addition to Indian education, most political leaders also called for each head of an Indian household to be given a plot of land as a way of sending the Indians on the road to becoming civilized farmers. To the politicians, this much-needed change would end the Indians' archaic concepts of com-munal lands and terminate their outdated tribal governments.

AMERICANIZATION AND INDIAN SCHOOLS

What would eventually turn into a massive industrial education and Americanization effort for young Native Americans began with the im-prisonment of Indian warriors. In the spring of 1875, the U.S. Army put Captain (later Brigadier General) Richard H. Pratt in charge of seventy-

two warriors of the Kiowa, Comanche, Cheyenne, Arapahoe, and Cad-
doe peoples. The army considered the men "ringleaders" of Indian
resistance and sought to separate them from their respective tribes when
it gave Pratt instructions that the warriors "should all be sent in chains
as prisoners to Florida, and held there indefinitely."[13] But Pratt had other
ideas when he argued that instead of endless days spent in a jail, the
warriors "should be industrially trained, educated and civilized so far
as possible, so that if returned to their people they would go back as
influences for good."[14] With the military's permission, Pratt began "un-
chaining" the prisoners. Dressed in army fatigues, the warriors traded
the jail cell for the classroom, where they learned English, Protestantism,
American civics, and an industrial trade. Pratt successfully convinced the
army to release the prisoners who were so trained. Some returned to
their tribes, while others attempted to live in white society.

Declaring success with the Indian warriors, Pratt launched into a new
Americanization effort by seeking and getting permission from the U.S.
Bureau of Indian Affairs, the U.S. military, and Congress to start a school
for Indian children. Pratt argued that missionary schools, designed to
Christianize Native Americans, failed to give them vocational training
and much-needed interaction with members of the white community.
For the first year, Pratt worked out of the Hampton Institute, a school
founded to offer vocational training to African Americans, but he soon
moved his Indian school to Carlisle Barracks, a relatively deserted army
station in south central Pennsylvania. The cost of running the school was
financed from the "Civilization Fund"—proceeds from selling off land
of the Osage Indians in Kansas.

Pratt began by gathering Indian boys and girls selected by Indian Bureau agents at the Sioux reservation in the South Dakota Territory, along
with children from other tribes, before heading east. Carlisle Indian
School began in the fall of 1879. The school separated children from their
parents and their native language and culture, and Pratt hoped to transform the children by cutting their hair, putting them in uniforms, and
renaming them from a list of biblical and common "American" names.
Some Indian children resisted Pratt's methods by creating disturbances,
running away, and in a few cases committing suicide. Therefore, discipline was harsh to ensure conformity. No longer allowed to speak their
native tongue, children spent hours learning to read and write English
and were taught Victorian etiquette and American civics. Instructors also
Christianized the Indian children, and reading the Protestant Bible became part of the Americanization routine. An important aspect of the
school was the time spent learning a vocational trade. Boys received
training in farming, carpentry, wagon making, harness making, shoe-
making, printing, tailoring, blacksmithing, and tinsmithing, while girls
learned sewing, cooking, housekeeping, and laundering. Vocational

skills became enhanced through contact with local craftsmen from the Carlisle community. According to Pratt, without becoming "skilled workmen," the Indians would "remain aboriginal and useless in this country only because of lack of opportunity to become anything else."[15]

The Carlisle concept had some critics in Congress. But far from speaking out against an educational system that resulted in the extermination of the Indian culture, these critics wanted to expand the system. Senator Henry Teller of Colorado, in a heated debate over Indian land allotments, expressed his concern with the Indian education program, contending that it "does not accomplish the great purposes of civilization to send a few wild Indians down to Hampton and a few up to Carlisle." Instead, Teller wanted to put Americanization schools directly in the Indian communities: "We must bring the influences where a whole Indian tribe or a whole band will be affected and influenced by them."[16] Senator H.L. Dawes of Massachusetts, who later drafted the Dawes Act providing for the division of Indian land into privately owned plots, agreed that the government should create schools on Indian reservations instead of removing the children to off-reservation schools. Pratt answered these critics, "I do not believe that amongst his people an Indian can be made to feel all the advantages of a civilized life, nor the manhood of supporting himself and of standing out alone and battling for life as an American citizen. To accomplish that, his removal and personal isolation is necessary."[17]

Since the majority of Congress embraced the idea of Indian schools both off and on reservations, appropriations poured into the efforts, and thousands of Indian children went through the Americanization process. For many in the white society, the Indian school's "publicity and appreciation grew, and the Carlisle beacon, 'to civilize the Indian; get him into civilization; to keep him civilized, [and] let him stay, was confirmed.' "[18]

INDIAN RESPONSE TO INDUSTRIAL EDUCATION

Many tribes followed the new government land reforms and did not resist the Americanization of their children, since they hoped that the effort to conform would bring acceptance and peace. Others fought back and sought their own answer to the "Indian Question"—freedom. Resistance to Indian schools came from a variety of tribes. According to a government agent's report, the Crow were "bitterly opposed to sending their children to school and invent[ed] all kinds of excuses to get the children out or keep from sending them." Likewise, the Idaho Lemhi people were "constantly at rebellion against civilizing elements," especially connected to the education of their children.[19] Many tribes drafted and sent petitions to Congress, while some sent delegations to the Indian

Bureau to battle against the Americanization efforts. Tribal leaders also undermined the process by instilling cultural traditions whenever possible. Some tribes split over the issue. In 1902 writer and social reformer Hamlin Garland observed:

> Upon close study . . . each tribe, whether Sioux, or Navajo, or Hopi will be found to be divided . . . into two parties, the radicals and the conservatives—those who are willing to change, to walk the white man's way; and those who are deeply, sullenly skeptical of all civilization measures, clinging tenaciously to the traditions and lore of their race. These men are often the strongest and bravest of their tribe, the most dignified and the most intellectual. . . . Though in rags, their spirits are unbroken; from the point of view of their sympathizers, they are patriots.[20]

NEZ PERCE RESISTANCE TO AMERICANIZATION

One of the most outspoken Indian leaders was Chief Joseph of the Wallowa Nez Perce. While he was held captive with his tribe at Fort Leavenworth, Kansas, Chief Joseph began a long and tireless struggle for justice. When Pratt visited the fort in 1879, the commander of Leavenworth, General John Pope, asked him to take fifty Nez Perce children to his Indian school, but Chief Joseph refused to allow the tribe's children to participate in the program, and Pratt did not want to take the youngsters by force. Not wanting to give up on the idea, Pope asked Pratt to stay in the area to duplicate his successful "Florida experience" with the Nez Perce prisoners. But Pratt acknowledged the strong resistance of the Nez Perce people and concluded that the "conditions and facilities were so little conducive to success" that he asked to be excused from the task. In Pratt's words, "Chief Joseph and his subchiefs . . . all persisted in refusing their children until they knew their own fate. Chief Joseph was noted as an orator, and his long speech was full of impressive arraignment of our government and people for mistreatment of his people."[21] (Much later, in 1904, several Nez Perce Indian children did attend the Carlisle School.)

Shortly after their capture in 1877, the Nez Perce leader and his band continued to fight for their freedom by writing a petition to the U.S. government asking for permission to return to Oregon, but the petition was rejected. Soon the band was exiled in a malaria-ridden area of Oklahoma—set aside for Native American tribes—where it faced new and daunting hardships.

THE DAWES ACT

Many political, military, and social reformers wanted to go beyond the Indian educational system and argued that individual property ownership was the next step in "uplifting" the Indians. For a number of years, Congress considered several land-allotment plans, including Texas senator Richard Coke's bill, which divided reservation land without giving Indians citizenship. But not everyone agreed to the division of Indian reservations. In May 1880, a minority view was issued from the Committee on Indian Affairs of the House of Representatives, calling the Coke bill "wrong, ill-timed, and unstatesmanlike." Congressmen Russell Errett, Charles E. Hooker and T.M. Gunter signed the minority opinion and asserted that the real intention of the bill—disguised "in the name of Humanity"—was to open up additional western lands to white settlers. Furthermore, land allotments would not "civilize" the Indian or improve his situation: "The whole training of an Indian from his birth, the whole history of the Indian race, and the entire array of Indian traditions, running back for at least four hundred years, all combine to predispose the Indian against this scheme for his improvement, devised by those who judge him exclusively from *their* standpoint instead of from *his*."[22] Even this minority view was framed by the prevailing ideological consensus of the day, since the three congressmen acknowledged that eventually the weaker culture "must in the end be supplanted by the strong." But they warned that the Indian culture "cannot be violently wrenched out of place and cast aside," but must be changed with "time, patience, and the skill as well as the benign spirit of Christian statesmanship."[23]

Congress eventually passed a land-allotment bill in February 1887, this time sponsored by Senator Dawes. The Dawes Act called for the division of Indian lands into small, privately owned plots, mirroring the system of independent white farmers. Reformers "considered the private ownership of land to be an indispensable means for the acculturation of the Indians and their eventual assimilation into white society."[24] Therefore, this system sought to end the long-standing Indian concept of communal ownership of land and the tribal leadership system—both thousands of years old. Citizenship was "conferred" on all Indians who abandoned the way of the Indian and adopted "the habits of civilized life."[25] Supporters theorized that once land allotment and citizenship were set in place, the Indians—as individuals—would be firmly under the management of the U.S. government. Indian Bureau agents, working throughout the western reservations, strove to convince the Indians to accept this change.

Not everyone applauded the new act. Congressman J. Hale Sypher joined a small faction in the House to chastise Congress and called the

Dawes Act a "deliberate scheme to destroy the autonomy" of the Indian tribes. "It is a bold and audacious scheme, planned with consummate cunning, to destroy the constitutional governments of the Indian nations and to establish in their stead the domination of the white man in the Indian Territory."[26] The minority voice in Congress also predicted that the Dawes Act would lead to further loss of lands for the Native Americans.

INDIAN OBJECTIONS TO LAND ALLOTMENTS

The Cherokee Nation challenged the Dawes Act. They could never "dream that, without their consent, they should ever be forced to dissolve their Government, change the tenure of their lands and become subject to a Government altogether administered by the whites." In a carefully worded resolution, the Cherokee attempted to turn the tables on the U.S. government by using the rhetoric of the white man. The Indians explained that they were not "savages" or "uncivilized," but a carefully organized social and political unit. The Cherokee contended that "the white man's Bible says God gave the lands of Canaan to the children of Israel. The Indian's Bible, which is held in the form of tradition, says the Great Spirits gave America to the Indian" and their right to govern themselves stretched far beyond British or American history.[27] The chief of the Creek Indians also protested the Dawes Act and began his address to the U.S. government by explaining how the Creek people had already adapted to the white system through public education, industrial training, and teachings on the "principles of a constitutional republican form of government." But assimilation had to stop with the allocation of tribal lands, since "the holding of [Creek] lands in common is a custom among the Creeks as old as the history and traditions of the tribe. . . . Under it they have prospered and been happy."[28] The Creek leader urged the Dawes Commission to reconsider the new federal Indian policies.

CHIEF JOSEPH'S CONTINUED PROTESTS

In January 1879, Chief Joseph received permission to travel to Washington, D.C., to speak to U.S. political leaders about Indian land policies, the continued encroachment of white settlers, and his hopes of returning to his ancestral homeland in the Wallowa Valley. Speaking to President Rutherford B. Hayes, cabinet members, and various congressmen and diplomats, Chief Joseph attempted to educate the American leaders about his people. "I want the white people to understand my people. Some of you think an Indian is like a wild animal. This is a great mistake."[29] The Indian leader spoke out against the lies of the American leaders and the many broken promises. He also described the laws of his people that taught the Nez Perce not to break a bargain or tell a lie, and to "treat all men as they treated us." Chief Joseph criticized the Indian schools, Christianization efforts, and the reservation policy:

> You might as well expect the rivers to run backward as that any man who was born a free man should be contented penned up and denied liberty to go where he pleases. If you tie a horse to a stake, do you expect he will grow fat? If you pen an Indian up on a small spot of earth, and compel him to stay there, he will not be contented nor will he grow and prosper. I have asked some of the great white chiefs where they get their authority to say to the Indian that he shall stay in one place, while he sees white men going where they please. They cannot tell me. . . . Let me be a free man—free to travel, free to stop, free to work, free to trade, where I choose, free to choose my own teachers, free to follow the religion of my fathers, free to think and talk and act for myself—and I will obey every law, or submit to the penalty.[30]

Over the years, Chief Joseph continued to bring important Indian issues to the American public, and many became sympathetic to the plight of the Nez Perce as he made his people's case through speeches, interviews, and writings. He also received assistance from General Miles, who had overseen the surrender of the Nez Perce a few years earlier and had grown to know and respect the Indian leader. Now Miles pressured the authorities to allow the Nez Perce band to return to Oregon. C.E.S. Wood, the former lieutenant who recorded Chief Joseph's surrender statement in 1877, started a letter-writing campaign to convince the government to send the Nez Perce home. The Indian Rights Association, the Presbyterian church, and many newspaper editors also took up the cause. Their efforts paid off when letters and telegrams poured into the nation's capital in support of returning the Nez Perce to their homeland. In May 1883, the government, unwilling to send Chief Joseph and the Nez Perce to Wallowa Valley in Oregon, the land of their ancestors, instead took the Indian tribe to an Idaho Indian reservation. In 1897, Chief Joseph once again ventured east, this time to meet with President William McKinley to complain about white settlers moving onto the lands of his Colville Reservation in Idaho.

Over the years, the Nez Perce leader continued to challenge government policies and tried to keep white educators and missionaries away from his tribe. Chief Joseph also spoke out against the Dawes Act. If any member did not pick his land lot, a government agent would make the selection in the name of the Indian. Most of Chief Joseph's Nez Perce did not appear in person to receive their allotments in protest of the system and in the hope of being sent back to the Wallowa Valley.

Chief Joseph's gallant fight ended suddenly when he died from a heart attack on September 21, 1904. The Indian Bureau physician "reported simply that he had died of a broken heart."[31] But Yellow Bull, who fought with Chief Joseph against the white encroachment and often accompanied the leader, vividly glimpsed the future when he concluded, "Joseph is dead but his words will live forever."[32]

CONCLUSION

At the end of the Indian Wars, a new battle began—a battle for the soul of the American Indian. This marked a new chapter in the history of the U.S. military as key officers joined with political and social reformers to fashion a nonmilitary solution to the "Indian Question." They concluded that the only way for the Indian to survive in the dawning age of the twentieth century would be through conformity to the white man's way of life. But in reality, U.S. government policies created a generation of Indians who struggled to understand the contradictions in cultures and grew angry at the abuses of their people. The Indian schools often left children rejected by white society and isolated from their indigenous people. The Dawes Act undermined tribal connections and forced the Indian to adhere to what white Americans believed to be a rational pragmatic system of landowners and government. Much like the Indian schools, the Dawes Act refused to acknowledge any value in the centuries-old traditions of Native Americans. As predicted, most of the land split into allotments—and often the best land—went to white settlers and speculators. The Indians fought back. They challenged U.S. government policies and tried valiantly to keep their cultural traditions alive. It would be decades before the Indians could begin to secure the right of self-determination when it came to their children's education and their tribal government. Some of the changes came with the 1970s AIM, the American Indian Movement, designed to regain respect, political power and cultural heritage of the various Indian tribes.

By the turn of the twentieth century, the United States would fight another war growing out of the continued blindness of America's ethnocentric attitudes, its paternalistic role of civilizing the "uncivilized," and its unwillingness to understand and respect other cultures. This time the war took place on a far-off island in the Pacific—the Philippines. As for the Nez Perce, the tribe continues to struggle to reclaim its culture. In 1998, its prudent fund-raising efforts resulted in the purchase of a large collection of tribal artifacts—key to reclaiming its cultural heritage and passing down traditions to its children. But with a new century on the horizon, the Nez Perce have also continued to embrace modernity, complete with their own official Web page.

NOTES

1. Brigadier-General O.O. Howard, *Supplementary Report (Non-Treaty Nez-Perce Campaign)*, Department of the Columbia, January 26, 1878, p. 57. In the collection of the U.S. Army Military History Institute, Carlisle Barracks, Pennsylvania.

2. David Wallace Adams, *Education for Extinction: American Indians and the Boarding School Experience, 1875–1928* (Lawrence: University Press of Kansas, 1995), p. 52.

3. Brigadier General N.A. Miles, U.S. Army, "Our Indian Question," *Journal of the Military Service Institute of the United States*, Vol. II, no. 7 (1881): 290. In the collection of the Nelson Miles Papers, Nez Perce Box, U.S. Army Military History Institute, Carlisle Barracks, Pennsylvania.

4. David Wallace Adams, *Education for Extinction: American Indians and the Boarding School Experience, 1875–1928* (Lawrence: University Press of Kansas, 1995), p. 19.

5. Ibid., p. 9.

6. Allan R. Millett and Peter Maslowski, *For the Common Defense: A Military History of the United States of America* (New York: Free Press, 1984), p. 237.

7. J.W. Wright, *Chivington Massacre of the Cheyenne Indians* (Gideon & Pearson, 186?), p. 2; Pamphlets in American History, I 37.

8. Sherman quoted in Millett and Maslowski, *For the Common Defense*.

9. Ibid.

10. Howard, *Supplementary Report (Non-Treaty Nez-Perce Campaign)*, p. 57.

11. Miles, "Our Indian Question," p. 279.

12. Miles, "Our Indian Question," p. 291.

13. R.H. Pratt, Brig. Gen., U.S.A., *American Indians, Chained and Unchained*, Being an address before the Pennsylvania Commandery of the Military Order of the Loyal Legion at the Union League, Philadelphia, October 23, 1912, p. 5. In the Pamphlets in American History collection, no. I 236.

14. Ibid., p. 6.

15. Ibid., p. 13.

16. U.S. Congress, Senate, *Debate on the Bill to Provide Land in Severalty, Congressional Record*, 46th Cong., 3rd sess., January 20, 1881, Senate Report 1773.

17. Correspondence between General Pratt and Senator Dawes, reprinted in Richard Henry Pratt, *Battlefield and Classroom: Four Decades with the American Indian, 1867–1904* (New Haven: Yale University Press, 1964), p. 266.

18. R.H. Pratt, Brig. Gen., U.S.A., *American Indians, Chained and Unchained*, p. 15.

19. Adams, *Education for Extinction*, p. 210.

20. Quoted from a 1902 report by Hamlin Garland, ibid., p. 212.

21. Pratt, *Battlefield and Classroom*, p. 196.

22. U.S. Congress, House of Representatives, Committee on Indian Affairs,

Lands in Severalty to Indians: Report to Accompany, HR 5038, 46th Cong., 2nd sess., May 28, 1880, H. Report 1576, p. 8.

23. Ibid.

24. D.S. Otis, *The Dawes Act and the Allotment of Indian Lands,* ed. Francis Paul Prucha (Norman: University of Oklahoma Press, 1973), p. ix.

25. Quoted in Otis, *The Dawes Act,* p. 7.

26. *Committee on Indian Affairs, House of Representatives, Remarks of Mr. Sypher,* March 6, 1896. Pamphlets in American History, no. I 254, p. 1.

27. *Communication to the United States Commissioners in Relation to a Conference on Propositions of the Government,* by Commission on Part of the Cherokee Nation, 1896 (St. Louis: R. & T.A. Ennis Stationery Company, 1896), pp. 8–9. Pamphlets in American History, no. I 721.

28. *Message of the Chief of the Muskogees, and Reply of the National Council in Extraordinary Session April 4, 1894, to the Dawes Commission* (Okla.: Eufaula Journal, 1894?), p. 5. Pamphlets in American History, I 848.

29. Chief Joseph, "Chief Joseph's Own Story" (St. Paul: 1925?), p. 11. Reprinted in Pamphlets in American History, no. I 432. Originally printed as "An American Indian's View of Indian Affairs," *North American Review* 128 (April 1879).

30. Ibid., pp. 29–30.

31. Merrill D. Beal, *"I Will Fight No More Forever": Chief Joseph and the Nez Perce War* (Seattle: University of Washington Press, 1966; reprint, 1995), pp. 300–301.

32. David Lavender, *Let Me Be Free: The Nez Perce Tragedy* (San Francisco: HarperCollins, 1992), p. 346.

DOCUMENTS

5.1. Proclamation by Governor John Evans of the Colorado Territory against Hostile Indians, August 11, 1864

On August 11, 1864, John Evans, governor of the Colorado Territory, issued a proclamation declaring that "most of the Indian tribes of the Plains are at war and hostile to the whites." He authorized all citizens of Colorado to pursue and "kill and destroy . . . hostile Indians." On November 29, 1864, Colonel John M. Chivington and his 3rd Regiment of Colorado Volunteers brutally attacked and killed a group of Indians made up mostly of defenseless women and children. Although Chivington was publicly denounced, his actions reflected the views of many other military and political leaders who had little regard for Native Americans. Not all military and political leaders felt this way. Some worked to integrate Indians into the white culture through the Americanization process or learned to honor and respect the Indian cultures. Evans's proclamation is reprinted here.

Having sent special messengers to the Indians of the Plains, directing the friendly to rendevouz [sic] at Fort Lyon, Fort Larnerd, Fort Laramie, and Camp Collins, for safety and protection, warning them that all hostile Indians would be pursued and destroyed, and the last of said messengers have now returned, and the evidence being conclusive that most of the Indian tribes of the Plains are at war and hostile to the whites and having to the utmost of my ability endeavored to induce all the Indians of the Plains to come to said places of rendevouz [sic], promising them subsistence, which with few exceptions they have refused to do.

Now, therefore, I, John Evans, Governor of Colorado, do issue this, my Proclamation, and authorize all citizens of Colorado, either individually, or in such parties as they may arrange, to go in pursuit of all hostile Indians on the Plains, scrupulously avoiding those who respond to the call to rendevouz [sic] at the points indicated; also, to kill and destroy as enemies of the country, wherever they may be found, all such hostile Indians.

And further, as the only reward I am authorized to offer for such services, I hereby empower such citizens to take captive and hold to their own private use and benefit, all the property of such hostile Indians, that they may capture, and to receive for all stolen property recovered from said Indians such reward as may be deemed proper and just therefore.

I further offer to all such parties as will organize under the militia law of the Territory for the purpose, to furnish them arms and ammunition and to present their account for pay as regular soldiers for themselves, their horses, their subsistence and transportation, to Congress under the assurance of the department commander that they will be paid.

The conflict is on us all, and all good citizens are called on to do their duty for the defense of their houses and families.

In testimony whereof, I have hereto set my hand and caused the great seal of the Territory of Colorado to be affixed, this 11th day of August, A.D. 1864.

By the Governor:

JOHN EVANS.

S.H. Elbert,
Sec'y of Col. Terr.

Source: J.W. Wright, *Chivington Massacre of the Cheyenne Indians* (Gideon & Pearson, 186?), p. 2. Pamphlets in American History, I 37.

5.2.   Chief Joseph's Own Story, 1879

Chief Joseph, the leader of the Wal-lam-wat-kin band of the Nez Perce, told his story to the North American Review *in April 1879. After the defeat of his tribe in 1877, Chief Joseph spent the rest of his life lobbying for Indian rights through interviews, public speeches, and visits to Washington, D.C. The following is an excerpt from his 1879 interview.*

My friends, I have been asked to show you my heart. I am glad to have a chance to do so. I want the white people to understand my people. Some of you think an Indian is like a wild animal. This is a great mistake. I will tell you all about our people, and then you can judge whether an Indian is a man or not. I believe much trouble and blood would be saved if we opened our hearts more. I will tell you in my way how the Indian sees things. The white man has more words to tell you how they look to him, but it does not require many words to speak the truth. What I have to say will come from my heart, and I will speak with a straight tongue. Ah-cum-kin-I-ma-me-hut (the Great Spirit) is looking at me, and will hear me.

My name is In-mut-too-yah-lat-lat (Thunder-traveling-over-the-mountain).

I am chief of the Wal-lam-wat-kin band of Chute-pa-lu, or Nez Perces (nose-pierced Indians). I was born in eastern Oregon, thirty-eight winters ago. My father was chief before me. When a young man he was called Joseph by Mr. Spaulding, a missionary. He died a few years ago. There was no stain on his hands of the blood of a white man. He left a good name on the earth. He advised me well for my people.

Our fathers gave us many laws, which they had learned from their fathers. These laws were good. They told us to treat all men as they treated us; that we should never be the first to break a bargain; that it was a disgrace to tell a lie; that we should speak only the truth; that it was a shame for one man to take from another his wife, or his property, without paying for it. We were taught to believe that the Great Spirit sees and hears everything, and that He never forgets; that hereafter He will give every man a spirit-home according to his desserts [sic]; if he has been a good man, he will have a good home; if he has been a bad man, he will have a bad home. This I believe, and all my people believe the same. . . .

At last I was granted permission to come to Washington and bring my friend Yellow Bull and our interpreter with me. I am glad we came. I have shaken hands with a great many friends, but there are some things I want to know which no one seems able to explain. I cannot understand how the Government sends a man out to fight us, as it did General Miles, and then breaks his word. Such a Government has something wrong about it. I cannot understand why so many chiefs are allowed to talk so many different ways, and promise so many different things. I have seen the Great Father Chief (the President); the next Great Chief (Secretary of the Interior); the Commissioner Chief (Hayt); the Law Chief (General Butler), and many other law chiefs (Congressmen), and they all say they are my friends, and that I shall have justice, but while their mouths all talk right I do not understand why nothing is done for my people. I have heard talk and talk, but nothing is done. Good words do not last long until they amount to something. Words do not pay for my dead people. They do not pay for my country, now overrun by white men. They do not protect my father's grave. They do not pay for my horses and cattle. Good words will not give me back my children. Good words will not make good the promise of your War Chief, General Miles. Good words will not give my people good health and stop them from dying. Good words will not get my people a home where they can live in peace and take care of themselves. I am tired of talk that comes to nothing. It makes my heart sick when I remember all the good words and all the broken promises. There has been too much talking by men who had no right to talk. Too many misrepresentations have been made, too many misunderstandings have come up between the white men about the Indians. If the white man wants to live in peace with the Indian he can live in peace. There need be no trouble. Treat all men alike. Give them all the same law. Give them all an even chance to live and grow. All men were made by the same Great Spirit Chief. They are all brothers. The earth is the mother of all people, and all people should have equal rights upon it. You might as well expect the rivers to run backward as that any man who was born a free man should be contented penned up and denied liberty to go where he pleases. If you tie a horse to a stake, do you expect he will grow fat? If you pen an Indian up on a small spot of earth, and compel him to stay there, he will not be contented nor will he grow and prosper. I have asked some of the great white chiefs where they get their authority to say to the Indian that he shall stay in one place, while he sees white men going where they please. They cannot tell me. . . .

I only ask of the Government to be treated as all other men are treated. If I cannot go to my own home, let me have a home in some country where my people will not die so fast. I would like to go to Bitter Root Valley. There my people would be healthy; where they are now they are dying. Three have died since I have left my camp to come to Washington.

When I think of our condition my heart is heavy. I see men of my race treated as outlaws and driven from country to country, or shot down like animals.

I know that my race must change. We cannot hold our own with the white men as we are. We only ask an even chance to live as other men live. We ask to be recognized as men. We ask that the same law shall work alike on all men. If the Indian breaks the law, punish him by the law. If the white man breaks the law, punish him also.

Let me be a free man—free to travel, free to stop, free to work, free to trade, where I choose, free to choose my own teachers, free to follow the religion of my fathers, free to think and talk and act for myself—and I will obey every law, or submit to the penalty. . . .

Whenever the white man treats the Indian as they treat each other, then we shall have no more wars. We shall be all alike—brothers of one father and one mother, with one sky above us and one country around us, and one government for all. Then the Great Spirit Chief who rules above will smile upon this land, and send rain to wash out the bloody spots made by brothers' hands upon the face of the earth. For this time the Indian race are waiting and praying. I hope that no more groans of wounded men and women will ever go to the ear of the Great Spirit Chief above, and that all people may be one people.

In-mut-too-yah-lat-lat has spoken for his people.

Young Joseph.

Source: Chief Joseph, "Chief Joseph's Own Story" (St. Paul: 1925?), pp. 11, 29–31. Reprinted in *Pamphlets in American History*, no. 1 432. Originally printed as

"An American Indian's View of Indian Affairs," *North American Review* 128 (April 1879): 412–433.

5.3.   Brigadier General Nelson Miles's Views on the Indian Question, 1881

Chief Joseph surrendered to General Nelson Miles in 1877, ending the Nez Perce war. But Miles got to know and respect the Indian leader and became Chief Joseph's advocate in the struggle of the Wallowa Nez Perce to return to their ancestral homelands. Miles also joined in the debate over the "Indian Question" through his writings and public speeches. Although Miles acknowledged that both white men and Indians were to blame for the war, he saw Indian assimilation through Americanization education as the answer to ending the western conflict.

To the Corresponding Secretary Military Service Institution, Governor's Island.

SIR: The generous offer made by your Society is a strong incentive to any one familiar with the subject, to present his views on "Our Indian Question;" at the same time there is another inducement that would prompt a response to your invitation, namely—the hope that some good results may be drawn from a fair and free discussion of this important subject, and with that view the following is most respectfully submitted for the consideration of the Honorable Board.

The real issue in the question which is now before the American people is, whether we shall continue the vacillating and expensive policy that has marred our fair name as a nation and a Christian people, or devise some practical and judicious system by which we can govern one quarter of a million of our population, securing and maintaining their loyalty, raising them from the darkness of barbarism to the light of civilization, and put an end to these interminable and expensive Indian wars.

The supposition that we are near the end of our Indian troubles is erroneous, and the fact that a condition of affairs now exists over an enormous area of country, in which an American citizen cannot travel, unguarded and unarmed, without the danger of being molested, is, to say the least, preposterous and unsatisfactory. . . .

The more we study the Indian character the more we appreciate the marked distinction between the civilized being and the real savage, yet we shall find that the latter is governed by the same impulses and motives that govern all other men. The want of confidence and the bitter hatred now existing between the two races have been engendered by the warfare that has lasted for centuries, and by the stories of bad faith, cruelty and wrong, handed down by tradition from father to son until they have become second nature in both. It is unfair to suppose that one party has invariably acted rightly, and that the other is responsible for every wrong that has been committed. We might recount the treachery of the red man, the atrocity of his crimes, the cruelties of his tortures, and the hideousness of his savage customs; we might undertake to estimate the number of his victims, and to picture the numberless valleys which he has illuminated by the burning homes of hardy frontiersmen, yet at the same time the other side of the picture might appear equally as black with injustice. . . .

The white race has now obtained such complete control of every quarter of the country and the means of communication with every section are now so ample that the problem resolves itself down to one or two modes of solution, viz., to entirely destroy the race by banishment and extermination, or to adopt some humane and practicable method of improving part and parcel of our great population. The first proposition, though it will be found to have thousands of advocates in different sections of the country, is too abhorrent to every sense of humanity to be considered. The other method is regarded as practicable, but its adoption is considered doubtful. . . .

As the Government has expended hundreds of thousands of dollars in building military posts that as the settlements advance are no longer occupied or required, and as there are at these places excellent buildings and large reservations, it would be well to utilize them for educational and industrial purposes. The present school system is regarded as too expensive, and productive of little good. The children are exposed to the degrading influence of camp-life, and the constant moving of the tribes destroys the best efforts of instructors. Several years ago the writer recommended the use of several of our unoccupied military posts, and that as many of the youth of the different tribes as could be gathered voluntarily be placed at these establishments, particularly the sons of chiefs, who will in a few years govern the different tribes. These could soon be taught the English language, habits of industry, the benefits of civilization, the power of the white race, and, after a few years; return to their people with some education, with more intelligence, and with their ideas of life entirely changed for the better. They would in turn become the educators of their own people, and their influence for good could not be estimated, while the expense of educating them would be less than at present, and thousands would be benefited thereby. The Indians, as they become civilized and educated, as they acquire property and pay taxes toward the support of the Government, should have the same rights of citizenship as all other men enjoy.

The white man and the Indian should be taught to live side by side, each respecting the rights of the other, and both living under wholesome laws, enforced with ample authority and exact justice.

Source: Brigadier General N.A. Miles, U.S. Army, "Our Indian Question," *Journal of the Military Service Institute of the United States*, vol II, No. 7 (1881): 278–292. In the collection of the Nelson Miles Papers, Nez Perce Box, U.S. Army Military History Institute, Carlisle Barracks, Pennsylvania.

5.4.   View of the Minority of the Committee on Indian Affairs of the House of Representatives, May 28, 1880

The debate over allotting land to western Indians raged in Congress for many years. The following excerpt reflects the minority opinion in the House of Representatives to the bill of Senator Richard Coke of Texas that called for individual ownership of land on the Indian reservations. Three minority leaders argued that the bill was just another way for white Americans to steal land from the Indians.

The undersigned, members of the Committee on Indian Affairs of the House of Representatives, are unable to agree with the majority of the committee in reporting favorably upon this bill. . . .

The plan of this bill is not, in our judgment, the way to civilize the Indian. However much we may differ with the humanitarians who are riding this hobby, we are certain that they will agree with us in the proposition that it does not make a farmer out of an Indian to give him a quarter-section of land. There are hundreds of thousands of white men, rich with the experiences of centuries of Anglo-Saxon civilization, who cannot be transformed into cultivators of the land by any such gift. . . . The whole training of an Indian from his birth, the whole history of the Indian race, and the entire array of Indian traditions, running back for at least four hundred years, all combine to predispose the Indian against this scheme for his improvement, devised by those who judge him exclusively from *their* standpoint instead of from *his*. From that time of the discovery of America, and for centuries probably before that, the North American Indian has been a communist. Not in the offensive sense of modern communism, but in the sense of holding property in common. The tribal system has kept bands and tribes together as families, each member of which was dependent on the other. The very idea of property in the soil was unknown to the Indian mind. . . .

We are free to admit that the two civilizations, so different throughout, cannot well co-exist, or flourish together. One must, in time, give way to the other, and the weak must in the end be supplanted by the strong. But it cannot be violently wrenched out of place and cast aside. Nations cannot be made to change their habits and methods and modes of thought in a day. To bring the Indian to look at things from our standpoint is a work requiring time, patience, and the skill as well as the benign spirit of Christian statesmanship. . . .

The real aim of this bill is to get at the Indian lands and open them up to settlement. The provisions of the apparent benefit of the Indian are but the pretext to get at his lands and occupy them. With that accomplished, we have securely paved the way for the extermination of the Indian races upon this part of the continent. If this were done in the name of Greed, it would be bad enough; but to do it in the name of Humanity, and under the cloak of an ardent desire to promote the Indian's welfare by making him like ourselves, whether he will or not, is infinitely worse. Of all the attempts to encroach upon the Indian, this attempt to manufacture him into a white man by act of Congress and the grace of the Secretary of the Interior is the baldest, the boldest, and the most unjustifiable.

Whatever civilization has been reached by the Indian tribes has been attained under the tribal system, and not under the system proposed by this bill. . . . Gradually, under that system they are working out their own deliverance, which will come in their own good time if we but leave them alone and perform our part of the many contracts we have made with them. But that we have never yet done and it seems from this bill we will never yet do. We want their lands and we are bound to have them. Let those take a part in despoiling them who will; for ourselves, we believe the entire policy of this bill to be wrong, ill-timed, and unstatesmanlike; and we put ourselves on record against it as about all that is now left us to do, except to vote against the bill on its final passage.

Russell Errett.

Chas. E. Hooker.

T.M. Gunter.

Source: U.S. Congress, House of Representatives, Committee on Indian Affairs, *Lands in Severalty to Indians: Report to Accompany*, HR 5038, 46th Cong., 2nd sess., May 28, 1880, House Report 1576, pp. 7–10.

5.5.   The Dawes Act, 1887

In 1887, Congress finally passed a long-debated act concerning Indian land allotments. The act was designed to further Americanize Indians by forcing them to become independent farmers. While some tribes accepted the new Indian policy, others fought

against the act since it served to undermine the role of the tribal
government and the concept of communal land ownership. The
following excerpt from the Dawes Act lays out its key provisions.

An act to provide for the allotment of lands in severalty to Indians on
the various reservations, and to extend the protection of the laws of the
United States and the Territories over the Indians, and for other purposes.

Be it enacted by the Senate and House of Representatives of the United States
of America in Congress assembled, That in all cases where any tribe or band
of Indians has been, or shall hereafter be, located upon any reservation
created for their use, either by treaty stipulation or by virtue of an act
of Congress or executive order setting apart the same for their use, the
President of the United States be, and he hereby is, authorized, whenever
in his opinion any reservation or any part thereof of such Indians is
advantageous for agricultural and grazing purposes, to cause said reservation, or any part thereof, to be surveyed, or resurveyed if necessary,
and to allot the lands in said reservation in severalty to any Indian located thereon on in quantities as follows:

To each head of a family, one-quarter of a section;

To each single person over eighteen years of age, one-eighth of a
section;

To each orphan child under eighteen years of age, one-eighth of a
section; and

To each other single person under eighteen years now living, or who
may be born prior to the date of the order of the President directing an
allotment of the lands embraced in any reservation, one-sixteenth of a
section: *Provided,* That in case there is not sufficient land in any of said
reservations to allot lands to each individual of the classes above named
in quantities as above provided, the lands embraced in such reservation
or reservations shall be allotted to each individual of each of said classes
pro rata in accordance with the provisions of this act: *And provided fur-*
ther, That where the treaty or act of Congress setting apart such reservation provided for the allotment of lands in severalty in quantities in
excess of those herein provided, the President, in making allotments
upon such reservation, shall allot the lands to each individual Indian
belonging thereon in quantity as specified in such treaty or act: *And*
provided further, That when the lands allotted are only valuable for grazing purposes, an additional allotment of such grazing lands, in quantities
as above provided, shall be made to each individual.

Approved, February 8, 1887.

Source: An Act to Provide for the Allotment of Lands in Severalty to Indians on
the Various Reservations (general Allotment act or Dawes Act), *United States*
Statutes at Large, 24: 388–391, 1887.

5.6.   The Cherokee Nation Opposes the Dawes Act, 1896

*The Cherokee Nation objected to the U.S. government's Indian
policies. In the following excerpt, members of the Commission
to the Five Tribes addressed the members of the Dawes Commission, asking them to reconsider the land-allotment act. The
Indian leaders argued that the Dawes Act would undermine their
tribes' traditional way of life.*

Our people are greatly alarmed, if not touched with panic, at the unexpected demands which have been recently made for the abolishment
of their Government and the erection of a Territorial Government in their
country. . . . They could not even dream that, without their consent, they
should ever be forced to dissolve their Government, change the tenure
of their lands and become subject to a Government altogether administered by the whites. . . . Notwithstanding the centuries of hardships our
people, the American Indians, have been required to pass through, we
have not lost all faith in the rectitude of mankind. We think the wrongs
inflicted upon our people since the landing of the Mayflower, have been
only such aberrations as in all ages have marked the path of the world's
civilization, while the real intent of that civilization has ever been to lift
the entire race to the higher excellence of character, that would enable
every member of society to extend to others the measure of consideration
he would demand for himself. . . .

We claim the right of self-government in its utmost extent, yet not so
as to conflict with the Constitution of the United States, nor the treaties
and laws made or enacted in pursuance thereof; the right in fee-simple
to our lands; and the right to object to the establishment of a territorial
government in our country without our consent.

1. In vindication of these rights we can appeal to no higher power
   than the law; nor should the United States, even in the infinitude
   of its power, desire to invoke any higher authority in its action
   toward our country and people. Arbitrary action does not well
   comport with the dignity of great States. As in the individual
   man, so in States, a sense of honor should be the supreme law
   of action.

2. The white man's Bible says God gave the lands of Canaan to the
   children of Israel. The Indian's Bible, which is held in the form
   of tradition, says the Great Spirit gave America to the Indians.
   At the founding of the United States the Government acknowledged the right of the Indians to the soil. . . .

3. The right to govern themselves was derived by the Cherokees, neither from Great Britain nor the United States. They always had that right. It is declared in the Act of Union between the Eastern and Western Cherokees: "Our fathers have existed as a separate and distinct Nation, in the possession and exercise of the essential attributes of sovereignty, from a period extending into antiquity beyond the records and memory of man; these attributes, with the rights and franchises which they involve, remain still in full force and virtue. . . ."

According to Webster, a tribe is "a nation of savages or uncivilized people; a body of rude people under one leader or government." But this definition does not fit the Cherokees. They have long been journeying along the same road as that which was traveled by the most polite nations.

We wish to say to you and to the American people, that there are ten thousand schemes and plots being laid—every plan that the human mind can devise—to get possession of our land for townsite and general land speculation. Speculation is the key that unlocks the secret of the great clamor for this country to be opened. . . .

We, like Caractacus, when we behold the "splendor and magnificence" of such American cities as Boston, New York, Chicago, Washington and other teeming millions of wealth, feel constrained to exclaim: "How is it possible that men possessed of such splendor and magnificence at home," should envy us our humble homes in Indian Territory, which we have bought, and to which we have a white man's title—a patent in fee simple?

We have the honor to be, gentlemen.

Your obedient servants,
WALTER A. DUNCAN,
JAMES W. DUNCAN,
WM. EUBANKS,
JOHN WICKLIFF,
BYRD JONES,
ROBIN PANN,
Commissioners.

Source: "Communication to the United States Commissioners *in* Relation to a Conference on Propositions of the Government, by Commission on Part of the Cherokee Nation" (St. Louis: R. & T.A. Ennis Stationery Company, 1896). Pamphlets in American History, no. I 721.

5.7.   Brigadier General Richard H. Pratt Describes His Americanization Work with Indians, October 23, 1912

Brigadier General Richard H. Pratt, the founder of the Indian School Movement designed to Americanize Indian students, promoted the concept through his writings and public speeches. The following is an excerpt from Pratt's October 23, 1912, address before the Pennsylvania Commandery of the Military Order of the Loyal Legion at the Union League in Philadelphia, Pennsylvania. In it, Pratt provides background on his Americanization work with Indian warrior prisoners in Florida and with children at the Carlisle Indian School in Carlisle Barracks, Pennsylvania.

It was then determined that the ringleaders and most criminals should all be sent in chains as prisoners to Florida, and held there indefinitely. . . . I had suggested to General [William Tecumseh] Sheridan that while under this banishment they should be industrially trained, educated and civilized so far as possible, so that if returned to their people they would go back as influences for good. . . .

Benevolent ladies, some of them skilled school-teachers, undertook their education, and the younger men and a number of older ones were under scholastic instruction in the casements of the old Fort fitted up crudely as schoolrooms. They learned to speak English, and many of the younger men to write creditable letters. Regular religious services were established, and eventually all who cared to were permitted to go to church services in town. They were dressed in the fatigue uniform of U.S. soldiers. . . . The daily contact with our kindly people brought amazing results in transforming them into capable civilized men.

Experience had shown that the few Indians, if properly handled, could easily and quickly be merged and assimilated in their interests with our white population, from whom they could best get the high and better ideas of life they all needed to become useful citizens. These views led to warm discussion between General [C.H.] Armstrong and me, until I finally declared I could not conscientiously remain on duty at Hampton, but was willing, if held to duty in Indian education, to undertake a school especially for Indians [children] and there work out my own ideas.

I went to Washington and suggested to Mr. [Carl] Schurz [Republican Representative from Missouri] that Carlisle Barracks, then unoccupied, located in the rich Cumberland Valley in Pennsylvania, whose industrious people would be examples for pupils, might be utilized for such a school. . . .

Repairs to the barracks were immediately started, and I went to Rosebud and Pine Ridge Agencies for pupils. . . . We reached Carlisle, October 6, 1879. Before starting to Dakota I had sent Etahdleuh, one of the Florida prisoners, to the Kiowa and Comanche Agency after pupils, and Making Medicine to the Cheyenne and Arapahoe Agency. These two, with the help of Agents Miles and Haworth, made up good parties in which I was much gratified to find a number of the children of my Florida prisoners, which proved their confidence in their former jailer.

Mr. A.J. Standing, whom I have known as a successful teacher among the Indians at the Wichita and Fort Still Agencies, was engaged to assist at the School. He was then in Kansas, and secured a party from the Pawnees. The children from these tribes enabled the school to open November 1, 1879, with 146 pupils, twenty-seven more than was authorized.

The expenses of the school were paid the first three years from what was called the "Civilization Fund," which was several hundred thousand dollars accumulated for the purpose of general Indian civilization from the sale of Osage Indian lands in Kansas. The success of the school led the Interior Department to help it to grow, and after three years Congress had confidence and passed the bill permanently to use Carlisle Barracks. . . .

Training in industries was to be no less a factor than general education in English. A farm was rented and shops were established for trades; a practical agriculturist and mechanics were employed to make farmers, printers, carpenters, blacksmiths, wagon-makers, shoemakers, harness-makers, tailors, tinsmiths, painters, etc., out of the boys, while suitable instructors taught the girls cooking, needlework, laundering, housekeeping, and all household duties. . . .

Indian boys and girls isolated from their fellows, surrounded by English-speaking people, advance in English and civilization far more rapidly than is possible in any Indian School. They earned money which was all theirs and which spurred their energies by giving to them many advantages the resources of the school could not supply. They were taught to save and place at interest, until their accumulated savings at the close of each summer's outing was over thirty-five thousand dollars, giving all savers good help to begin life on leaving school.

We early found at Carlisle that we could give young Indians the education in English which enabled them to read and understand the Bible and opened the way to all knowledge in English quite as quickly as the other system could give them education in their own language. Besides these limitations on the use of the hindering tribal systems in two and a half centuries only four of the more than eighty tribes and radically different languages had ever been provided with any kind of a vernacular system. . . .

In 1875 the Indians all held their lands in common and tribal masses. There were no allotments in severalty, but among the five civilized tribes and the Indians in New York State, and possibly some smaller aggregations, they could, under tribal laws, individually occupy indefinitely such of the tribal lands as they improved and built upon.

In 1904 a very large proportion of the Indians had received allotments aggregating many millions of acres, and the consent to and contentment of the Indians with these allotments was due very largely to the influence of the Indians who had been among the whites and learned the white man's system of individual ownership.

Source: R.H. Pratt, Brig. Gen., U.S.A., *American Indians, Chained and Unchained*, Being an Address before the Pennsylvania Commandery of the Military Order of the Loyal Legion at the Union League, Philadelphia, October 23, 1912, pp. 3–17. In Pamphlets in American History Collection, No. I 236.

ANNOTATED RESEARCH GUIDE

Books and Articles

Adams, David Wallace. *Education for Extinction: American Indians and the Boarding School Experience, 1875–1928*. Lawrence: University Press of Kansas, 1995. Provides a comprehensive history of the Indian school experience (particularly the Carlisle school) from the views of both the assimilators and the Native Americans.

Beal, Merrill D. *"I Will Fight No More Forever": Chief Joseph and the Nez Perce War*. Seattle: University of Washington Press, 1966; reprint, 1995. Retells the story of the Nez Perce war and the life of Chief Joseph's band in exile as they fought to return to their homeland.

Coleman, Michael C. *American Indian Children at School, 1850–1930*. Jackson: University Press of Mississippi, 1993. Presents an overview of the Indian educational experience. Includes a list of autobiographies and biographies written by or about those who participated in the programs.

Hampton, Bruce. *Children of Grace: The Nez Perce War of 1877*. New York: Henry

Holt, 1994. A comprehensive examination of the Nez Perce, particularly focusing on the 1877 war between Chief Joseph's Nez Perce and the U.S. Army.

Highberger, Mark. "The Death of Wilhautyah." *American History* 33, no. 5 (1998): 40–47. Traces the tension that grew between white settlers and the Nez Perce Indians and exploded with the killing of Nez Perce warrior Wilhautyah in 1876.

Howard, O.O., Duncan McDonald, and Chief Joseph (compiled by Linwood Laughy). *In Pursuit of the Nez Perce: The Nez Perce War of 1877*. Wrangell, AK: Mountain Meadow Press, 1993. Tells the story of the Nez Perce war through the words of three men: General Oliver O. Howard, the commanding officer who led the fight against the nontreaty Nez Perce; Duncan McDonald, a Montana newspaper reporter who covered the war; and Chief Joseph, the leader of the Wallowa band of the Nez Perce Indians.

Josephy, Alvin M., Jr. *The Nez Perce Indians and the Opening of the Northwest*. Boston: Houghton Mifflin, 1997. Comprehensive history of the Nez Perce Indians discussing the tribe's history, the encroachment of the white man, the Nez Perce war, and the return of Chief Joseph to the Idaho area.

Lavender, David. *Let Me Be Free: The Nez Perce Tragedy*. San Francisco: HarperCollins, 1992. Details the lives of the Nez Perce Indians, the U.S. Army's long chase before the surrender of Chief Joseph, and the eventual return of the Nez Perce band to Idaho.

McDermott, John D. *Forlorn Hope: The Battle of White Bird Canyon and the Beginning of the Nez Perce War*. Boise: Idaho State Historical Society, 1978. Examines the Nez Perce war, beginning with the large migration of white settlers into Indian Territory with the discovery of gold in 1860 and the tension that led to the Battle of White Bird Canyon.

O'Dell, Scott, and Elizabeth Hall (contributor). *Thunder Rolling in the Mountains*. Boston: Houghton Mifflin, 1992. Presents the Nez Perce story told by the daughter of Chief Joseph, Sound of Running Feet.

Otis, D.S. *The Dawes Act and the Allotment of Indian Lands*. Norman: University of Oklahoma Press, 1973. Provides a detailed history of the Dawes Act that allotted lands to individual Indians in an effort to assimilate Indians into the dominant culture.

Pratt, Richard Henry. *Battlefield and Classroom: Four Decades with the American Indian, 1867–1904*. New Haven: Yale University Press, 1964. Written by the founder of the Indian School movement, this book describes his role in the Americanization of the Indian warriors and the founding of the Carlisle Indian School. Includes copies of correspondence with key leaders as they pushed for the assimilation of the Native American.

Stadius, Martin. *Dreamers: On the Trail of the Nez Perce*. Caldwell, ID: Caxton Press, 1999. Traces the trek of the Nez Perce and the U.S. military as they did battle during their chase through Oregon and Idaho.

Witmer, Linda F. *The Indian Industrial School: Carlisle, Pennsylvania, 1879–1918*. Camp Hill, PA: Plank's Suburban Press, 1993. This photographic essay traces the history of the Carlisle Indian School by looking at pictures of the thousands of children who went through the Americanization process.

Video

"Fight No More Forever." Volume 6 of Ken Burns's *The West*: A Film by Stephen Ives. PBS Video. This volume traces the roots of the conflict that began the Nez Perce war, General Howard's pursuit of Chief Joseph, the Indian leader's eventual surrender to General Miles near Canada, and the exile of the tribe in Kansas and Oklahoma.

Web Sites

http://www.nezperce.org. Link to the official Web site of the Nez Perce tribe, which provides a brief history, information on the tribal government, and a listing of current community events.

http://www.uidaho.edu/nezperce/neemepoo.htm. A Web site designed by students from the University of Idaho that offers links to the history and current activities of the Nez Perce.

6

The Annexation of the Philippines: Imperialists versus Anti-Imperialists

The post–Civil War era was one of rapid and profound changes. With economic stress, rising nationalism, and a modernizing military, America began to look outward toward overseas expansion. Expansion was not new in U.S. history, nor was the notion of "American exceptionalism." From their first step on the new continent, European settlers saw themselves as God's chosen people and began to head west. By the 1840s, western expansion obtained its own name—Manifest Destiny—and with it a continued sense of America's God-given right, even duty, to spread from sea to sea. Although expansionist impulses were temporarily halted by the Civil War, they quickly returned at the war's end, leading to the trans-Mississippi Indian Wars and to overseas aspirations. As America looked abroad, its expansionist spirit now became entwined with a patriotic fever and the scientific notion of social Darwinism. However, in the 1890s, not everyone embraced this renewed conviction, and the nation found itself at a diplomatic crossroads.

Imperialists and anti-imperialists soon fought a war of words as they debated the future path of the United States. Many expressed concerns about the nation's involvement in the Spanish-American War in 1898, but the debate between imperialists and anti-imperialists reached its pinnacle with the annexation of the Philippine Islands in 1899. After successfully defeating the Filipino people who resisted annexation, America entered a period of military modernization and emerged as a new world power.

AMERICAN EXPANSIONISM

During the late nineteenth century, a growing number of political, military, and intellectual leaders began to advocate a more aggressive American foreign policy. Their motivations varied. Some, concerned with frequent economic depressions, argued that expansion into overseas markets would bring economic success, while others emphasized the need for strategic security and worldwide military bases. This became even more important when, during the last quarter of the century, the country endured some twelve years of economic instability complete with foreclosures, bankruptcies, agrarian revolts, industrial unemployment, and labor strife. Others, like historian Frederick Jackson Turner, mourned the end of the western frontier and feared that it meant an end to America's uniqueness, resourcefulness, and individualism. Expansionists looked with increasing concern at the continued global colonization by Great Britain, Germany, France, Italy, Belgium, Russia, and Japan. They argued that the key to the security of the nation was the creation of an American commercial empire that would rival European powers and expand the strength and influence of the United States. Early examples of American "outwards" expansion included the acquisition of Alaska and Midway Island, the opening of Japan to American trade, the control of Hawaiian politics and economy, and the partnership with Great Britain and Germany in the protectorate of the Samoan Islands. In 1890, Naval War College professor Captain Alfred Thayer Mahan persuasively connected economic success and world power with the necessity for a modern navy in his widely circulated book *The Influence of Sea Power upon History, 1660–1783*. By the end of the nineteenth century, the U.S. Navy was transformed into a world-class force.

Nationalism, Anglo-Saxonism, and social Darwinism lay at the roots of expansionists' ideology. The belief in the superiority of white Americans of northern European descent had a long history. It was used to justify the destruction of the Indian culture and the enslavement of African people. Post–Civil War nationalism was sparked by the desperate drive to reunify the nation after the bloody conflict that had divided the North and the South. Paralleling and often interweaving in late-nineteenth-century nationalism were Anglo-Saxonism and social Darwinism. English social philosopher Herbert Spencer adopted Charles Darwin's theories of natural selection and applied them to the human race. Social Darwinists argued that life was an unending struggle for existence, and only the strongest or fittest survived to procreate a "superior" bloodline. New racial theories claimed that white Anglo-Saxon Americans stood firmly at the top of society's pecking order. These social theories dominated the rising industrial landscape, which labeled African Americans and new immigrants as culturally inferior. It did not take long for these concepts to find their way into American foreign policy, especially since most political leaders claimed Anglo-Saxon ethnicity. Expansionists advocated a new role for America, one of securing, "uplifting," and "civilizing" countries deemed "unfit" to survive on their own. This new foreign policy dovetailed with the growing mission of Protestant churches to spread Christianity to "heathens" throughout the world. Often American commerce, Christianity, and culture went hand-in-hand, as when the founder of the Singer Sewing Machine Company, Isaac Singer, called for American commerce to follow closely on the heels of American missionaries heading for China. Singer, proud of overseas expansion of American products, advertised his sewing machine with a drawing of three "Ladies of Manila" sewing an American flag.[1]

TOWARD AN AMERICAN EMPIRE

Although the growing movement toward American global power and overseas expansion can be seen in conflicts in Samoa, Chile, Hawaii, and Venezuela, it was the Spanish-American War of 1898 that catapulted the nation into an overseas empire. The conflict began with the Cuban fight for independence from Spain. With an unrelenting war at hand, the Cuban revolutionaries sought American support. While U.S. businessmen worried over their Cuban investments and the disruption of trade with the island, humanitarian issues sparked the greatest response from the American people. Coverage of the war triggered a fierce competition between Joseph Pulitzer of the *New York World* and William Randolph Hearst of the *New York Journal* as both sought readers through sensationalized accounts of Spanish atrocities. A war fever known as "jingoism" gripped the nation, especially after the explosion of the U.S. battleship *Maine* on February 15, 1898. By April 1898, the United States was engaged in a "Splendid Little War" against Spain, a war that lasted only four months. Fighting took place both in Cuba and in the Philippines, where the new U.S. Navy crushed the Spanish fleet, and U.S. Army ground forces managed to defeat the enemy, despite critical problems with organization, supplies, and equipment. A public hungry for sensationalized war stories joyously celebrated the exploits of Theodore Roosevelt's "Rough Riders," a colorful group of cowboys and polo players who charged San Juan Hill overlooking Santiago de Cuba, secured a place in history, and catapulted their leader into the national spotlight. At the war's end, America gained the Spanish territories of Puerto Rico, Guam, and the Philippines (the latter for a payment of $20 million). This began a new chapter in U.S. history—empire building.

Creating an American overseas empire sparked a fierce debate between imperialists who supported the annexation of new territories and anti-imperialists who adamantly opposed such ventures. The national argument over the annexation of the Philippines saw a dramatic convergence of cultural attitudes and economic concerns. This debate was complicated by the obvious resentment of the Filipino people, who saw American ownership as simply replacing one oppressor with another and launched a fierce resistance to American claims on the archipelago.

IMPERIALISTS

Imperialists did not consider the Filipino people capable of self-government and viewed annexation as "benevolent assimilation." This group also applauded the acquisition of the Philippines as a sound economic decision and a prudent national security strategy. Finally, imperialists contended that the Constitution supported this decision. Republican politicians Henry Cabot Lodge, Albert Beveridge, Nelson Aldrich, and Theodore Roosevelt, Ambassador to Great Britain John Hay, Secretary of War Elihu Root, and navy captain Alfred T. Mahan led the charge for the imperialists. While some historians argue that President William McKinley stood at the vanguard of imperialism, others maintain that he reluctantly embraced the spirit. Probably McKinley's most stirring justification for annexation came when he addressed a group of Methodists on November 21, 1899. Adopting the philosophy of social Darwinists and Protestant missionaries, the president called the Philippines a "gift from the gods" and pledged "to educate the Filipinos, and uplift and civilize and Christianize them." He also contended that allowing "commercial rivals" to secure the islands would be "bad business" and maintained that the Filipino people "were unfit" to govern themselves.[2]

Senator Albert J. Beveridge extolled the retention of the Philippines as good economic sense because it represented the doorway to the lucrative Asian trade. Newly selected to Congress in 1899, Beveridge was an outspoken advocate of overseas expansion. He professed the superiority of America and saw annexation as a benevolent way of assimilating the Filipino people. In a speech to Congress riddled with Anglo-Saxon rhetoric, the Indiana senator claimed that the decision was greater than party politics and was, instead, a "divine mission." "God has not been preparing the English-speaking and Teutonic peoples for a thousand years for nothing. . . . He has made us adepts in government that we may administer government among savage and senile peoples."[3] While opponents of overseas expansion charged that annexation violated the Declaration of Independence and the Constitution, imperialists adamantly disagreed. Although they concurred that governments derive their authority from the consent of the governed, imperialists argued that only those "capable" of self-rule should have such rights. Beveridge rationalized, "We governed Indians without their consent, we govern our territories without their consent. . . . If England can govern foreign lands, so can America."[4]

Nationalism also played a key role in the imperialists' position. In a March 7, 1900, speech to Congress, Senator Henry Cabot Lodge of Massachusetts praised America's expansionist history and predicted great things for the growing nation if it continued on the "right path"—annexation. Before his appointment to Congress, Lodge had been the editor of the *North American Review* and had lectured on American history at Harvard University. As a senator, he became an influential leader of American foreign policy. An ardent imperialist, Lodge declared: "Thus far we have never failed to take the right path. . . . We shall stretch out into the Pacific; we shall stand in the front rank of the world powers."[5]

ANTI-IMPERIALISTS

Strong opposition to the annexation of the Philippines came from a very diverse group known as anti-imperialists that included politicians, reformers, and intellectuals from different political parties, socioeconomic classes, and regions of the country. Prominent among them were politicians William Jennings Bryan, George F. Hoar, William B. Bate, Richard Pettigrew, Grover Cleveland, and Benjamin Harrison; political independents and reformers Charles Francis Adams, Carl Schurz, and Jane Addams; academicians William Graham Sumner and William James; industrialist Andrew Carnegie; union leader Samuel Gompers; and writer Mark Twain. Anti-imperialists were diverse in their opinions of why American control should not expand into the Philippines. Strong supporters of self-determination maintained that annexation degraded both the Declaration of Independence and the Constitution. Some noted the hypocrisy in Christianizing the Filipinos, many of whom were Catholic. Others warned that permanent entanglements overseas could pull America into a worldwide crisis, which would require the United States to build up its military forces. Some anti-imperialists also argued that commercial expansion could threaten the domestic economy, asserting that cheap Filipino labor would put American workers on the streets. Perhaps ironically, some anti-imperialists held on to the same racist views as imperialists concerning the inferiority of the Filipino people. This xenophobic group fought against the inclusion of foreigners they deemed "unfit" to become Americans.

Like many anti-imperialists, Senate Majority Leader George Hoar unwaveringly argued that annexation violated the Declaration of Independence and the Constitution. The Massachusetts senator served as trustee for several universities, was a regent of the Smithsonian Institution, and studied the classics. Hoar was also a long-standing and influential member of Congress. He strongly objected to imperialists who compared the control over the American Indians (without their consent) to the situation in the Philippines. Hoar challenged imperialist senators: You have no right at the cannon's mouth to impose on any unwilling people . . . your Declaration of Independence and your Constitution and your notions of freedom and notions of what is good."[6] "The people of the Philippine Islands are clearly a nation. . . . The people there have got a government, with courts and judges. . . ."

Carl Schurz, president of the Anti-imperialist League, became a well-known and adamant supporter of self-determination in the Philippines. Schurz had fled Germany as one of the revolutionaries known as the '48ers; once in America, he ran unsuccessfully for governor of Wisconsin, spent one year as the minister to Spain, and served in the Union army before branching out as a social reformer and a newspaper editor. Schurz began his long service as the U.S. senator from Missouri in 1869. In 1877, Schurz joined the cabinet of President Rutherford Hayes as secretary of the interior, and from 1892 to 1901 he headed the National Civil Service Reform League. The liberal Republican called the American war in the Philippines "illegal and unconstitutional." Schurz declared that it was "the plain duty of the American people to stop the bloody war against the inhabitants of the Philippines, to recognize their right and title to freedom and independence . . . and to withdraw our armed forces from those islands as soon as they may no longer be needed to . . . protect the people thereof in setting up and maintaining an independent government."[7] In an October 1899 speech, Schurz argued, "We hold with Abraham Lincoln, that 'no man is good enough to govern another man without that man's consent,' " and "to do so would be despotism."[8]

Episcopal pastor and Yale University professor William Graham Sumner "served as a spokesman for the professorial anti-imperialists at Harvard and Yale."[9] Although Sumner was a principal exponent of social Darwinism, he challenged the assumptions made by imperialists that the Filipino people wanted to adopt the American way of life. "They hate our ways. They are hostile to our ideas. Our religion, language, institutions, and manners offend them." Sumner pointedly noted, "Each national laughs at all the others when it observes these manifestations of national vanity. You may rely upon it that they are all ridiculous by virtue of these pretensions, including ourselves. The point is that each of them repudiates the standards of the others, and the outlying nations, which are to be civilized, hate all the standards of civilized men. We assume that what we like and practice, and what we think better, must come as a welcome blessing to Spanish-Americans and Filipinos."[10]

Popular writer Mark Twain, an active member of the Anti-imperialist League, wrote passionate and satirical pieces to wake the public to the hypocrisies and dangers of imperialism. "True, we have crushed a deceived and confiding people; we have turned against the weak and the friendless who trusted us; we have stamped out a just and intelligent and well-ordered republic; we have stabbed an ally in the back and slapped the face of a guest . . . we have robbed a trusting friend of his land and his liberty . . . we have debauched America's honor and blackened her face before the world."[11]

Samuel Gompers, president of the American Federation of Labor, noted the irony of hanging the Declaration of Independence on the walls of schoolhouses in the Philippines, while at the same time forbidding independence. Gompers served as the vice president of a number of anti-imperialist organizations in the late nineteenth and early twentieth centuries. In his writings and speeches, Gompers warned Americans of the economic dangers associated with the annexation of the Philippines. Although he supported self-determination for the Filipino people, he did not see them as his equals. Labor unionists particularly feared the immigration of cheap, unprotected labor into the United States. Gompers observed the animosity currently directed at the American worker who demanded fair and just treatment and asked, "How much more difficult will it be to arouse any sympathy, and secure relief for the poor semi-savages in the Philippines?"[12] Senator William B. Bate of Tennessee held similar racist views of the Filipino people. The former Tennessee governor called them "a heterogeneous mass of mongrels," and pleaded, "Do not let them become a part of us with their idolatry, polygamous creeds, and harem habits."[13]

Anti-imperialists remained a diverse group with often-contradictory viewpoints. Most favored "acquisitions within the Western Hemisphere and the retention of naval bases elsewhere," but they coalesced in their protest against overseas expansion.[14] There was one thing that remained constant with anti-imperialists—their vigilance against imperialism.

ELECTION OF 1900

The debate of imperialists versus anti-imperialists filtered into the presidential race of 1900. The Philippine insurrection was still raging when McKinley ran for reelection. McKinley had served in the Union army during the Civil War before pursuing a career as an attorney and a politician, becoming a U.S. congressman, the governor of Ohio, and the president of the United States. Fearing that Theodore Roosevelt, now a popular Spanish-American War hero, would run for president in 1900 and thus undermine McKinley's aspirations, the Republican party convinced the "cowboy" to join the McKinley ticket as the vice presidential candidate. Roosevelt had previously served in the New York State Assembly before moving to a ranch in North Dakota. When he returned to New York in 1886, he served in a number of state political positions before being appointed McKinley's secretary of the navy during the president's first term. Roosevelt resigned from this position to lead the Rough Riders in the Spanish-American War.

Although the Republicans tried to keep the Pacific war from becoming the dominant issue in the campaign, they continued to justify the Philippine-American War when they were under attack. Senator Beveridge called the conflict a military "necessity" and a matter of "American honor." McKinley declared that "our sons [were in the Philippines] because in the providence of God, who moved mysteriously, that great archipelago had been placed in the hand of the American people." He added that the war would end when the American flag "float[ed] triumphantly in every island of the archipelago under the undisputed and acknowledged sovereignty of the republic of the United States."[15] Despite this discourse, the Republican strategy called for avoiding the topic of imperialism or deflecting it back to their opponents by blaming Democrats for embracing the anti-imperialists' position—freedom for the Filipino people.

The Democratic presidential candidate, William Jennings Bryan, attempted to focus his campaign on problems in the economy and the plight of the western farmers. Nevertheless, he wasted no time in criticizing McKinley for leading the country in the wrong direction by trying to subjugate the Filipino people. Bryan, a former senator from Nebraska, had run unsuccessfully for president in 1896; he also led the Nebraska Volunteer Infantry in the Spanish-American War. In his bid for the presidency, Bryan associated the oppression of the Filipino people with slavery, declaring that Abraham Lincoln had abolished slavery only to have McKinley bring it back.

The Republicans could not escape their association with the Philippine-American War and imperialism. With aspirations of becoming the next vice president, Republican candidate Theodore Roosevelt hit the campaign trail. There he contended that "only fools would confuse the healthy and historic expansion of America with imperialism, and the anti-imperialists were worse than fools. They were champions of Filipino bandits and 'miscreants' who urged cowardly surrender."[16] Bryan's defeat in the 1900 presidential election produced the clear understanding that the Democratic party needed to disassociate itself from anti-imperialism. But fierce debates continued in Congress as Democrats and Republicans argued about what was to be done with the Philippines once the insurrection was over.

While Americans debated the pros and cons of annexation and fought over the future of the Philippines, the Filipino people took action. Led by Emilio Aguinaldo, they battled against the U.S. military for their independence from 1899 to 1902. Atrocities on both sides turned the conflict into a horrific nightmare that shocked America. The war ended on July 4, 1902, with the military surrender of the Filipino rebels.

MILITARY REFORM

Both the Spanish-American War and the Philippine insurrection brought to light major inadequacies in America's military preparedness. Fighting the Spanish-American War revealed serious problems, including outdated weapons, inappropriate (wool) uniforms, inadequate transportation, lack of supplies, uneatable and unhealthy food, and rampant disease, resulting in internal conflict and complete chaos. Engaging in a long-distance war in the Philippines only compounded many of these problems. With the assassination of President McKinley by an anarchist in September 1901, Roosevelt took the reins of government and pushed for much-needed military improvements. At the forefront of military reform, which continued during the early twentieth century, were Secretary of War Elihu Root and Major General Leonard Wood, who helped to bring an unprecedented modernization to the military system. Changes included the incorporation of innovative weaponry, new training methods, improved military education, tighter reserve (formerly militia) regulations, and the creation of the General Staff. The expansion and improvement of both the U.S. Army and Navy also helped propel America into a new world-power status.

CONCLUSION

The Philippine-American conflict cost the lives of over 4,000 American troops and 20,000 Filipino troops. Approximately 200,000 Filipino civilians also died, mostly from famine, diseases, and counterinsurgency warfare. Although some historians argue that the United States made substantial improvements in the Philippines during its years of tenure by establishing schools, building railroads, and introducing public health measures, others note that much of this was done under the auspices of Americanization and criticize the United States for its refusal to grant the Philippines its freedom until after World War II.

U.S. interest in expansion did not stop with the Philippine insurrection but continued as America extended its control into Latin America, several Pacific islands, and part of the Southeast Asian arena. The nation's global recognition continued to grow with America's involvement in the Venezuela Dispute over the border between British Guiana and Venezuela, the Boxer Rebellion, the Russo-Japanese War, and other international events, and the new century was moving forward when the United States joined the fight against the Kaiser in World War I.

NOTES

1. Advertisement: "Ladies of Manila," *Literary Digest* (September 3, 1898).

2. Charles S. Olcott, *William McKinley* (Boston: Houghton Mifflin, 1916; reprint, New York: Ams Press, 1972), p. 111.

3. U.S. Congress, Senate, "In Support of an American Empire," speech by Senator Albert J. Beveridge of Indiana, 56th Cong., 1st sess., *Congressional Record* 33 (January 9, 1900): 710.

4. Albert Beveridge, "The March of the Flag," *Indianapolis Journal*, September 17, 1898. Excerpts reprinted in Claude G. Bowers, *Beveridge and the Progressive Era* (New York: The Literary Guild, 1932), p. 72. Reprint of campaign speech given September 16, 1898.

5. U.S. Congress, Senate, "The Retention of the Philippine Islands," speech by Senator Henry Cabot Lodge of Massachusetts, 56th Cong., 1st sess., *Congressional Record* 33 (March 7, 1900): 42–43.

6. U.S. Congress, Senate, "The Lust of Empire," speech by Senator George Hoar of Massachusetts, reprinted from the Senate Proceedings in the *Congressional Record*, April 17, 1900, Library of American Civilization, LAC 16720, p. 2.

7. Richard E. Welch, Jr., *Response to Imperialism: The United States and the Philippine-American War, 1899–1902* (Chapel Hill: University of North Carolina Press, 1979), p. 48.

8. Carl Schurz, *Speeches, Correspondence, and Political Papers of Carl Schurz* (New York: G.P. Putnam's Sons, 1913), Library of American Civilization, LAC 20837-4p. selected by Frederic Bancroft on behalf of the Carl Schurz Memorial Committee, n.p.

9. Welch, *Response to Imperialism*, p. 119.

10. William Graham Sumner, *War and Other Essays* (New Haven: Yale University Press, 1911), p. 304.

11. Mark Twain, "To the Person Sitting in Darkness," *North American Review* 172 (February 1901): 168.

12. Samuel Gompers, "Imperialism—Its Dangers and Wrongs," in *Republic or Empire? The Philippine Question*, ed. William Jennings Bryan (Chicago: Independence Company, 1899), p. 210.

13. Quoted in Leonard Schlup, "Imperialist Dissenter: William B. Bate and the Battle against Territorial Acquisitions, 1889–1900," *Southern Studies* 6 (Summer 1995): 78.

14. Allan R. Millett and Peter Maslowski, *For the Common Defense: A Military History of the United States of America* (New York: Free Press, 1984), p. 284.

15. Welch, *Response to Imperialism*, p. 59.

16. Ibid., p. 67.

DOCUMENTS

6.1. President William McKinley's Philippine Annexation Prayer, November 21, 1899

President William McKinley's conversation about the Philippines with a group from the General Missionary Committee of the Methodist Episcopal Church perhaps best exemplified the imperialists' position. In it, the undercurrents of American superiority and social Darwinism foretold the future of the Philippine Islands.

Before you go I would like to say just a word about the Philippine business. I have been criticized a good deal about the Philippines, but don't deserve it. The truth is I didn't want the Philippines, and when they came to us as a gift from the gods, I did not know what to do with them. . . .

"When next I realized that the Philippines had dropped into our laps I confess I did not know what to do with them. I sought counsel from all sides—Democrats as well as Republicans—but got little help. . . . I walked the floor of the White House night after night until midnight; and I am not ashamed to tell you, gentlemen, that I went down on my knees and prayed almighty God for light and guidance more than one night.

And one night late it came to me this way—I don't know how it was, but it came: (1) that we could not give them back to Spain—that would be cowardly and dishonorable; (2) that we could not turn them over to France and Germany—our commercial rivals in the Orient—that would be bad business and discreditable; (3) that we could not leave them to themselves—they were unfit for self-government—and they would soon have anarchy and misrule over there worse than Spain's was; and (4) that there was nothing left for us to do but to take them all, and to educate the Filipinos, and uplift and civilize and Christianize them, and by God's grace do the very best we could by them, as our fellowmen for whom Christ also died. And then I went to bed, and went to sleep, and slept soundly, and the next morning I sent for the chief engineer of the War Department (our map-maker), and I told him to put the Philippines on the map of the United States, . . . and there they are, and there they will stay while I am President!"

Source: Quoted in Charles S. Olcott, *William McKinley* (Boston: Houghton Mifflin, 1916, reprinted by New York: Ams Press, 1972), Vol. II, pp. 110–111.

6.2.   Senator Albert J. Beveridge Claims That the Philippines Belong to the United States Forever, January 9, 1900

Progressive reformer and zealous imperialist, Senator Albert J. Beveridge of Indiana helped to lead the charge for the annexation of the Philippines. In his January 1900 speech before the Senate, Beveridge expounded the position of imperialists who contended that annexation would be good for the American economy and global position. His belief in Anglo-Saxon supremacy resounded from the speech as he argued that annexation would not violate the principles of American democracy.

The times call for candor. The Philippines are ours forever, "territory belonging to the United States," as the Constitution calls them. And just beyond the Philippines are China's illimitable markets. We will not retreat from either. We will not repudiate our duty in the archipelago. We will not abandon our opportunity in the Orient. We will not renounce our part in the mission of our race, trustee, under God of the civilization of the world. And we will move forward to our work, not howling out regrets like slaves whipped to their burdens, but with gratitude for a task worthy of our strength, and thanksgiving to Almighty God that He has marked us as His chosen people, henceforth to lead in the regeneration of the world. . . .

Our largest trade henceforth must be with Asia. The Pacific is our ocean. More and more Europe will manufacture the most it needs, secure from its colonies the most it consumes. Where shall we turn for consumers of our surplus? Geography answers the question. China is our natural customer. She is nearer to us than England, Germany, or Russia, the commercial powers of the present and the future. They had moved nearer to China by securing permanent bases on her borders. The Philippines give us a base at the door of all the East. . . .

The Declaration of Independence does not forbid us to do our part in the regeneration of the world. If it did, the Declaration would be wrong. . . . And the sense in which "consent" is used in the Declaration is broader than mere understanding; for "consent" in the Declaration means participation in the government "consented" to. And yet these people who are not capable of "consenting" to any form of government must be governed. . . . And so the authors of the Declaration themselves governed the Indians without their consent [and] the inhabitants of Louisiana without their consent. . . .

Mr. President, this question is deeper than any question of party politics; deeper than any question of the isolated policy of our country even; deeper even than any question of constitutional power. It is elemental. It is racial. God has not been preparing the English-speaking and Teutonic peoples for a thousand years for nothing but vain and idle self-contemplation and self-admiration. No! He has made us the master organizers of the world to establish system where chaos reigns. He has given us the spirit of progress to overwhelm the forces of reaction throughout the earth. He has made us adepts in government that we may administer government among savage and senile peoples. Were it not for such a force as this the world would relapse into barbarism and night. And of all our race He has marked the American people as His chosen nation to finally lead in the regeneration of the world. This is the divine mission of America, and it holds for us all the profit, all the glory, all the happiness possible to man. We are trustees of the world's progress, guardians of its righteous peace. The judgement of the Master is upon us: "Ye have been faithful over a few things; I will make you ruler over many things. . . ."

That flag has never paused in its onward march. Who dares halt it now—now, when history's largest events are carrying it forward; now, when we are at last one people, strong enough for any task, great enough for any glory destiny can bestow?

Source: U.S. Congress, Senate, "In Support of an American Empire," speech by Senator Albert J. Beveridge of Indiana, 56th Cong., 1st sess., *Congressional Record* 33 (January 9, 1900): 704–712.

6.3.   Senator Henry Cabot Lodge Argues That the United States Should Retain the Philippine Islands, March 7, 1900

One of the leading proponents of the annexation of the Philippines was Senator Henry Cabot Lodge, a Republican from Massachusetts, head of the Foreign Relations Committee. In his March 1900 speech before Congress, Lodge outlined the key reasons why the United States should govern the Philippines. Filled with nationalistic sentiment, the speech applauds America's expansionist spirit.

Call up your own history as witness. It was not inevitable that we should take Louisiana. We could have remained shut up between the

Mississippi and the Atlantic and allowed another people to build the great city where New Orleans stands. But it was inevitable, if we followed the true laws of our being, that we should be masters of the Mississippi and spread from its mouth to its source. It was not inevitable that the union of States should endure. Had we so chosen we could have abandoned it, but if we had abandoned it we should have gone down to nothingness, a disintegrated chaos of petty republics. We determined that the Union should live, and then it was inevitable that it should come to what it is to-day. There was nothing inevitable about the Monroe Doctrine. We need never have asserted it, need never have maintained it. Had we failed to do both we should have had Europe established all about us; we should have been forced to become a nation of great standing armies; our growth and power would have been choked and stifled. But we have declared and upheld it. We have insisted that all the world should heed it, and it is one of the signs of the times that in The Hague Convention we have obtained at last a formal recognition of it from all the nations of Europe.

Yet the Monroe Doctrine is far more than a proposition of international law which we have laid down. Millions of men are ready to fight for that doctrine who could not define its terms, and who have never read, perhaps, the famous message which announced it. That is because the instinct of the people recognizes in that doctrine a great principle of national life. Without clinging to it we should be in constant peril, our evolution would be retarded, our existence menaced. The European power which attempts to establish itself in new possessions in the Americas, whether on a little island or in a continental state, from Patagonia to the Rio Grande, is our enemy. We are ready to fight upon that "theme until our eyelids do no longer wag." Is it because we want territory to the south of us? Far from it. It is because we know by instinct that it is a law of our being, a principle of our national life, that no power from over seas shall come into this hemisphere to thwart our policy or to cross our path. The Monroe doctrine [*sic*], with all it implies, is inevitable if we are to be true to the laws of our being.

Like every great nation, we have come more than once in our history to where the road of fate divided. Thus far we have never failed to take the right path. Again are we come to the parting of the ways. Again a momentous choice is offered to us. Shall we hesitate and make, in coward fashion, what Dante calls, "the great refusal?" Even now we can abandon the Monroe doctrine [*sic*], we can reject the Pacific, we can shut ourselves up between our oceans, as Switzerland is inclosed among her hills, and then it would be inevitable that we should sink out from among the great powers of the world and heap up riches that some stronger and bolder people, who do not fear their fate, might gather them. Or we may follow the true laws of our being, the laws in obedience to which we have come to be what we are, and then we shall stretch out into the Pacific; we shall stand in the front rank of the world powers; we shall give to our labor and our industry new and larger and better opportunities; we shall prosper ourselves; we shall benefit mankind.

Source: U.S. Congress, Senate, "The Retention of the Philippine Islands," speech by Senator Henry Cabot Lodge of Massachusetts, 56th Cong., 1st sess., *Congressional Record* 33 (March 7, 1900): 42–43.

6.4. Senator George F. Hoar Opposes the Lust for Empire, April 17, 1900

In Senator George F. Hoar's April 17, 1900 speech before the U.S. Senate, he confronted imperialists who contended that the annexation of the Philippines would not violate American principles. The Massachusetts Republican argued that the annexation dishonored both the Declaration of Independence and the Constitution.

It is not my purpose . . . to discuss the general considerations which affect any acquisition of sovereignty by the American people over the Philippine Islands, which has been or may be proposed. I am speaking today only of the theory of constitutional interpretation propounded by the senator [Orville Platt] from Connecticut. . . .

The question is this: Have we the right, as doubtless we have the physical power, to enter upon the government of ten or twelve million subject people without constitutional restraint? Of that question the senator from Connecticut takes the affirmative. And on that question I desire to join issue. . . .

Now, I claim that under the Declaration of Independence you cannot govern a foreign territory, a foreign people, another people than your own; that you cannot subjugate them and govern them against their will, because you think it is for their good, when they do not; because you think you are going to give them the blessings of liberty. You have no right at the cannon's mouth to impose on an unwilling people your Declaration of Independence and your Constitution and your notions of freedom and notions of what is good. That is the proposition which the senator asserted. He does not deny it now.

If the senator gets up and says, "I will not have those people in Iloilo subdued; I'll not govern the Philippine Islands unless the people consent; they shall be consulted at every step," he would stand in a different position. That is what I am complaining of. When I asked the senator during his speech whether he denied that just governments rested on the consent of the governed, he said, in substance, that he did deny it—that is, his answer was "some of them"; and he then went on to specify places where government did not so rest.

The senator says, "Oh, we governed the Indians against their will when we first came here," long before the Declaration of Independence. I do not think so. I am speaking of other people. Now, the people of the Philippine Islands are clearly a nation—a people three and one-third times as numerous as our fathers were when they set up this nation. If gentlemen say that because we did what we did on finding a great many million square miles of forests and a few hundred or thousand men roaming over it without any national life, without the germ of national life, without the capacity for self-government, without self-government, without desiring self-government, was a violation of your principle, I answer, if it was a violation of your principle it was wrong.

It does not help us out any to say that 150 years ago we held slaves or did something else. If it be a violation of your principle, it is wrong. But if, as our fathers thought and as we all think, it was not a violation of the principle because there was not a people capable of national life or capable of government in any form, that is another thing.

But read the account of what is going on in Iloilo. The people there have got a government, with courts and judges, better than those of the people of Cuba, who, it was said, had a right to self-government, collecting their customs; and it is proposed to turn your guns on them, and say, "We think that our notion of government is better than the notion you have got yourselves." I say that when you put that onto them against their will and say that freedom as we conceive it, not freedom as they conceive it, public interest as we conceive it, not as they conceive it, shall prevail, and that if it does not we are to force it on them at the cannon's mouth—I say that the nation which undertakes that plea and says it is subduing these men for their good when they do not want to be subdued for their good will encounter the awful and terrible rebuke, "Beware of the leaven of the Pharisees, which is hypocrisy."

Source: U.S. Congress, Senate, "The Lust of Empire," speech by Senator George Hoar of Massachusetts, reprinted from the Senate Proceedings in the *Congressional Record*, April 17, 1900, Library of Civilization, LAC 16720, pp. 1–2.

6.5.   William Graham Sumner Opposes Imperialism, January 16, 1899

William Graham Sumner, an Episcopal minister and Yale University professor, presented the following lecture to Yale's Phi Beta Kappa Society on January 16, 1899. In it, Sumner expressed his anti-imperialist position as he challenged America's ethnocentric view of colonization.

I intend to show that, by the line of action now proposed to us, which we call expansion and imperialism, we are throwing away some of the most important elements of the American symbol and are adopting some of the most important elements of the Spanish symbol.

There is not a civilized nation which does not talk about its civilizing mission just as grandly as we do. The English, who really have more to boast of in this respect than anybody else, talk least about it, but the Phariseeism with which they correct and instruct other people has made them hated all over the globe. The French believe themselves the guardians of the highest and purest culture, and that the eyes of all mankind are fixed on Paris, whence they expect oracles of thought and taste. The Germans regard themselves as charged with a mission, especially to us Americans, to save us from egoism and materialism. The Russians, in their books and newspapers, talk about the civilizing mission of Russia in language that might be translated from some of the finest paragraphs of imperialistic newspapers. . . .

We assume that what we like and practice, and what we think better, must come as a welcome blessing to Spanish-Americans and Filipinos. This is grossly and obviously untrue. They hate our ways. They are hostile to our ideas. Our religion, language, institutions, and manners offend them. They like their own ways, and if we appear amongst them as rulers, there will be social discord in all the great departments of social interest. The most important thing which we shall inherit from the Spaniards will be the task of suppressing rebellions.

If the United States takes out of the hands of Spain her mission, on the ground that Spain is not executing it well, and if this nation in its turn attempts to be schoolmistress to others, it will shrivel up into the same vanity and self-conceit of which Spain now presents an example. To read our current literature one would think that we were already well on the way to do it.

Now, the great reason why all these enterprises which begin by saying to somebody else, "We know what is good for you better than you know yourself and we are going to make you do it," are false and wrong is that they violate liberty; or, to turn the same statement into other words, the reason why liberty, of which we Americans talk so much, is a good thing is that it means leaving people to live out their own lives in their own way, while we do the same.

If we believe in liberty, as an American principle, why do we not stand by it? Why are we going to throw it away to enter upon a Spanish policy of dominion and regulation? . . . The point which I have tried to make in this lecture is that expansion and imperialism are at war with the best traditions, principles, and interests of the American people.

Source: William Graham Sumner, *War and Other Essays* (New Haven: Yale University Press, 1911), p. 304.

6.6.   Samuel Gompers Warns of the Dangers and Wrongs of Imperialism, 1899

Samuel Gompers, president of the American Federation of Labor and an ardent anti-imperialist, presided over a number of anti-imperialist organizations. In this essay, he warned the public that if the Philippines were annexed, immigration would increase and cheap labor would surely undermine the American worker. Gompers's Anglo-Saxon views on race were also clearly expressed in this piece.

It is worse than folly, aye, it is a crime, to lull ourselves into the fancy that we shall escape the duties which we owe to our people by becoming a nation of conquerors, disregarding the lessons of nearly a century and a quarter of our national existence as an independent, progressive, humane and peace-loving nation. We cannot with safety to ourselves, or justice to others keep the workers and the lovers of reform and simple justice divided, or divert their attention, and thus render them powerless to expose abuses and remedy existing injustice. . . .

If the Philippines are annexed what is to prevent the Chinese, the Negritos and the Malays coming to our country? How can we prevent the Chinese coolies from going to the Philippines and from there swarm into the United States and engulf our people and our civilization? If these new islands are to become ours, it will be either under the form of Territories or States. Can we hope to close the flood-gates of immigration from the hordes of Chinese and the semi-savage races coming from what will then be part of our own country? Certainly, if we are to retain the principles of law enunciated from the foundation of our Government, no legislation of such a character can be expected.

In a country such as ours the conditions and opportunities of the wage-earners are profoundly affected by the view of the worth or dignity of men who earn their bread by the work of their hands. The progress and improvement in the condition of the wage-earners in the former slave States have been seriously obstructed by decades in which manual labor and slave labor were identical. The South now, with difficulty, respects labor, because labor is the condition of those who were formerly slaves, and this fact operates potentially against any effort to secure so-cial justice by legislative action or organized movement of the workers. If these facts have operated so effectually to prevent necessary changes in the condition of our own people, how difficult will it be to quicken our conscience so as to secure social and legislative relief for the semi-savage slave or contract laborers of the conquered islands?

If we attempt to force upon the natives of the Philippines our rule, and compel them to conform to our more or less rigid mold of govern-ment, how many lives shall we take? Of course, they will seem cheap, because they are poor laborers. They will be members of the majority in the Philippines, but they will be ruled and killed at the convenience of the very small minority there, backed up by our armed land and sea forces. The dominant class in the islands will ease its conscience because the victims will be poor, ignorant and weak. When innocent men can be shot down on the public highways as they were in Lattimer, Pa., and Virden, Ill., men of our own flesh and blood, men who help to make this homogeneous nation great, because they dare ask for more humane con-ditions at the hands of the moneyed class of our country, how much more difficult will it be to arouse any sympathy, and secure relief for the poor semi-savages in the Philippines, much less indignation at any crime against their inherent and natural rights to life, liberty and pursuit of happiness?

Source: Samuel Gompers, "Imperialism—Its Dangers and Wrongs," in *Republic or Empire? The Philippine Question*, ed. William Jennings Bryan (Chicago: Inde-pendence Company, 1899), pp. 209–211.

ANNOTATED RESEARCH GUIDE

Books and Articles

Bain, David Haward. *Sitting in Darkness: Americans in the Philippines*. Boston: Houghton Mifflin, 1984. Examines the history and politics of the United States and the Philippines and analyzes their historic intersection with the Philippine-American War.

Beisner, Robert L. "1898 and 1968: The Anti-imperialists and the Doves." *Political Science Quarterly* 85, no. 2 (1970): 187–216. Compares and contrasts the anti-imperialist movements that grew out of both the Spanish-American War and the Vietnam War.

———. *Twelve against Empire: The Anti-imperialists, 1898–1900.* New York: McGraw-Hill, 1968. Explores the careers and writings of twelve leading anti-imperialists, including independent Mugwumpers and Republican leaders.

Crichton, Judy. *America 1900: The Turning Point.* New York: Henry Holt, 1998. This book is the companion to the PBS documentary with the same name. Both provide an extensive, though impressionistic, look at major political, economic, cultural, and technological changes that occurred at the turn of the century, beginning with the Spanish-American and Philippine-American wars.

Foner, Philip S., ed. *The Anti-imperialist Reader: A Documentary History of Anti-imperialists in the United States.* New York: Holmes & Meier, 1984. A comprehensive compilation of writings by leading anti-imperialists of the late nineteenth and early twentieth centuries.

Gates, John M. "Philippine Guerrillas, American Anti-imperialists, and the Election of 1900." *Pacific Historical Review* 46, no. 1 (1977): 51–64. Looks at how Filipino guerrillas misunderstood the complexities of American politics when they increased their resistance under the assumption that anti-imperialists would seize power in the 1900 election.

Hawkins, Hunt. "Mark Twain's Anti-imperialism." *American Literary Realism* 25, no. 2 (1993): 31–45. Analyzes Mark Twain's anti-imperialistic literature as it intersected with the writer's pessimistic view of the world.

Hoganson, Kristin L. *Fighting for American Manhood: How Gender Politics Provoked the Spanish-American and Philippine-American Wars.* New Haven: Yale University Press, 1998. Explores cultural beliefs surrounding gender roles (e.g., manhood and war) and connects this with imperialism and motives for fighting both wars.

Karnow, Stanley. *In Our Image: America's Empire in the Philippines.* New York: Ballantine Books, 1990. Pulitzer Prize–winning book about America's attempt at colonization. Takes a complex look at issues of cultural, political, and religious assimilation.

Langellier, J. Phillip. *Uncle Sam's Little Wars: The Spanish-American War, Philippine Insurrection, and the Boxer Rebellion, 1898–1902.* London: Greenhill Books, 1999. This illustrated history focuses on American foreign policy in the late nineteenth and early twentieth centuries as America became a global power.

Linn, Brian McAllister. *The Philippine War, 1899–1902.* Lawrence: University Press of Kansas, 2000. Examines the complex military aspect of the war and the new challenges faced by the U.S. Army.

Markowitz, Gerald E., ed. *American Anti-imperialism, 1895–1901.* New York: Garland Publishing, 1976. Provides reprints of speeches, editorials, and articles from leading anti-imperialists from both the conservative and radical branches of the movement.

Miller, Stuart Creighton. *"Benevolent Assimilation": The American Conquest of the Philippines, 1899–1903.* New Haven: Yale University Press, 1982. Explores the military conflict in the Philippine-American War and connects it to racism, Anglo-Saxonism, and the American effort to "Christianize" and "civilize" the Filipino people.

Paterson, Thomas G., ed. *American Imperialism and Anti-imperialism: Problem Studies in American History*. New York: Thomas Y. Crowell, 1973. Includes essays by leading historians of the 1970s that examine the Spanish-American War and the anti-imperialist movement that followed.

Smith, Edwina C. "Southerners on Empire: Southern Senators and Imperialists, 1898–1899." *Mississippi Quarterly* 31, no. 1 (1977–78): 89–108. Contends that racism and resentment over Reconstruction influenced southern senators and led to their objections over U.S. policies in the Philippines.

Welch, Richard E., Jr. *Response to Imperialism: The United States and the Philippine-American War, 1899–1902*. Chapel Hill: University of North Carolina Press, 1979. Analyzes the reaction of various groups (business leaders, unionists, missionaries, supremacists, intellectuals, and anti-imperialists) to the decision to annex the Philippines.

Zimmermann, Warren. "Jingoes, Goo-Goos, and the Rise of America's Empire." *Wilson Quarterly* 22, no. 2 (1998): 42–65. Examines the history of American empire building from 1893 (annexation of Hawaii) to 1903 (Panama Canal Treaty) and explores both the supporters and protesters of expansionism into Samoa, Guam, the Philippines, and the Panama Canal Zone.

Videos

The American Experience: America 1900 (PBS). Among many topics discussed in this film on the United States in 1900 is the nation's rise to world power. See PBS website for teacher resources and film: PBS.org

As It Happened: The Spanish-American War (The History Channel). Examines the reporting of the Spanish-American War and the rise of "Yellow Journalism." See Historychannel.com

Crucible of Empire: The Spanish-American War (PBS). Using original documents and film footage, this documentary explores war and society during the Spanish American War. See PBS website for teacher resources and film purchase information: PBS.org

Web Sites

http://www.history.ohio-state.edu/projects/uscartoons. Online political cartoons, including cartoons on the subject of expansion and imperialism.

http://www.mtholyoke.edu/acad/intrel/feros-pg.htm. Extensive collection of primary sources related to American international relations provided by Mount Holyoke College professor Vincent Ferraro. Includes government documents and writings of both imperialists and anti-imperialists.

7

The Espionage and Sedition Acts: Promoting War and Suppressing Dissent in World War I

The pervasive class, ethnic, and ideological diversity of American society, along with the unpopular nature of World War I, brought a new crisis to the United States. Convinced of the need to mobilize public opinion in support of the war, President Woodrow Wilson created the Committee on Public Information (CPI), the government's official propaganda machine. CPI used new advertising and marketing methods and worked with a small army of volunteers in an attempt to unify the nation in a common support for the war effort. But, fueled by superpatriotism, CPI instead created a jingoistic fever that escalated into mass hysteria. The Espionage Act of 1917 and the Sedition Act of 1918—which made it a crime to write or say anything against the U.S. government, the Constitution, or the flag, aid the enemy, or obstruct recruiting—added to the intensity of the day. Radicals, pacifists, conscientious objectors, and members of ethnic communities found themselves targets of imprisonment, harassment, violence, and even death. Although many Americans argued that gaining public support for the war was vital to the success of the allied forces, others condemned the restrictive atmosphere found in the home front, as "liberties won by ages of struggle [were] breaking down under the pressure of war." The blatant violations of civil liberties caused the American Union against Militarism (AUAM) pointedly to ask, "Is the Constitution a Scrap of Paper?" The "Spirit of '76 [was] under fire."[1]

The Great War officially began with the June 1914 assassination of Archduke Franz Ferdinand when he and his wife visited Sarajevo. The archduke was the heir to the Austro-Hungarian throne, and his assassination was part of a much larger resistance movement against the Austro-Hungarian Empire. However, an intense global atmosphere of economic competition, heightened nationalism, and rising militarism that had been building up for decades quickly turned the incident into a world war.

The Democratic party's rallying theme for Woodrow Wilson in the 1916 presidential election, "He Kept Us out of War," reflected the view of many Americans at the time who thought that the United States should stay out of the European conflict. In fact, isolationism had long been the fiber of American foreign policy. Yet shortly after his reelection, Wilson joined military reformers and a select group of Americans to promote the controversial "preparedness movement," which called for "universal military training" for America's young men. In response, "agrarians, immigrants, industrial workers, liberal pacifists, members of the women's movement, political and economic radicals, anarchists, and socialists" cried out in protest.[2] Many from these groups also joined their voices to demand a continued path of American neutrality. But tension mounted when Germany sank the *Lusitania* (1915) with the loss of many American lives and resumed unrestricted German U-boat warfare against all vessels in war zones. These actions, combined with the Zimmerman telegram (which supposedly revealed Germany's efforts to take up sides against the United States), the political instability in Russia, and other events, finally convinced Wilson to secure a declaration of war against Germany—a war he now called a struggle for democracy and freedom.

Many argued that democracy and freedom faced their biggest struggles on the American home front, since civil liberties became the first casualty of the war. Freedom of speech and freedom of the press— carefully protected under the First Amendment to the Constitution— were victims of the American war mobilization effort as debates raged between the U.S. government and war dissenters. The government, backed by the Supreme Court and the Espionage and Sedition acts, stood firm in its belief that a wartime emergency required unity of cause and the silencing of dissent. What was considered freedom in peacetime was now labeled "a clear and present danger" in war.

THE PEACE COMMUNITY

Before America's entrance into the war, peace activists spoke out against the European conflict and pushed for American neutrality. Many expressed frustration over the senselessness of war, the high cost of modern weapons, and the clear misuse of people's natural talents and energies. As tension in Europe exploded into war, social reformers and religious pacifists united with some members of the business and academic communities in a struggle to achieve peace. In April 1915, an American delegation of forty-seven women—mostly social, labor, and educational reformers—sailed through dangerous waters on their way to The Hague in the Netherlands to offer a proposal for peace. Among them was Jane Addams, the well-known Progressive reformer who devoted her life to helping the urban poor. Business leader Henry Ford also played a visible role in the peace movement and pledged, "I will do everything in my power to prevent murderous, wasteful war in America and in the world; I will devote my life to fight this spirit of militarism." War, said Ford, "is murder."[3] In December 1915, Ford backed up his commitment with his "Peace Ship" voyage, sent on a mission to Europe in an attempt to end the Great War. Although both the visit to The Hague and the "Peace Ship" journey were unsuccessful, they reflected the determination of these activists. Peace supporters also worried about the possibility of a future draft if America went to war—a draft that would ultimately force religious pacifists into military service despite their nonviolent beliefs. Conscientious objectors, who held moral, ethical, or religious beliefs in opposition to war, faced an uncertain future.

Once America officially entered the conflict in April 1917, Progressive reformers, especially the social justice workers who devoted their energy to humanitarian issues and urban and labor reform—divided over the war. While many played a key role in the peace movement, others chose to assist the U.S. government in its mobilization efforts. The latter group of reformers hoped that by working with the government, they could eventually meet their humanitarian goals. But Progressive Randolph Bourne asked, "If the war is too strong for you to prevent, how is it going to be weak enough for you to control and mold to our liberal purposes?"[4] Throughout the war, the pacifist community continued to work toward peace through meetings, writings, and public debates.

ETHNIC COMMUNITIES

Early in the European conflict, German and Irish Americans united to try to convince the United States to stay on a neutral course. While German Americans feared a fight against their own "brothers," Irish Americans adamantly opposed supporting Great Britain, the long-time oppressor of the Irish people. As the war in Europe escalated, ethnic organizations such as the National German-American Alliance (founded as an educational society to preserve the German language, literature, and culture) turned their efforts to keeping America out of the war. The Ancient Order of Hibernians, editors of Irish newspapers, and other Irish groups assisted in this goal, objecting to the growing current of "Anglo-

Saxon internationalism." Through rallies, speeches, demonstrations, newspaper editorials, and resolutions, German and Irish Americans attempted to educate the public about British violations of international law such as mining neutral harbors, raiding neutral merchant ships, blockading international waters, and harassing American citizens of German descent. They also objected to America's violation of the laws of neutrality, especially the inequity of selling munitions and providing loans in favor of Great Britain. The height of German and Irish American protests came with their powerful, but ultimately unsuccessful campaign against the reelection of President Wilson. Once war began, most German and Irish Americans joined in support of the war, and many young men from both of these ethnic groups served in the U.S. Army. But much smaller groups in the German and Irish American communities still attempted to get their voice of protest heard in the deafening atmosphere of conformity.

Not all ethnic groups sought American neutrality. In fact, immigrants from the oppressed areas of the Austro-Hungarian Empire hoped that a war against the Central Powers would finally free their homelands. The Czech and Slovak Americans united as early as 1914 to work toward the creation of an independent Czechoslovakia. Many other immigrant groups dreamed of creating democratic states in their homelands. The Polish Americans worked toward the establishment of an independent Poland, and Jewish Americans hoped to form a Jewish homeland in Palestine. With America's declaration of war, leaders from the Czech, Slovak, Polish, and Jewish American communities encouraged members of their ethnic groups to serve in the U.S. Army or the Czechoslovak, Polish, or Jewish legions attached to the French and British armies. Eventually, more than 18 percent of the American army consisted of foreign-born soldiers.[5]

RADICALS

American radicals saw the war as an inevitable battle among imperialist powers that for far too long had exploited people through harsh global colonization. They too took an antiwar stance. By 1917, the Socialist party had made significant gains by obtaining almost 600,000 votes for their presidential candidate—the largest vote ever given a Socialist leader—and a considerable number of Socialists took their elected positions as mayors and city officials throughout the United States. Since the Socialist party passionately spoke out against the exploitation of the American working class—pervasive in factories, railroads, and coal mines throughout the United States—not surprisingly, their supporters often came from this group. Once America entered the war, the Socialist party denounced the conflict and called the national draft "undemocratic" and a clear violation of the Thirteenth Amendment, which ended "involuntary servitude." As one Socialist party pamphlet asserted:

> A conscript is little better than a convict. He is deprived of his liberty and of his right to think and act as a free man. A conscripted citizen is forced to surrender his right as a citizen and become a subject. He is forced into involuntary servitude. He is deprived of the protection given him by the Constitution of the United States. He is deprived of all freedom of conscience in being forced to kill against his will. . . . In a democratic country each man must have the right to say whether he is willing to join the army. Only in countries where uncontrolled power rules can a despot force his subjects to fight.[6]

Radicals warned that this war, like past wars, would become a poor man's war. They argued that although the capitalists declared the war, it would be working-class sons who would needlessly die in it; workers were merely pawns in the capitalists' struggle for world power.

Not all workers supported the Socialists' position. The American Federation of Labor (AFL), the largest and most powerful union, backed America's entrance into the war. Known for his procapitalist stance, AFL president Samuel Gompers took center stage in the mobilization effort, lending his name to the massive propaganda campaign to get America's workers securely behind the war effort.

AN APPEAL TO PATRIOTISM

The initial lack of widespread support for the conflict prompted President Wilson to conduct a "war for the American mind."[7] With the April 1917 congressional declaration of war, the government not only had to muster up an effective fighting force and move the nation toward a war economy, but also it had to galvanize public opinion in support of the war. To many American leaders, creating a unified home front seemed even more critical, considering the prewar debates.

The Committee on Public Information, headed by Progressive journalist George Creel, utilized the skills of writers, historians, filmmakers, artists, journalists, advertising executives, marketing managers, and tens of thousands of speakers. They enthusiastically presented the war as an emotional crusade and painted anyone who did not support the cause as a danger to America. As historian David M. Kennedy revealed, Creel "unashamedly" admitted that he was fighting "for the minds of men [and] for the 'conquest of their convictions.' "[8]

The Liberty Loan Campaign, tied closely to CPI's efforts, took on the dual role of raising money for the war and eliciting patriotic support.

Both agencies used conformity and fear as finely honed weapons. Liberty Loan posters used animalistic portrayals of the German "Hun" as a predator of children and destroyer of virtuous women. Volunteer speakers known as "Four Minute Men"—75,000 strong—sought to drum up war fever in quick speeches before clubs, social gatherings, motion-picture showings, and other public events. Supplied with carefully prepared lines from CPI pamphlets, the volunteer speakers packed their speeches with superpatriotic rhetoric. Typical of the feverish appeals of the CPI Four Minute Men was the following, from a Pennsylvania speech: "With the world menace of Kaiserism towering above us larger, bloodier than ever, American's morale has strengthened tremendously. Issues are clearer, the will to victory is spreading. . . . The spirit of American liberty is [being] challenged. . . . The spirit of America and America herself are threatened. Who of us then can hesitate to give every ounce of American blood and treasure for the defense of American homes NOW?"[9] CPI and the Liberty Loan Campaign also worked with clergymen who urged their congregations to demonstrate their patriotism by buying liberty bonds. One sermon published in a CPI pamphlet declared, "You can not be a tightwad and a Christian at the same time. If Christ rules the world, Kaiserism must go; if the Kaiser rules the world, the Christ spirit is lost. As you value your Christianity, buy these bonds."[10]

CPI and the Liberty Loan Campaign also directed their propaganda efforts at the millions of newly arrived immigrants. Knowing little of the lives, traditions, or politics of ethnic communities, the native-born population also knew little about the immigrants' view of the war. Long-established preconceptions and prejudices forged into anti-immigrant nativism and turned the drive for patriotism into a drive for Americanization. CPI and the Liberty Loan Campaign tapped into this nativist strain and demanded "no more hyphens in America." They asked immigrants to prove their loyalty—"Are you 100% American? Prove It! Buy U.S. Government Bonds." Loan posters written in various languages, designed to elicit patriotism, included symbols of the American flag, the Statue of Liberty, and Ellis Island.[11]

After the 1917 Communist Revolution in Russia, CPI also attacked radical Bolshevik philosophy and declared that "the true American ideal is that Bolshevism stands for all that is subversive of law and order." In public speeches, CPI's instructions told Four Minute Men to "explain carefully that Bolshevism is the antithesis of what we have fought for [and] explain how opposite it is to true Democracy."[12] CPI pamphlets poured into working-class communities, refuting Socialists' claims that the war was a struggle between oppressive capitalist countries at the expense of the workers.

CIVIL LIBERTIES—THE FIRST CASUALTY OF THE WAR

CPI rhetoric helped to feed a mass frenzy as the superpatriotic environment turned ugly. But the war of words took on a new and even more dangerous direction with the Espionage and Sedition acts. These acts were used as weapons against members of the peace movement, various ethnic groups, and those deemed radical, and in the hysteria of the day, the pressure to conform created an unconcealed, repressive atmosphere where civil liberties became a sacrificial victim of the war.

Although elements of the acts reflect mature security concerns of a nation at war, other sections clearly trampled the First Amendment. The Espionage Act of 1917, taking up fourteen pages in *United States Statutes at Large*, mandated heavy penalties for anyone found guilty of transmitting information about U.S. national defense to any foreign powers, interfering with military recruiting, encouraging disloyalty among the U.S. armed forces, using U.S. mail for treasonous materials, and many other infractions. The 1918 amendment to Section 3 of the Espionage Act, commonly known as the Sedition Act, made it unlawful to

> incite insubordination, disloyalty, mutiny, or refusal of duty, in the military or naval forces of the United States or shall willfully obstruct ... the recruiting or enlistment service of the United States, or ... willfully utter, print, write, or publish any disloyal, profane, scurrilous, or abusive language about the form of government of the United States, or the Constitution of the United States, or the military or naval forces of the United States or the flag ... or the uniform of the Army or Navy of the United States.[13]

Title XII, Section 2, expanded the act even further and stated that "every letter, writing, circular, post card, picture, print engraving, photograph, newspaper, pamphlet, book or other publication, matter or thing of any kind, containing any matter advocating or urging treason, insurrection, or forcible resistance to any law of the United States, is hereby declared to be non-mailable."[14] Those found guilty were liable to punishments of up to twenty years in prison and up to $10,000 in fines.

Postmaster General Albert S. Burleson used the acts to suppress the writings of radicals, pacifists, and ethnic leaders through censorship and restriction of second-class-mail privileges. The latter restriction could bankrupt a press that could not afford the expense of first-class mass mailings. Throughout the war, it became clear that Burleson, an anti-radical superpatriot—"the foremost official enemy of dissidents"—continually overstepped his authority in a personal crusade for conformity.[15] Although he claimed that socialist papers would be banned only if they included "treasonable or seditious matter," Burleson concluded, "Most socialist papers do contain this matter."[16] Thus he and his team of postal censors unfairly targeted the radical press, shutting down, delaying, or censoring radical publications throughout the United States. These included papers that questioned capitalism, advocated a world government, quoted "dangerous" philosophers, reprinted antiwar cartoons, and promoted consumer guilds and a more equitable economy. Burleson also attacked the writings of the radical union Industrial Workers of the World (IWW). This misuse of the Espionage Act prompted Socialist leader Norman Thomas to remark that the postmaster general didn't "know socialism from rheumatism."[17]

Burleson also overstepped his authority by cutting off the second-class-mailing privileges of many ethnic presses without just cause. This created economic problems for the small presses, and many faced a shutdown. He required foreign-language newspapers to submit English translations of articles—adding to their expenses, delaying publication, and indirectly censoring the ethnic presses. Although all ethnic newspapers faced scrutiny, editors of radical ethnic presses, who continued to blame Great Britain for the war or who published articles on both America's and Germany's war efforts, faced threats of imprisonment. Eventually, the U.S. government jailed a number of editors of foreign-language newspapers and shut down their presses. Burleson closely monitored the writings of peace activists as well.

As the supercharged public atmosphere turned into hysteria, immigrants, pacifists, and radicals became targets of violence and even death. The American Protection League, with a membership of over 250,000 volunteers, worked with the Justice Department as loyalty watchdogs, reporting dissent or any "suspicious" activities to the U.S. attorney general. Tens of thousands of reports poured into city offices as the war progressed. Vigilantes hunted down conscientious objectors in "slacker raids," opened private mail, burned "pro-German" books, spied on neighbors, and attacked and even killed immigrants and radicals. Robert Prager fell victim to an irate mob in Missouri that wrapped him in an American flag, dragged him through town, and then lynched him. His only crime— he was born in Germany. At a postwar victory loan pageant in Chicago, a U.S. Navy sailor got into an armed confrontation with a man who "did not stand and remove his hat while the band was playing the Star-Spangled Banner." After exchanging heated words, the sailor shot the man. As if to justify the shooting, the *Washington Post* reported, "It was believed by the authorities he had come here for the I.W.W. convention."[18]

During the war, hysteria reached the absurd when hamburgers, sauerkraut, and German measles became "liberty sandwiches," "liberty cabbage," and "liberty measles." Some even renamed dachshunds "liberty pups." Schools supplied children with scissors to cut away all references to Germany from their textbooks and canceled the German language from the curriculum. Libraries removed German books from their shelves. Museums took down German artwork, and many urban officials instructed city orchestras not to play Bach, Wagner, and Beethoven or other German music.

In an attempt to quiet the hysteria, President Wilson issued a plea to the American public in which he condemned "the mob spirit" and called for an end to lynching and other violent acts occurring throughout the nation. "No man who loves America, no man who really cares for her fame and honor and character, or who is truly loyal to her institutions, can justify mob action. . . . We are at this very moment fighting lawless passion."[19]

FIGHTING BACK

War dissenters fought back. The American Union against Militarism, reacting to the blatant violations of civil liberties, announced the creation of the Civil Liberties Bureau "for the maintenance in war time of the rights of free press, free speech, peaceful assembly, liberty of conscience, and freedom from unlawful search and seizure." Roger N. Baldwin led the group of lawyers who, without a fee, worked to protect the rights of the American people. "War or no war, civil liberty must be maintained in America."[20] AUAM also distributed pamphlets throughout the United States that clearly spelled out rights guaranteed by the First Amendment and contended that "the Constitution permits citizens to criticize officials, the conduct of the war and war legislation, to oppose war and even to express sympathy with the enemy. The Constitution is not suspended by a declaration of war."[21] AUAM also created the Conscientious Objectors' Bureau, designed to defend the rights of pacifists. Although the Selective Service Board made provisions for "any well recognized religious sect or organization" to be exempted from combat service, "in practice [the policy] frequently proved unfair and harsh."[22] Eventually, the U.S. government offered proven conscientious objectors a noncombatant classification for military service or furloughed pacifists to civilian work. Those who refused either choice found themselves in military prisons.

Women from the pacifist and suffragette communities funded the Bureau of Legal Advice, located in New York City, to protect the rights of conscientious objectors and to fight against the "enemy alien" status assigned to immigrants born under the reign of the Central Powers. After a long struggle for rights, some conscientious objectors found success in court, but most were inducted into the army.

Socialists, pacifists, and other war dissenters persisted in speaking out against the war and the growing loss of civil rights. But freedom of speech continued to be a fatality in the war, and those who spoke out faced harassment and imprisonment. The Department of Justice prosecuted more than two thousand people under the Espionage and Sedition acts. Socialist leader Eugene Debs, the new director of the Civil Liberties Bureau, Roger N. Baldwin, and well-known suffragette and pacifist Alice Paul, among many others, were jailed for their antiwar stance. Debs was arrested after a two-hour speech that focused on socialism and the American economic system, but included a brief mention of the war: "The master class has always declared the wars; the subject class has always fought the battles. The master class has had all to gain and nothing to lose, while the subject class has had nothing to gain and all to lose—especially their lives."[23] Debs, an outspoken war dissenter, failed to convince the judge that his comments were protected under the First Amendment. In sentencing Baldwin for violating the Selective Service Act, the judge concluded, "I think that you have lost sight of one very fundamental and essential thing for the preservation of that American liberty of which by tradition you feel that you are a genuine upholder. A Republic can last only so long as its laws are obeyed."[24]

The Justice Department deported or jailed IWW leaders, investigated the New York City branch of the Women's Peace party, and kept peace activist Jane Addams under surveillance. Addams, once known as "Saint" Jane, now became "the most dangerous woman in America."[25] As the war continued, AUAM and many other peace organizations began to tone down their rhetoric as the pacifists, fearful of prosecution, divided between less and more militant members.

Some dissenters fought back through the court system. Perhaps the most famous wartime case involved Charles T. Schenck, sentenced under the Espionage Act for printing and distributing leaflets to draftees urging them to resist conscription. Schenck took his case to the U.S. Supreme Court, arguing protection under the First Amendment. However, in *Schenck v. United States*, Justice Oliver Wendell Holmes, Jr., concluded, "When a nation is at war many things which might be said in time of peace are such a hindrance to its efforts that their utterance will not be endured so long as men fight. . . . No court could regard them as protected by any constitutional rights." According to Holmes, Schenck's conviction should stand, since his actions represented "a clear and present danger" to the nation.[26]

CONCLUSION

The first attempt to silence Americans' right of free speech under the Constitution came in 1798, when the Federalist-dominated Congress passed the Sedition Act, making it a crime to defame falsely U.S. government officials or hamper the policies of the government. The act reflected the stress and strain of a young nation facing its first major foreign policy crisis as it became a pawn in a war between Great Britain and France. Federalists used the Sedition Act to quiet the protests of Republican opponents, particularly newspaper editors who attacked Federalist policy.

The Espionage and Sedition acts of World War I represented a much more extensive effort at forced conformity. As historian Stephen Vaughn explained, "Democratic government is worth having, and it is also very difficult to maintain, and herein lies an essential awkwardness in judging the activities of the United States government's first large-scale propaganda agency."[27] The Committee on Public Information tried to rally public support for the war through massive campaigns extolling American virtues and sacred duties to "make the world safe for democracy." It successfully promoted American national unity, a much-needed force in winning wars. However, in its "great crusade to save democracy" throughout the world, it injured American democracy. The Espionage and Sedition acts and the jingoistic fever created by CPI and the Liberty Loan Campaign became powerful weapons used against dissenters, seriously wounding American civil liberties.

Unity of spirit and purpose was essential in fighting World War I, particularly considering how new weapons—courtesy of modern industrial technology—had turned the war into a deadly stalemate. George Creel later bragged that "there was no part of the great war machinery that we did not touch, no medium of appeal that we did not employ. The printed word, the spoken word, the motion picture, the telegraph, the cable, the wireless, the poster, and the sign-board—all these were used in our campaign to make our own people and all other peoples understand the causes that compelled America to take arms."[28] But in the emotionally charged atmosphere of superpatriotism, the voices of many radicals, pacifists, and the foreign born were stifled. The U.S. government's propaganda campaign and the Espionage and Sedition acts silenced dissenters and trampled the First Amendment. At the war's end, the hysteria that made many "suspect" to the "American cause" did not simply end. In fact, much of the emotion of the day was redirected into a Red Scare—an early-twentieth-century witch-hunt to purge the country of "dangerous" radicals. Democracy, the Constitution, and the "Spirit of '76" continued to be under fire. But the excesses of superpatriotism spurred institutional responses too. The American Civil Liberties Union, for example, owes its origins to efforts to protect free speech rights during the war. Conscientious objectors and other wartime dissenters did not let the government have the last word on what counted as good Americanism.

During World War II, Franklin Roosevelt purposely avoided taking the same path as Woodrow Wilson when he considered the need to mobilize public opinion. Roosevelt's Office of War Information (OWI) similar to CPI, hired thousands of writers, artists, and advertisers to sell war, but instead of directing its effort at forcing conformity, OWI underscored the barbarism of the Axis powers when it asked Americans to help the nation achieve victory. Although World War II America avoided widespread hysteria, not everyone escaped the loss of civil liberties. More than 110,000 Japanese Americans spent the war in U.S. internment camps. Although no formal charges or trials took place, this group, made up of some 40,000 Japanese immigrants and 70,000 American citizens of Japanese ancestry, found themselves in desert prison camps, most for the duration of the war.

NOTES

1. *The Spirit of '76—Under Fire*, American Union against Militarism, May 1917, Jane Addams Papers, American Peace Society, 1906–1928, Reel 43. Swarthmore College Peace Collection, Swarthmore College Peace Library. (Hereafter cited as Jane Addams Papers, Swarthmore College Peace Library).

2. John Whiteclay Chambers II, *To Raise an Army: The Draft Comes to Modern America* (New York: Free Press, 1987), pp. 107, 109.

3. Barbara S. Kraft, *The Peace Ship: Henry Ford's Pacifist Adventure in the First World War* (New York: Macmillan, 1978), pp. 33, 51.

4. David M. Kennedy, *Over Here: The First World War and American Society* (Oxford and New York: Oxford University Press, 1980), p. 52.

5. Nancy Gentile Ford, *Americans All: Foreign-born Soldiers in World War I* (College Station: Texas A and M University Press, 2001), see Chapter 1, pp. 16–44.

6. *Long Live the Constitution of the United States*, Socialist Party, Pennsylvania, Eastern District Office File, Record Group 118, Records of United States Attorneys, National Archives, Mid Atlantic Region, Philadelphia, Pennsylvania.

7. Kennedy, *Over Here*, p. 45.

8. Ibid., p. 61.

9. "Danger of America," Committee on Public Information, Division of Four Minute Men, Bulletin no. 31, May 27, 1918, p. 1. The Pennsylvania Four Minute Men, Clarence B. Brinton Collection, World War I Liberty Loan Drive Records, 1917–1919. In the collection of the Historical Society of Pennsylvania. (Hereafter cited as Pennsylvania Four Minute Men, HSP.)

10. "The Third Liberty Loan," Committee on Public Information, Division of Four Minute Men, Bulletin no. 29, April 6, 1918, p. 1. Pennsylvania Four Minute Men, HSP.

11. Kennedy, *Over Here*, pp. 64–68.

12. *Victory Liberty Loan Handbook for Speakers* (Washington, DC: Treasury Department War Loan Organization, 1919), pp. 24–25. Pennsylvania Four Minute Men, HSP.

13. *United States Statutes at Large* (Washington, D.C., 1918), 40:553.

14. William H. Rehnquist, *All the Laws But One: Civil Liberties in Wartime* (New York: Vintage Books, 2000), p. 173.

15. Kennedy, *Over Here*, p. 75.

16. James R. Mock, *Censorship 1917* (Princeton, NJ: Princeton University Press, 1941), p. 145.

17. Kennedy, *Over Here*, p. 76.

18. "Chicagoans Cheer Tar Who Shot Man," *Washington Post*, May 7, 1919, p. 1.

19. "The President on Mob Violence," American Union against Militarism, July 26, 1918, Jane Addams Papers, American Peace Society, 1906–1928, Reel 43, Swarthmore College Peace Library.

20. *The Spirit of '76—Under Fire*, p. 3.

21. *Constitutional Rights in War-time*, (Washington, DC: American Union Against Militarism, May 1917), Jane Addams Papers, American Peace Society: 1906–1928, Reel 43, Swarthmore College Peace Collection Swarthmore College Peace Library.

22. Kennedy, *Over Here*, p. 163.

23. Quoted in Ray Ginger, *The Bending Cross: A Biography of Eugene Victor Debs* (New Brunswick, NJ: Rutgers University, 1949), pp. 376–377.

24. *The Individual and the State: The Problem as Presented by the Sentencing of Roger N. Baldwin*, November 1918, American Civil Liberties, 1918 National Civil Liberties Bureau folder, Swarthmore College Peace Collection, Swarthmore College Peace Library.

25. Allen F. Davis, *American Heroine: The Life and Legend of Jane Addams* (London: Oxford University Press, 1973), pp. 232, 251.

26. Rehnquist, *All the Laws But One*, p. 174.

27. Stephen Vaughn, *Holding Fast the Inner Lines: Democracy, Nationalism and the Committee on Public Information* (Chapel Hill: University of North Carolina Press, 1980), p. xi.

28. George Creel, *How We Advertised America* (New York: Harper & Brothers, 1920), p. 2.

DOCUMENTS

7.1. The Committee on Public Information Promotes Its View of the Meaning of America, June 29, 1918

The U.S. government's propaganda machine, the Committee on Public Information, issued a series of instructions for the Four Minute Men who volunteered to give short (four-minute) patriotic speeches before public gatherings. The following is a reprint of CPI's "Americanization" statements that were used to elicit loyalty when Four Minute Men were speaking to America's immigrant communities.

A result of this war will be a wonderful amalgamation of races within America. The melting pot is boiling now.

At this time we know only Old Americans and New Americans. The hyphen is gone. It changed to vapor in the melting pot. No American may owe a secret heart allegiance to some foreign country. This is home. Here are our ties, and the ties of all those we love most.

There may be sentiment, justly so, for the former home. Even if you fled from a tyranny over there. All the finer the sentiment, if you yearn to see the old folks freed from tyranny and living amid the blessings of liberty that you enjoy. But America must come first in your inner heart.

THE OATH OF NATURALIZATION

None of us who were born abroad will ever forget the oath of allegiance we took. . . . Note that the oath of naturalization particularly mentions giving up allegiance to the old country. A man can not serve two masters. If he votes, acts, or talks in the interest of that old country for any reason whatsoever against the interests of his new allegiance he is a cheat, a perjurer; he is legally and morally a man without a country.

WANTED: LOYALTY FROM WITHIN

There is only one person that can make me all American, all-loyal at heart, true blue. That man is myself. We may have heard threats from some Americans who themselves do not understand Americanism. But the leaders of the country, while insisting upon observance of laws, do not want to force outward loyalty. They want us to feel our loyalty inwardly; feel it of our own accord. They want to help, whenever we want help—in understanding.

OUR DUTY TO "NEW AMERICANS"

(Avoid patronizing attitude in speeches. Likewise avoid warning "Old Americans" against patronizing manner. Simply assume equality.)

It is the duty of the American born to recognize the good brought to our country by our new brethren; for this is our common home. Employers should help the foreign born in their plans of Americanization when they seek opportunities for study. Night school facilities should be enlarged. The wicked habit of giving nicknames to foreigners and their descendants must be abandoned. Stop it among children as you would stop any other unpatriotic utterance.

Old Americans should set an example, too, in the little things that spell patriotism. How many of us know the words of the Star Spangled Banner? May we all learn them this week. Observe respect to the symbol of our country, the flag; never forget the salute.

Source: "The Meaning of America," Committee on Public Information, Division of Four Minute Men, Bulletin no. 33, June 29, 1918, pp. 5–7. The Pennsylvania Four Minute Men, Clarence B. Brinton Collection, World War I Liberty Loan Drive Records, 1917–1919, in the collection of the Historical Society of Pennsylvania.

7.2.   The American Union against Militarism Defends the Spirit of '76, May 1917

This pamphlet from the American Union against Militarism expressed concern over the repressive direction of the country and announced the formation of the Civil Liberties Bureau, designed to protect the constitutional rights of Americans.

For the maintenance in war time of the rights of free press, free speech, peaceful assembly, liberty of conscience, and freedom from unlawful search and seizure.

Liberties won by ages of struggle are breaking down under the pressure of war. Those who criticize war policies or discuss terms of peace are subject to continual persecution by petty officials determined to force their conception of patriotism upon all citizens. It is necessary, in order to preserve our constitutional rights, to organize effectively throughout the nation.

The American Union Against Militarism has therefore established a

CIVIL LIBERTIES BUREAU, advised by a group of lawyers, with local committees and attorneys assisting in the leading cities. It is the object of this Bureau to act as a clearinghouse of free information, advice and legal aid to citizens whose constitutional rights are assailed by reason of the war.

In undertaking this responsibility we depend on the fullest co-operation of local anti-militarist organizations, of able lawyers all over the country who for the sake of justice and freedom are willing to defend cases of this kind without fee, and of individual citizens who care enough for their country to insist that, war or no war, civil liberty must be maintained in America.

Directing Committee
L. Hollingsworth Wood, Chairman
Roger N. Baldwin, Director
John Lovejoy Elliot
Norman M. Thomas
Agnes Brown Leach
Amos Pinchot
John Haynes Holmes

IS THE CONSTITUTION A SCRAP OF PAPER?

First Amendment to the Constitution

"Congress shall make no law respecting an establishment of religion, or prohibiting the free exercise thereof; or abridging the freedom of speech, or of the press; or the right of the people peaceably to assemble and to petition the Government for a redress of grievances."

Fourth Amendment to the Constitution

"The right of the people to be secure in their persons, houses, papers, and effects, against unreasonable searches and seizures, shall not be violated, and no warrants shall issue but upon probable cause, supported by oath or affirmation, and particularly describing the place to be searched and the persons or things to be seized."

Source: The Spirit of '76—Under Fire, American Union against Militarism, May 1917, Jane Addams Papers, American Peace Society, 1906–1928, Reel 43, Swarthmore College Peace Collection, Swarthmore College Peace Library.

7.3.   The American Union against Militarism Upholds Constitutional Rights in Wartime, May 1917

In May 1917, the American Union against Militarism, fearful of widespread violations of American civil liberties, especially un-

der the impending Espionage Act, distributed pamphlets empha-
sizing the constitutional rights of Americans. In this pamphlet, the
AUAM discussed freedom of speech, freedom of the press, and
freedom of assembly. Despite resistance, Congress enacted the
Espionage Act on June 15, 1917.

Constitutional rights are being seriously invaded throughout the United States under pressure of war. Men are arrested and fined for criticizing the Government or the President. Halls are refused for meetings; meetings are broken up; pamphlets and literature opposing war are confiscated and the authors haled into court.

In short, the guarantees of the Federal Constitution have been suspended at the dictate of petty officials who would compel conformity on the part of all citizens to their conception of war policies.

Such a time is a challenge to all patriots to maintain the liberties guaranteed by the Constitution. . . .

(1) FREE SPEECH AND FREE PRESS

The Constitution permits citizens to criticize officials, the conduct of the war and war legislation, to oppose war and even to express sympathy with the enemy. The Constitution is not suspended by a declaration of war.

The theory of the first amendment of the Constitution is that a citizen may say anything he pleases, but that he is liable for any injury, which his utterances may cause and may be proceeded against for such injury. Congress may by statute attempt to define in war-time what are seditious or treasonable utterances, but the validity of such legislation is extremely doubtful. There are a few legal points in this connection which need to be made clear.

(1) No man can be tried for treason for anything that he may say or write. . . .

(2) RIGHT OF ASSEMBLY IN PRIVATE PLACES

The police have no legal right to enter private meetings held on private property, nor to break up orderly public meetings held on private property, nor to confiscate literature or papers without a warrant. . . .

(3) RIGHT OF ASSEMBLY IN PUBLIC PLACES

The police have no right to break up meetings held on the street or other public places, or to prevent a man from speaking before he says anything on which to make a charge. The police have not the right to stop the distribution of literature either on the streets or in meetings. . . .

The police have no more legal right to stop the distribution of literature on the street than they have to stop the distribution of newspapers on the street. Some cities have ordinances which forbid the distribution of literature on the street for the purpose of preventing the streets from being littered. But it has been held by a number of courts that only the person who throws the literature on the street, not the person who hands it to him, can be found guilty under such an ordinance.

(4) INVASIVE ACTS BY PROSECUTING OFFICIALS

In addition to interference by the police, the rights of free speech and free press may be invaded by prosecuting officials and district attorneys who in some cases summon persons to appear before them and to produce their records, literature, names of members of an organization, and the like. In some cases offices are raided and literature and papers taken in charge by federal or local officials. No prosecuting official or district attorney has the right to summon citizens to answer inquiries, or to enter a private office to take papers without warrant. They have no right to question citizens about their activities or utterances until a formal charge has been made in court.

The only way to meet such interference by prosecuting officials is to assert constitutional rights, to decline to give information or give up papers without a warrant, and to consult an attorney at once.

(5) THE "SPY BILL"

The effect on constitutional rights of the so-called "Spy" or Espionage bill, pending in Congress at the time this pamphlet is being printed, will be considerable. A special statement will be issued later dealing with the provision of that bill in relation to the statements made in this pamphlet. It seems likely, however, that no provision of the bill will abridge these rights definitely, and that if any provision does, it will be taken at once into the courts.

Much will depend on how such war-time legislation is administered. The administration at Washington professes a desire to be liberal, and it is to be hoped that the federal authorities who will enforce the provisions of this act, will not undertake seriously to interfere with established rights.

Source: Constitutional Rights in War-time (Washington, DC: American Union Against Militarism, May 1917), Jane Addams Papers, American Peace Society, 1906–1928, Reel 43, Swarthmore College Peace Collection, Swarthmore College Peace library.

7.4.   The Socialist Party Opposes the Draft

The Socialist Party of America spoke against the national draft, calling it unconstitutional. In the following leaflet, the Philadel-

*phia branch of the Socialist party explained its position and called
for a repeal of the Conscription Act.*

The 13th Amendment, Section 1, of the Constitution of the United
States says: "Neither slavery nor involuntary servitude, except as a punishment for crime whereof the party shall have been duly convicted, shall
exist within the United States, or any place subject to their jurisdiction."

The Constitution of the United States is one of the greatest bulwarks
of political liberty. It was born after a long, stubborn battle between king-
rule and democracy. (We see little or no difference between arbitrary
power under the name of a king and under a few misnamed "representatives.") In this battle the people of the United States established the
principle that freedom of the individual and personal liberty are the most
sacred things in life. Without them we become slaves. . . .

The Thirteenth Amendment to the Constitution of the United States
. . . embodies this sacred idea. The Socialist Party says that this idea is
violated by the Conscription Act. When you conscript a man and compel
him to go abroad to fight against his will, you violate the most sacred
right of personal liberty, and substitute for it what Daniel Webster called
"despotism in its worst form."

A conscript is little better than a convict. He is deprived of his liberty
and of his right to think and act as a free man. A conscripted citizen is
forced to surrender his right as a citizen and become a subject. He is
forced into involuntary servitude. He is deprived of the protection given
him by the Constitution of the United States. He is deprived of all freedom of conscience in being forced to kill against his will.

Are you one who is opposed to war, and were you misled by the venal
capitalist newspapers, or intimidated or deceived by gang politicians and
registrars into believing that you would not be allowed to register your
objection to conscription? Do you know that many citizens of Philadelphia insisted on their right to answer the famous question twelve, and
went on record with their honest opinion of opposition to war, notwithstanding the deceitful efforts of our rulers and the newspaper press to
prevent them from doing so? Shall it be said that the citizens of Philadelphia, the cradle of American liberty, are so lost to a sense of right and
justice that they will let such monstrous wrongs against humanity go
unchallenged?

In a democratic country each man must have the right to say whether
he is willing to join the army. Only in countries where uncontrolled
power rules can a despot force his subjects to fight. Such a man or men
have no place in a democratic republic. This is tyrannical power in its
worst form. It gives control over the life and death of the individual to
a few men. There is no man good enough to be given such power.

Conscription laws belong to a bygone age. Even the people of Germany, long suffering under the yoke of militarism, are beginning to de-

mand the abolition of conscription. Do you think it has a place in the United States? Do you want to see unlimited power handed over to Wall Street's chosen few in America? If you do not, join the Socialist Party in its campaign for the repeal of the Conscription Act. Write to your congressman and tell him you want the law repealed. Do not submit to intimidation. You have a right to demand the repeal of any law. Exercise your rights of free speech, peaceful assemblage and petitioning the government for a redress of grievances. Come to the headquarters of the Socialist Party, 1326 Arch Street, and sign a petition to congress for the repeal of the Conscription Act. Help us wipe out this stain upon the Constitution!

Help us re-establish democracy in America. Remember, "eternal vigilance is the price of liberty." Down with autocracy! Long live the Constitution of the United States! Long live the Republic!

Source: Long Live the Constitution of the United States, Socialist Party, Pennsylvania, Eastern District Office File, Record Group 118, Records of United States Attorneys, National Archives, Mid Atlantic Region, Philadelphia, Pennsylvania.

7.5.   Judge Mayer Remarks on the Problem of the Individual and the State in Imposing Sentence on Roger N. Baldwin, November 1918

A federal court judge sentenced Roger N. Baldwin, director of the Civil Liberties Union, to one year in prison for violation of the Selective Service Law after Baldwin read a prepared statement to the court. Excerpts from the judge's remarks are presented here.

In all that you have said, I think that you have lost sight of one very fundamental and essential thing for the preservation of that American liberty of which by tradition you feel that you are a genuine upholder. A Republic can last only so long as its laws are obeyed. The freest discussion is permitted, and should be invited in the processes that lead up to the enactment of a statute. There should be the freest opportunity of discussion as to the methods of the administration of the statutes. But the Republic must cease to exist if disobedience to any law enacted by the orderly process laid down by the constitution is in the slightest degree permitted. That is, from my point of view, fundamental. That is the sense, not only from an ideal standpoint, but from a practical standpoint. We should not be able, as I think most Americans believe, to maintain what we regard as a Government of free people, if some individual, whether from good or bad motives, were able successfully to violate a statute, duly and constitutionally and properly passed, because his own view of the same might differ from that entertained by the law makers who have enacted the law, and from that of the Executive who has given it his approval.

Now that is my point of view, based upon a system whose perpetuity rests upon obedience of the law. It may often be that a man or woman has greater foresight than the masses of the people. And it may be that in the history of things, he, who seems to be wrong today, may be right tomorrow. But with those possible idealistic and academic speculations a Court has nothing to do.

I don't take into consideration any of the details of the organization with which you were connected. I cannot and will not endeavor to arrive at any conclusion as to whether its activities were good, bad, or indifferent. If it should come before the Court sometime, why then, the Court, however composed, will deal with the subject matter as the evidence may justify. I am concerned only with your perfectly definite, frank statement that you decline to take a step which the law provides. I am directing my mind solely to the indictment to which you plead guilty. You are entirely right. There can be no compromise. There can be neither compromise by you as the defendant, as you say, because you don't wish to compromise. Nor can there be compromise by the Court, which, for the moment, represents organized society as we understand it in this Republic. He who disobeys the law, knowing that he does so, with the intelligence that you possess, must, as you are prepared to—take the consequences. . . .

The case is one, from the standpoint of the penalty to be imposed, no different from that which has been imposed in many similar cases. The maximum penalty, as I understand it, is one year in the penitentiary. You have already spent twenty days in imprisonment. You ask for no compromise. You will get no compromise. You are sentenced to the penitentiary for eleven months and ten days.

Source: The Individual and the State: The Problem as Presented by the Sentencing of Roger N. Baldwin, November 1918, American Civil Liberties, 1918 National Civil Liberties Bureau folder, Swarthmore College Peace Collection, Swarthmore College Peace Library.

7.6.   The *Washington Post* Reports That a Sailor Wounded a Pageant Spectator Who Was Disrespectful to the Flag, May 7, 1919

As mass hysteria gripped the nation, vigilantes attacked pacifists, immigrants, radicals, and anyone who did not openly display loyalty to the United States. Tension remained at the war's end.

The following is a Washington Post *report of an American sailor
who got into an armed struggle with a man who refused to stand
and remove his hat during the playing of the "Star-Spangled Banner," at a victory loan Pageant. After an exchange of words, the
sailor shot the man.*

Chicago, May 6—Disrespect for the American flag and a show of resentment toward the thousands who participated in a victory loan pageant here tonight may cost George Goddard his life. He was shot down
by a sailor of the United States navy when he did not stand and remove
his hat while the band was playing the "Star-Spangled Banner."

Goddard had a seat of vantage in the open amphitheater. When he
failed to stand he was the most conspicuous figure among the throng.
When he fell at the report of the "sailor's" gun the crowd burst into
cheers and hand-clapping. When Goddard failed to respond to the first
strains of the national anthem Samuel Hagerman, sailor in the guard of
honor asked him to get up.

"What for?" demanded Goddard.

"Hagerman touched him with his bayonet."

"Get up. Off with your hat."

Goddard muttered and drew a pistol.

With military precision Hagerman stepped back a pace and slipped a
shell into his gun.

Goddard started away. As the last notes of the anthem sounded the
sailor commanded him to halt. Then he fired into the air.

"Halt!"

Goddard paid no attention.

The sailor aimed and fired three times. Goddard fell wounded. Each
shot found its mark.

When he [Goddard] was searched, an automatic pistol, in addition to
the one he had drawn, was found. Another pistol and fifty cartridges
were found in a bag he carried. He said he was a tinsmith, out of work.
Papers showed he had been at Vancouver and Seattle and it was believed
by the authorities he had come here for the I.W.W. convention.

Source: "Chicagoans Cheer Tar Who Shot Man," *Washington Post*, May 7, 1919,
p. 2.

7.7.   President Woodrow Wilson on Mob Violence, July 26, 1918

*Fearing social disorder in a divided nation, President Woodrow
Wilson pleaded with Americans not to give in to mob violence.*

*He also spoke out against lynchings, calling it "a blow at the heart
of ordered law and humane justice." The National Civil Liberties
Bureau reprinted Wilson's speech and distributed it throughout
the United States.*

My Fellow Countrymen:

I take the liberty of addressing you upon a subject which so vitally
affects the honor of the nation and the very character and integrity of
our institutions that I trust you will think me justified in speaking very
plainly about it.

I allude to the mob spirit which has recently here and there very frequently shown its head among us, not in any single region, but in many
and widely separated parts of the country. There have been many lynchings, and every one of them has been a blow at the heart of ordered law
and humane justice. No man who loves America, no man who really
cares for her fame and honor and character, or who is truly loyal to her
institutions, can justify mob action while the courts of justice are open
and the governments of the states and the nation are ready and able to
do their duty. We are at this very moment fighting lawless passion.

Germany has outlawed herself among the nations because she has dis-
regarded the sacred obligations of law and has made lynchers of her
armies. Lynchers emulate her disgraceful example. I, for my part, am
anxious to see every community in America rise above that level, with
pride and a fixed resolution which no man or set of men can afford to
despise.

We proudly claim to be the champions of democracy. If we really are,
in deed and in truth, let us see to it that we do not discredit our own. I
say plainly that every American who takes part in the action of a mob
or gives it any sort of countenance is no true son of this great democracy,
but its betrayer, and does more to discredit her by that single disloyalty
to her standards of law and right than the words of her statesmen or the
sacrifices of her heroic boys in the trenches can do to make suffering
peoples believe her to be their savior.

How shall we commend democracy to the acceptance of other peoples,
if we disgrace our own by providing that it is, after all, no protection to
the weak? Every mob contributes to German lies about the United States
what her most gifted liars cannot improve upon by the way of calumny.
They can at least say that such things cannot happen in Germany except
in times of revolution, when law is swept away.

I therefore very earnestly and solemnly beg that the Governors of all
the states, the law officers of every community, and, above all, the men
and women of every community in the United States, all who revere
America and wish to keep her name without stain or reproach, will co-
operate—not passively, merely, but actively and watchfully—to make

an end of this disgraceful evil. It cannot live where the community does not countenance it.

I have called upon the nation to put its great energy into this war and it has responded—responded with a spirit and genius for action that has thrilled the world. I now call upon it, upon its men and women everywhere, to see to it that its laws are kept inviolate, its fame untarnished. Let us show our utter contempt for the things that have made this war hideous among the wars of history by showing how those who love liberty and right and justice and are willing to lay down their lives for them upon foreign fields stand ready also to illustrate to all mankind their loyalty to the things at home which they wish to see established everywhere as a blessing and protection to the peoples who have never known the privileges of liberty and self-government.

I can never accept any man as a champion of liberty either for ourselves or for the world, who does not reverence and obey the laws of our own beloved land, whose laws we ourselves have made. He has adopted the standards of the enemies of his country, whom he affects to despise.

Woodrow Wilson
Reprinted by the National Civil Liberties Bureau

Source: "The President on Mob Violence," American Union against Militarism, July 26, 1918, Jane Addams Papers, American Peace Society, 1906–1928, Reel 43, Swarthmore College Peace Collection, Swarthmore College Peace Library.

ANNOTATED RESEARCH GUIDE

Books and Articles

Chambers, John Whiteclay, II. *To Raise an Army: The Draft Comes to Modern America*. New York: Free Press, 1987. Examines the history of the U.S. draft system. Much of the book focuses on the complexities of the World War I draft and includes an analysis of actions taken by critics, pacifists, and draft resisters.

Cottrell, Robert C. "Roger Nash Baldwin, The National Civil Liberties Bureau, and Military Intelligence during World War I." *Historian* 60 (1997): 87–106. Examines the U.S. Military Intelligence Division's investigation of Robert Baldwin, the director of the Civil Liberties Bureau. Baldwin worked to protect the rights of conscientious objectors, radicals, and other Americans during World War I.

DeBauche, Leslie Midkiff. *Reel Patriotism: The Movies and World War I*. Madison: University of Wisconsin Press, 1997. Analyzes the role of the American film industry during World War I, which worked closely with the U.S. government to promote patriotism.

Early, Frances H. "Feminism, Peace, and Civil Liberties: Women's Role in the Origins of the World War I Civil Liberties Movement." *Women's Studies*

18, nos. 2–3 (1990): 95–115. Discusses the work of the Bureau of Legal Advice, founded by women pacifists and suffragettes. The bureau, located in New York City, assisted conscientious objectors and also spoke out against the "enemy alien" status given to immigrants born in the Central Powers.

Ford, Nancy Gentile. *"Americans All!" Foreign-born Soldiers in World War I*. College Station: Texas A&M University Press, 2001. Although this book primarily focuses on immigrant soldiers who fought in the American army during World War I, it includes a chapter on home-front activities in ethnic communities in the United States and analyzes both the immigrants' patriotic efforts and their homeland objectives.

Higham, John. *Strangers in the Land: Patterns of American Nativism, 1860–1925*. New York: Atheneum, 1970. This classic work examines anti-immigrant sentiment and nativist fever that rose during the late nineteenth and early twentieth centuries. It includes two chapters on the "100 percent Americanism" and antiradicalism campaign prevalent during World War I.

Josephson, Harold, ed. *Biographical Dictionary of Modern Peace Leaders*. Westport, CT: Greenwood Press, 1985. Provides biographies of peace activists from 1800 to 1980.

Kennedy, David M. *Over Here: The First World War and American Society*. Oxford and New York: Oxford University Press, 1990. Presents a detailed account of the World War I home front, including the U.S. government's mobilization and propaganda efforts and the resulting mass hysteria.

Luebke, Frederick C. *Bonds of Loyalty: German-Americans and World War I*. De Kalb: Northern Illinois University Press, 1974. Discusses the experiences of German Americans during World War I.

Oukrop, Carol. "The Four Minute Men Became a National Network during World War I." *Journalism Quarterly* 52, no. 4 (1975): 632–637. Analyzes the role of the Committee on Public Information's Four Minute Men, who gave short patriotic speeches in motion-picture houses and at other public gatherings.

Rehnquist, William H. *All the Laws But One: Civil Liberties in Wartime*. New York: Vintage Books, 2000. Written by the chief justice of the United States, this book provides an overview of the history of civil liberties in America. Although most of the book focuses on the Civil War era, it includes a chapter on the threat to civil liberties found during World War I.

Walker, Samuel. *In Defense of American Liberties: A History of the ACLU*. New York: Oxford University Press, 1990. Provides a comprehensive history of the American Civil Liberties Union from World War I through the 1990s. Focuses on the ACLU's struggle to protect the civil liberties of Americans.

Zecker, Robert. "The Activities of Czech and Slovak Immigrants during World War I." *Ethnic Forum* 15, nos. 1–2 (1995): 35–54. Describes how Czech and Slovak Americans demonstrated their loyalty to America while supporting their homelands' fight for independence.

Video

The Great War and the Shaping of the 20th Century (PBS). Examines World War I from a military, political, social, and cultural perspective. Eight videos capture the words and images of the war. PBS Web site includes teacher resources, including interviews and maps. See PBS.org.

Web Site

http://www.lib.byu.edu. World War I Document Archives administered by Brigham Young University. Includes official government documents, memorials, photographs, maps, and personal reminiscences.

8

Hiroshima and Nagasaki: The Decision to Drop the Atomic Bomb in World War II

"Within four months we shall in all probability have completed the most terrible weapon ever known in human history, one bomb of which could destroy a whole city," wrote Secretary of War Henry L. Stimson to President Harry S. Truman on April 25, 1945.[1] On August 6, less than four months later, America's newest weapon, the atomic bomb, destroyed the Japanese city of Hiroshima with the force of more than "20,000 tons of T.N.T." The bomb hit with "more than two thousand times the blast power of the British 'Grand Slam' "—the largest bomb ever used in war to that date.[2] Hiroshima, a nine-mile-wide city, virtually disappeared. Three days later, the United States dropped another atomic bomb, this time on Nagasaki. Both bombs killed over 150,000 people and left hundreds of thousands struggling to survive. Japan soon surrendered. After World War II, America's brief period of atomic monopoly helped to fuel the emerging Cold War, but the nuclear arms race that followed threatened to put the two superpowers, the United States and the Soviet Union, on a direct path of mutual destruction. Ultimately, the development of this powerful weapon brought in a new era for humankind and unleashed a force that eventually had the potential of destroying not just a city, but civilization.

Even during the developmental stages of the atomic bomb, political leaders, military officials, and the nation's top scientists deliberated on how to use the new weapon. At the close of World War II, the debate over atomic energy took place in the U.S. Congress and in the United Nations as leaders struggled over the issue of international control. But in the end, the world had to settle for indistinct and incomplete attempts at nuclear arms limitations. Today, as in the decades since its deployment, historians ask, "Was it necessary to drop the atomic bomb?"

THE MANHATTAN PROJECT

In the late 1930s, with Europe embroiled in major turmoil, Japan saw an opportunity to accelerate the expansion of its power and influence throughout the Pacific, including encroaching into the European colonial empire in Asia. Tension mounted as the United States attempted to prevent the Japanese advancement through economic sanctions and military threats. When the United States entered World War II after the Japanese surprise attack on Pearl Harbor in December 1941, it quickly found itself fighting a two-front war. The U.S. military joined the British and Russian forces in Europe in their fight against Adolf Hitler, and American troops with British assistance did battle with the Japanese in the Pacific. Even after the Allies successfully defeated Hitler in the spring of 1945, the United States feared a protracted war in Asia. Therefore, at Yalta, the United States asked for help from the Soviet Union in ending the Asian conflict. The USSR agreed to remobilize its troops to the Asian border and to declare war on Japan by mid-August 1945.

Even before the United States entered World War II, President Franklin D. Roosevelt created the Office of Scientific Research and Development (OSRD) in 1941 and tasked it with the responsibility of creating new weapons. OSRD succeeded in bringing new equipment and medicine to the Allied forces in both Europe and Asia, including radar, sonar, rocket launchers, proximity fuses, blood plasma, and penicillin. Scientist Albert Einstein, a Jewish refugee from Hitler's terror, had previously cautioned the president that German physicists hoped to harness atomic energy into a weapon of mass destruction. In response, Roosevelt soon put scientists to work on developing the atomic bomb, and the Manhattan Project was born. General Leslie R. Groves headed the top-secret project, which drew together the preeminent scientists of the day from leading American and European universities and scientific organizations. Some 120,000 people worked on various elements of the project, and over the next three years, the U.S. government spent two billion dollars in thirty-seven different research facilities. Most employees did not know that their work was associated with the atomic bomb, especially since Grove compartmentalized the developmental stages to keep it top secret. Only the most prominent scientists involved in the project knew the ultimate goal. Perhaps at no other time in history did science and war connect in such a profound way.

THE TRUMAN ADMINISTRATION AND THE DECISION TO
DROP THE BOMB

Roosevelt's sudden death in April 1945 forced Vice President Harry S. Truman to assume a leadership position he was neither trained nor equipped to handle. In fact, Roosevelt had kept Truman in the dark about many military matters, perhaps the most important being the Manhattan Project. On April 25, Stimson briefed Truman and explained the progress of the atomic bomb. Truman then met with key political, military, and scientific leaders, privileged by knowledge of the Manhattan Project, to discuss future possibilities. These included the members of the Interim Committee, a top-secret advisory board. The committee consisted of Stimson (secretary of war), Ralph A. Bard (under secretary of the navy), William L. Clayton (assistant secretary of state), James F. Byrnes (soon to be appointed the new secretary of state), Vannevar Bush (director, OSRD), Karl T. Compton (Office of Field Service, OSRD), and James B. Conant (chairman, National Defense Research Committee). A special scientific panel attached to the committee included nuclear physicists J. Robert Oppenheimer, Arthur H. Compton, Ernest O. Lawrence, and Enrico Fermi. Two assistants to the secretary of war, George L. Harrison and Harvey H. Bundy, also played an important advisory role. In addition, Groves and George Marshall (army chief of staff) attended many of the meetings on the atomic bomb.

The Truman administration limited the options available in ending the war in Asia when it refused to accept anything less than Japan's unconditional surrender. Anticipating that an invasion might be necessary, the Joint Chiefs of Staff (JCS) directed General Douglas MacArthur to design a plan, code-named Olympic. The invasion, set for November 1, 1945, called for the involvement of some 400,000 troops and would require an enormous amphibious landing on the southernmost Japanese island of Kyushu. American military leaders feared that if the invasion became a reality, it could easily result in a bloody and prolonged military deadlock. U.S. intelligence, with access to enemy codes, warned that the Japanese military was actively fortifying Kyushu. This included mining the bays, evacuating civilians, and moving a number of Japanese military divisions into the area. Intelligence predicted that some 100,000 Japanese troops would be used as a counterinvasion force, with an additional 130,000 troops placed throughout Kyushu. American combatants had already experienced the determination and fortitude of Japanese soldiers on various Pacific islands, and American military leaders expected that the Japanese people would put up an even greater fight in defending their homeland.[3]

Truman and his advisors also discussed postwar diplomatic concerns. Although the Soviet Union and the United States fought in World War

II as allies, tension and mistrust isolated the two nations. In fact, Truman told key British officials about the atomic bomb, but he chose not to directly inform Soviet leader Joseph Stalin. Discussions that took place between Truman and his team of advisors also centered on the Soviets' future prospects for nuclear capability. Although scientists predicted that the USSR would have its own atomic bombs in three to four years, Groves insisted that it would more likely be twenty years. Groves argued that the Soviets did not have access to uranium, the key component of the bomb, especially since the United States was securing deposits around the world. But scientists found this notion unlikely. As the conflict against Germany came to a close, it became clear that the war had caused a serious shift in global power. European empires that for centuries had wielded enormous influence and authority now struggled just to survive. In their wake, the United States and the Soviet Union—with opposing political and economic systems—stood ready to fill the vacuum. Truman and his advisors recognized the importance of the atomic bomb in postwar foreign policy.

Scholars argue about how much influence the Interim Committee had on the final decision to drop the bomb. Most contend that the committee discussions deliberated on "how" to use the atomic bomb, not "if" the weapon should be used, since few connected with the Truman administration challenged the assumption that if the war continued, the bomb would be deployed once it was perfected. Nevertheless, on May 31, the group concluded that the atomic bomb should be used on Japan as soon as possible and without prior notice. On June 16, the Scientific Panel of the Interim Committee recommended that "not only Britain, but also Russia, France, and China be advised that we have made considerable progress in our work on atomic weapons." Arthur Compton, Lawrence, Oppenheimer, and Fermi also "welcome[d] suggestions as to how we can cooperate in making this development contribute to improved international relations." But while the panel acknowledged alternatives to dropping the bomb on Japan, such as a demonstration of the weapon's awesome power without loss of life, in the end it saw "no acceptable alternative to direct military use."[4] Later, Oppenheimer recalled, "We didn't know beans about the military situation in Japan. We didn't know whether they could be caused to surrender by other means or whether the invasion was really inevitable. But in [the] backs of our minds was the notion that the invasion was inevitable because we had been told that."[5]

As scientists worked feverishly on the new weapon, American planes continued their massive conventional bombing of Japan, successfully reducing a large number of cities to rubble. International law technically protected civilian populations from attack, but early in World War II, violations of this agreement led to strategic bombing raids by both sides over major cities in Europe and Asia. One of the worst raids took place against Tokyo, Japan. On March 9, 1945, Major General Curtis E. LeMay gave the order for American B-29s to drop two thousand tons of bombs on Tokyo during an incendiary-bombing raid. "In loss of life this was the most destructive air raid in history, without exception; it killed 83,793 people while injuring 40,918, destroying about a quarter of Tokyo's buildings and leaving more than a million homeless."[6] Other American bombing raids followed against Nagoya, Osaka, Kobe, and other cities and industrial sites in Japan. As the bombing of cities became common-place and the American military and society became inured to such high losses of civilian life, the use of the atomic bomb became even more acceptable. In a discussion between Byrnes and members of the Scientific Panel, "it was pointed out that the deaths resulting from dropping the bomb on a Japanese city 'would not be greater in order of magnitude than the number already killed in fire raids.' "[7]

ATOMIC SCIENTISTS AND THE DECISION TO DROP THE BOMB

Although the atomic bomb was originally planned as a defensive weapon against Hitler, the focus of its use shifted to Japan after the defeat of Germany in the spring of 1945. However, not everyone working on the Manhattan Project agreed on the new future of the bomb. Most of the scientists had joined the project in a race against Germany's top scientists and saw the creation of the new weapon as a defensive mea-sure, a counterforce to Hitler, who would surely drop an atomic bomb on the United States once it was in his arsenal. Since the European war ended before Germany's scientists completed their task, some OSRD sci-entists questioned the humanitarian consequences of using such a de-structive weapon as an aggressive measure.

In May 1945, scientists Leo Szilard, Harold Urey, and Walter Bartky tried to convince future Secretary of State James F. Byrnes that a staged demonstration of the bomb would be adequate to warn Japan of the deadly consequences of such power if it were used against them. De-ploying the bomb in a deserted area would save lives and still deliver an effective message. But they failed to persuade Byrnes. Next, Szilard and six other scientists working in the Metallurgical Laboratory at the University of Chicago formed the Committee on Political and Social Problems. This committee, led by Professor James Franck, sent a report to the secretary of war on June 11, 1945, noting that the "main motiva-tion" for building the bomb—the race against German nuclear scien-tists—no longer existed. Franck and his associates argued that "the military advantages and the saving of American lives achieved by the sud-den use of atomic bombs against Japan may be outweighed by the ensuing loss of confidence and by a wave of horror and repulsion sweeping over the rest of the world" if the bomb was dropped on the people of Japan.[8] Instead, the Franck report asked, why not demonstrate the new weapon to Japanese officials by exploding it on a deserted island? This would save both American and Japanese lives, but still bring an end to the war. The scientists also warned of an imminent nuclear arms race once the weapon was complete, cautioning that atomic energy could not stay "secret for an indefinite time."

The Franck Report's solution was to put the bomb under international control and declare a moratorium on nuclear weapons. But, the scientists warned, convincing the world to do this after dropping the bomb on Japan would be difficult. However, if the United States demonstrated the destructiveness of the bomb on an uninhabited island, America could later argue effectively for international control and a freeze on all future manufacture and development. The scientists asserted that the only way to "be diverted from a path which must lead to total mutual destruction" would be to establish an "international agreement barring a nuclear armament race."[9] Despite their convictions, these scientists had difficulty in getting both Stimson and Truman to hear their points of view.

A few key political and military leaders also spoke out against the planned use of the atomic bomb. Navy Under Secretary Bard asked the secretary of war to reconsider a surprise attack. Bard was a member of the Interim Committee, but broke ranks and questioned the committee's decision to drop the bomb without first warning Japan of its destructive nature. In his memo of June 27 to Stimson, Bard explained that "ever since I have been in touch with this program I have had a feeling that before the bomb is actually used against Japan that Japan should have some preliminary warning for say two or three days in advance of use." Bard advised that "the stakes [were] so tremendous," and he was sure that Japan was "searching for some opportunity which they could use as a medium of surrender."[10] Later, General Dwight Eisenhower claimed that when he had learned that the atomic bomb was finally ready to use on Japan, he had "protested vehemently that 'the Japanese were ready to surrender and it wasn't necessary to hit them with that awful thing.' "[11] A few years after the bomb was dropped, Admiral William D. Leahy also publicly questioned the use of the "barbarous" weapon."[12]

But most political and military leaders stood by their convictions that the atomic bomb would end the war quicker than conventional methods and allow America to avoid the costly invasion of Japan. Furthermore, with only two bombs available, they refused to consider using one as a demonstration, particularly fearing the ramifications of a failed explosion during such a display. The atomic bomb, the leaders argued, could save American and Japanese lives, and the plan was to drop the bomb on "purely military targets."

DROPPING "THE MOST TERRIBLE BOMB"

At the break of dawn on July 16, 1945, OSRD scientists tested the first atomic bomb near Alamogordo, New Mexico. Scientist E.O. Lawrence described the event as he got out of his car: "Just as I put my foot on the ground I was enveloped with a warm brilliant yellow white light—from darkness to brilliant sunshine in an instant, and as I remember I momentarily was stunned by the surprise.... Through my dark sun glasses there was a gigantic ball of fire rising rapidly from the earth—at first as brilliant as the sun, growing less brilliant as it grew boiling and swirling into the heavens."[13] It was now just a matter of time until this imposing force would be released on the world.

In another petition sent to the president on July 17, 1945, sixty-nine Chicago scientists, led by Leo Szilard, involved in the Manhattan Project asked Truman to rethink using the bomb on Japan and to consider the moral obligations of restraint. Once this destructive power was released, they warned, "it would then be more difficult for us to live up to our responsibility of bringing the unloosened forces of destruction under control."[14] It is believed that the petition, given to Groves (July 25) and Stimson (August 1) in Washington, D.C., was never seen by the president, who "was about to leave Europe on the return voyage home from Potsdam."[15]

Just over a week after the test, on July 25, President Truman officially gave the directive to drop the first atomic bomb as soon as weather permitted. That night, writing in his diary, Truman called the new weapon "the most terrible bomb in the history of the world," with the destructive force "prophesied in the Euphrates Valley Era, after Noah and his fabulous Ark." Truman also noted that "military objectives and soldiers and sailors are the target and not women and children."[16] Yet, according to the bombing order, the targets chosen included Hiroshima, Kokura, Niigata, and Nagasaki, all major cities populated with civilian men, women, and children; none were "purely military targets." Kyoto was dropped from the original list, despite the city's military activities, because it held great cultural significance for the Japanese people, and any destruction of it would no doubt galvanize Japanese resistance and make any postwar accommodations difficult if not impossible. Once the political decision was made, the directive was turned over to the military for execution.

On August 6, 1945, the first atomic bomb exploded in Hiroshima. In reality, the atomic bomb was very different from conventional weapons, and its destructive force was unmatched in human history. Temperatures in the fireball exceeded fifty million degrees Fahrenheit, and those closest to the explosion virtually disintegrated. One bomb instantly killed some 80,000 people, left tens of thousands more seriously injured, and destroyed over a quarter of a million homes. Within the year, 60,000 more died from the effects of the bomb, many from the radiation. Three days later, another atomic bomb destroyed Nagasaki. Michihiko Hachiya, a Japanese physician, recorded his experiences in his *Hiroshima Diary*:

> Suddenly, a strong flash of light startled me—and then another. . . . All over the right side of my body I was cut and bleeding. A large splinter was protruding from a mangled wound in my thigh, and something warm trickled into my mouth. My cheek was torn. . . . Embedded in my neck was a sizable fragment of glass. . . . Getting to my feet, I discovered that I had tripped over a man's head. . . . Fires sprang up and whipped by a vicious wind began to spread. . . . It was all a nightmare.[17]

Nagasaki survivor Tatsue Urata described a Nagasaki victim. "The skin was peeling off his face and chest and hands. He was black all over . . . his whole body was coated with it and the blood trickling from his wounds made red streaks in the black."[18] In a brilliant flash of light, "the most terrible bomb in the history of the world" had ushered in a new and terrifying era for mankind.

THE DEBATE CONTINUES

In 1946, nuclear policy advisor James B. Conant asked Karl Compton and Stimson to write articles explaining why the United States had dropped the atomic bomb. Compton's *Atlantic Monthly* article argued "with complete conviction, that the use of the atomic bomb saved hundreds of thousands—perhaps several millions—of lives, both American and Japanese; that without its use the war would have continued for many months."[19] In his *Harper's Magazine* article, Stimson concurred: "*As long as the Japanese government refused to surrender*, we should be forced to take and hold the ground, and smash the Japanese ground armies, by close-in fighting of the same desperate and costly kind that we had faced in the Pacific islands for nearly four years."[20]

The debate over whether the United States should have dropped the atomic bomb continues today. Traditional scholars argue that the atomic bomb was a military necessity and conclude that Truman made the right decision. They agree with the conclusion of Compton and Stimson and maintain that this powerful weapon was necessary to end the war quickly and to save American lives. One only had to look at the difficult military engagements in the Pacific theater, such as in Okinawa, for proof that the Japanese would hold firm in an invasion of their country. According to military historian Edward J. Drea, "Japan's military leaders seemed determined to go down fighting and take as many Americans with them as possible."[21] Official and popular estimates of the number of Americans who would have died in the invasion of Japan ranged from some thirty thousand to one million, but this group of scholars argues that any American deaths in an amphibious landing would have been unacceptable. They ask, would American mothers forgive the U.S. government for not using all weapons in its arsenal if their sons died on the shores of Kyushu? Could the U.S. government justify spending two billion dollars on the weapon's development and then not use the perfected bomb? Traditionalists also contend that the atomic bomb was a natural extension of the regularly conducted conventional bombing, which took tens of thousands of lives. Traditionalists assert that a demonstration of the bomb in a deserted area might have led to a political disaster if the bomb failed to explode. Furthermore, the U.S. weapon supply was very limited. Finally, the historians argue that military hard-liners in Japan ignored the emperor's pleas to surrender until the United States dropped the atomic bombs. Since World War II ended shortly after the United States dropped the second bomb on Japan, a perceived assumption that the bomb brought an immediate peace is ingrained in the popular belief system—an assumption that is difficult to challenge.

Revisionist scholars argue that the atomic bomb was not necessary to end the war in the Pacific. Prior to this, Japan was clearly in a grim situation and for all purposes was a defeated nation. In June 1945, Japanese leaders asked the Soviet Union to negotiate peace. American leaders should have modified their conditions and pursued other alternatives to unconditional surrender, such as allowing the Japanese to retain their emperor. Many revisionists would agree with Admiral William D. Leahy, who concluded, "It is my opinion that the use of this barbarous weapon at Hiroshima and Nagasaki was of no material assistance in our war against Japan. The Japanese were already defeated and ready to surrender. . . . Being the first to use it, we had adopted an ethical standard, common to the barbarians of the Dark Ages. I was not taught to make war in that fashion, and wars cannot be won by destroying women and children."[22] In the end, the United States did modify the terms of unconditional surrender by allowing Japan to maintain its emperor, albeit now as a symbolic rather than a real political leader. Many also argue that despite the risks of failure, demonstrating the bomb to Japanese military leaders would most likely have led to a quick end of the war without the cost of so many Japanese civilian lives. Some historians contend that Truman's advisors never debated whether or not to use the atomic bomb, but simply assumed that they would use it once it was complete. It was only later that the advisors provided the public with specific reasons for its use in an effort to stifle growing discontent. Thus policymakers sought out government-sponsored public releases (such as the ones by Compton and Stimson) to justify unleashing such a destructive power into the world.

Other revisionists argue that the rising Cold War played a key role in the decision to drop the bomb. Truman used the bomb as a diplomatic weapon in an effort to warn the Soviets that the United States would be a formidable enemy in the future. The mid-August date of the Russian agreement to enter the war against Japan was approaching quickly. The Soviet invasion of Manchuria already had pushed Japan toward surrender, and many revisionists contend that a Soviet war against Japan would have quickly shaken the enemy into giving up their fight. Therefore, the bomb allowed America to end the Japanese war before the USSR officially entered the conflict and intentionally blocked the Soviet Union from making key postwar demands in Asia, and it also warned the Soviets against aggression in Europe. Even before the close of the war with Germany, the Soviet Union and the United States did not completely agree on Stalin's desire to control the Soviet Union's border states as a method of defense. In a 1960 interview, Leo Szilard explained the connection between the atomic bomb and the USSR: "Byrnes was concerned about Russia's having taken over Poland, Rumania and Hungary, and so was I. Byrnes thought that the possession of the bomb by America would render the Russians more manageable in Europe. I failed to see how sitting on a stockpile of bombs, which in the circumstances we could not possibly use, would have this effect, and I thought it even conceivable that it would have the opposite effect."[23]

CONCLUSION

At the war's end, many atomic scientists renewed their efforts to secure an international system of nuclear control and gave radio addresses, visited community groups, participated in school assemblies, and presented public lectures, all to educate the public on their ideas of nuclear disarmament. In 1946, the Chicago team created the journal *Bulletin of the Atomic Scientists* "in an effort to prevent nuclear disasters." Einstein stood with his fellow scientists in their efforts. Burdened by his part in putting the atomic bomb in motion, Einstein later called the letter he wrote Roosevelt the one "great mistake in my life." Oppenheimer also lamented the "blood" on his hands, concluding that he and his fellow physicists "have known sin" for their part in the weapon's development.[24] Despite the hard work, the scientists failed in their efforts to put the atomic bomb under international control. Some scientists even became targets of Cold War hysteria and the radical purges of the 1950s, accused of aiding the Soviet Union in its atomic bomb development. But just as the Manhattan Project scientists had predicted, America's atomic monopoly was short lived. In 1949, the Soviet Union successfully tested its own nuclear weapon, and an arms race of epic proportions followed.

Historians will no doubt continue their debate over the decision to drop the atomic bomb, and the answer may never be crystal clear. What is clear is that the new weapon had a profound effect on the future of the United States, and the bomb's impact on the political, economic, and military affairs of the country is a landmark event. The atomic bomb helped to escalate the Cold War, fuel an already-rabid anti-Communist scare, and force an unprecedented weapons buildup. The new weapon technology and the subsequent nuclear arms race helped to give birth to the military-industrial complex, which dominated the economy for decades to come. Acute fear of the Soviet Union created a new emphasis on civil defense, and fallout shelters and air-raid drills became commonplace. Perhaps most important, the atomic bomb changed the nature of warfare. With the impending fear of nuclear annihilation, future wars would be fought for limited objectives, for balance, not victory, and the Korean and Vietnam conflicts would be defined by that fateful day in August 1945 when the United States dropped the atomic bomb on Japan.

After witnessing the testing of the first atomic bomb, scientist Ernest O. Lawrence concluded, "We have this day crossed a great milestone in human progress." J. Robert Oppenheimer had a different reaction to the demonstration as he remembered the line from the Hindu Scripture, "Now I am become Death, the destroyer of worlds."[25] The unleashing of atomic energy forever transformed the future, and its significance is still unknown—human progress or the destroyer of worlds?

NOTES

1. "Henry L. Stimson's Memorandum Discussed with President Truman, April 25, 1945," in *The Atomic Bomb over Japan: Development, Decisions, & Delivery*, Pamphlet no. 7 (Sandia Base, Albuquerque: Field Command AFSWP, 1974), p. 6. In the collection of the U.S. Army Military History Institute, Carlisle Barracks, Carlisle, Pennsylvania.

2. "Statement by the President Announcing the Use of the A-Bomb at Hiroshima, August 6, 1945," *Public Papers of the Presidents of the United States: Harry S. Truman: Containing the Public Messages, Speeches, and Statements of the President, April 12 to December 31, 1945* (Washington, DC: U.S. Government Printing Office, 1961), p. 197.

3. Edward J. Drea, "Previews of Hell," *MHQ: The Quarterly Journal of Military History* 7, no. 3 (Spring 1995): 74–81.

4. "Recommendations on the Immediate Use of Nuclear Weapons, by the Scientific Panel of the Interim Committee on Nuclear Power, June 16, 1945," Records of the Office of the Chief of Engineers, Manhattan Engineering District, Harrison-Bundy Files Record Group 77, Folder 76, National Archives.

5. Gar Alperovitz, *The Decision to Use the Atomic Bomb* (New York: Vintage Books, 1996), p. 165.

6. Russell F. Weigley, *The American Way of War: A History of United States Military Strategy and Policy* (New York: Macmillan, 1977), p. 364.

7. Alperovitz, *The Decision to Use the Atomic Bomb*, p. 164.

8. "A Report to the Secretary of War, June 1945," *Bulletin of the Atomic Scientists*, vol. 1, no. 10 (May 1, 1964): 3.

9. Ibid., p. 2.

10. Ralph A. Bard, "Memorandum on the Use of S-1 Bomb," June 27, 1945, Records of the Chief of Engineers, Manhattan Engineering District, Harrison-Bundy Files Record Group, Folder 77, Roll 6, M1108, National Archives.

11. Robert James Maddox, "The Biggest Decision: Why We Had to Drop the Atomic Bomb," in *Taking Sides: Clashing Views on Controversial Issues in American History since 1945*, ed. Larry Madaras (Guilford, CT: McGraw-Hill/Dushkin, 2001), p. 8. Maddox questions this statement and thinks that Eisenhower's "recollections grew more colorful as the years went on."

12. Gar Alperovitz, *The Decision to Use the Atomic Bomb*, p. 326.

13. "Thoughts by E.O. Lawrence," in *The Atomic Bomb, 1942–1945: Reproductions of Some of the Critical Documents Pertaining to the Development and Use of the Atomic Bomb*, p. 1. Papers of Leslie R. Groves, Jr., in the collection of the U.S. Army Military History Institute, Carlisle Barracks, Carlisle, PA.

14. Members of the Metallurgical Laboratory, Chicago, "A Petition to the President of the United States," July 17, 1945, Records of the Chief of Engineers, Manhattan Engineering District, Harrison-Bundy Files Record Group 77, Folder 76, Roll 6, M1108, National Archives.

15. Alperovitz, *The Decision to Use the Atomic Bomb*, p. 191.

16. Truman's diary from the Secretary's File, Truman Library. Available online from the Truman Library Web site: http://www.trumanlibrary.org.

17. Michihiko Hachiya, M.D., *Hiroshima Diary: the Journal of a Japanese Physician*, August 6–September 30, 1945 (Chapel Hill: University of North Carolina Press, 1955), pp. 1–3.

18. Allan M. Winkler, *Life under a Cloud: American Anxiety about the Atom* (New York: Oxford University Press, 1993), p. 23.

19. Karl T. Compton, "If the Atomic Bomb Had Not Been Used," *Atlantic Monthly* 178 (December 1946): 54–56.

20. Henry L. Stimson's Memorandum Discussed with President Truman, April 25, 1945, *The Atomic Bomb over Japan*, p. 6.

21. J. Drea, "Previews of Hell," p. 75.

22. Alperovitz, *The Decision to Use the Atomic Bomb*, p. 3.

23. "President Truman Did Not Understand," *U.S. News and World Report*, August 15, 1960, p. 69.

24. Winkler, *Life under a Cloud*, pp. 36–38.

25. "Thoughts by E.O. Lawrence," p. 2.

DOCUMENTS

8.1. Henry L. Stimson's Memorandum to President Truman on the Atomic Bomb, April 25, 1945

After Franklin D. Roosevelt's sudden death in April 1945, Secretary of War Henry L. Stimson informed Roosevelt's vice president, now president, Harry S. Truman, about the development of the atomic bomb. The following is an excerpt from Stimson's memorandum.

Within four months we shall in all probability have completed the most terrible weapon ever known in human history, one bomb of which could destroy a whole city. Although we have shared its development with the U.K., physically the U.S. is at present in the position of controlling the resources with which to construct and use it and no other nation could reach this position for some years. Nevertheless it is practically certain that we could not remain in this position indefinitely.

a. Various segments of its discovery and production are widely known among many scientists in many countries, although few scientists are now acquainted with the whole process which we have developed.

b. Although its construction under present methods requires great scientific and industrial effort and raw materials, which are temporarily mainly within the possession and knowledge of U.S. and U.K., it is extremely probable that much easier and cheaper methods of production will be discovered by scientists in the future, together with the use of materials of much wider distribution. As a result, it is extremely probable that the future will make it possible for atomic bombs to be constructed by smaller nations or even groups, or at least by a larger nation in a much shorter time.

As a result, it is indicated that the future may see a time when such a weapon may be constructed in secret and used suddenly and effectively with devastating power by a willful nation or group against an unsuspecting nation or group of much greater size and material power. With its aid even a very powerful unsuspecting nation might be conquered within a very few days by a very much smaller one. . . .

The world in its present state of moral advancement compared with its technical development would be eventually at the mercy of such a weapon. In other words, modern civilization might be completely destroyed.

To approach any world peace organization of any pattern now likely to be considered, without an appreciation by the leaders of our country of the power of this new weapon, would seem to be unrealistic. No system of control heretofore considered would be adequate to control this menace. Both inside any particular country and between the nations of the world, the control of this weapon will undoubtedly be a matter of the greatest difficulty and would involve such thorough going rights of inspection and internal controls as we have never heretofore contemplated.

Furthermore, in the light of our present position with reference to this weapon, the question of sharing it with other nations and, if so shared, upon what terms, becomes a primary question of our foreign relations. Also our leadership in the war and in the development of this weapon has placed a certain moral responsibility upon us which we cannot shirk without very serious responsibility for any disaster to civilization which it would further.

On the other hand, if the problem of the proper use of this weapon can be solved, we would have the opportunity to bring the world into a pattern in which the peace of the world and our civilization can be saved.

Source: Henry L. Stimson's Memorandum Discussed with President Truman, April 25, 1945, *The Atomic Bomb over Japan: Development, Decisions, and Delivery*, Pamphlet no. 7 (Sandia Base, Albuquerque: Field Command AFSWP, 1947). In the collection of the U.S. Army Military History Institute, Carlisle Barracks, Carlisle, Pennsylvania.

8.2.   The Franck Report on the Use of the Atomic Bomb, June 11, 1945

Atomic scientists James Franck (chairman), Donald J. Hughes, J.J. Nickson, Eugene Rabinowitch, Glenn T. Seaborg, J.C. Stearns, and Leo Szilard formed the Committee on Political and Social Problems, which submitted a report to the secretary of war objecting to dropping the atomic bomb on Japan without warning.

We found ourselves, by the force of events, during the last five years, in the position of a small group of citizens cognizant of a grave danger for the safety of this country as well as for the future of all other nations, of which the rest of mankind is unaware. We therefore feel it our duty to urge that the political problems, arising from the mastering of nuclear power, be recognized in all their gravity, and that appropriate steps be taken for their study and the preparation of necessary decisions. . . . In the past, science has often been able to provide also new methods of protection against new weapons of aggression it made possible, but it cannot promise such efficient protection against the destructive use of nuclear power. . . . In the absence of an international authority which would make all resort to force in international conflicts impossible, nations could still be diverted from a path which must lead to total mutual destruction, by a specific international agreement barring a nuclear armament race. . . .

It is true that some irrational element in mass psychology makes gas poisoning more revolting than blasting by explosives, even though gas warfare is in no way more "inhuman" than the war of bombs and bullets. Nevertheless, it is not at all certain that American public opinion, if it could be enlightened as to the effect of atomic explosives, would approve of our own country being the first to introduce such an indiscriminate method of wholesale destruction of civilian life.

Thus, from the "optimistic" point of view—looking forward to an international agreement on the prevention of nuclear warfare—the military advantages and the saving of American lives achieved by the sudden use of atomic bombs against Japan may be outweighed by the ensuing loss of confidence and by a wave of horror and repulsion sweeping over the rest of the world and perhaps even dividing public opinion at home.

From this point of view, a demonstration of the new weapon might best be made, before the eyes of representatives of all the United Nations, on the desert or a barren island. The best possible atmosphere for the achievement of an international agreement could be achieved if America could say to the world, "you see what sort of a weapon we have but did not use. We are ready to renounce its use in the future if other nations join us in this renunciation and agree to the establishment of an efficient international control."

After such a demonstration, the weapon might perhaps be used against Japan if the sanction of the United Nations (and of public opinion at home) were obtained, perhaps after a preliminary ultimatum to Japan to surrender or at least to evacuate certain regions as an alternative to their total destruction. This may sound fantastic, but in nuclear weapons we have something entirely new in order of magnitude of destructive power, and if we want to capitalize fully on the advantage their possession gives us, we must use new and imaginative methods.

James Franck (Chairman), Donald J. Hughes, J.J. Nickson,
Eugene Rabinowitch, Glenn T. Seaborg, J.C. Stearns, Leo Szilard

Source: Franck Report reprinted in "A Report to the Secretary of War, June 1945," *Bulletin of the Atomic Scientists* 1, no. 10 May 1, 1946, pp. 1–5.

8.3. The Scientific Panel of the Interim Committee Recommends the Immediate Use of Nuclear Weapons, June 16, 1945

The special Scientific Panel attached to the Interim Committee on Nuclear Power recommended "direct military use" of the atomic bomb. The following is a reprint of the report from the panel, which included scientists J.R. Oppenheimer, A.H. Compton, E.O. Lawrence, and E. Fermi.

You have asked us to comment on the initial use of the new weapon. This use, in our opinion, should be such as to promote a satisfactory adjustment of our international relations. At the same time, we recognize our obligation to our nation to use the weapons to help save American lives in the Japanese War.

(1) To accomplish these ends we recommend that before the weapons are used not only Britain, but also Russia, France, and China be advised that we have made considerable progress in our work on atomic weapons, that these may be ready to use during the present war, and that we would welcome suggestions as to how we can cooperate in making this development contribute to improved international relations.

(2) The opinions of our scientific colleagues on the initial use of these weapons are not unanimous: they range from the proposals of a purely technical demonstration to that of the military application best designed to induce surrender. Those who advocate a purely technical demonstration would wish to outlaw the use of atomic weapons, and have feared that if we use the weapons now our position in future negotiations will be prejudiced. Others emphasize the opportunity of saving American lives by immediate military use, and believe that such use will improve the international prospects, in that they are more concerned with the prevention of war than with the elimination of this specific weapon. We find ourselves closer to these latter views; we can propose no technical demonstration likely to begin an end to the war; we see no acceptable alternative to direct military use.

(3) With regard to these general aspects of the use of atomic energy, it is clear that we, as scientific men, have no proprietary rights. It is true that we are among the few citizens who have had occasion to give thoughtful consideration to these problems during the past few years. We have, however, no claim to special competence in solving the political, social, and military problems which are presented by the advent of atomic power.

J.R. Oppenheimer, A.H. Compton, E.O. Lawrence, E. Fermi
June 16, 1945
For the Panel

Source: "Recommendations on the Immediate Use of Nuclear Weapons, by the Scientific Panel of the Interim Committee on Nuclear Power, June 16, 1945," Records of the Office of the Chief of Engineers, Manhattan Engineering District, Harrison Bundy Files Record Group 77, Folder 76, National Archives.

8.4. Memorandum by Under Secretary of the Navy Ralph A. Bard to Secretary of War Henry L. Stimson on the Use of the Atomic Bomb, June 27, 1945

In June 1945, Under Secretary of the Navy Ralph A. Bard, a member of Truman's Interim Committee, wrote to Secretary of War Henry L. Stimson suggesting that the United States should consider an alternative to dropping the atomic bomb on Japan.

SECRET—TOP SECRET—SECRET

MEMORANDUM ON THE USE OF S-1 BOMB:

Ever since I have been in touch with this program I have had a feeling that before the bomb is actually used against Japan that Japan should have some preliminary warning for say two or three days in advance of use. The position of the United States as a great humanitarian nation and the fair play attitude of our people generally is responsible in the main for this feeling.

During recent weeks I have also had the feeling very definitely that the Japanese government may be searching for some opportunity which they could use as a medium of surrender. Following the three-power conference emissaries from this country could contact representatives from Japan somewhere on the China Coast and make representations with regard to Russia's position and at the same time give them some information regarding the proposed use of atomic power, together with whatever assurances the President might care to make with regard to the Emperor of Japan and the treatment of the Japanese nation following unconditional surrender. It seems quite possible to me that this presents the opportunity which the Japanese are looking for.

I don't see that we have anything in particular to lose in following such a program. The stakes are so tremendous that it is my opinion [that] very real consideration should be given to some plan of this kind. I do not believe under present circumstances existing that there is anyone in this country whose evaluation of the chances of the success of such a program is worth a great deal. The only way to find out is to try it out.

Ralph A. Bard
27 June 1945

Source: Ralph A. Bard, "Memorandum on the Use of S-1 Bomb," June 27, 1945, Records of the Chief of Engineers, Manhattan Engineering District, Harrison-Bundy File Record Group 77, Folder 77, M1108, National Archives.

8.5.   Scientists Petition the President of the United States Not to Use the Atomic Bomb Unless the Japanese Refuse to Surrender, July 17, 1945

In July 1945, Leo Szilard and sixty-eight other scientists from the Metallurgical Laboratory at the University of Chicago sent a petition asking the president not to use the atomic bomb unless surrender terms were clearly explained to the Japanese and all other alternatives failed. It is believed that the petition, given to Groves (July 25) and Henry L. Stimson (August 1) in Washington, D.C., was never seen by the president, who "was about to leave Europe on the return voyage home from Potsdam."

Discoveries of which the people of the United States are not aware may affect the welfare of this nation in the near future. The liberation of atomic power which has been achieved places atomic bombs in the hands of the Army. It places in your hands, as Commander-in-Chief, the fateful decision whether or not to sanction the use of such bombs in the present phase of the war against Japan.

We, the undersigned scientists, have been working in the field of atomic power. Until recently we have had to fear that the United States might be attacked by atomic bombs during this war and that her only defense might lie in a counterattack by the same means. Today, with the defeat of Germany, this danger is averted and we feel impelled to say what follows:

The war has to be brought speedily to a successful conclusion and attacks by atomic bombs may very well be an effective method of warfare. We feel, however, that such attacks on Japan could not be justified, at least not until the terms which will be imposed after the war on Japan were made public in detail and Japan were given an opportunity to surrender.

If such public announcement gave assurance to the Japanese that they could look forward to a life devoted to peaceful pursuits in their homeland and if Japan still refused to surrender our nation might then, in certain circumstances, find itself forced to resort to the use of atomic bombs. Such a step, however, ought not to be made at any time without seriously considering the moral responsibilities which are involved.

The development of atomic power will provide the nations with new means of destruction. The atomic bombs at our disposal represent only the first step in this direction, and there is almost no limit to the destructive power which will become available in the course of their future development. Thus a nation which sets the precedent of using these newly liberated forces of nature for purposes of destruction may have to bear the responsibility of opening the door to an era of devastation on an unimaginable scale.

If after this war a situation is allowed to develop in the world which permits rival powers to be in uncontrolled possession of these new means of destruction, the cities of the United States as well as the cities of other nations will be in continuous danger of sudden annihilation. All the resources of the United States, moral and material, may have to be mobilized to prevent the advent of such a world situation. Its prevention is at present the solemn responsibility of the United States—singled out by virtue of her lead in the field of atomic power.

The added material strength which this lead gives to the United States brings with it the obligation of restraint and if we were to violate this obligation our moral position would be weakened in the eyes of the world and in our own eyes. It would then be more difficult for us to live up to our responsibility of bringing the unloosened forces of destruction under control.

In view of the foregoing, we, the undersigned, respectfully petition: first, that you exercise your power as Commander-in-Chief to rule that the United States shall not resort to the use of atomic bombs in this war unless the terms which will be imposed upon Japan have been made public in detail and Japan knowing these terms has refused to surrender; second, that in such an event the question whether or not to use atomic bombs be decided by you in the light of the considerations presented in this petition as well as all the other moral responsibilities which are involved.

Signed by Sixty-nine Scientists.

Source: Members of the Metallurgical Laboratory, Chicago, "Petition to the President of the United States," July 17, 1945, Records of the Chief of Engineers, Manhattan Engineering District, Harrison-Bundy File Record Group 77, Folder 76, Roll 6, M1108, National Archives.

8.6.   Statement by President Harry S. Truman Announcing the Use of the Atomic Bomb at Hiroshima, August 6, 1945

On August 6, 1945, President Harry S. Truman announced to the American public that the United States had dropped an atomic bomb on Hiroshima. Although the president described Hiroshima as "an important Japanese Army base," it was also a city filled with hundreds of thousands of civilians.

Sixteen hours ago an American airplane dropped one bomb on Hiro-shima, an important Japanese Army base. That bomb had more power than 20,000 tons of T.N.T. It had more than two thousand times the blast power of the British "Grand Slam" which is the largest bomb ever yet used in the history of warfare.

The Japanese began the war from the air at Pearl Harbor. They have been repaid many fold. And the end is not yet. With this bomb we have now added a new and revolutionary increase in destruction to supple-ment the growing power of our armed forces. In their present form these bombs are now in production and even more powerful forms are in development.

It is an atomic bomb. It is a harnessing of the basic power of the universe. The force from which the sun draws its power has been loosed against those who brought war to the Far East.

Before 1939, it was the accepted belief of scientists that it was theoret-ically possible to release atomic energy. But no one knew any practical method of doing it. By 1942, however, we knew that the Germans were working feverishly to find a way to add atomic energy to the other en-gines of war with which they hoped to enslave the world. But they failed. We may be grateful to Providence that the Germans got the V-1's and V-2's late and in limited quantities and even more grateful that they did not get the atomic bomb at all.

The battle of the laboratories held fateful risks for us as well as the battles of the air, land and sea, and we have now won the battle of the laboratories as we have won the other battles. . . .

We are now prepared to obliterate more rapidly and completely every productive enterprise the Japanese have above ground in any city. We shall destroy their docks, their factories, and their communications. Let there be no mistake; we shall completely destroy Japan's power to make war.

It was to spare the Japanese people from utter destruction that the ultimatum of July 26 was issued at Potsdam. Their leaders promptly rejected that ultimatum. If they do not now accept our terms they may expect a rain of ruin from the air, the like of which has never been seen on this earth. Behind this air attack will follow sea and land forces in such numbers and power as they have not yet seen and with the fighting skill of which they are already well aware. . . .

The fact we can release atomic energy ushers in a new era in man's understanding of nature's forces. Atomic energy may in the future sup-plement the power that now comes from coal, oil, and falling water, but at present it cannot be produced on a basis to compete with them com-mercially. Before that comes there must be a long period of intensive research.

It has never been the habit of the scientists of this country or the policy of this Government to withhold from the world scientific knowledge. Normally, therefore, everything about the work with atomic energy would be made public.

But under present circumstances it is not intended to divulge the technical processes of production or all the military applications, pending further examination of possible methods of protecting us and the rest of the world from the danger of sudden destruction.

I shall recommend that the Congress of the United States consider promptly the establishment of an appropriate commission to control the production and use of atomic power within the United States. I shall give further consideration and make further recommendations to the Congress as to how atomic power can become a powerful and forceful influence towards the maintenance of world peace.

Source: "Statement by the President Announcing the Use of the A-Bomb at Hiroshima, August 6, 1945," *Public Papers of the Presidents of the United States: Harry S. Truman: Containing the Public Messages, Speeches, and Statements of the President, April 12 to December 31, 1945* (Washington, DC: U.S. Government Printing Office, 1961), pp. 197–200.

8.7.   The Hiroshima Diary of Doctor Michihiko Hachiya, August 6, 1945

Dr. Michihiko Hachiya recorded the experiences of his family and friends after the United States dropped the atomic bomb on Hiroshima. The following is an excerpt from his diary of August 6, 1945.

The hour was early; the morning still, warm, and beautiful. Shimmering leaves, reflecting sunlight from a cloudless sky, made a pleasant contrast with shadows in my garden as I gazed absently through wide-flung doors opening to the south.

Clad in drawers and undershirt, I was sprawled on the living room floor exhausted because I had just spent a sleepless night on duty as an air warden in my hospital.

Suddenly, a strong flash of light startled me—and then another. So well does one recall little things that I remember vividly how a stone lantern in the garden became brilliantly lit and I debated whether this light was caused by a magnesium flare or sparks from a passing trolley.

Garden shadows disappeared. The view where a moment before all had been so bright and sunny was now dark and hazy. Through swirling dust I could barely discern a wooden column that had supported one corner of my house. It was leaning crazily and the roof sagged dangerously. . . .

What had happened?

All over the right side of my body I was cut and bleeding. A large splinter was protruding from a mangled wound in my thigh, and something warm trickled into my mouth. My cheek was torn, I discovered as I felt it gingerly, with the lower lip laid wide open. Embedded in my neck was a sizable fragment of glass which I matter-of-factly dislodged, and with the detachment of one stunned and shocked I studied it and my blood-stained hand.

Where was my wife? Suddenly thoroughly alarmed, I began to yell for her: "Yaeko-san! Yaeko-san! Where are you?"

Blood began to spurt. Had my carotid artery been cut? Would I bleed to death? Frightened and irrational, I called out again: "It's a five-hundred-ton bomb! Yaeko-san, where are you? A five-hundred-ton bomb has fallen!"

Yaeko-san, pale and frightened, her clothes torn and bloodstained, emerged from the ruins of our house holding her elbow. Seeing her, I was reassured. My own panic assuaged, I tried to reassure her. "We'll be all right," I exclaimed. "Only let's get out of here as fast as we can."

She nodded, and I motioned for her to follow me.

The shortest path to the street lay through the house next door so through the house we went—running, stumbling, falling, and then running again until in headlong flight we tripped over something and fell sprawling into the street. Getting to my feet, I discovered that I had tripped over a man's head. "Excuse me! Excuse me, please!" I cried hysterically. There was no answer. The man was dead. The head had belonged to a young officer whose body was crushed beneath a massive gate.

We stood in the street, uncertain and afraid, until a house across from us began to sway and then with a rending motion fell almost at our feet. Our own house began to sway, and in a minute it, too, collapsed in a cloud of dust. Other buildings caved in or toppled. Fires sprang up and whipped by a vicious wind began to spread. . . .

Our progress towards the hospital was interminably slow, until finally, my legs, stiff from drying blood, refused to carry me farther. The strength, even the will, to go on deserted me, so I told my wife, who was almost as badly hurt as I, to go on alone. This she objected to, but there was no choice. She had to go ahead and try to find someone to come back for me.

Yaeko-san looked into my face for a moment, and then, without saying a word, turned away and began running towards the hospital. Once, she looked back and waved and in a moment she was swallowed up in the gloom. It was quite dark now, and with my wife gone, a feeling of dreadful loneliness overcame me.

I must have gone out of my head lying there in the road because the next thing I recall was discovering that the clot on my thigh had been dislodged and blood was again spurting from the wound. I pressed my hand to the bleeding area and after a while the bleeding stopped and I felt better. Could I go on? I tried. It was all a nightmare—my wounds, the darkness, the road ahead. My movements were ever so slow, only my mind was running at top speed....

All who could were moving in the direction of the hospital. I joined in the dismal parade when my strength was somewhat recovered, and at last reached the gates.

Source: Michihiko Hachiya, M.D., *Hiroshima Diary: The Journal of a Japanese Physician, August 6–September 30, 1945* (Chapel Hill: University of North Carolina Press, 1955), pp. 1–9.

8.8.   Karl T. Compton Defends the Decision to Drop the Atomic Bomb, December 16, 1946

After the war, James B. Conant asked Karl T. Compton, a member of Truman's Interim Committee, to write an article defending America's decision to drop the atomic bomb on Japan. It appeared in the Atlantic Monthly *in December 1946.*

About a week after V-J Day I was one of a small group of scientists and engineers interrogating an intelligent, well-informed Japanese Army officer in Yokohama. We asked him what, in his opinion, would have been the next major move if the war had continued. He replied: "You would probably have tried to invade our homeland with a landing operation on Kyushu about November 1. I think the attack would have been made on such and such beaches."

"Could you have repelled this landing?" we asked, and he answered: "It would have been a very desperate fight, but I do not think we could have stopped you." "What would have happened then?" we asked.

He replied: "We would have kept on fighting until all Japanese were killed, but we would not have been defeated," by which he meant that they would not have been disgraced by surrender.

It is easy now, after the event, to look back and say that Japan was already a beaten nation, and to ask what therefore was the justification for the use of the atomic bomb to kill so many thousands of helpless

Japanese in this inhuman way; furthermore, should we not better have kept it to ourselves as a secret weapon for future use, if necessary? This argument has been advanced often, but it seems to me utterly fallacious. . . .

I believe, with complete conviction, that the use of the atomic bomb saved hundreds of thousands—perhaps several millions—of lives, both American and Japanese; that without its use the war would have continued for many months; that no one of good conscience knowing, as Secretary Stimson and the Chiefs of Staff did, what was probably ahead and what the atomic bomb might accomplish could have made any different decision. Let some of the facts speak for themselves.

Was the use of the atomic bomb inhuman? All war is inhuman. Here are some comparisons of the atomic bombing with conventional bombing. At Hiroshima the atomic bomb killed about 80,000 people, pulverized about five square miles, and wrecked an additional ten square miles from the city, with decreasing damage out to seven or eight miles from the center. At Nagasaki the fatal casualties were 45,000 and the area wrecked was considerably smaller than at Hiroshima because of the configuration of the city.

Compare this with the results of two B-29 incendiary raids over Tokyo. One of these raids killed about 125,000 people, the other nearly 100,000.

Of the 210 square miles of greater Tokyo, 85 square miles of the densest part was destroyed as completely, for all practical purposes, as were the centers of Hiroshima and Nagasaki; about half the buildings were destroyed in the remaining 125 square miles; the number of people driven homeless out of Tokyo was considerably larger than the population of greater Chicago. These figures are based on information given us in Tokyo and on a detailed study of the air reconnaissance maps. They may be somewhat in error but are certainly of the right order of magnitude.

Was Japan already beaten before the atomic bomb? The answer is certainly "yes" in the sense that the fortunes of war had turned against her. The answer is "no" in the sense that she was still fighting desperately and there was every reason to believe that she would continue to do so; and this is the only answer that has any practical significance.

General MacArthur's staff anticipated about 50,000 American casualties and several times that number of Japanese casualties in the November 1 operation to establish the initial beachheads on Kyushu. After that they expected a far more costly struggle before the Japanese homeland was subdued. There was every reason to think that the Japanese would defend their homeland with even greater fanaticism than when they fought to the death on Iwo Jima and Okinawa. No American soldier who survived the bloody struggles on these islands has much sympathy with the view that battle with the Japanese was over as soon as it was clear that their ultimate situation was hopeless. No, there was every reason to expect a terrible struggle long after the point at which some people can now look back and say, "Japan was already beaten." . . .

Did the atomic bomb bring about the end of the war? That it would do so was the calculated gamble and hope of Mr. Stimson, General Marshall, and their associates. The facts are these. On July 26, 1945, the Potsdam Ultimatum called on Japan to surrender unconditionally. On July 29 Premier Suzuki issued a statement, purportedly at a cabinet press conference, scorning as unworthy of official notice the surrender ultimatum, and emphasizing the increasing rate of Japanese aircraft production. Eight days later, on August 6, the first atomic bomb was dropped on Hiroshima; the second was dropped on August 9 on Nagasaki; on the following day, August 10, Japan declared its intention to surrender, and on August 14 accepted the Potsdam terms.

On the basis of these facts, I cannot believe that, without the atomic bomb, the surrender would have come without a great deal more of costly struggle and bloodshed.

Source: Karl T. Compton, "If the Atomic Bomb Had Not Been Used," *Atlantic Monthly* 178 (December 16, 1946): 54–56.

ANNOTATED RESEARCH GUIDE

Books and Articles

Allen, Thomas B., and Norman Polmar. "Code-Name Downfall." *American History* 30, no. 4 (1995): 50–61. Supports the traditional argument that the atomic bomb saved a substantial number of American lives, since it made a major invasion of Japan unnecessary.

Alperovitz, Gar. *The Decision to Use the Atomic Bomb*. New York: Vintage Books, 1996. Using extensive primary documents, the author focuses on the complexities of the decision to drop the atomic bomb. This includes Truman's use of the bomb as a diplomatic weapon against the Soviet Union and the rewriting of postwar history in an attempt to justify unleashing a new destructive weapon.

———. "Hiroshima: Historians Reassess." *Foreign Policy* 99 (1995): 15–34. Provides a historiographical essay on the decision to drop the bomb by focusing on scholarly interpretations between 1955 and 1993.

Bernstein, Barton J. "The Atomic Bombings Reconsidered." *Foreign Affairs* 74, no. 1 (January/February 1995): 135–152. Examines assumptions made by political leaders that the bomb would be used once it was developed. Explores alternatives to dropping the bomb and argues that Japan would have probably surrendered without a costly land invasion.

———. "Seizing the Contested Terrain of Early Nuclear History: Stimson, Conant, and Their Allies Explain the Decision to Use the Atomic Bomb." *Diplomatic History* 17, no. 1 (1993): 35–72. Examines the efforts of James B. Conant, Truman's nuclear policy advisor, to justify the dropping of the atomic bomb to the American people in the postwar years through fact-filled publications that portrayed the decision as a carefully thought-out process.

————. "Writing, Righting, or Wronging the Historical Record: President Truman's Letter on His Atomic-Bomb Decision." *Diplomatic History* 16, no. 1 (1992); 163–173. Examines the confusion associated with the date of Truman's decision to drop the atomic bomb.

Davidson, James West, and Mark Hamilton Lytle. *After the Fact: The Art of Historical Detection.* New York: Alfred A. Knopf, 1982. Designed to help students understand how history is written and revised. Includes a chapter on "The Decision to Drop the Atomic Bomb."

Dower, John W. "The Bombed: Hiroshimas and Nagasakis in Japanese Memory." *Diplomatic History* 19, no. 2 (1995): 275–295. Explores the Japanese culture and the atomic bomb and argues that because information on the bomb was restricted by both the Japanese and U.S. governments, the Japanese reaction to the bomb was fashioned and influenced by the Cold War.

Drea, Edward J. "Previews of Hell." *MHQ: The Quarterly Journal of Military History* 7, no. 3 (spring 1995): 74–81. Examines the extensive Japanese military buildup in Kyushu in preparation for a possible American invasion, noting that a costly amphibious landing would have occurred if it were not for the atomic bomb.

Erwin, Robert. "Oppenheimer Investigated." *Wilson Quarterly* 18, no. 4 (1994): 34–45. Examines unsubstantiated charges that Oppenheimer collaborated with the Soviet Union in its atomic bomb development by using the memoirs of a former Cold War Soviet spy.

Estes, Allen C. "General Leslie Groves and the Atomic Bomb." *Military Review* 72, no. 8 (1992): 41–52. Provides a positive assessment of Groves's leadership role in the Manhattan Project.

Goldberg, Stanley. "Racing to the Finish: The Decision to Bomb Hiroshima and Nagasaki." *Journal of American–East Asian Relations* 4, no. 2 (1995): 117–128. Examines General Leslie Groves's efforts to use the atomic bomb, concerned that Congress would question the success of the two-billion-dollar research project if the weapon was not used.

Maddox, Robert James. "The Biggest Decision: Why We Had to Drop the Atomic Bomb." *Taking Sides: Clashing Views on Controversial Issues in American History Since 1945,* ed. Larry Madaras. Guilford, CT: McGraw-Hill/Dushkin, 2001, pp. 4–12. Argues that it was the atomic bomb that forced hard-liners in Japan to surrender. As a result, Truman's use of the bomb saved both American and Japanese lives that would have been lost in a prolonged invasion of Japan.

Maslowski, Peter. "Truman, the Bomb, and the Numbers Game." *MHQ: The Quarterly Journal of Military History* 7, no. 3 (1995): 103–107. Explores the various options considered by military leaders in their determination to end the war with the least number of casualties.

Wainstock, Dennis. *The Decision to Drop the Atomic Bomb.* Westport, CT: Praeger, 1996. Using both Japanese and American primary documents, refutes the possibility of Japan surrendering before the bomb was dropped.

Weintraub, Stanley. *The Last Great Victory: The End of World War II, July–August 1945*. New York: Dutton, 1995. Puts the bomb in context with broader political and military issues from both the American and the Japanese perspectives.

Winkler, Allan M. *Life under a Cloud: American Anxiety about the Atom*. New York: Oxford University Press, 1993. Provides a comprehensive political and cultural overview of nuclear weapons from the atomic bomb to the present.

Videos

Hiroshima: The Decision to Drop the Bomb. A&E documentary examines the debate over the use of the atomic bomb and asks whether it was really necessary for ending the war quickly.

J. Robert Oppenheimer: Father of the Atomic Bomb. A&E biography examines the life of the scientist and his important role in the Manhattan Project and the postwar nuclear world. Includes secret footage of the project and atomic tests and newsreels of the Senator Joseph McCarthy hearings.

Race for the Superbomb. Documentary by the American Experience traces the history of nuclear weapons and puts it into perspective with Cold War politics, civil defense, and science and technology.

Web Sites

http://www.mtholyoke.edu/acad/intrel/hiroshim.htm. Extensive collection of primary sources related to American international relations provided by Mount Holyoke College professor Vincent Ferrano. Includes government documents, reports from scientists, and academic articles related to the atomic bomb.

http://www.trumanlibrary.org The Truman Library's online archives provide primary documents related to the atomic bomb, as well as teaching units, lesson plans, and classroom activities.

9

The Recall of General Douglas MacArthur: The Debate over Limited War in Korea

On April 20, 1951, some 550,000 people lined the streets of the nation's capital in a joyous welcome home for General Douglas MacArthur. "No old soldier ever put his sword away with such a resounding bang. None ever moved to the side-lines amidst such pageantry," noted the *Washington Post*.[1] Many who cheered along the parade path were angered by President Harry S. Truman's recall of MacArthur when the two tangled over military policy in the Korean War. The general public greeted the Korean conflict, coming close on the heels of the victorious World War II, with bewilderment and confusion. The Cold War had altered the nature of American warfare and turned the Korean War into a war for balance, not victory. For a country used to fighting "total wars" that ended in unconditional surrender, this new Asian conflict was baffling. The dispute between Truman and MacArthur on how to conduct the war only added to the nation's anxiety. Tension escalated on the Senate floor when the secretary of defense and key military leaders went head-to-head with MacArthur over foreign policy. The Truman-MacArthur controversy, played out in the public forum, represented a command crisis that challenged civil-military authority and shook the nation at a critical time in its history.

The roots of the Cold War can be traced back to World War II and the growing distrust between the Allied forces—especially between the United States and the Soviet Union. This distrust was magnified by disagreements over each country's vision of the postwar world. Mistrust escalated when the Soviet Union began to secure border states in Eastern

Europe, and the United States attempted to promote capitalism in the same area. Wars of national liberation played out in the Third World as small countries attempted to break free from colonial rule, only to find themselves embroiled in the fierce struggle between the superpowers. The Soviet Union's development of the atomic bomb and the "fall of China" to Communist forces under Mao Zedong (Mao Tse-tung) convinced many in the United States that communism must be stopped at all costs. President Truman's "Containment Policy" established a defense perimeter around the world—like a line in the sand—and the American leader called for a massive buildup of American conventional and atomic forces. The Cold War had begun.

THE KOREAN WAR

Just five years after the close of World War II, the United States found itself once again at war, this time in Korea. In many ways, this conflict resulted directly from postwar tensions and Cold War politics, but its roots can be traced back to World War II, when Japanese soldiers surrendered to Soviet troops in northern Korea and the American army in southern Korea. Attempts to unify the country proved unsuccessful, and Korea remained separated at the thirty-eighth parallel, a dividing line established by the Americans. Both the United States and the Soviet Union removed their troops by 1949, but not before influencing their respective areas. The United States supported American-educated Syngman Rhee, a politically conservative, staunch anti-Communist, to lead the Republic of Korea in the south. The Soviet Union recognized a northern government, the Democratic People's Republic of Korea, under Kim Il Sung, an ardent Communist and former commander of guerrilla forces who had fought against the Japanese in World War II.

On June 25, 1950, North Korea attempted to reunite the country by force when the North Korean People's Army (NKPA) crossed the thirty-eighth parallel into South Korea. Looking through Cold War lenses, Truman tended to see all global conflicts as attempts by the Communists to spread their long tentacles throughout the world, and Korea was no exception. Although the small country was not part of America's original defense perimeter, Truman reconsidered its importance and asked the United Nations to support a "police action" to remove North Korean troops out of the Republic of Korea. Since the world agency sanctioned the action, Truman was able to avoid asking Congress for a declaration of war. However, in reality, the Korean conflict was clearly an American war, as 90 percent of the UN's ground troops and the entire naval and air support came from the United States. Also, President Truman and the Joint Chiefs of Staff, not the United Nations, directed General Douglas MacArthur, the head of the Korean operation. MacArthur, the colorful commander of the Pacific theater during World War II and the head of the occupation forces in Japan, had reached hero status in America. Now he was in charge of a new kind of warfare—one that he later claimed caused him to fight "with one arm tied behind his back," and one that would bring an end to his long and illustrious career.[2]

The Korean conflict proved difficult. At first, North Korean troops had the UN forces on the run, finally pushing them back to the southern point of the Korean peninsula. After several months of fighting, MacArthur made a risky, but brilliant amphibious landing behind enemy lines at Inchon, surprising the North Korean army with an attack on its rear forces. The successful maneuver sent the enemy reeling back across the thirty-eighth parallel. With Truman's approval, MacArthur went on the chase, hoping to defeat the North Koreans and even force the "reunification of Korea under UN supervision."[3] But MacArthur pushed too far. Even before the troops crossed the dividing line between the two nations, the Joint Chiefs of Staff (JCS) warned MacArthur not to place UN soldiers close to the Manchurian border, fearing that this would appear as a threat to Communist China. Stretching the order to its limit, the general put the troops close at hand, but shortly, to the astonishment of the JCS, ordered them "to drive forward with all speed and full utilization of their forces . . . to secure all of North Korea."[4] When MacArthur was asked for an explanation for defying the order, he said that he saw no conflict between his actions and the directive, which stated, "These instructions . . . may require modification in accordance with developments."[5] As MacArthur's successful advance put him closer and closer to the Yalu River, China issued a number of warnings to halt and threatened to intercede in the Korean War if necessary. In mid-October, as tension mounted, and as numbers of Chinese "volunteers" were discovered fighting with the North Koreans, Truman and MacArthur met on Wake Island to discuss their options. MacArthur remained adamant that the Chinese were bluffing and assured the president that he would win the war and bring the "boys home by Christmas." The general convinced the president that even if the Chinese did attack, the UN forces would prevail. He was wrong.

Late in the cold wintry month of November 1950, 300,000 Chinese troops crossed the frozen Yalu River and hit the UN troops with full force, hurling them past the thirty-eighth parallel and down the Korean peninsula. The Chinese attack had changed the nature of the war and had turned it from an effort to liberate South Korea from North Korean troops into a dangerous political game with the potential of devastating global consequences. As UN soldiers retreated, a dramatic disagreement erupted between Truman and MacArthur over the next military move. As they debated throughout the winter, the UN forces began to resecure lost ground, but the war soon turned into an icy cold and bloody stalemate—a limited war with limited objectives—to keep the North Korean troops above the thirty-eighth parallel. All the while, American casualties mounted and the American public wondered why American soldiers suffered and died in a far-off place.

THE TRUMAN-MACARTHUR DEBATE

As soon as he learned of the November attack by the Chinese troops, Truman called an emergency meeting of the National Security Council (NSC). General Omar Bradley, the head of the Joint Chiefs of Staff, read a cablegram from MacArthur describing the adverse evolution of the war. Historian Burton I. Kaufman has described the "somber" mood at the White House, where everyone "was troubled and angered by the fact that MacArthur had badly misjudged the capacity and willingness of China to invade Korea."[6] Considering the new turn of events, the Truman administration considered three possible military options: (1) escalate the war, (2) withdraw UN troops from Korea, or (3) resecure the line at the thirty-eighth parallel and negotiate peace. Secretary of State Dean Acheson supported the latter and argued for an end of the U.S. involvement in Korea once UN troops secured the southern territory. Acheson feared that an escalation of the war would take America away from its primary objective. Like other key advisors, he remained adamant that the focus of American foreign policy must remain on Europe, not Asia.

The president, the secretary of defense, and the joint chiefs of staff agreed. Still convinced that the Soviet Union was behind the North Korean invasion, they feared a possible third world war, which threatened to detonate from the chaos in Korea. To make matters worse, the Soviet Union now had atomic weapons, which, if they were brought into play, could turn a small war in the Korean peninsula into a nuclear nightmare. Even if a world war could be averted, they worried that any armed conflict with China would leave Europe vulnerable to Soviet expansion. General Bradley would later call the Korean War "the wrong war, at the wrong place, at the wrong time, and with the wrong enemy."[7]

Truman's advisors understood all too well that if China chose to escalate the war, they would have no options left except to respond despite the alarming dangers. With this in mind, the military conducted a top-secret study on the use of the atomic bomb on military targets in Korea and China. In an effort to shake up the Chinese, Truman let it be known that the United States would consider using the atomic bomb. In response, Western Europe exploded with indignation. Newspaper editorials criticized the American administration; British prime minister Clement Attlee personally protested the possible use of the weapon; and the Labour party in Parliament called for the removal of British troops from Korea. Allied nations strongly advised against further provoking Communist China. They also agonized over the possibility that if the Soviet Union became aggravated by the Korean situation, an attack on Western Europe could follow. Acheson now worried that America might lose the support of its allies. In one fell swoop, the Korean War had escalated into an international crisis, leaving Truman scurrying to calm the waters.

Truman now needed to walk a delicate line between showing strength in Asia and forcing a global conflict. To assure the allies of U.S. support, Truman put the foreign policy focus back on Europe when he strengthened the American forces in key positions on the continent. He also attempted to calm the allies concerning Korea by once again committing to the original UN objective—to contain communism in North Korea.

But the crisis was far from over. The situation worsened when the State Department and the Department of Defense found themselves at odds. Examining the situation from a military stance, the Department of Defense suggested that the best option would be a complete withdrawal of UN troops. But the State Department refused to give up on South Korea and pointed out Japan's vulnerable position if America showed weakness in Asia. Truman continued to side with the State Department, for, as historian Callum A. MacDonald has noted, by December 1950 it became clear that the "administration would accept a stalemate and a return to the status quo as the price of avoiding a wider war."[8]

The Republican party, a longtime critic of Truman's foreign policy, went on a political attack and "turned Truman's own Cold War propaganda against himself."[9] Republicans also blamed Democrats for the "fall of China" to Communist leadership. They also questioned the resolve of the Democrats to stand strong against the Soviet Union and demanded to know why the president hesitated at Korea's thirty-eighth parallel when he had previously advocated a strong aggressive response to the spread of communism. The situation in the Korean War became even more complex because of the intensity of the Cold War atmosphere created by a Red Scare. The debate over Korea was conducted amid House Un-American Activities Committee (HUAC) hearings and Wisconsin senator Joseph McCarthy's accusation that communism had "infiltrated" the State Department, universities, Hollywood, and eventually the army. McCarthy charged that the "Reds" and their "pinko" fellow travelers had wormed into the Truman administration and had weakened its commitment to fight communism. This made any "retreat" in Asia considerably more difficult for Truman to explain. Looking for a way to overcome the jumbled mess without surrendering its position in the Far East, the United States stood firm at the thirty-eighth parallel, continued to balance power in Korea, and sought a cease-fire agreement.

MacArthur was incensed. The old World War II hero—the general who was taught to fight and triumphantly win all-out wars, to meet force with counterforce—just could not conceive of a war for balance, not victory. But to MacArthur, the choice was never as simple as world war or limited war. Instead, he insisted that a controlled escalation of the Korean War was possible without turning the conflict into a major international quarrel.

MacArthur saw no reason to abandon his strategy of reunifying Korea, and he strongly disagreed with Truman that Europe was of more strategic importance than Asia. He also remained convinced that the Soviet Union would not enter the Korean War, since it was not in its strategic interest to do so. Although MacArthur did not advocate an all-out war against China or suggest the use of UN ground troops in Manchuria, he steadfastly argued for the full use of American naval and air power. This included bombing both military bases in Manchuria and industrial targets on the mainland, destroying bridges and hydroelectric plants along the Yalu River, and blockading the Chinese coast. The justification was pure and simple to MacArthur—China had started the war against UN forces. The general's monolithic assumptions about communism convinced him that China, not North Korea, was the author of the attack. Even before the November setback, the general proposed asking for help from the former Chinese leader Jiang Jieshi (Chiang Kai-shek), who had escaped to Formosa (Taiwan) when Mao secured China in 1949. Now MacArthur renewed his cause to employ Chinese Nationalist troops in Korea and the Chinese mainland. Finally, MacArthur urged that UN airmen be allowed to pursue enemy planes as they flew across the Manchurian border.

MacArthur also believed adamantly that when political means failed and leaders turned the situation over to the military, the military, not the politicians, must be in control. He later testified in Congress, "A theater commander, in any campaign, is not merely limited to the handling of his troops; he commands that whole area politically, economically, and militarily. You have got to trust at that stage of the game when politics fails, and the military takes over, you must trust the military, or otherwise you will have the system that the Soviet once employed of the political commissar, who would run the military as well as the politics of the country."[10] Such thinking governed MacArthur's policy and action in Korea.

THE DEBATE GOES PUBLIC

Disgruntled by Truman's new Korean policy that chose balance over victory, MacArthur went public with his objections through press releases, letters, and interviews. Truman warned the general to stop in a December 6, 1950, directive that instructed all overseas American officials not to discuss foreign or military policy with the U.S. media. But the Truman administration and MacArthur remained on a collision course, especially after China denounced America's attempts for a cease-fire and negotiations stalled. On January 13, 1951, Truman once again "personally warned" General MacArthur "that extension of the Korean conflict was contrary to United States policy."[11] But in March, MacArthur stunned the State Department when he released an unauthorized proclamation concerning the war in Korea. The general began by applauding the success of UN troops in their removal of Communist forces from South Korea and carefully spelled out the inferiority of the enemy's industrial and military capabilities. Then he went too far:

> The enemy therefore must by now be painfully aware that a decision of the United Nations to depart from its tolerant effort to contain the war to the area of Korea through expansion of our military operation to his coastal areas and interior bases would doom Red China to the risk of imminent military collapse. These basic facts being established, there should be no insuperable difficulty arriving at a decision on the Korean problem if the issues are resolved on their own merit without being burdened by extraneous matters not directly related to Korea.[12]

Later that same month, after receiving a letter from Congressman Joseph W. Martin, Jr., of Massachusetts, MacArthur broke his public silence once again. Martin, the Republican minority leader in the House of Representatives, had questioned Truman's foreign policy: "I think it is imperative to the security of our Nation and for the safety of the world that policies of the United States embrace the broadest possible strategy and that in our earnest desire to protect Europe we not weaken our position in Asia."[13] Martin also advocated the use of Chinese Nationalist troops from Formosa in the fight against the North Korean and Communist Chinese forces, and he asked the general for "his views on this point." In his response to the Martin, MacArthur contended that he could not understand why the U.S. government was willing to fight conflict "with arms" in Europe while diplomats in Asia "still fight it with words." The general argued that the "Communist conspirators have elected to make their play for global conquest" in Korea, and if Asia fell to communism, Europe would follow. MacArthur adamantly concluded, "We must win. There is no substitute for victory."[14] Martin inadvertently sealed MacArthur's fate when he read the letter aloud in the House of Representatives. In an April 6 diary entry, Truman wrote, "MacArthur shot another political bomb through Joe Martin. . . . This looks like the last straw. Rank insubordination."[15]

MacArthur's strong personality and arrogant behavior were not new to political and military leaders in Washington, and he had a number of run-ins during his many years of service in the U.S. military. General Matthew Ridgway, who replaced MacArthur in Korea, expressed profound respect for his predecessor and acknowledged the general's military genius, but he also saw another side of MacArthur's "complex character" and recognized that the same "headstrong quality" led to the general's success and caused his defiant behavior:

> The hunger for praise that led [MacArthur] on some occasions to claim or accept credit for deeds that he had not performed, or to disclaim responsibility for mistakes that were clearly his own; the love of the limelight that continually prompted him to pose before the public as the actual commander on the spot at every landing and at the launching of every major attack in which his ground troops took part . . . a faith in his own judgment that created an aura of infallibility . . . finally led him close to insubordination.[16]

This time, MacArthur had crossed the line. After meeting with key advisors, President Truman made the decision to dismiss General MacArthur as the commander of the UN forces in Korea.

In April 1951, MacArthur returned to a hero's welcome. Hundreds of thousands of people lined city streets; people took off from work, left school, and closed down civic meetings, all to greet the great military leader. Full-page ads in city newspapers celebrated the general's contributions. The majority of Americans had greeted the news of his recall with anger and disbelief. Although some agreed that Truman had no choice but to recall the general, most did not. Thousands of irate telegrams poured into the White House; letters to the editor called Truman a traitor to democracy and admonished the president for discrediting the great general. Others called the dismissal a victory for "Godless" communism. In Congress, a number of Republicans talked of impeachment proceedings. Newspaper editorials carried the debate to the public. The editor of the *Chicago Daily Tribune* called the general "a great man, a sincere man, a patriot" and asked why the Truman administration did not accept MacArthur's military plans. "What can that mean, except that the nation's greatest military man was overruled by Truman, by Secretary of State Acheson, by the state department appeasers who think that Communism can be jollied into good behavior, by the British foreign office, which seeks the preservation of its Asiatic colonial interests and its trade [and] by the United Nations, an organization of global Micawbers." [17] Not all reporters agreed. Former Secretary of the Interior Harold L. Ickes, writing in the *New Republic*, compared MacArthur to Revolutionary War hero Nathan Hale, whom Ickes called "loyal to his Commander-in-Chief." MacArthur "would do well to disassociate him-

self from the designation 'hero' or 'patriot.' . . . No man should be regarded as a hero, especially if he wears the uniform of his country, who
is willing to lead those who would destroy the unity of the American
people and divide them into contending factions for political purposes."[18] In a radio address to the American people, Truman explained
his decision to recall General MacArthur:

> In the simplest terms, what we are doing in Korea is this: We are
> trying to prevent a third world war. . . . Why don't we bomb Man-
> churia and China itself? Why don't we assist the Chinese Nation-
> alist troops to land on the mainland of China? If we were to do
> these things we would be running a very grave risk of starting a
> general war. . . . I believe that we must try to limit the war to Korea.
> . . . A number of events have made it evident that General Mac-
> Arthur did not agree with that policy. . . . General MacArthur is one
> of our greatest military commanders. But the cause of world peace
> is much more important than any individual.[19]

COMMAND CRISIS VERSUS VIOLATION OF CIVIL-MILITARY AUTHORITY?

The drama continued on the floor of the U.S. Congress when Mac-
Arthur gave an emotional farewell address to his country, but not before
criticizing the direction of American foreign policy. His speech ended
with the now-immortal words "old soldiers never die; they just fade
away." Since Congress remained "sharply divided" over the Truman-
MacArthur controversy, a combined Senate Armed Services Committee
and Foreign Relations Committee conducted an inquiry into the military
situation in Asia and the events surrounding the relief of General Douglas MacArthur.[20] At first, the senators seemed sympathetic to the general,
but the testimony of the Joint Chiefs turned the tide. General Bradley
"put the case for containment in Korea forcibly and clearly: Russia, not
China, was America's main enemy; Europe, not Asia, was the most important region of American interest."[21]

The Senate debate also centered on the charges of insubordination.
Secretary of Defense George C. Marshall testified that although MacArthur was unable to give his "wholehearted support" to U.S. military
policies, he never violated a military order. Marshall agreed, however,
that MacArthur disobeyed a directive given to him by the president concerning releasing public statements. Many questioned whether this constituted an infraction of the American democratic principle that placed
civilian authority above military power. When America's "Founding Fathers" sought to safeguard the young nation against possible military
oppression, they made this edict clear. Certainly, Truman argued with

conviction that MacArthur's insubordination equated to a challenge of civilian control. "If I allowed [MacArthur] to defy the civil authorities in this manner, I myself would be violating my oath to uphold and defend the Constitution."[22] Some historians, like D. Clayton James, disagree with the idea that MacArthur's insubordination "seriously threatened" the principle of civil-military authority. Instead, they see it as a crisis in command. "In short, an officer disobeyed and defied his superior and was relieved of command." Truman's response to the situation made it "clear that the principle was still safe and healthy."[23]

CONCLUSION

Regardless of whether MacArthur was guilty of undermining civil-military authority, his defiance, made public with his own hands, tore the nation apart. But the question remains, who was correct in his analysis of the Korean War? Did the Truman administration, "using a wide-angle lens," with access to important information on Soviet atomic capabilities and a keen understanding of the impact of an expanded war of global politics, have "a much clearer view of the realities and responsibilities of the day"?[24] Could the general have escalated the war with North Korea and China, contained it to a regional conflict, and successfully removed the Korean Communists from power in North Korea? No one knows for sure.

Some historians praise Truman's policies and argue that his decisions ultimately "contained" the Korean War and allowed the United States to keep its focus and resources fixed on Europe, where the Communist "advance" was checked. Others counter that MacArthur was justified in his criticisms of the president who put European defense first, thus withholding much-needed military strength that could have quickly ended the Korean War. They also harshly condemn any military strategy that called for balance as a substitute for victory. Other scholars question Truman's foreign policies, maintaining that the president gravely misunderstood the "spread of communism" and unnecessarily escalated the Cold War to dangerous levels. In the end, the Korean War turned into a prolonged and bloody stalemate at the thirty-eighth parallel—a war for balance. Although truce talks began in July 1951, peace would not be declared for another two years. This limited war ultimately cost the lives of 54,246 Americans, with more than 103,000 wounded or missing. In addition, the United States spent $54 billion on the war.

What is plainly understood is that the Korean conflict helped to alter radically the American way of war. The Cold War polarized the world into two armed camps, both now equipped with atomic bombs. The Korean War, with the potential of expanding into a world conflict, provided a chilling possibility of what could happen if either of the two superpowers chose to go head-to-head over political ideology. They did not in this instance because the United States recognized its interests dictated another course in Asia and a renewed focus on the Soviet Union. The Soviet Union was hardly ready to make a stand for Korea or China, where its influence was strong but not determinative. The Cold War shifted back to Europe. Still, this conflict helped stimulate an unprecedented expansion of the American military buildup throughout the world as "the United States turned from a crisis-oriented military policy toward concepts and programs designed to last as long as the rivalry with the Soviet Union."[25] America's renewed efforts to strengthen its conventional military forces and to build up its nuclear capability put the political giants face-to-face in a number of dangerous political games. Within a few years, Cold War politics would force America to fight another war for balance, not victory, as the legacy of the Korean War cast a long, dark shadow on the next Asian conflict—the Vietnam War.

NOTES

1. "550,000 See Hero at Monument and in Parade along Avenue," *Washington Post*, April 20, 1951, p. 1.

2. Geoffrey Perret, *Old Soldiers Never Die: The Life of Douglas MacArthur* (New York: Random House, 1996), p. 532.

3. Allan R. Millett and Peter Maslowski, *For the Common Defense: A Military History of the United States of America* (New York: Free Press, 1984), p. 488.

4. Quoted in D. Clayton Jones, *Refighting the Last War: Command and Crisis in Korea, 1950–1953* (New York: Free Press, 1993), p. 198.

5. Ibid.

6. Burton I. Kaufman, *The Korean War: Challenges in Crisis, Credibility, and Command* (Philadelphia: Temple University Press, 1986), p. 109.

7. "Testimony of General of the Army Omar N. Bradley," *Military Situation in the Far East, Hearings before the Committee on Armed Services and the Committee on Foreign Relations, United States Senate, 82nd Cong., 1st sess.* TO CONDUCT AN INQUIRY INTO THE MILITARY SITUATION IN THE FAR EAST AND THE FACTS SURROUNDING THE RELIEF OF GENERAL OF THE ARMY DOUGLAS MACARTHUR FROM HIS ASSIGNMENT IN THAT AREA, Part II, May 15, 1951 (Washington, D.C.: Government Printing Office, 1951), p. 732.

8. C. A. MacDonald, *Korea: The War before Vietnam* (New York: Free Press, 1987), p. 91.

9. Walter Karp, "Truman vs. MacArthur," *American Heritage* 35, no. 3 (April/May 1984): 90.

10. "Testimony of General of the Army Douglas MacArthur," *Military Situation in the Far East, Hearings before the Committee on Armed Services and the Committee on Foreign Relations, United States Senate, 82nd Cong., 1st sess.* TO CONDUCT AN INQUIRY INTO THE MILITARY SITUATION IN THE FAR EAST AND THE FACTS SURROUNDING THE RELIEF OF GENERAL OF THE ARMY DOUGLAS MACARTHUR FROM HIS ASSIGNMENTS IN THAT AREA, Part 1, May 3–14, 1951 (Washington, DC: U.S. Government Printing Office, 1951), p. 45.

11. Marshall's Senate testimony, reported in "Courses under Contingencies Were Defined, Marshall Says," *Washington Post*, May 10, 1951, p. 1.

12. John P. Glennon, Harriet D. Schwar, and Paul Claussen, eds., *Foreign Relations of the United States 1951, Korea and China* (Washington, DC: Department of State Publications, 1982), pp. 264–266.

13. Ibid., pp. 298–299.

14. Ibid, p. 299.

15. D. Clayton James with Anne Sharp Wells, *Refighting the Last War: Command and Crisis in Korea, 1950–1953* (New York: Free Press, 1953), p. 210.

16. Matthew B. Ridgway, *The Korean War* (Garden City, NY: Doubleday, 1967), p. 142.

17. "An American Speaks," *Chicago Daily Tribune*, April 10, 1951, p. 18.

18. Harold L. Ickes, "Nathan Hale and MacArthur," *New Republic*, May 7, 1951, p. 15.

19. Harry S. Truman, "Radio Report to the American People on Korea and on U.S. Policy in the Far East, April 11, 1951," *Public Papers of the Presidents of the United States: Harry S. Truman: Containing the Public Messages, Speeches, and Statements of the President, January 1 to December 31, 1951* (Washington, DC: U.S. Government Printing Office, Washington, 1965), p. 226.

20. "Congress Salutes MacArthur But Divides Sharply on Views," *Washington Post*, April 20, 1951, p. 1.

21. George Donelson Moss, *America in the Twentieth Century*, 3rd ed. (Upper Saddle River, NJ: Prentice Hall, 1997), p. 332.

22. Russell F. Weigley, *History of the United States Army* (New York: Macmillan, 1967), p. 517.

23. D. Clayton James, "Command Crisis: MacArthur and the Korean War, Harmon Memorial Lecture," U.S. Air Force Academy, November 12, 1981, p. 4.

24. Ridgway, *The Korean War*, p. 149.

25. Millett and Maslowski, *For the Common Defense*, p. 508.

DOCUMENTS

9.1.   **Statement by President Truman on the Situation in Korea, June 27, 1950**

On June 27, 1950, President Truman announced to the nation that North Korean troops had crossed the thirty-eighth parallel and invaded South Korea. Shortly afterward, Truman sent General Douglas MacArthur to South Korea to lead UN troops.

In Korea the Government forces, which were armed to prevent border raids and to preserve internal security, were attacked by invading forces from North Korea. The Security Council of the United Nations called upon the invading troops to cease hostilities and to withdraw to the 38th parallel. This they have not done, but on the contrary have pressed the attack. The Security Council called upon all members of the United Nations to render every assistance to the United Nations in the execution of this resolution. In these circumstances I have ordered United States air and sea forces to give the Korean Government troops cover and support.

The attack upon Korea makes it plain beyond all doubt that communism has passed beyond the use of subversion to conquer independent nations and will now use armed invasion and war. It has defied the orders of the Security Council of the United Nations issued to preserve international peace and security. In these circumstances the occupation of Formosa by Communist forces would be a direct threat to the security of the Pacific area and to United States forces performing their lawful and necessary functions in that area.

Accordingly I have ordered the 7th Fleet to prevent any attack on Formosa. As a corollary of this action I am calling upon the Chinese Government on Formosa to cease all air and sea operations against the mainland. The 7th Fleet will see that this is done. The determination of the future status of Formosa must await the restoration of security in the Pacific, a peace settlement with Japan, or consideration by the United Nations.

I have also directed that United States Forces in the Philippines be strengthened and that military assistance to the Philippine Government be accelerated.

I have similarly directed acceleration in the furnishing of military assistance to the forces of France and the Associated States in Indochina and the dispatch of a military mission to provide close working relations with those forces.

I know that all members of the United Nations will consider carefully the consequences of this latest aggression in Korea in defiance of the Charter of the United Nations. A return to the rule of force in international affairs would have far-reaching effects. The United States will continue to uphold the rule of law.

I have instructed Ambassador Austin, as the representative of the United States to the Security Council, to report these steps to the Council.

Source: Harry S. Truman, "Statement by the President on the Situation in Korea, June 27, 1950," *Public Papers of the Presidents of the United States: Harry S. Truman: Containing the Public Messages, Speeches, and Statements of the President, January 1 to December 31, 1950* (Washington, DC: U.S. Government Printing Office, 1965), p. 492.

9.2.   Letters Exchanged by Joseph W. Martin, Jr., and General MacArthur, March 1951

Correspondence between Congressman Joseph W. Martin, Jr., and General Douglas MacArthur proved to be the "last straw" for Truman, who recalled the general after Martin made the letters public.

LETTER FROM HON. JOSEPH W. MARTIN, JR., TO GENERAL
MACARTHUR, MARCH 8, 1951:
(FROM *DAILY CONGRESSIONAL RECORD*, APRIL 13, 1951, p. 3938)

OFFICE OF THE MINORITY LEADER,
HOUSE OF REPRESENTATIVES,
Washington, D.C., March 8, 1951.
General of the Army Douglas MacArthur,
Commander in Chief, Far Eastern Command.

My Dear General: In the current discussions of foreign policy and over-all strategy many of us have been distressed that, although the European aspects have been heavily emphasized, we have been without the views of yourself as Commander in Chief of the Far Eastern Command.

I think it is imperative to the security of our Nation and for the safety of the world that policies of the United States embrace the broadest possible strategy and that in our earnest desire to protect Europe we not weaken our position in Asia.

Enclosed is a copy of an address I delivered in Brooklyn, N.Y., February 12, stressing this vital point and suggesting that the forces of Generalissimo Chiang Kai-shek on Formosa might be employed in the opening of a second Asiatic front to relieve the pressure on our forces in Korea.

I have since repeated the essence of this thesis in other speeches, and intend to do so again on March 21, when I will be on a radio hook-up.

I would deem it a great help if I could have your views on this point, either on a confidential basis or otherwise. Your admirers are legion, and the respect you command is enormous. May success be yours in the gigantic undertaking which you direct.

Sincerely yours,

Joseph W. Martin, Jr.

REPLY THERETO BY GENERAL MACARTHUR, MARCH 20, 1951:
(FROM *DAILY CONGRESSIONAL RECORD*, APRIL 13, 1951, p. 3938.
SEE ALSO *DAILY CONGRESSIONAL RECORD*, APRIL 5, 1951, p. 3482)

GENERAL HEADQUARTERS,
SUPREME COMMANDER FOR THE ALLIED POWERS,
Tokyo, Japan, March 20, 1951.
Hon. Joseph W. Martin, Jr.
House of Representatives, Washington, D.C.

Dear Congressman Martin: I am most grateful for your note of the 8th forwarding me a copy of your address of February 12. The latter I have read with much interest, and find that with the passage of years you have certainly lost none of your old-time punch.

My views and recommendations with respect to the situation created by Red China's entry into war against us in Korea have been submitted to Washington in most complete detail. Generally, these views are well known and clearly understood as they follow the conventional pattern of meeting force with maximum counterforce, as we have never failed to do in the past. Your view with respect to the utilization of the Chinese forces on Formosa is in conflict with neither logic nor this tradition.

It seems strangely difficult for some to realize that here in Asia is where the Communist conspirators have elected to make their play for global conquest and that we have joined the issue thus raised on the battlefield; that here we fight Europe's war with arms while the diplomatic (*diplomats?*) there still fight it with words; that if we lose the war to communism in Asia the fall of Europe is inevitable, win it and Europe most probably would avoid war and yet preserve freedom. As you pointed out, we must win. There is no substitute for victory.

With renewed thanks and expressions of most cordial regard, I am

Faithfully yours,

Douglas MacArthur

Source: John P. Glennon, Harriet D. Schwar, and Paul Claussen, eds., *Foreign Relations of the United States, 1951, Korea and China* (Washington, DC: Department of State Publications, 1982), pp. 298–299.

9.3.   President Truman's Radio Report to the American People on Korea and on U.S. Policy in the Far East, April 11, 1951

In response to the public outrage at the dismissal of General Mac-Arthur, President Truman addressed the American people in a radio broadcast from the White House.

My fellow Americans:

I want to talk to you plainly tonight about what we are doing in Korea and about our policy in the Far East.

In the simplest terms, what we are doing in Korea is this: We are trying to prevent a third world war.

I think most people in this country recognized that fact last June. And they warmly supported the decision of the Government to help the Republic of Korea against the Communist aggressors. Now, many persons, even some who applauded our decision to defend Korea, have forgotten the basic reason for our action.

It is right for us to be in Korea now. It was right last June. It is right today. I want to remind you why this is true.

The Communists in the Kremlin are engaged in a monstrous conspiracy to stamp out freedom all over the world. If they were to succeed, the United States would be numbered among their principal victims. It must be clear to everyone that the United States cannot—and will not—sit idly by and await foreign conquest. The only question is: What is the best time to meet the threat and how is the best way to meet it?

The best time to meet the threat is in the beginning. It is easier to put out a fire in the beginning when it is small than after it has become a roaring blaze. And the best way to meet the threat of aggression is for the peace-loving nations to act together. If they don't act together, they are likely to be picked off, one by one. . . .

We do not want to see the conflict in Korea extended. We are trying to prevent a world war—not to start one. And the best way to do that is to make it plain that we and the other free countries will continue to resist the attack.

But you may ask why can't we take other steps to punish the aggressor. Why don't we bomb Manchuria and China itself? Why don't we assist the Chinese Nationalist troops to land on the mainland of China?

If we were to do these things we would be running a very grave risk of starting a general war. If that were to happen, we would have brought about the exact situation we are trying to prevent.

If we were to do these things, we would become entangled in a vast conflict on the continent of Asia and our task would become immeasurably more difficult all over the world. What would suit the ambitions of the Kremlin better than for our military forces to be committed to a full-scale war with Red China?

It may well be that, in spite of our best efforts, the Communists may spread the war. But it would be wrong—tragically wrong—for us to take the initiative in extending the war.

The dangers are great. Make no mistake about it. Behind the North Koreans and Chinese Communists in the front lines stand additional millions of Chinese soldiers. And behind the Chinese stand the tanks, the planes, the submarines, the soldiers, and the scheming rulers of the Soviet Union.

Our aim is to avoid the spread of the conflict.

The course we have been following is the one best calculated to avoid an all-out war. It is the course consistent with our obligation to do all we can to maintain international peace and security. . . .

I have thought long and hard about this question of extending the war in Asia. I have discussed it many times with the ablest military advisors in the country. I believe with all my heart that the course we are following is the best course.

I believe that we must try to limit the war to Korea for these vital reasons: to make sure that the precious lives of our fighting men are not wasted; to see that the security of our country and the free world is not needlessly jeopardized; and to prevent a third world war.

A number of events have made it evident that General MacArthur did not agree with that policy. I have therefore considered it essential to relieve General MacArthur so that there would be no doubt or confusion as to the real purpose and aim of our policy. It is with the deepest personal regret that I found myself compelled to take this action. General MacArthur is one of our greatest military commanders. But the cause of world peace is much more important than any individual.

The change in commands in the Far East means no change whatever in the policy of the United States. We will carry on the fight in Korea with vigor and determination in an effort to bring the war to a speedy and successful conclusion. The new commander, Lt. Gen. Matthew Ridgway, has already demonstrated that he has the great qualities of military leadership needed for this task.

We are ready, at any time to negotiate for a restoration of peace in the area. But we will not engage in appeasement. We are only interested in real peace. . . .

The struggle of the United Nations in Korea is a struggle for peace. Free nations have united their strength in an effort to prevent a third world war. That war can come if the Communist rulers want it to come. But this Nation and its allies will not be responsible for its coming. We do not want to widen the conflict. We will use every effort to prevent that disaster. And in so doing, we know that we are following the great principles of peace, freedom, and justice.

Source: Harry S. Truman, "Radio Report to the American People on Korea and on U.S. Policy in the Far East, April 11, 1951," *Public Papers of the Presidents of the United States: Harry S. Truman: Containing the Public Messages, Speeches, and Statements of the President, January 1 to December 31, 1951* (Washington, DC: U.S. Government Printing Office, 1965), pp. 223–227.

9.4.   General Douglas MacArthur's Address to Congress, April 19, 1951

The public greeted the returning general with parades, luncheons, and other celebrations that honored MacArthur for his many years of service for his country. Such public accolades further convinced MacArthur and his supporters to take his case directly to the people. The general conveyed the essence of his argument in a farewell address before a joint session of Congress.

MR. PRESIDENT, MR. SPEAKER, AND DISTINGUISHED MEMBERS OF THE CONGRESS: I stand on this rostrum with a sense of deep humility and great pride—humility in the wake of those great American architects of our history who have stood here before me, pride in the reflection that this forum of legislative debate represents human liberty in the purest form yet devised.

Here are centered the hopes and aspirations and faith of the entire human race. I do not stand here as advocate for any partisan cause, for the issues are fundamental and reach quite beyond the realm of partisan consideration. They must be resolved on the highest plane of national interest if our course is to prove sound and our future protected. I trust, therefore, that you will do me the justice of receiving that which I have to say as solely expressing the considered viewpoint of a fellow American. I address you with neither rancor nor bitterness in the fading twilight of life with but one purpose in mind: to serve my country.

The issues are global and so interlocked that to consider the problems of one sector, oblivious to those of another, is but to court disaster for the whole. While Asia is commonly referred to as the gateway to Europe, it is no less true that Europe is the gateway to Asia, and the broad influence of the one cannot fail to have its impact upon the other. There are those who claim our strength is inadequate to protect on both fronts, that we cannot divide our effort. I can think of no greater expression of defeatism. If a potential enemy can divide his strength on two fronts, it is for us to counter his effort. The Communist threat is a global one. Its successful advance in one sector threatens the destruction of every other sector. You cannot appease or otherwise surrender to Communism in Asia without simultaneously undermining our efforts to halt its advance in Europe. Beyond pointing out these simple truisms, I shall confine my discussion to the general areas of Asia. . . .

[Korea] created a new war and an entirely new situation—a situation not contemplated when our forces were committed against the North Korean invaders—a situation which called for new decisions in the diplomatic sphere to permit the realistic adjustment of military strategy. Such decisions have not been forthcoming. While no man in his right mind would advocate sending our ground forces into continental China, and such was never given a thought, the new situation did urgently demand a drastic revision of strategic planning if our political aim was to defeat this new enemy as we had defeated the old.

Apart from the military need as I saw it to neutralize the sanctuary protection given the enemy north of the Yalu, I felt that military necessity in the conduct of the war made mandatory [1] The intensification of our economic blockade against China; [2] The imposition of a naval blockade against the China coast; [3] Removal of restrictions on air reconnaissance of China's coastal areas and of Manchuria; [4] Removal of restrictions on the forces of the republic of China on Formosa, with logistical support to contribute to their effective operation against the Chinese mainland.

For entertaining these views, all professionally designed to support our forces in Korea and to bring hostilities to an end with the least possible delay and at a saving of countless American and Allied lives, I have been severely criticized in lay circles, principally abroad, despite my understanding that from a military standpoint the above views have been fully shared in the past by practically every military leader concerned with the Korean campaign, including our own joint chiefs of staff. . . .

But once war is forced upon us, there is no other alternative than to apply every available means to bring it to a swift end. War's very object is victory, not prolonged indecision. In war there can be no substitute for victory. . . .

I have just left your fighting sons in Korea. They have met all tests there, and I can report to you without reservation that they are splendid in every way. It was my constant effort to preserve them and end this savage conflict honorably and with the least loss of time and minimum sacrifice of life. Its growing bloodshed has caused me the deepest anguish and anxiety. Those gallant men will remain often in my thoughts and in my prayers always. I am closing my 52 years of military service. When I joined the army, even before the turn of the century, it was the fulfillment of all of my boyish hopes and dreams. The world has turned over many times since I took the oath on the plain at West Point, and the hopes and dreams have long since vanished, but I still remember the refrain of one of the most popular barrack ballads of that day which proclaimed most proudly that old soldiers never die; they just fade away. And, like the old soldier of that ballad, I now close my military career and just fade away, an old soldier who tried to do his duty as God gave him the light to see that duty. Good-by.

Source: Douglas MacArthur, *A Soldier Speaks: Public Papers and Speeches of General of the Army Douglas MacArthur*, Prepared for the United States Military Academy, West Point, New York, by the Department of the Military Art and Engineering (New York: Praeger, 1965), p. 243.

9.5.   Douglas MacArthur's Testimony on the Military Situation in the Far East, Hearings before the Committee on Armed Services and the Committee on Foreign Relations, May 1951

In May 1951, General MacArthur appeared before Congress to answer questions concerning his recall as the commander of the UN forces in Korea. The general explained his view of how the war should be conducted in the following excerpt.

CARRYING OUT MILITARY ORDERS

Senator Bridges. Have you ever, to your knowledge, refused to carry out a military order given you?

General MacArthur. Senator, I have been a soldier for 52 years. I have in that time, to the best of my ability, carried out every order that was ever given me. No more subordinate soldier has ever worn the American uniform. I would repudiate any concept that I wouldn't carry out any order that was given me. If you mean to say that the orders I have carried out I was in agreement with, that is a different matter. Many of the orders that I have received, I have disagreed with them, both their wisdom and their judgement; but that did not affect in the slightest degree my implementing them to the very best and maximum of my ability. Any insinuation by anyone, however high his office, that I have ever in any way failed, to the level of my ability, to carry out my instructions, is completely unworthy and unwarranted. . . .

POLITICAL DECISIONS IN KOREA

Senator Wiley. You have indicated in your public addresses that there has been a failure to take certain needed political decisions in the Korean matter. Can you tell us what you think those decisions might well have been?

General MacArthur. I can tell you what I would have done.

Senator Wiley. Yes.

General MacArthur. I would have served—as soon as it became apparent that Red China was throwing the full might of its military force against our troops in Korea, I would have served warning on her that if she did not within a reasonable time discuss a cease-fire order, that the entire force of the United Nations would be utilized to bring to an end the predatory attack of her forces on ours. In other words, I would have supplied her with an ultimatum that she would either come and talk terms of a cease fire within a reasonable period of time or her actions in Korea would be regarded as a declaration of war against the nations engaged there and that those nations would take such steps as they felt necessary to bring the thing to a conclusion. That is what I would have done, and I would still do it, Senator. . . .

REASONS FOR RECALL

Senator Wiley. General, when you were recalled when the message came through, were there any reasons assigned to your recall?

General MacArthur. The only reasons were contained in the order that I received and the reason that was given was that it was felt that I could not give my complete support to the policies of the United States and of the United Nations. That reason seems to be to me—there was no necessity to give any reason.

Senator Wiley. I understand.

General MacArthur. But it seems to me to be completely invalid. I have not carried out every directive that I have ever received, but what I was trying to do was to find out what the directives were to be for the future.

OBJECTIVES IN KOREA

[*General MacArthur.*] I was operating in what I call a vacuum. I could hardly have been said to be in opposition to policies which I was not aware of even. I don't know what the policy is now. You have various potentials. First is that you can go on and complete this war in the normal way and bring about just and honorable peace at the soonest time possible with the least loss of life by utilizing all of your potential. The second is that you bring this thing to an end in Korea by yielding to the enemy's terms and on his terms. The third is that you go on indecisively, fighting, with no mission for the troops except to resist and fight in this accordion fashion—up and down—which means that your cumulative losses are going to be staggering. It isn't just dust that is settling in Korea, Senator; it is American blood. Now, my whole effort has been since Red China came in there to get some definition, military definition, of what I should do. There has been no change from the directions that I had— to clear North Korea. As far as the United Nations are concerned, as far as the Joint Chiefs of Staff are concerned, my directives have been changed and I have been informed that my main objective, which takes precedence over everything else, was the security of my forces and the protection of Japan. And I have been operating on that. Now, that is not a mission. Now, when you say that I have enunciated my recommendations, they are plain and clear. The only reason that you can logically say that I would disagree was the concept that something else than what I recommended was going to be done. Now, I don't know what is going to be done, but I can assure you had I stayed in command, whatever was ordered to be done I would have done it to the best of my ability. . . .

REDUCING AMERICAN LOSSES IN KOREA

General MacArthur. Now you speak of American forces being sucked into China, ground forces. I invite your attention to the fact that hundreds of thousands of American Ground Forces have already been committed in Korea, and if you keep on this indecisive fighting, hundreds of thousands of more of them will go there. Our losses already, the battle casualties are approaching 65,000. This conflict in Korea has already lasted almost as long as General Eisenhower's decisive campaign, which brought the European War to an end. And yet the only program that I have been able to hear is that we shall indecisively go on resisting aggression, whatever that may mean. And if you do, you are going to have thousands and thousands and thousands of American lives that will fall, and in my own opinion events finally will catch up with you, so that you will have to stop it in some way; and then the great question is— Where does the responsibility of that blood rest? This I am quite sure—It is not going to rest on my shoulders.

Senator Green. As I understand it, the pressure that could be brought in the south, you count upon to reduce the pressure in Korea to such an extent that it would be a quick victory in Korea?

General MacArthur. What I said, Senator, was that if you use the Chinese forces on Formosa for a diversionary effect, and force the enemy to operate on another front, you will unquestionably diminish the pressure upon our forces in Korea, and thereby you will save American blood and American efforts.

EFFECT OF MILITARY VICTORY IN KOREA ON POLITICAL VICTORY IN CHINA

Senator Green. I understand how it might save that in Korea, but would it not increase it in China by more than what you save in Korea? If you get or you could get thereby a quick victory in Korea, it does not assure, or does it assure, you of a quick victory in China? Have we not substituted a greater problem for a lesser one? That is the thing that bothers me, and that is the reason I am asking these questions.

General MacArthur. I believe that if you will hit the Chinese and stop their potentials for war, you will bring peace not only to Korea but you will bring peace to China—that is as far as you can bring it. . . .

WAR AS THE ULTIMATE PROCESS OF POLITICS

General MacArthur. The general definition which for many decades has been accepted was that war was the ultimate process of politics; that when all other political means failed, you then go to force; and when you do that, the balance of control, the balance of concept, the main interest involved, the minute you reach the killing stage, is the control of the military. A theater commander, in any campaign, is not merely limited to the handling of his troops; he commands that whole area politically, economically, and militarily. You have got to trust at that stage of the game when politics fails, and the military takes over, you must trust the military, or otherwise you will have the system that the Soviet once employed of the political commissar, who would run the military as well as the politics of the country.

Source: "Testimony of General of the Army Douglas MacArthur," *Military Situation in the Far East, Hearings before the Committee on Armed Services and the Committee on Foreign Relations, United States Senate, 82nd Cong.*, 1st sess. *TO CONDUCT AN INQUIRY INTO THE MILITARY SITUATION IN THE FAR EAST AND THE FACTS SURROUNDING THE RELIEF OF GENERAL OF THE ARMY DOUGLAS MACARTHUR FROM HIS ASSIGNMENTS IN THAT AREA*, Part 1, May 3–14, 1951 (Washington, DC: U.S. Government Printing Office, 1951), pp. 3, 27–31, 44–45.

9.6. George C. Marshall's Testimony on the Military Situation in the Far East, Hearings before the Committee on Armed Services and the Committee on Foreign Relations, May 1951

The secretary of defense, the secretary of war, and members of the Joint Chiefs of Staff also testified before Congress. The following is an excerpt from the testimony of Secretary of Defense George C. Marshall, who explains how MacArthur was "out of step" with the Truman administration's military policies in Korea.

Secretary Marshall. I have a brief statement to make, but first I would like to observe that it is a very distressing necessity, a very distressing occasion, that compels me to appear here this morning and in effect in almost direct opposition to a great many of the views and actions of General MacArthur. He is a brother Army officer, a man for whom I have tremendous respect as to his military capabilities and military performances and from all I can learn, as to his administration of Japan. I am here primarily to answer whatever questions you and members of the committees may care to ask me. However, I think it may be helpful if, at the outset, I make a brief preliminary statement which I think will clarify some of the issues raised in the course of your hearings last week. . . .

BASIC DIFFERENCES ON EXTENSION OF CONFLICT

Secretary Marshall. Now, as to the basic differences of judgment which exist between General MacArthur on the one hand, and the Joint Chiefs of Staff, the Secretary of Defense, and the President, on the other hand. Our objective in Korea continues to be the defeat of the aggression and the restoration of peace. We have persistently sought to confine the conflict to Korea and to prevent its spreading into a third world war. In this effort, we stand allied with the great majority of our fellow-members of the United Nations. Our efforts have succeeded in thwarting the aggressors, in Korea, and in stemming the tide of aggression in southeast Asia and elsewhere throughout the world. Our efforts in Korea have given us some sorely needed time and impetus to accelerate the building of our defenses and those of our allies against the threatened onslaught of Soviet imperialism. General MacArthur, on the other hand, would have us on our own initiative, carry the conflict beyond Korea against the mainland of Communist China, both from the sea and from the air. He would have us accept the risk involvement not only in an extension of the war with Red China, but in an all-out war with the Soviet Union. He would have us do this even at the expense of losing our allies and wrecking the coalition of free people throughout the world. He would have us do this even though the effect of such action might expose Western Europe to attack by the millions of Soviet troops poised in Middle and Eastern Europe. This fundamental divergence is one of judgment as to the proper course of action to be followed by the United States. This divergence arises from the inherent difference between the position of a field commander, whose mission is limited to a particular area and a particular antagonist, and the position of the Joint Chiefs of Staff, the Secretary of Defense, and the President, who are responsible for the total security of the United States, and who, to achieve and maintain this security, must weigh our interests and objectives in one part of the globe with those in other areas of the world so as to attain the best over-all balance.

PUBLIC VOICING OF THE DISAGREEMENT

Secretary Marshall. It is their [Joint Chiefs of Staff, secretary of defense, and the president] responsibility to determine where the main threat to our security lies, where we must fight holding actions, and where and how we must gain time to grow stronger. On the other hand, the responsibilities and the courses of action assigned to a theater commander necessarily apply to his own immediate area of responsibility. It is completely understandable and, in fact, at times commendable that a theater commander should become so wholly wrapped up in his own aims and responsibilities that some of the directives received by him from higher authority are not those that he would have written for himself. There is nothing new about this sort of thing in our military history. What is new, and what has brought about the necessity for General MacArthur's removal, is the wholly unprecedented situation of a local theater commander publicly expressing his displeasure at and his disagreement with the foreign and military policy of the United States. It became apparent that General MacArthur had grown so far out of sympathy with the established policies of the United States that there was grave doubt as to whether he could any longer be permitted to exercise the authority in making decisions that normal command functions would assign to a theater commander. In this situation, there was no other recourse but to relieve him.

IMPORTANCE OF CASUALTIES IN KOREA

Secretary Marshall. As to the question of the specific campaign in Korea, as to the casualties that are daily occurring there, with our troops, and those of our allies, no one, I believe, is more conscious of them than I am. I realize, though, that the commander on the spot, who actually witnesses the casualties, is even more impressed by what is going on. However, during some very painful years, I had a daily question of casualties from all over the world, and it is an agonizing procedure, so I can fully understand the reaction of a commander in General MacArthur's position, to the struggle in Korea, unless he could clearly see an early and victorious way out. But there are many other considerations that this Government has to take into account; and it becomes the hard duty of those responsible to consider what is the wisest course to follow in such matters. What our troops have done has really been magnificent. Thank goodness, a few of them are now coming back and they will return in much larger numbers beginning the end of this month; but we have small choice at the moment in the matter; and what we can do is appreciate to the full the heroism, the endurance, and the skillful fighting that those men are doing for us.

ADEQUACY OF REASONS FOR MACARTHUR REMOVAL

Senator Wiley. MacArthur, on the ground 10,000 miles away, had a different idea as to how the battle should be carried on. He gave those different ideas to his supervisors here in Washington, and they must have given them to the allies, and they disagreed with his ideas. Because they disagreed with MacArthur's ideas, you people came to the conclusion that he was violating a directive of some kind, which justified his removal?

Secretary Marshall. I'll say this, Senator: By his public statement he has created a feeling of great uneasiness among our allies, as to the consequent results from his proposals.

He was creating a feeling of uncertainty with our allies as to who was directing these affairs—that our Chief Executive, as the executive agent for those allies, or otherwise—when he proposed the utilization of the Chinese Nationalist troops from Formosa, he was setting up a very serious consideration, entirely remote from the quality of those troops, which is a matter that the Chief of Staff can talk to you more definitely in regard to than I can, because the employment of Chinese Nationalist troops in Korea set up a possible political consequence of great importance to those allies. . . .

Senator Wiley. He didn't use them.

Secretary Marshall. He was proposing their use, sir.

Senator Wiley. Was that a sufficient crime to take a man of this position out of that job?

Secretary Marshall. When you create the feeling among your allies that you are on the verge of doing something which they feel is of great misfortune to them and a hazard to them, you are now involved in a question of policy, and the President of the United States by the Constitution is the only one who should interpret that.

Source: "Testimony of Secretary of Defense George C. Marshall," *Military Situation in the Far East, Hearings before the Committee on Armed Services and the Committee on Foreign Relations, United States Senate, 82nd Cong., 1st sess., TO CONDUCT AN INQUIRY INTO THE MILITARY SITUATION IN THE FAR EAST AND THE FACTS SURROUNDING THE RELIEF OF GENERAL OF THE ARMY DOUGLAS MACARTHUR FROM HIS ASSIGNMENTS IN THAT AREA,* Part 1, May 3–14, 1951 (Washington, DC: U.S. Government Printing Office, 1951), pp. 322–326, 416–417.

9.7.   Harold L. Ickes Compares Nathan Hale and Douglas MacArthur, May 7, 1951

A well-known Republican leader, Harold L. Ickes, wrote an editorial in the New Republic *in which he sharply criticized Mac-*

Arthur. Ickes served as the secretary of the interior under both Presidents Franklin D. Roosevelt and Harry Truman. In his article, Ickes contended that MacArthur violated the principles of civil-military authority and demonstrated disloyalty to the President of the United States.

Many generations of American youth have known the story of Nathan Hale. They have revered and honored his memory. He is regarded, almost above any other American who has ever lived, as the highest exponent of selflessness and of devotion to country, even unto death. His heroism was particularly distinguished. It was heroism of service, of self-abnegation, of devotion to his country, of willingness to pay the supreme price of life itself in the ignominious form of hanging. If this sincere and devoted patriot had come through the Revolutionary War alive, one cannot conceive of his touring the country to receive the stimulated adulation of the populace. One cannot think of him as willingly lending himself to political partisans seeking political control and pelf for themselves. Least of all can one imagine his ignoring or defying the orders of his military superiors. If he had, fortunately for his country, survived to become a citizen of the newly created United States, it is not to be imagined that he would have appealed to the people over the head of the duly elected President of the United States.

Nathan Hale exemplified the word "loyal." He was loyal to his comrades in arms; he was loyal to his immediate commanding officers; he was loyal to his Commander-in-Chief; he was loyal to his political ideals.

If Nathan Hale were alive today, he would merely be one of a million or more "heroes," many of them self-acclaimed or at least willing to plead "guilty" to the flattering impeachment. The word hero has become disgustingly cheap.

Gen. Douglas MacArthur would do well to disassociate himself from the designation "hero" or "patriot." There is nothing of the hero about this man if the word is supposed to connote selflessness and willingness to sacrifice one's self. Nor can man be a patriot unless he loves his country and zealously supports its authority and interests. No man should be regarded as a hero, especially if he wears the uniform of his country, who is willing to lead those who would destroy the unity of the American people and divide them into contending factions for political purposes. MacArthur and Sen. Robert Taft (R, Ohio) would take half of American strength and resources, if necessary, to throw behind Chiang Kai-shek in waging a war against Communist China, a war that has already been lost overwhelmingly by Chiang Kai-shek and which he can never win, even if we should support him with all of our strength. Others, under President Truman's leadership, would marshal our might and conserve it to defend against Russia, which is the real foe of all that America is and should be.

Whether President Truman is right or wrong, either as a military tactician or as an international politician, can probably only be proved by the event. But there can be no disputing the fact that he is the chosen civilian leader of the country, that he will hold office at least until January 20, 1953, and that, in the meantime, unless our Constitution is to be violated, as MacArthur has deliberately violated all of the principles of his profession, he will be Commander-in-Chief of our armed forces during his term as President.

What would MacArthur have done if, while fighting was in progress in Korea and he was serving as supreme commander, a general had written a letter to a pestiferous and miserable little politician by the name of Joe Martin, taking issue publicly with some policy laid down by him? The answer is simple. Even if such an insubordinate wrecker of morale were a lieutenant general, he would quickly be relieved of his command and court-martialed.

The spirit of Nathan Hale, who was willing to submit to the most disgraceful form of death possible in our civilization, still, thank God, pervades the rank and file, as well as the upper echelons, of the American army. MacArthur's insubordination, his unrebuked defiance of his Commander-in-Chief, his unrequited defiance of all military traditions, his open attempt to make a mock of civic as well as of military virtue, is a bad example for troops and civilians alike. He is said to regard himself as a man of destiny. At times he has seemed to stretch his stature to that of God. Certainly there is nothing to shrink him to earthly proportions when one considers the sacrilegious words of Rep. Dewey Short, the former minister of the Gospel from Missouri, who said, after General MacArthur's speech before Congress: "We heard God speak here today, God in the flesh, the voice of God."

General MacArthur is said to be sure of a place in history. There are times when we Americans can show less common sense and sound judgment than any other people on earth. But whenever we madly shout "Hosanna" to some imitation god, we usually quickly discover the clay feet and, as unobtrusively as possible, slip back into the ranks of those who are loyal to their country and jealous of its reputation for sanity even during a time of hysterical stress that is due to the machinations of our Joe Martins, our Styles Bridges's and our Cains and McCarthys.

Source: Harold L. Ickes, "Nathan Hale and MacArthur," *New Republic*, May 7, 1951, p. 15.

9.8.   The *Stars and Stripes* Criticizes the Firing of MacArthur, April 19, 1951

Americans debated whether Truman's dismissal of MacArthur was justifiable. The editors of the military newspaper Stars and Stripes—*"The Voice of the Veterans of the United States"— praised the general's military skills and inferred that Truman, not MacArthur, should have been "fired."*

Never have the people of this country been so shocked as they were last week when President Truman relieved Gen. Douglas MacArthur of his Far East commands. They have experienced great emotions, it is true, but the conflagration of public opinion resulting from the MacArthur ouster pales them all. It would seem that the organized veterans of the Nation might have sprung to their feet in roaring indignation, but even they and their spokesmen were so nonplused and their sentiment was so divided by the issues involved that they either crawled into their shells or else issued mild and inconclusive statements to tide them over until their heads clear a little and until the hysteria subsides and things come a little more clearly into focus. An idol has fallen, but we suggest that knowing the General as we do and understanding at least to some degree the temper of the Chief Executive and his advisors, this incident is not settled by long odds.

We believe it behooves everybody to attempt to look upon this incident as dispassionately as possible and to dig down to the bottom of the controversy to find its fundamentals, analyze them and guardedly reach such conclusions as might best serve our citizenry. Certainly nobody can deny that Mr. Truman, as Commander in Chief of the armed forces in time of emergency, had the right and power to remove anybody who does not go along with him in following out national policy. He had that privilege, and he exercised it with, we believe, honest reluctance. Realizing that there were material differences in the thinking of the two men, it could have been hoped that the President would first recall Mac-Arthur to this country for conferences in an effort to get together, but attempts to compose conflicting ideas were otherwise followed and, having failed, the boss fired a subordinate. The fact that a mediocre artillery captain dismissed a five-star general with a world-wide reputation as a master strategist is beside the point. MacArthur was a loose spoke in Truman's policy wheel and it was removed for repairs in accordance with protocol. World War II was lost at the gates of Berlin, and another war may be lost in Korea, but no Presidential prerogatives were violated and, if Mr. Truman is to be held to account, it must be shown that his monumental action is a terrible error of judgment. The final outcome of the controversy and whatever may happen in reprisal must be determined by calm study and honest decision, not by emotional and political retaliation. . . .

As veterans, we must look to the issues rather than become lost in a debate over personalities, and we are gladdened by the purpose expressed by the Congress, and agreed to by the President, to investigate the issue and we hope, to reach a definition of policy that is best suited to the national needs. . . .

It is our firm conviction that the military must always be subordinated to civilian control if this Government is to survive, but we can not help but conclude that not only is Gen. MacArthur the victim of a gang of internationalists in the Department of State who are attempting to take the United States into a World Federation by which our sovereignty and individual liberties will be lost, but also that our President is going to lose his political head for permitting them to influence his judgment.

Source: "Fired the Wrong Man," *The Stars and Stripes*, April 19, 1951, p. 1.

ANNOTATED RESEARCH GUIDE

Books and Articles

Belmonte, Laura. "Anglo-American Relations and the Dismissal of MacArthur." *Diplomatic History* 19, no. 4 (1995): 641–667. Explores Britain's opposition to and frustration with MacArthur from his appointment as head of the UN forces to his recall from the command.

Christensen, Thomas J. "Threats, Assurances, and the Last Chance for Peace: The Lessons of Mao's Korean War Telegrams." *International Security* 17, no. 1 (1992): 122–154. Provides a new perspective on the Korean War by utilizing telegrams, letters, and other primary documents from Mao Zedong to Joseph Stalin and Chinese military leaders.

Donaldson, Gary A. *America at War since 1945: Politics and Diplomacy in Korea, Vietnam, and the Gulf War*. Westport, CT: Praeger, 1996. Examines the difficulties of fighting the Korean and Vietnam wars and connects these conflicts to how the United States fought the Gulf War.

Fehrenbach, T.R. *This Kind of War: The Classic Korean War History*. Washington, DC: Brassey's, 1998. Detailed book on the military actions in the Korean War that includes a fact-filled chapter on the Truman-MacArthur debate.

Jones, D. Clayton. *Refighting the Last War: Command and Crisis in Korea, 1950–1953*. New York: Free Press, 1993. Includes a chapter on the Truman-MacArthur debate and argues that the differences between the two leaders were far more complex than just total war versus limited war.

Karp, Walter. "Truman vs. MacArthur." *American Heritage* 35, no. 3 (April/May 1984): 84–95. Provides an overview of the Truman-MacArthur controversy, focusing primarily on the public reaction, the Republican response, and the congressional hearings.

Kaufman, Burton I. *The Korean War: Challenges in Crisis, Credibility, and Command.* Philadelphia: Temple University Press, 1986. Examines the Korean War and the Truman-MacArthur controversy from the general's viewpoint.

Lutzker, Michael A. "Presidential Decision Making in the Korean War: The British Perspective." *Presidential Studies Quarterly* 26, no. 4 (1996): 978–995. Looks at the problems in the Korean War from the perspective of the British and discusses their anxiety about MacArthur's military actions and proposed plans.

MacArthur, Douglas. *Reminiscences.* New York: McGraw-Hill, 1964. MacArthur recounts his military career and devotes a chapter of his book to the "frustration in Korea."

———. *A Soldier Speaks: Public Papers and Speeches of General of the Army Douglas MacArthur.* New York: Praeger, 1965. Prepared for the U.S. Military Academy, West Point, New York, this book includes General MacArthur's public papers and speeches.

MacDonald, C.A. *Korea: The War before Vietnam.* New York: Free Press, 1987. Explores the roots of the Korean War and the Cold War and examines the problems associated with fighting a limited war. Includes a discussion of the Truman-MacArthur debate.

Perret, Geoffrey. *Old Solders Never Die: The Life of Douglas MacArthur.* New York: Random House, 1996. Details the life and career of General MacArthur. Includes an examination of the Cold War as a new kind of war and connects this to the difficulties in fighting the Korean War.

Ridgway, Matthew B. *The Korean War.* Garden City, NY: Doubleday, 1967. Written by the general who replaced MacArthur as the commander of the UN forces in Korea, this book includes a chapter on the dismissal of MacArthur. Although Ridgway shows respect to MacArthur, he explains why the president's decision was correct.

Smith, Robert. *MacArthur in Korea: The Naked Emperor.* New York: Simon and Schuster, 1982. Focuses on MacArthur's complex personality, his leadership in Korea, and the debate between the general and the president.

Toland, John. *In Mortal Combat: Korea, 1950–1953.* New York: William Morrow, 1991. Discusses many of the controversies surrounding the Korean War, including the arguments between Truman and MacArthur over Korean military policies.

Weintraub, Stanley. *MacArthur's War: Korea and the Undoing of an American Hero.* New York: Free Press, 2000. Provides a complete account of important military actions that took place during MacArthur's command in the Korean War.

Video

Reda, Lou, prod. *General Douglas MacArthur*. Lou Reda Production for A&E Television Network. This video traces MacArthur's military career from World War I through the Korean War. Distributed by A&E Home Video, South Burlington, VT.

Web Sites

http://korea50.army.mil/teachers.html. "Just for Teachers" includes a story on the war for young readers and a word-search game.

http://mcel.pacificu.edu/as/students/stanley/home.html. Includes book reviews, oral histories, maps, senior thesis, and links to other related sites.

http://school.discovery.com/lessonplans/programs/koreanwar. Provides K-12 lesson plans, vocabulary words, suggested reading, and student questions on the Korean War.

http://www.whistlestop.org/index.html. Official Web site of the Truman Presidential Library, "Whistlestop." Includes primary sources concerning the Korean War. Also found at http://Trumanlibrary.org.

10

The My Lai Massacre: Crossing the Line in Vietnam

America's twenty-five-year involvement in the Vietnam War thrust the nation into a long, dark tunnel that never seemed to end. One of the darkest moments occurred with the My Lai Massacre. In the early hours of March 16, 1968, American soldiers from Charlie Company of the 1st Battalion, 20th Infantry, opened fire on unarmed villagers in the small hamlet of My Lai. The next four hours saw unspeakable terror. Soldiers lined up women, children, and old men in front of ditches and mowed them down with gunfire. The unthinkable continued—the mass execution of families, children gunned down with M-16s, young women brutally raped before being shot to death—and in the end, the death toll was four hundred Vietnamese civilians. The officers covered up the reality of the morning's events, and despite reports of the incident from other sources, the military did not formally investigate the massacre until the incident became public in November 1969. As Americans struggled to understand the actions, debates began to rage. Was My Lai the cold reality of an undefined war, or did the soldiers cross the line? When does war become murder?

What caused Company C to lose control that March morning? Military investigators, scholars, and journalists who have attempted to understand the massacre look at a number of explanations, including the psychological breakdown of the soldiers, poor military leadership, and the common acceptance of unrestrained violence as a consequence of war. Others put the blame on civilian and military policymakers who promoted an atmosphere where war crimes became a de facto policy. The general public also debated the My Lai incident, and its reactions reflected a nation struggling to understand the perplexity of the Vietnam War.

The Vietnamese people had long struggled for their independence. Their centuries-old fight against Chinese domination shifted to the French when the European empire colonized Vietnam in the late nineteenth century. During World War II, Ho Chi Minh and the Vietnamese Independence League (Vietminh) resisted the Japanese who occupied the country. The Vietnamese rebels also helped the United States by providing intelligence information and rescuing downed American pilots. At the war's end, when the French reasserted their control over the Vietnamese colony, Ho Chi Minh and the Vietminh fought back. Ho Chi Minh had become a Communist in the 1920s, but he was principally a nationalist determined to free his country from foreign rule. Although President Franklin D. Roosevelt had considered recognizing Vietnam's independence, the rising Cold War convinced President Harry S. Truman to support the French, since a strong European power could help balance the Soviet presence in the region. American economic aid and covert support followed. The French defeat at Dienbienphu in 1954 resulted in the division of Vietnam at the seventeenth parallel and ushered in a new and eventually a demoralizing chapter in U.S. history.

America's efforts at "nation building" failed when it attempted to shore up an increasingly corrupt South Vietnamese government under the leadership of Ngo Dinh Diem, the anti-Communist president of the Republic of Vietnam (South Vietnam). As Diem's abuses continued, resistance by the Vietcong rebels increased. During the Dwight Eisenhower and John F. Kennedy administrations, American advisors, sent to assist the South Vietnamese army, grew rapidly to reach more than 16,000 by the fall of 1963. A series of coups brought new leadership to a failing South Vietnamese government, while the strength of the Vietcong increased from the support of Ho Chi Minh, now the leader of the Democratic People's Republic of Vietnam (North Vietnam). During the Lyndon Johnson administration, combat troops replaced advisors, and the conflict—still framed by Cold War ideology—became a war to stop the spread of communism. Eventually, some 2.8 million Americans served in the Vietnam War, a conflict filled with confusion, frustration, and division, a war that included the disturbing massacre in a small hamlet known as My Lai.

MY LAI MASSACRE

In the early part of 1968, shortly after the United States experienced a major humiliation during the Communists' Tet offensive, Task Force Barker of the American Division attempted to chase down and secure the

Vietcong in Quang Ngai Province. This dangerous mission took Charlie Company far from its base camp and into the hazardous interior of the well-known enemy stronghold of the 48th Vietcong Battalion. Captain Ernest L. Medina, the leader of Charlie Company, gave the orders to secure My Lai, part of the Son My Village. On March 16, helicopters landed the first platoon, led by Lieutenant William L. Calley. They were later followed by the second and third platoons. Although Charlie Company had experienced little combat prior to My Lai, it had lost two men in a minefield in February. Thirteen soldiers were injured in the same incident. A few days before the My Lai mission, Charlie Company's second platoon lost a popular sergeant from a booby trap. Three others were wounded at the same time.

From the testimony later taken at Calley's court martial, it is clear that confusion reigned once the men entered the hamlet. Expecting heavy enemy fire and experiencing none, the men were uncertain of their next move. Instead of Vietcong soldiers, they found women, children, and old men. Some soldiers rounded up the villagers, while others destroyed property and livestock. However, Calley soon set the stage for the massacre when he instructed his men "to take care of the people. . . . I mean kill them." Others remember that Calley yelled, "Why haven't you wasted them yet?" before he fired into a group of "unarmed, unresisting villagers."[1] (Later, Calley claimed he was only following Medina's orders when the commanding officer told Calley to "waste" the Vietnamese villagers if he could not move them in time to set up a defensive position.)

According to later testimonies, Calley and others lined up villagers in front of a ditch and shot them with automatic weapons. Specialist Charles Hall recalled looking in the ditch. "They were dead. There was blood coming from them. They were just scattered all over the ground. . . . They were very old people, very young children, and mothers. . . . There was blood all over them."[2] Specialist Charles Sledge saw Calley grabbing a small child—"a little baby"—running toward the village and "threw it into the ditch and fired."[3]

Mayhem followed confusion as other soldiers in the first platoon joined in the killings. Soldiers from the second and third platoons followed suit. Sergeant Charles West explained the loss of control this way: "When the attack started, it couldn't have been stopped by anyone." West continued, "We were mad and we had been told that only the enemy would be there when we landed. . . . We were going in for a fight and for our dead buddies. . . . We started shooting everything and everybody we saw. . . . It was like our ammunition would never run out."[4] In addition to the executions, some twenty women were raped, some in front of their children. Soldiers killed many of the women and children after they violated the women.

Not everyone participated in the massacre. "Many soldiers took no action at all, but stood passively by while others destroyed My Lai. A few, after witnessing inexplicable acts of violence against defenseless villagers, affirmatively refused to harm them."[5]

Helicopter pilot Hugh C. Thompson and his gunner, Larry Colburn, were horrified by what they saw on the ground at My Lai and reported the incident by radio to headquarters. Risking their own lives, the two rescued over a dozen children from the area. During the rescue of a small child, Thompson and Calley exchanged words. After the pilot instructed his gunner to shoot Calley if he interfered, he was able to save the child.

Thompson reported what he saw to his company commander, Major Frederick Watke. Watke advised the task force commander, Lieutenant Colonel Frank Barker, of the massacre. However, after Barker returned from visiting the area, he told Watke that "he could find nothing to substantiate Thompson's allegations."[6] After hearing "rumors" of the massacre and receiving written complaints from Vietnamese officials, Washington ordered an investigation. American Division Commander Major General Samuel W. Koster instructed Brigade Commander Colonel Oran Henderson to investigate. Henderson reported that "20 non-combatants were inadvertently killed when caught in the area of preparatory fires and in the cross fires of the US and VC forces on 16 March 1968."[7] Soon after the March incident, Lieutenant Calley was relieved of his position as platoon commander, and his request to be transferred out of the company was honored.

Things quieted down until early 1969, when Vietnam veteran Ron Ridenhour, a former helicopter gunner, made the incident public. Ridenhour had heard about My Lai from a member of Charlie Company and substantiated the massacre after discussions with others. After writing to some thirty different congressmen and Pentagon officials with no success, Ridenhour contacted journalist Seymour Hersh, and soon news of My Lai soon shook the nation.

PSYCHOLOGICAL BREAKDOWN OF THE SOLDIERS

Was Vietnam so different from previous wars in its ferocity that bloodshed of this proportion could result? Some argue that to truly understand My Lai, one must understand the distinguishing nature of the Vietnam War and the immeasurable frustration experienced by both the individual soldier and the nation as a whole. To a country gleaming with the success of World War II—a "good" war complete with clear moral objectives and war heroes—Vietnam was exhausting in its complexities. Like the Korean War, Vietnam was a war for balance, not victory. However, in many ways, the Korean conflict was still a traditional war. Success could be measured in territories lost or gained and in the position and strength of the enemy troops. Although the objective was not popular, it was clear—confine the enemy in the north above the thirty-eighth parallel.

The Vietnam War was a vastly different war—a war often fought against an unseen enemy. Body counts replaced territories gained in a war of attrition. For American ground troops, Vietnam meant guerrilla warfare, booby traps, land mines, sniper fire, and ambushes. It also meant surviving in the intense heat of the jungles, swamps, and rice paddies. American soldiers sent to fight the spread of communism found it difficult to discern its presence, and their inability or unwillingness to understand the language, culture, and objectives of the Vietnamese people only added to the confusion. Were the innocent farmers by day actually the snipers at night? Were country villagers loyal to the rebel forces? Were the Vietnamese working in the American camps really Vietcong? As historian George C. Herring notes, "Ironically and tragically, America's allies—the South Vietnamese—became the target of much of the anger and frustration that built up during the war."[8]

Historian Stephen E. Ambrose asserts that war is the most "extreme experience" a person can encounter, and under such pressure, soldiers sometimes snap. Describing the war in Vietnam, he explains: "What happens to men in combat is that they see their buddy with his brains oozing out of a hole in his head. . . . They see men trying to stuff his guts back into his stomach. They see a man carry his left arm in his right hand. They see men who have lost their manhood to a piece of shrapnel."[9] According to Ambrose, "Lieutenant Calley lost control, as did his men."[10]

The report from the House Armed Services Investigating Subcommittee contended that "extenuating circumstances" played a role in My Lai. Soldiers in Vietnam lived "for extended periods of time in the shadow of violent death and in constant fear" caused by a war against an unseen enemy. "Understandably such conditions can warp attitudes and mental processes causing temporary deviation from normality of action, reason and sense of value."[11] Historians James S. Olson and Randy Roberts concluded that under such circumstances reality became blurred, and Charlie Company

drift[ed] swiftly into a culture of violence in which anything seemed permissible. Cut off from the civilization and rules of conduct that they had learned in the United States, isolated on long patrols through Vietnamese villages, frustrated at seeing their friends and comrades killed or maimed, many soldiers adopted a new code of behavior, one that permitted the killing of prisoners, the torture of suspects, the cutting off of ears of the dead, the rough treatment and rape of civilians.[12]

POOR LEADERSHIP

Others argue that poor leadership played a key role in the My Lai Massacre. Captain Medina set the tone by making it clear that the villagers could not be trusted. Although there are various accounts of the captain's orders, many soldiers felt that the message was clear—revenge. His preattack "pep talk" was more like an eerie ceremony than an attempt to instill esprit de corps in the troops. The men of Company C should "settle some scores" for the death of their friends, and Medina recited the names of each man who had died. Lieutenant Calley was at best an incompetent platoon commander with few leadership and military skills. Medina continually ridiculed the young man despite the lieutenant's attempt to impress him. After the massacre, Calley claimed that Medina had given him the order to "neutralize" My Lai before and during the attack, telling him to "make sure there was no one left alive."[13] The cover-up by Task Force Commander Barker, Brigade Commander Henderson, and Division Commander Koster brought in even higher levels of deficient leadership unwilling to deal with a serious situation.

Some argue that the responsibility for My Lai should lie with the commander of the American troops in Vietnam, General William C. Westmoreland. When the American media attacked the military in the early 1970s for violating international rules of war in Vietnam, they claimed that General Westmoreland could be punished for war crimes. In response, the Department of the Army produced an investigative report. In it, the army acknowledged "isolated acts" of violence against Vietnamese civilians, but argued that General Westmoreland was "keenly aware of humanitarian considerations" in Vietnam and instructed his commanders to adhere to the "Rules of Engagement," which call for the protection of civilian lives and property. The army also counterargued that "terror and intimidation are basic tools of the Communist forces in Vietnam. . . . The bestial conduct of the Communist forces in no way excuses or mitigates the criminality of isolated acts by the US Forces. It does raise the question why those who criticize the US conduct of the war in Vietnam on humanitarian grounds fail to point the finger of guilt at the Communist forces."[14]

CIVILIAN AND MILITARY POLICY

Others argue that the indiscriminate killing of Vietnamese civilians had become a routine practice emanating from an "official and quasi-official climate" of excessive force created by American policymakers measuring the war's success in body counts and "kill ratios." Social scientists Edward M. Opton, Jr., and Nevitt Sanford maintained that "free fire zones" or "kill zones" were often "inhabited villages" when destruction occurred. "Winning the hearts and minds" of the Vietnamese people had quickly deteriorated, in the words of one Marine Corps officer, into one of "bombing and shelling them from their villages, assassinating their leaders, breaking up their families by removing the men, and removing the rural population to concentration camps euphemistically called 'refugee camps.' "[15] Journalists also joined the debate. According to Jonathan and Orville Schell's 1969 article in the *New York Times*, My Lai was not an "isolated atrocity." The two journalists exposed what they contended were common army practices. When the "pacification camps" were filled to capacity, search-and-destroy missions continued. "Only now peasants were not warned before an air strike was called in on their village."[16] According to the Schells, "It was under these circumstances of official acquiescence to the destruction of the countryside and its people that the massacre of [My Lai] occurred. Such atrocities were and are the logical consequences of a war directed against an enemy indistinguishable from the people."[17]

UNRESTRAINED VIOLENCE AS A CONSEQUENCE OF WAR

Some scholars and military investigators argue that soldiers who participated in the My Lai incident were products of a culture that advocated extreme violence, racism, and Machiavellianism in the American style of foreign policy and in wars throughout the world. In historian Ambrose's words, "Do not think that My Lai was an exception or an aberration when you consider war from the time of the ancient Greeks up to the present. Atrocity is a part of war that needs to be faced and discussed."[18] Certainly, American history includes examples of war atrocities with racial overtones, such as those in the Indian Wars and the Philippine-American War.

Rules of war have changed significantly during the twentieth century. Noncombatant immunity—the international agreement that war is fought between combatants, not civilians—began to erode during World War I, especially with the use of the submarine. However, it was the policy of strategic bombing during World War II that made it acceptable for civilians to be targets of war and led to the dropping of the atomic bomb on two Japanese cities. The 1971 army report on the conduct of the war in Vietnam urges readers not to "disregard history" when evaluating what the report claimed were isolated instances of "criminal acts" in Vietnam. "Civilian suffering, though tragic, is an unavoidable consequence of war. Time has fogged the memory of the great allied offensives of World War II which liberated Axis-occupied territories and the heavy losses of friendly civilian lives and property that accompanied these massive drives. There has been nothing in the war in Vietnam to compare with the total devastation of St. Lo or the over 100,000 estimated casualties incurred during the recapture of Manila."[19]

PUBLIC DEBATE

The initial public reaction was one of shock and bewilderment when Americans heard Paul Meadlo's confession on the *CBS Evening News* with Walter Cronkite on November 21, 1969. Newspapers and magazines throughout the nation quickly picked up the story. Reporters interviewed members of the general public as well as their political leaders. Response ranged from disbelief to apathy to anger. Americans directed blame at the individual soldier, the nation, or antiwar protesters. Others contended that the story was simply not true and was in fact "planted" by Vietcong "sympathizers."

The *Philadelphia Inquirer* called My Lai "the kind of atrocity generally associated with the worst days of Hitler and Stalin and other cruel despotism." The *Washington Star* called it "simply appalling." My Lai became the cover story for both *Newsweek* and *Time*, and *Life* carried photographs taken by one of the soldiers along with "extensive accounts." Conservative newspapers also responded. The *Chicago Tribune*'s reaction to the statements of other presses warned the public that "Americans should not be deceived by the contemptible lamentations that we are all guilty and that our troops in Viet Nam [*sic*] have been brutalized by war and are just as inhuman as Communists." The *National Observer* dismissed any notion that the fault lay with the system, emphasizing that "individual responsibility" for the killings "must be fixed."[20]

A *Minneapolis Tribune* "statewide poll" taken before Christmas 1969 revealed that "49 percent of 600 persons interviewed thought the reports of mass murder at My Lai 4 were false." Others saw the killings as either a natural outcome of war or an isolated exception. One Bostonian argued, "What do they give soldiers bullets for—to put in their pockets?" Senator Allen Ellender, a Democrat from Louisiana, told a reporter that the "slain" Vietnamese "got just what they deserved." Governor George Wallace of Alabama, publicly supported Calley and declared that investigators "ought to spend the time trying folks who are trying to destroy this country instead of trying those who are serving their country." A poll taken by *Time* magazine of "1,600 households indicated that 65 percent of the American public believed such incidents were bound to happen in any war." Although President Richard Nixon thought that "under no circumstances was [the massacre] justified, he concluded that it was 'an isolated incident.' " In Jacksonville, Florida, six American Legion posts "announced plans to raise a $200,000 defense fund for Calley."[21]

Some expressed anger at the media. When the *Cleveland Plain Dealer* printed photos of the massacre, one woman angrily responded, "Your paper is rotten and anti-American." Another woman pointedly asked, "How can I explain these pictures to my children?" After the CBS interview, one caller sent a telegram that read, "[Mike] Wallace is pimping for the protesters." Senator Peter H. Dominick, a Republican from Colorado, attacked the media, concluding that reporters sensationalized the incident.[22] But many were still stunned by the killing of innocent civilians and struggled to understand.

After looking at the photos of the massacre, Congressman Leslie C. Arends, a Republican from Illinois, told a reporter that he had to leave the room: "The pictures were pretty gruesome." The chairman of the Senate Armed Services Committee, John C. Stennis, called My Lai "a shocking affair . . . contrary to every rule and instruction the army has issued."[23] Senator George S. McGovern of South Dakota maintained, "What this incident has done is to tear the mask off the war. . . . I think that for the first time millions of Americans are realizing that we have stumbled into a conflict where we not only of necessity commit horrible atrocities against the people of Vietnam, but where in a sense we brutalize our own people and our nation." The senator concluded that "national policy" was "on trial." In 1972, McGovern ran for president with the promise to end the war in Vietnam, but his bid for the White House was unsuccessful. "Dove voices" and antiwar protesters clearly saw My Lai as further proof that the United States should not be in Vietnam. The subsequent cover-up provided additional evidence to this group that the government and the military could not be trusted.[24]

The American public debate continued during and after the congressional investigation of My Lai, which began in November 1969. An official military investigation followed. In March 1970, General William R. Peers, who headed the inquiry, released *The Report of the Department of the Army Review of the Preliminary Investigation into the My Lai Incident*. This report uncovered a four-year military cover-up and recommended that charges be brought against twenty-eight commissioned officers and two noncommissioned officers. However, eventually, army lawyers decided to bring criminal charges against only four officers (Capt. Medina, Lt. Calley, Capt. Eugene Kotouc, and Lt. Thomas K. Willingham) along with nine enlistees. Two generals received a reduction in rank. On March 29, 1971, after careful deliberation, the jury at Calley's court-martial trial "announced they had found Calley guilty of premeditated murder. Two days later, on March 31, after considering the matter for nearly seven hours, the jury returned to a crowded but hushed courtroom and declared that Calley should be confined at hard labor for the length of his natural life."[25] Other soldiers received reprimands.

A national survey taken in April 1971 revealed that 58 percent of the public did not think that Calley should have been brought to trial. Most of those who disapproved of the trial thought it "unfair to send a man to fight in Vietnam and then put him on trial for doing his duty."[26] Among those who disapproved of the trial, 43 percent thought that it kept the nation from "facing the real issue: what's wrong with the war and the way it's being fought." Of the 34 percent who approved of the trial, 53 percent felt that soldiers, even in combat situations, should not kill "defenseless civilians." Some 48 percent of those who approved of the trial agreed that "every man must bear responsibility for his own actions." When Calley was found guilty of premeditated murder, a 1971 *Newsweek* poll disclosed that 79 percent of those polled did not agree with the verdict, and some 81 percent of those polled considered life imprisonment "too harsh."[27]

CONCLUSION

In reaching their decision to sentence Calley to life imprisonment, the United States military justices acknowledged the frustrating nature of the Vietnam War, the difficulties of fighting against an unseen enemy, and violence as a consequence of war. It also acknowledged the lieutenant's "deficiencies" as a leader. However, in the March 1971 sentencing of the lieutenant, the military justices concluded:

Destructive as war is, war is not an occasion for the unrestrained satisfaction of an individual soldier's proclivity to kill. An officer especially must exert his mind to keep his emotions in check, so that his judgement is not destroyed by fear, hate, or frustration. Probably Lieutenant Calley's judgement, perception, and stability were lesser in quality than the average lieutenant's. . . . However, the deficiencies did not even approach the point of depriving him of the power of choice. The approved sentence is not too severe a consequence of his choosing to commit mass murder.[28]

Just three days after Calley's 1971 sentencing to life imprisonment, President Richard Nixon ordered that the lieutenant be released from prison on "house arrest" waiting appeal. For the next thirty-five months, Calley's "jail" was an apartment at Fort Benning, Georgia. On August 20, 1971, the commanding general of the 3rd U.S. Army reduced Calley's sentence to twenty years. Calley's lawyers continued to fight for a review of *U.S. v. Calley*, asking for a new trial. However, the Court of Military Review denied this petition in 1973. But in April 1974, the Secretary of the Army, Howard Calloway, reduced Calley's sentence to ten years.

Any attempt by Nixon to rethink Vietnam strategy and mollify the antiwar movement came to a dramatic halt with the Watergate scandal and the president's subsequent resignation in August 1974. "His successor, Gerald R. Ford, inherited a crippled presidency and defense policy," which soon saw a dramatic reduction in military spending.[29]

Calley served only four and a half months in jail at Leavenworth before Calloway officially paroled him on November 9, 1974. The My Lai trials came during an exceptionally turbulent time in American history, as the nation struggled to deal with government deception over the Vietnam War and Watergate. Did the leniency shown toward the accused soldiers represent their innocence, or did it represent a nation's desperate desire to bring closure to the pain and confusion associated with America's first military defeat? Only one thing was certain: the former members of the 1st Battalion, 20th Infantry, Charlie Company were free. America's disillusionment with Vietnam continued for decades to come, and the cry "no more Vietnams" resonated throughout the next war in the Persian Gulf.

NOTES

1. Court of Military Review, *United States v. First Lieutenant William L. Calley, Jr.* Extracts from Vol. 46, *Court-Martial Reports,* United States Army War College (USAWC), February 16, 1973, p. 1169. U.S. Army Military History Institute, Carlisle Barracks, Pennsylvania. Hereafter cited as *United States v. Calley.* Testimonies from Calley's 1971 court martial trial are reprinted in this Court of Military Review document.

2. Ibid., p. 1171.

3. Ibid., p. 1173.

4. Quoted in Jerold M. Starr and Christopher W. Wilkens, *When War Becomes a Crime: The Case of My Lai* (Washington, DC: Center for Social Studies Education, 1988; revised, 1991), n.p.

5. *United States v. Calley,* p. 1165.

6. Joseph Goldstein, Burke Marshall, and Jack Schwartz, *The My Lai Massacre and Its Cover-up: Beyond the Reach of the Law? The Peers Commission Report with a Supplement and Introductory Essay on the Limits of Law* (New York: Free Press, 1976), p. 47. Reprint of the report of the Department of the Army review of the preliminary investigations into the My Lai incident.

7. Memo to Commanding General American Division, from Oran K. Henderson, Col., Infantry Commanding, SUBJECT: Report of Investigation APO SF 96374, 24 April 1968, Peers investigation government documents, reprinted in Lt. Gen. W.R. Peers, *The My Lai Inquiry* (New York: W.W. Norton, 1979), pp. 272–273.

8. George C. Herring, "What Kind of War Was the Vietnam War?" in *Facing My Lai: Moving beyond the Massacre,* ed. David L. Anderson (Lawrence: University Press of Kansas, 1998), pp. 98–99.

9. Stephen E. Ambrose, "Atrocities in Historical Perspective," in *Facing My Lai: Moving beyond the Massacre,* ed. David L. Anderson (Lawrence: University Press of Kansas, 1998), p. 109.

10. Ibid., p. 118.

11. From the House Armed Services Investigations Subcommittee Report, quoted in *United States v. Calley*, p. 1196.

12. James S. Olson and Randy Roberts, *My Lai: A Brief History with Documents* (Boston: Bedford Books of St. Martin's Press, 1998), p. 17.

13. *United States v. Calley*, p. 1180; Olson and Roberts, *My Lai*, p. 19.

14. U.S. Department of the Army, Office of the Deputy Chief of Staff for Military Operations, *Final Report of the Research Project on Conduct of the War in Vietnam* (Washington, DC: U.S. Government Printing Office, May 1971), pp. 96–97, U.S. Army Military History Institute, Carlisle Barrarks, Carlisle, Pennsylvania. Hereafter cited as *Conduct of War in Vietnam, Final Report*.

15. Edward M. Opton, Jr., and Nevitt Sanford, "Lessons of Mylai," in *The American Military*, ed. Martin Oppenheimer (Chicago: Aldine Publishing Company, 1971), pp. 109, 111.

16. Orville Schell and Jonathan Schell, "Slaughter in Songmy," *New York Times*, November 26, 1969, p. 44.

17. Ibid.

18. Ambrose, "Atrocities in Historical Perspective," p. 108.

19. *Conduct of the War in Vietnam, Final Report*, p. 95.

20. Quoted in Seymour M. Hersh, *My Lai 4: A Report on the Massacre and Its Aftermath* (New York: Random House, 1970), p. 141.

21. Ibid., pp. 151–160.

22. Ibid., p. 152.

23. Ibid., pp. 157–158.

24. Ibid.

25. Michael Bilton and Kevin Sim, *Four Hours in My Lai* (New York: Penguin Group, 1992), pp. 337–338.

26. For a reprint of the public opinion polls, see Starr and Wilkens, *When War Becomes a Crime*, pp. 22–24.

27. Ibid.

28. *United States v. Calley*, p. 1196.

29. Allan R. Millett and Peter Maslowski, *For the Common Defense: A Military History of the United States of America* (New York: Free Press, 1984), p. 565.

DOCUMENTS

10.1.   **Colonel Oran Henderson's Report of the Investigation, April 24, 1968**

Some critics of the My Lai Massacre contend that military leaders must share some of the blame for the tragedy. Critics also express outrage at the cover-up by high-ranking officers. The following report was submitted by Brigade Commander Colonel Oran K. Henderson. In it, the colonel explained that Task Force Commander Lieutenant Colonel Frank Barker, Company Commander Captain Ernest Medina, and other officers claimed that "at no time were any civilians gathered together and killed by US soldiers." Henderson also reported only twenty Vietnamese civilian casualties at My Lai, which he said occurred when civilians were "caught" in a "battle area." Henderson also denied that American troops killed between 450 and 500 Vietnamese and called the information "Viet Cong" propaganda.

SUBJECT: Report of Investigation
Commanding General
American Division
APO SF 96374

1. (U) An investigation has been conducted of the allegations cited in Inclosure I. The following are the results of this investigation.

2. (C) On the day in question, 16 March 1968, Co C 1st Bn 20th Inf and Co B 4th Bn 3rd Inf as part of Task Force Barker, 11th Inf Bde, conducted a combat air assault in the vicinity of My Lai Hamlet (Son My Village) in eastern Son Tinh District. This area has long been an enemy strong hold, and Task Force Barker had met heavy enemy opposition in this area on 12 and 23 February 1968. All persons living in this area are considered to be VC or VC sympathizers by the District Chief. Artillery and gunship preparatory fires were placed on the landing zones used by the two companies. Upon landing and during their advance on the enemy positions, the attacking forces were supported by gunships from the 174th Avn Co and Co B, 23rd Avn Bn. By 1500 hours all enemy resistance had ceased and the remaining enemy forces had withdrawn. The results of this operation were 128 VC soldiers KIA [Killed in Action]. During preparatory fires and the ground action by

the attacking companies 20 non-combatants caught in the battle area were killed. US Forces suffered 2 KIA and 10 WIA [wounded in action] by booby traps and 1 man slightly wounded in the foot by small arms fire. No US soldier was killed by sniper fire as was the alleged reason for killing the civilians. Interviews with LTC Frank A. Barker, TF Commander; Maj Charles C. Calhoun, TF S_3; CPT Ernest L. Medina, Co Co C, 1–20; and CPT Earl Michles, Co Co B, 4–3 revealed that at no time were any civilians gathered together and killed by US soldiers. The civilian habitants in the area began withdrawing to the southwest as soon as the operation began and within the first hour and a half all visible civilians had cleared the area of operations.

3. (C) The Son Tinh District Chief does not give the allegations any importance and he pointed out that the two hamlets where the incident is alleged to have happened are in an area controlled by the VC since 1964. COL Toan, Cmdr 2d ARVN Div reported that the making of such allegations against US Forces is a common technique of the VC propaganda machine. Inclosure 2 is a translation of an actual VC propaganda message targeted at the ARVN soldier and urging him to shoot Americans. This message was given to this headquarters by the CO, 2d ARVN Division o/a 17 April 1968 as matter of information. It makes the same allegations as made by the Son My Village Chief in addition to other claims of atrocities by American soldiers.

4. (C) It is concluded that 20 non-combatants were inadvertently killed when caught in the area of preparatory fires and in the cross fires of the US and VC forces on 16 March 1968. It is further concluded that no civilians were gathered together and shot by US soldiers. The allegation that US Forces shot and killed 450–500 civilians is obviously a Viet Cong propaganda move to discredit the United States in the eyes of the Vietnamese people in general and the ARVN soldier in particular.

5. (C) It is recommended that a counter-propaganda campaign be waged against the VC in eastern Son Tinh District.

Oran K. Henderson
COL, Infantry
Commanding

Source: From Peers investigation government documents, reprinted in Lt. Gen. W.R. Peers, *The My Lai Inquiry* (New York: W.W. Norton, 1979), pp. 272–273; Joseph Goldstein, Burke Marshall, and Jack Schwartz, *The My Lai Massacre and Its Cover-up: Beyond the Reach of Law? The Peers Commission Report with a Supplement and Introductory Essay on the Limits of Law* (New York: Free Press, 1976), pp. 285–286.

10.2.   Journalists Jonathan and Orville Schell Assign Responsibility for the My Lai Massacre, November 26, 1969

Shortly after the news of the My Lai incident became public, journalists began to analyze the cause of the massacre. In the following article, Jonathan and Orville Schell, who experienced the Vietnam War firsthand as journalists in Quang Ngai Province, argued that the United States had a de facto policy that made the killing of Vietnamese civilians not only acceptable, but a relatively common practice. They further argued that Calley and the other men from Charlie Company should not shoulder the blame alone.

To the Editor:

Many Americans are justifiably horrified by reports of mass execution of civilians in Vietnam. The most recent incident at Songmy [My Lai], or "Pinkville," in Quangngai Province now centers around two servicemen, Lieut. William Calley and Staff Sgt. David Mitchell, who stand accused of murder. Experience in Vietnam and Quangngai Province as journalists has led us to write this letter in hopes of dispelling two possible misapprehensions; that such executions are the fault of men like Calley and Mitchell alone, and that the tragedy of Songmy is an isolated atrocity.

We both spent several weeks in Quangngai some six months before the incident. We flew daily with the F.A.C.'s (Forward Air Control). What we saw was a province utterly destroyed. In August 1967, during Operation Benton, the "pacification" camps became so full that army units in the field were ordered not to "generate" any more refugees. The army complied. But search and destroy operations continued.

Only now peasants were not warned before an air strike was called in on their village. They were killed in their villages because there was no room for them in the swamped pacification camps. The usual warnings by helicopter loudspeaker or air-dropped leaflets were stopped. Every civilian on the ground was assumed to be enemy by the pilots by nature of living in Quangngai, which was largely a free fire zone.

Pilots, servicemen not unlike Calley and Mitchell, continued to carry out their orders. Village after village was destroyed from the air as a matter of *de facto* policy. Air strikes on civilians became a matter of routine. It was under these circumstances of official acquiescence to the destruction of the countryside and its people that the massacre of Songmy [My Lai] occurred.

Such atrocities were and are the logical consequences of a war directed against an enemy indistinguishable from the people.

Orville Schell
Jonathan Schell
Berkeley, Calif., Nov. 19, 1969

Source: Orville Schell and Jonathan Schell, "Slaughter in Songmy," *New York Times*, November 26, 1969, p. 44.

10.3.   Final Report of the Army on the Conduct of the War in Vietnam, May 1971

During the war, critics questioned U.S. practices in Vietnam and alleged that American troops committed atrocities against the Vietnamese people that constituted war crimes. Some critics suggested that General William C. Westmoreland, head of the American forces, could also be guilty of war crimes. In response, the U.S. Department of the Army put together a Research Project Task Force to investigate. Its report, excerpted here, acknowledged that some isolated cases of atrocities did occur in Vietnam, but argued that Westmoreland directed the American troops to protect Vietnamese civilians and abide by the rules of war. In addition, the report argued, "Civilian suffering, though tragic, is an unavoidable consequence of war," and cited examples from World War II. The army also counterattacked, asking why critics did not criticize war atrocities committed by the Communist forces.

Critics of the United States military assistance effort in Vietnam have, from the beginning, charged that the United States Government has violated international law by committing its armed forces in support of the Government of the Republic of Vietnam. Coincidentally, many of them have alleged that the US Forces under General Westmoreland's command conducted hostilities in a manner which violated internationally accepted norms. They have also charged that high US commanders, including General Westmoreland, could be punishable as war criminals under the principles applied to Axis commanders after World War II.

This paper addresses itself to the second and third type of allegations mentioned. Its purpose is to show that General Westmoreland conducted the war in Vietnam in a manner consistent with the requirements of international law and that he fulfilled his obligation as commander by requiring the forces under his command to comply with the laws of war. . . .

The history of General Westmoreland's conduct of the war in Vietnam shows that as a commander he conformed to the laws of war and was keenly aware of humanitarian considerations. MACV [Military Assistance Command, Vietnam] directives governing the conduct of air and ground operations in South Vietnam promulgated by General Westmoreland provided the restraints necessary to minimize noncombatant casualties and civilian property damage. Operations in Specified Strike Zones were subject to the law of war and the Rules of Engagement, and search and destroy operations were carried out under similar restrictions. General Westmoreland continuously instructed his commanders of the need to abide by the rules of governing the protection of civilian lives and property.

While it is true that Vietnamese civilians were relocated, in some instances against their will, it is clear that the relocations conducted by US Forces were made for good and cogent military reasons and in a manner in keeping with the spirit and intent of General Westmoreland's directives and guidance. It is further clear that General Westmoreland's directives were established to provide protection for the civilian and his property and that the relocation programs conducted in Vietnam were neither war crimes nor crimes against humanity.

General Westmoreland, no less than his critics, has pointed out that the care and treatment of refugees and civilian war casualties have sometimes been less than desirable. However, it is equally true that through the combined efforts of the Government of Vietnam, the United States military, United States Aid to International Development, and many other volunteer activities, the care and treatment of these individuals has improved vastly and has been as humane as possible under the circumstances.

Although International Committee of the Red Cross inspections of the South Vietnamese PW camps during General Westmoreland's tenure disclosed some minor administrative discrepancies, US military authorities took reasonable and effective steps to secure the proper treatment of all captured enemy personnel. They fulfilled their humanitarian as well as their legal obligation concerning the treatment and well being of personnel originally captured or detained by US units. Moreover, the South Vietnamese authorities have been both willing and able to handle prisoners of war in the manner required by the Geneva Conventions.

In the absence of clear and convincing evidence that there were widespread, patently criminal violations of the law of war in Vietnam during the period 24 June 1964–3 July 1968, and that the preventive/corrective actions taken by General Westmoreland were so inadequate as to constitute criminal negligence in the supervision of his subordinates, the

Nuremberg principles would not constitute any precedent for the conclusion that General Westmoreland could be found guilty of war crimes.

The military effort in Vietnam has been the focus of controversy from the outset. Critics have argued that since the US purpose in Vietnam is to guarantee the liberty of the Vietnamese people, the incidence of civilian casualties and the destruction of civilian property are proof that US strategy is inappropriate and ill conceived. Such civilian suffering, though tragic, is an unavoidable consequence of war. Time has fogged the memory of the great allied offensives of World War II which liberated Axis-occupied territories and the heavy losses of friendly civilian lives and property that accompanied these massive drives. There has been nothing in the war in Vietnam to compare with the total devastation of St. Lo or the over 100,000 estimated casualties incurred during the recapture of Manila.

The facile use of the term "war crimes" as a rhetorical device to discredit the US effort in Vietnam manifests a like ignorance of or disregard for history. Axis commanders were not punished because, as an incident of combat operations, civilians were injured or killed, or non-military property was destroyed. They were tried because they implemented a policy of deliberate extermination and intimidation which included mass executions and other forms of calculated brutality. Some individual members of the US Forces have committed criminal acts in Vietnam, but those who so readily charge that the US Forces have committed war crimes on a wide scale would do well to read the charges and judgements, and review the evidence in the World War II cases. It might well serve to place the matter in proper perspective. Such a study will also reveal that the tactics and policies of the VC mirror those of the Axis powers in WW II. Terror and intimidation are basic tools of the Communist forces in Vietnam. The torture, abduction, and murder of teachers and civilian officials of the village and provincial governments has been a standard VC tactic. The deliberate destruction of civilian refugee centers and harassment by fire of hamlets and villages were widespread. The systematic mass murder of over 4,000 civilians at Hue during the Tet offensive has been publicized, but the grim chronicle of cumulative atrocities is less widely known. Excluding incidents during the 1968 Tet offensive, more than 18,000 South Vietnamese were assassinated by the Communist forces in 1968, 1969, and 1970, according to Department of Defense statistics. In the same time period, more than 23,000 South Vietnamese were abducted by the enemy. These tragic figures include the murder of approximately 400 persons and the abduction of more than 600 others who were already victims of war and classified as refugees. The Communists deliberately attacked at least twenty refugee centers and 56 medical facilities and hospitals during the period 1968 to 1970.

Unlike the enemy's medical facilities, those of the GVN and US Forces are clearly marked and identifiable. In addition, the Communist forces compelled thousands of South Vietnamese to serve as battlefield laborers, just as the Germans forced millions of people to work as slave laborers in the war industries of the Reich. . . .

The bestial conduct of the Communist forces in no way excuses or mitigates the criminality of isolated acts by the US Forces. It does raise the question why those who criticize the US conduct of the war in Vietnam on humanitarian grounds fail to point the finger of guilt at the Communist forces. Why does the media ignore all but the most massive Communist atrocities, but distort legitimate acts of war by the US Forces to find criminality where there is none, and leap upon reports of isolated criminal acts, real or imagined, as irrefutable evidence of widespread American war crimes? If there is to be an inquiry related to the Vietnam war, it should be into the reasons why enemy propaganda was so widespread in this country and why the enemy was able to condition the public to such an extent that the best educated segments of our population have given credence to the most incredible allegations, and, more like the children of Hamelin than the most sophisticated members of our society, have fallen over themselves in their haste to follow wherever they should be led.

Source: U.S. Department of the Army, Office of the Deputy Chief of Staff for Military Operations, Final Report of the Research Project on Conduct of the War in Vietnam" (Washington, DC: U.S. Government Printing Office, May 1971), pp. 93–97.

10.4.   Court-Martial Report on *United States v. Calley*, November 17, 1970–March 29, 1971

Members of Charlie Company provided graphic details about the attack on My Lai during the trial of Lieutenant William Calley. Testimonies from the American soldiers described the four hours of horror.

As previously described, some of the villagers rooted out of their homes were placed in a group guarded by PFC Paul Meadlo and PFC Dennis Conti. PFC Dursi, who was about fifteen feet from PFC Meadlo watching his own group of Vietnamese, saw Lieutenant Calley come onto the trail and heard him ask Meadlo "if he could take care of that group." A couple of minutes later the appellant returned and, as Dursi remembered, yelled to Meadlo, "Why haven't you wasted them yet?" PFC Dursi turned and started to move his group down the trail when he heard M-16 fire from his rear.

PFC Conti recounted that Lieutenant Calley told him and Meadlo "To take care of the people," left, and returned:

> "Then he came out and said, 'I thought I told you to take care of them.' Meadlo said, 'We are watching them' and he said 'No, I mean kill them.' "

Conti testified that he saw Lieutenant Calley and Meadlo fire from a distance of ten feet with M-16 rifles on automatic fire into this group of unarmed, unresisting villagers. . . .

Meadlo testified that he was guarding a group of villagers with Conti when Lieutenant Calley approached him and said, "You know what to do with them, Meadlo." He assumed at the time this meant only to continue guarding them. However, appellant returned in ten or fifteen minutes and said, "How come they're not dead?" Meadlo replied, "I didn't know we were supposed to kill them," after which Lieutenant Calley directed, "I want them dead." Meadlo remembered that appellant backed away and began firing into the group before he did the same. . . .

Specialist Four Hall collected thirty or forty people, pushed them forward through My Lai (4) to the ditch, left them there, and proceeded to a position in the paddies beyond. He noticed that Sergeant Mitchell, Lieutenant Calley, the platoon's RTO's and several others stayed behind. Sometime after he got into position Hall heard fully automatic fire behind him coming from the area of the ditch. He saw a helicopter land and appellant converse with its aviator, after which he heard slow, semi-automatic fire from the ditch. Later, when he crossed the ditch on a wooden foot bridge, he saw thirty or forty people in it:

> "They were dead. There was blood coming from them. They were just scattered all over the ground in the ditch, some in piles and some scattered out 20, 25 meters perhaps up the ditch. . . . They were very old people, very young children, and mothers. . . . There was blood all over them . . ."

Other members of the first platoon saw Vietnamese placed into a ditch and appellant and others fire into it. Some members of the third platoon also saw the bloody bodies. Also, the observations of witnesses who were in the supporting helicopters portray a telling, and ghastly, overview of the slaughter at the ditch. Aviators and crew members saw from the air numbers of bodies they variously estimated from about thirty to about one hundred. One aviator, a Lieutenant (then Warrant Officer) Thompson, actually landed near the scene three times. The second time, he spoke with someone, who from the evidence must have been Lieutenant Calley. Thompson succeeded in evacuating a few living Vietnamese despite appellant's deprecations. The evidence from others is certainly persuasive that Lieutenant Calley boasted, "I'm the boss here," after he spoke with an aviator. . . .

According to Specialist Four Sledge, five or ten minutes after Lieutenant Calley returned from speaking with a helicopter aviator, he and Calley encountered a forty to fifty year old man dressed in white robes as they moved north up the ditch. Appellant repeatedly questioned the man, "Viet Cong adou?" (Are you Viet Cong), to which the man continually replied, "No viec." Suddenly Lieutenant Calley shot the man in the face at point blank range, blowing half of his head away. Immediately after this incident Sledge remembered that:

"Someone hollered, 'there's a child,' You know, running back toward the village. Lieutenant Calley ran back, the little—I don't know if it was a girl or boy—but it was a little baby, and he grabbed it by the arm and threw it into the ditch and fired."

Sledge observed this from a distance of twenty to thirty feet. He recalled that only one shot was fired at the child from a distance of four or five feet. He did not see whether the round struck.

Source: Court of Military Review, *United States v. First Lieutenant William L. Calley, Jr.* Extracts from Vol. 46, *Court-Martial Reports,* United States Army War College, February 16, 1973, pp. 1163–1173. Testimonies from Calley's 1971 court martial trial are reprinted in this Court of Military Review document.

10.5.   The Sentencing of First Lieutenant William L. Calley, March 29, 1971

In the sentencing of Lieutenant William L. Calley, the military court took into consideration the frustrating nature of the Vietnam War, the difficulties of fighting against an unseen enemy, and violence as a consequence of war. It also noted Calley's "deficiencies" as a leader. Still, in 1971, the military court sentenced Calley to life imprisonment. President Richard Nixon released Calley from prison and he was put on "house arrest" during the appeal process. The secretary of the Army, Howard Calloway, paroled Calley in 1974. The following is an excerpt from the court-martial report.

In the report of the House Armed Services Investigating Subcommittee many of the extenuating circumstances affecting Lieutenant Calley are identified:

"In a war such as that in Vietnam, our forces in the field must live for extended periods of time in the shadow of violent death and in constant fear of being crippled or maimed by booby traps and mines. And added to this is the fact that this is not war in the conventional sense. The enemy is often not in uniform. A farmer or a housewife or a child by day may well be the enemy by night, fashioning or setting mines and booby traps, or giving aid, comfort and assistance to the uniformed enemy troops. Under such circumstances, one can understand how it might become increasingly difficult for our troops to accept the idea that many of those who kill them by night somehow become 'innocent civilians' by day. Understandably such conditions can warp attitudes and mental processes causing temporary deviation from normality of action, reason or sense of values. And the degree of deviation may vary with each individual."

These general circumstances, and mitigating factors personal to Lieutenant Calley, were specifically considered by the convening authority who substantially reduced the confinement portion of the sentence to twenty years.

No doubt Lieutenant Calley would never have directed or participated in a mass killing in time of peace. Nevertheless, he committed an atrocity in time of war and it is in the context of war that we judge him. Destructive as war is, war is not an occasion for the unrestrained satisfaction of an individual soldier's proclivity to kill. An officer especially must exert his mind to keep his emotions in check, so that his judgement is not destroyed by fear, hate, or frustration. Probably Lieutenant Calley's judgement, perception, and stability were lesser in quality than the average lieutenant's and these deficiencies are mitigating to some extent. However, the deficiencies did not even approach the point of depriving him of the power of choice. The approved sentence is not too severe a consequence of his choosing to commit mass murder.

Source: Court of Military Review, *United States v. First Lieutenant William L. Calley, Jr.* Extracts from Vol. 46, *Court-Martial Reports*, United States Army War College, February 16, 1973, p. 1196. Calley's March 29, 1971, sentencing is reprinted in this Court of Military Review document.

ANNOTATED RESEARCH GUIDE

Books and Articles

Anderson, David L., ed. *Facing My Lai: Moving beyond the Massacre*. Lawrence: University Press of Kansas, 1998. Summarizes roundtable discussions and debates that were part of the 1994 Tulane University Conference on the My Lai Massacre. The conference brought together historians, journalists, and Vietnam veterans, including Ron Ridenhour, the soldier who told Congress and the media about My Lai, and Hugh C. Thompson, Jr., the helicopter pilot who rescued a number of My Lai villagers.

Bilton, Michael, and Kevin Sim. *Four Hours in My Lai*. New York: Viking, 1992. Provides a detailed examination of the My Lai tragedy and explains how the incident still affects the nation and veterans today.

French, Peter A., ed. *Individual and Collective Responsibility: Massacre at My Lai*. Cambridge, MA: Schenkman Publishing Company, 1972. French and other philosophers examine ethical questions surrounding My Lai and ask if the blame should be on the individual soldier or society.

Goldstein, Joseph, Burke Marshall, and Jack Schwartz. *The My Lai Massacre and Its Cover-up: Beyond the Reach of Law?* New York: Free Press, 1976. Lt. General W.R. Peers's 1974 My Lai report for the Department of the Army with an introductory essay by Goldstein, Marshall, and Schwartz.

Hart, Franklin A. "Yamashita, Nuremberg, and Vietnam: Command Responsibility Reappraised." *Naval War College Review* 25 (1972): 19–36. Hart challenges Professor Telford Taylor's argument that General Westmoreland and other senior officers should be held responsible for the My Lai Massacre.

Hersh, Seymour M. *Cover-up*. New York: Random House, 1972. Written by the journalist who brought the My Lai Massacre to the public forum. Examines the cover-up of My Lai, using official transcripts and other military records.

Kelman, Herbert C., and Lee H. Lawrence. "American Response to the Trial of Lt. William L. Calley." In *The Military in America: From the Colonial Era to the Present*, ed. Peter Karsten. New York: Free Press, 1980, pp. 431–446. Provides an analysis of the public debate over Lieutenant William L. Calley's trial.

McCarthy, Mary. *Medina*. New York: Harcourt Brace Jovanovich, 1972. Utilizing newspaper accounts, McCarthy examines the trial of Charlie Company commander Captain Ernest L. Medina.

Olson, James S., and Randy Roberts. *My Lai: A Brief History with Documents*. Boston: Bedford Books of St. Martin's Press, 1998. A complete summary of My Lai is followed by a large selection of primary sources, including military correspondence, briefings, testimonies, investigation materials, newspaper accounts, and other related sources.

Opton, Edward M., Jr., and Nevitt Sanford. "Lessons of Mylai." In *The American Military*, ed. Martin Oppenheimer. Chicago: Aldine Publishing Company,

1971, pp. 104–116. The authors argue that the killing of civilians had become a de facto policy long before the My Lai Massacre and that American society is also to blame for the incident.

Peers, Lt. Gen. W.R. *The My Lai Inquiry*. New York: W.W. Norton, 1979. General Peers headed the investigation of My Lai, and this book shares his findings with the public. The book includes reprints of official military documents.

Starr, Jerold M., and Christopher W. Wilkens. *When War Becomes a Crime: The Case of My Lai*. N.p.: Center for Social Studies Education, 1988. This well-organized lesson plan for teachers provides a brief discussion on various topics related to My Lai followed by discussion questions. Photos, maps, and reprints of public opinion polls are also included.

Wilson, William. "I Had Prayed to God That This Thing Was Fiction." *American Heritage* 41, no. 1 (1990): 44–53. Written by one of the primary investigators of the My Lai cover-up about his experience. Summarizes Wilson's reaction when he read a letter written by Vietnam veteran Ron Ridenhour describing the massacre.

Web Sites

http://www.law.umkc.edu/faculty/projects. Professor Doug Linder, University of Missouri-Kansas City School of Law, Famous Trials Page, includes reprints of government documents related to My Lai.

http://www.pbs.org/wgbh/pages/amex/vietnam/trenches/mylai.html. PBS/ The American Experience. Includes summary of the history of the My Lai tragedy along with teacher guides.

http://www.ttu.edu/~vietnam/mylai.htm. This Tulane University site provides copies of oral histories from its conference on My Lai. A video of interviews with Hugh Thompson, Ron Ridenhour, and others are available for purchase on this Web site.

11

The Bombing of Iraq: The Debate over America's Growing Dependence on Technology in the Persian Gulf War

"If the war in the gulf ends the way it began—with a dazzling display of American technological superiority, individual grit and, most unexpectedly for Saddam Hussein, national resolve—we will no longer speak of post-Vietnam America. A new, post-gulf America will emerge, its self-image, sense of history, even its political discourse transformed," predicted Charles Krauthammer in the January 28, 1991, issue of *Time* magazine.[1] America's belief in technology is ingrained in its national culture. Technology helped to connect the continent, make the United States a global power, and put a man on the moon. Technology also created new and destructive weapons that pushed the death toll in the two world wars well into the tens of millions and escalated a nuclear arms race of epic proportions.

During the Persian Gulf War (January–February 1991), scholars, military leaders, and defense analysts continued an intense debate over America's growing reliance on high-tech weapons. Many military and political leaders saw high-technology air power as a way to achieve a quick military success and, at the same time, restore national confidence, damaged in both Korea and Vietnam. They predicted that air power would prove worthy by swiftly ending the Gulf War and sparing the lives of thousands of soldiers and civilians. But others pointedly asked, would this be a clean "antiseptic war," or "was the surgical face of battle, 1991 style, a mask over the familiar maw of death?"[2] These political leaders and defense analysts questioned whether new technological advances could really help America avoid a protracted war, keep losses to a minimum, and emerge as a credible military power. They warned Americans to look more closely at the success of Desert Storm's new "robowar" and cautioned them not to be lulled into a "techno-euphoria," or a false sense that computer-driven precision weapons could bring quick and easy victories in all future conflicts. Technology did provide a sense of distance from the fighting, which led to a renewed debate over women in combat. Ultimately, the Persian Gulf War brought with it a ghost from the past as the nation called for "no more Vietnams."

THE CRISIS

In 1989, President George Bush welcomed the end of the Cold War by declaring a "New World Order" free of conflict and full of hope for world peace. But in the summer of 1990, jubilation was marred by trouble in the Middle East. On August 2, President Saddam Hussein of Iraq ordered the invasion of Kuwait, a wealthy nation with an extremely lucrative oil industry. Saddam Hussein claimed that this small neighboring country had once been part of Iraq before British imperialists reshaped the Ottoman Empire in the 1920s. Controlling Kuwait would provide Iraq with much-needed easy access to the Persian Gulf. When Kuwait pleaded for help, a coalition of United Nations forces, led by the United States, answered the call.

American involvement in the Middle East can be traced to World War II, when the United States joined its allies, Britain and the Soviet Union, in the occupation of oil-rich Iran. At the war's end, the Soviet Union went head-to-head with its former allies over postwar oil rights, but the Communists found themselves out in the cold. In 1953, the American Central Intelligence Agency (CIA) overthrew the new Iranian prime minister, Mohammed Mossadegh, when he began to nationalize the British-controlled oil fields in Iran. The Dwight Eisenhower administration felt justified in toppling Mossadegh since the United States feared that the new Iranian government might sell oil to America's chief enemy, the Soviet Union. The CIA-backed coup restored the shah, Reza Pahlavi, protected British oil rights, and provided American oil companies control of 40 percent (a significant increase) of Iran's petroleum holdings. To secure this vital interest for the future, the U.S. government provided the shah with financial and military support for years to come and ultimately helped to create one of the most brutal regimes in the world. But by 1979, the Iranian people had had enough. Tired of being oppressed by the shah, the Iranians turned to Islamic fundamentalist Ayatollah Ruholla Khomeini as their new leader. In an effort to balance the ayatollah and protect foreign oil interests in other countries in the Middle East, the United States joined its European allies in advancing Saddam

Hussein's power. During the 1980s, when Iran and Iraq were engaged in a bloody war, the United States helped European powers turn an unimpressive Iraqi military into a large and treacherous force. Yet the situation became even more complex when members of the Ronald Reagan administration secretly sold weapons to Iran in order to free American hostages taken by Muslin extremists in Lebanon. The weapons were subsequently used in Iran's war with Iraq.

After eight years of brutal warfare with Iran that ended in a stalemate in 1988, Saddam Hussein hoped to improve the economy of his struggling country by taking over the oil-rich sheikdom of Kuwait. If he were successful, Iraq would control 25 percent of the world's oil industry and could dramatically drive up the price of petroleum. Within a few weeks, Iraqi forces took control of Kuwait and stationed troops along the Saudi Arabian border. If Iraq also secured Saudi Arabia, it could add another 20 percent of the world's oil reserve to its empire, subsequently holding hostage petroleum used by industrialized nations throughout the globe. Saddam Hussein also received world criticism for human rights violations. The future safety of Israel would also be in question if Iraq succeeded in its expansion.

At first, the United Nations Security Council unanimously objected to Iraq's actions and implemented economic sanctions against the nation. When that policy failed, a coalition of some 250,000 troops from the United States, Britain, France, Italy, Saudi Arabia, Egypt, Syria, Morocco, Oman, and the United Arab Emirates gathered at Saudi military bases. On November 29, 1990, the Security Council issued a final ultimatum to Saddam Hussein, giving him until January 15, 1991, to remove his troops from Kuwait. If he failed or refused to do so, Iraq would face the full force of the UN troops. The United Nations also called for world condemnation of Iraq and was pleased when Russian leader Mikhail Gorbachev joined in the chorus of global voices protesting Iraqi aggression. Even this did not convince Saddam Hussein to retreat. Dark clouds gathered in the Iraqi sky—a desert storm was approaching.

In the U.S. Congress, Democrats and Republicans participated in a passionate debate that sharply divided them into two camps: those who supported the continuation of economic sanctions against Iraq versus those who wanted to use immediate military force. On January 12, 1991, after much discussion, the House and Senate issued a joint resolution authorizing the use of American military troops against Iraq. U.S. Army General Norman Schwarzkopf headed Operation Desert Storm, which included more than half a million American soldiers, the largest military force deployed since the Vietnam War. They were joined by troops from more than twenty nations forming a united coalition against Saddam Hussein. The coalition began with a massive air assault.

AIR-POWER DOCTRINE

American air-power doctrines can be traced back to the 1920s, when General Billy Mitchell adopted the ideas of British and Italian military leaders Hugh Trenchard and Giulio Douhet, both of whom promoted the concept of air superiority. Searching for an alternative to the long stalemate and human carnage of the World War I trenches, these military theorists looked to the skies for answers. They argued that airplanes used on civilian populations could destroy the enemy's ability to make war by crushing its urban and industrial centers—its war-making machinery—and thus shattering the will of the people. Proponents concluded that air power was more humane and could win wars without protracted and costly ground battles. In 1926, Mitchell predicted that "future wars would be won by air power alone, through bombing campaigns reaching over the enemy's armies and navies to its vital centers of production and population, paralyzing the vital centers, making productive activity in them impossible, and destroying the enemy people's will to resist."[3] Throughout the 1920s, Mitchell pushed for the development of new airplane technology and the modernization of the American air service, but when he tangled with his superiors, he was court-martialed and subsequently resigned from the army. During the 1920s and 1930s, the doctrine of air pioneers was deemed unacceptable, even barbaric, since it violated long-established rules of war, which protected civilians in military conflicts.

However, during World War II, both Allied and Axis powers resorted to indiscriminate bombing of populated areas, demolishing numerous European and Japanese cities and killing hundreds of thousands of civilians. In the end, this terror bombing did not break the will of the people and may, in fact, have increased their determination to win. World War II strategic bombing brought to the forefront an important debate concerning ethics and war. Clearly, the "specter" of the multitude of civilians killed in World War II has "haunted U.S. presidents who have contemplated the use of strategic bombing since."[4]

THE SHADOW OF PAST WARS

The Vietnam War also left unanswered questions for many Americans as the long cast of the Asian war's shadow continued to fall over the Persian Gulf. Before and during Desert Storm, politicians, scholars, and journalists continually warned Americans against falling into the same snare as the Vietnam War. Historian Robert Dallek cautioned, "Americans have a very difficult time understanding and accepting limited war."[5] He noted that as the years of involvement in the Vietnam War lengthened and casualties increased, support for the war diminished.

Tom Wicker of the *New York Times* joined others in counseling that there must be clearly communicated objectives in the Gulf War, or the Vietnam experience would likely stand in the way of cohesive support for Desert Storm. Judging "by Korea and Vietnam, the lack of a clear-cut, widely accepted and easily understood war aim may be the factor that could undermine American unity in the gulf war."[6]

In the January congressional debates over Iraq, congressmen and senators made numerous references to the failure of the Vietnam War and warned that the next war must not turn out like the last one. Congressman Thomas J. Manton, a Democrat from New York, concluded, "The memories of Vietnam remain painfully clear in Woodside. Before my constituents are willing to sacrifice a new generation they must be convinced war is our only alternative." The delegate from American Samoa, Eni Faleomavaega (Democrat), spoke of the "horrors of war" and of the more than 50,000 American lives "sacrificed in Vietnam." When Faleomovaega had served in Vietnam, he had "never doubted for any moment the possibility that [he] might return either in a body bag or as a cripple for life." Congressman Randall "Duke" Cunningham (Republican, California) criticized the restrictions placed on the military in the Asian war and concluded that "in Vietnam our hands were tied, and over 55,000 Americans were killed," and Senator Sam Nunn, Democrat from Georgia, told the *Washington Post* that America had learned lessons from the Vietnam War. "We should hit military targets with awesome power at the beginning of any conflict, as well as knocking out power and communications, electrical, nuclear and chemical facilities."

Others disagreed with the impact of Vietnam on the Persian Gulf. Congressman Cass Ballenger, a Republican from North Carolina, declared that "the Persian Gulf [was] not Vietnam." Democratic congressional leader Charles Wilson agreed: "Before we mindlessly shout 'another Vietnam!' and get swept up in heady anti-war rhetoric, we need to ponder again." However, the Texas congressman added that any "military action should be quick and decisive.... The American people will not stand for American casualties mounting month after month from a prolonged conflict."[7]

AIR-WAR STRATEGY DEBATE

President George Bush, Secretary of Defense Dick Cheney, and Joint Chiefs of Staff Chairman Colin Powell approved four major criteria for the Persian Gulf War: (1) push Iraqi troops out of Kuwait; (2) eliminate the Iraqi military's nuclear, biological, and chemical weapons capability; (3) avoid the destruction of Kuwaiti cities and industry and avoid injuring Kuwaiti civilians; and (4) end the war quickly, with a low rate of friendly casualties. Air power lay at the center of Operation Desert

Storm. "This was done with the full knowledge that in previous conflicts where air power had been used (i.e. World War II, Korea, . . . Vietnam), the results [had] been less than decisive."[8] The coalition also designed a three-phase air war. Phase one focused on the destruction of Iraqi command, control, and communications, its air power, and its chemical, biological, and nuclear capacities. Phase two called for an aerial attack on Iraqi munitions, supplies, and transportation in an effort to separate the Iraqi troops from their supply lines. Phase three planned to target Iraqi ground forces and the elite Republican Guard.

Between January 17 and February 28, the coalition engaged in an extraordinary thirty-eight-day aerial blitz against Iraq, using a revolutionary new generation of high-tech weaponry. Satellites, computers, sensors, and guidance mechanisms reflected breakthroughs in modernized warfare used in the Gulf. The air attack called for "stealth bombers," shrouded from their enemy's radar detection, to deliver their payloads; laser-guided rockets, complete with computerized settings to hit with pinpoint accuracy; and "smart bombs" capable of taking a circuitous route to find their mark. Patriot missiles needed to intercept Iraqi Scud missiles headed for Israel, and Tomahawk cruise missiles—"essentially flying computers capable of sailing through the goalposts on a football field from a range of several hundred miles"—needed to glide into their Iraqi targets.[9]

During the conflict, a public debate ensued over the effectiveness of the air war. Many applauded its success, convinced that the massive bombardment would make it easier for the ground troops that might be necessary to push the Iraqi army out of Kuwait. Others went so far as to argue that a ground war in the Gulf would be unnecessary since "over time, air power [could] force an Iraqi withdrawal from Kuwait."[10] To this second group, a ground war was "foolish" and unnecessary, since "air power [would] win the war without exposing U.S. and allied troops to Iraq's formidable artillery, minefields and chemical weapons."[11] Air-war proponents also noted that precision bombing had improved substantially since World War II, with accuracy rates reduced from miles to feet. During World War II, "the typical allied bombing accuracy was about one mile—meaning bombers sent against an urban military target such as a rail yard would be almost certain to hit school yards and homes."[12] But Desert Storm bombing raids "were 9,000 times as accurate as those in World War II."[13] Therefore, air-war proponents maintained that because new modern weapons were capable of a much greater precision and far less destruction, they would result in far fewer civilian casualties. Smarter bombs with "less bang . . . reflect the virtue of being more threatening to an enemy military yet less threatening to civilians."[14]

Well-known military strategists were among those who argued against the need for a ground war. James Blackwell, deputy director for political military studies at the Center for Strategic and International Studies in Washington, D.C., contended that there was "no need" to use ground forces if the United States took an early initiative in its bombing raids. "The key is to strike the enemy with accurate firepower deep behind his lines as he is marshalling his forces or while they are still in their defensive positions." Blackwell concluded that technology was the key to achieving victory "without marching [UN troops] into Armageddon."[15] Eliot A. Cohen, professor of strategic studies at the Johns Hopkins University School for Advanced International Studies, maintained that a successful air war could result in an Iraqi withdrawal from Kuwait, considering the power and accuracy of the new weapons, "capable of paralyzing life in Iraq." Cohen also warned that it was much easier to begin a ground war than it was to end one. Edward N. Luttwak, a military historian at the Center for Strategic and International Studies in Washington, contended that precision bombing had not gone far enough; that bombing should be extended to "all roads, supply lines and supply trucks" that supported the Iraqi army with food and water in order to starve out the enemy. Luttwak concluded, "I would rather bomb them for months from the air rather than have thousands of Americans coming home in wheelchairs."[16]

Others agreed that a ground war should be avoided at all costs because of the possibility of the devastating consequences it could inflict on American soldiers. Former Assistant Secretary of Defense during the Reagan Administration, Richard Perle, in his *U.S. News & World Report* commentary, warned that a ground war would put American troops too close to both Iraqi guns and chemical weapons. Historian Arthur M. Schlesinger, Jr., agreed: "I don't think anything out there is worth the life of a single American soldier, but if we have to do something, I prefer to rely on air power and a blockade to starve them out."[17]

Opponents in the public debate over the success of the air war cautioned against overdependence on expensive air-power technology, warning that no previous war had been won by air power alone. Those who questioned the effectiveness of the air campaign noted "the overblown claims for precision bombing" in World War II, and critics concluded that "even in the face of new technologies, . . . precision bombing [was] a contradiction in terms."[18] Some questioned the cost, effectiveness, and control of the massive bombardment raids, noting that the sheer number of bombs used in the war dramatically surpassed those of previous wars by astonishing margins. According to a postwar congressional report, "The U.S. bomb tonnage dropped per day [on Iraqi targets] was equivalent to 85 percent of the average daily bomb tonnage dropped by the United States on all of Germany and Japan during the course of World War II."[19]

Former Senator Gary Hart, a Colorado Democrat who had served on the Senate Armed Services Committee from 1975 to 1987 and had run unsuccessfully for president in 1984 and 1988, advised that it was "too soon to worship high tech" military equipment. "Two myths have already emerged from this war: One is that technology in itself is a battlefield determinant. The other is that 'high quality' weapons have proved their superiority over 'low quality' weapons." Hart argued that the United States had lost as many expensive, high-tech "superior planes" as the Iraqis' "inferior" ones. He also questioned the actual success rate of "smart" precision-guided bombs used against "well-protected" targets. The former senator warned that virtually all electronic weapons could be "confused or defeated by a substantially cheaper" countermeasure. Hart concluded that technology could not act as a substitute for skilled military leadership and planning. "Military reformers have warned for more than a decade against substituting technology for *thinking*. If our strategy, tactics or doctrine are wrong, no amount of computers or sophisticated technology will fix them...."[20]

Critics also noted that the air war, despite its arsenal of precision weaponry and the coalition's promise to keep the Iraqi civilian population as safe as possible, still killed too many civilians and destroyed too many homes and factories. According to one report, "friendly fire" led to the deaths of 35 American soldiers and the wounding of 467 others. Military leaders enforced rigorous restrictions on the media during the Gulf War, since many still blamed televised broadcasts that showed the horrors of Vietnam as a key reason why the nation had lost confidence in its last war. Few journalists had access inside of Iraq. CNN was the first to bring news and images of Iraqi civilian deaths, and correspondent Peter Arnett concluded, "Viewers will have to get used to reports of this nature . . . massive bombing campaigns inevitably produce civilian casualties."[21] Throughout the war, Saddam Hussein claimed that aerial bombing caused a multitude of civilian deaths and alleged that the coalition purposely targeted cultural buildings. On January 29, 1991, the Iraqi leader condemned the American-led alliance and contended that bombing raids took the lives of 324 Iraqi civilians, injured another 416, and "damaged and destroyed religious, cultural and residential buildings." Saddam Hussein told the United Nations secretary general, "You, personally, bear responsibility to history and to mankind for the horrendous crimes being committed against the noble people of Iraq who are fighting for their freedom."[22] Darkness, confusion, and intelligence errors led to hundreds of civilian deaths, such as the destruction of a baby-milk factory, mistakenly thought by intelligence to house a biological weapons installation. Bombing raids also killed civilians and demolished homes in a number of neighborhoods, including Najaf, Al Dour, and Athiriya.

The U.S. Department of Defense (DOD) countered that the allied military minimized noncombatant injuries by carefully selecting military targets, using weapons specifically known for their precision, and sending support-mission aircraft to protect attacking aircrews so they could concentrate on the precise targets. Although coalition air power destroyed specific military installations in populated areas (permitted by the law of war), DOD asserted that "at no time were civilian areas as such attacked." In some cases, the coalition chose "not to attack many military targets in populated areas or in or adjacent to cultural (archaeological) sites." DOD accused Saddam Hussein of using cultural centers to protect military equipment and argued that civilian deaths resulted when Iraq did not evacuate civilians in close "proximity to legitimate military targets." Unintentional civilian deaths were more likely from faulty U.S. intelligence than from American aircrew mistakes or weapon failures.[23]

On February 24, 1991, in the final phase of Operation Desert Storm, the UN coalition put more than 200,000 ground troops into Kuwait with the mission of driving the Iraqi army out of the small country. By February 28, enemy forces fled across the border to their homeland or surrendered to UN troops. America experienced its first significant military victory since World War II.

THE DEBATE OVER THE PATRIOT

In April 1992, the House Committee on Governmental Operations began oversight hearings on the performance of the Patriot missile in the Gulf War. The hearings reflected the ongoing debate over war and technology. According to a summary of the hearings, reprinted by the Henry L. Stimson Center, the army's assessment of the Patriots' success began with a claim of 96 percent, but after a closer examination, Major General Jay M. Garner, deputy chief of staff, concluded, "The Army's new effectiveness assessment was that the Patriot had hit, though not necessarily destroyed, 40 percent of the Scuds it engaged in Israel and 70 percent in Saudi Arabia. Of the Scuds intercepted, the Army had high confidence that Patriots had destroyed 25 percent of the warheads."[24] This success assessment was challenged after an independent review of videotapes, reports from the Israeli air force and the Missile and Space Intelligence Center, and the testimony of experts. Expert testimony came from military officials, defense analysts from strategic-studies institutes and major universities, and officials from the Raytheon Company, which developed the Patriot. The House report noted, "A strong case can be made that Patriots hit only 9 percent of the Scud warheads engaged, and there are serious questions about these few hits." Much confusion arose because "the Patriot is not designed to explode upon impact with its targets, thus the explosions in the sky were a misleading indicator of success for both troops and the public."[25]

Critics of the growing dependence on technological warfare noted the exceedingly high cost of the new weapons and argued that their complexity sometimes made them unreliable. Others maintained that not only did most of the new high-tech weapons work with resounding success in the Gulf War, "this new military capability [also] adds an important dimension to the ability of the United States to deter war."[26]

WOMEN IN THE PERSIAN GULF

"For the first time in American history, U.S. combat units went into action with a lot of women officially in the ranks." Technological advances and the air war provided a sense of distance from "frontline" combat and thus made deploying women more acceptable to a society struggling over the issue of women in combat or near combat areas. The American military also brought in female soldiers "to the scene of recent, or imminent, combat."[27] Women were fully integrated into their units, held "combat-support jobs, and experienced the hardship of desert life along with their male counterparts." Some 37,000 women (6 percent of the U.S. troops) served in the Gulf as "administrators, air traffic controllers, logisticians, engineer equipment mechanics, ammunition technicians, ordinance specialists, communicators, radio operators, drivers, law enforcement specialists and guards." Many of their jobs were connected to the new technological revolution. Women also flew helicopters and reconnaissance aircraft, and several commanded combat-support brigades, battalions, companies, and platoon units.[28]

During the conflict, the idea of women serving in the military became a fiery topic for public debate. Some periodicals, like the conservative newspaper *Human Events*, argued that women belonged at home with their children and quoted female soldiers who questioned their decision to leave their children for war. Sgt. Lori Moore of Ft. Benning, Georgia, told *New York Times* reporter Jane Gross, "Our mission is combat, sending my kids (to relatives) was just part of the job—until they left. Then I was overwhelmed with guilt." Elaine Donnelly, a former member of the Defense Advisory Committee on Women in the Service, warned against an increasingly complex army as women entered the ranks. She asked, "Are we going to wind up with child care centers in Saudi Arabia?"[29]

Others strongly disagreed. Historian and retired Major General Jeanne Holm's study of female soldiers in the Persian Gulf War concluded that women were very capable and qualified. "They were as committed to fulfilling their military obligations as their male counterparts . . . [and] they did the jobs they had been trained to do and did them well."[30] Holm also argued that although some sexual tension and harassment occurred in the Gulf, men and women, in fact, worked as a team. The Department of Defense applauded the "vital" and "highly successful" role that women played in Operation Desert Storm, where they "performed admirably and without substantial friction or special consideration." In its final report to Congress, DOD concluded, "U.S. women performed a wide range of critical missions. This fact alone clearly set up a visible example of U.S. principles."[31]

CONCLUSION

Many scholars and military analysts agree that the success of the Persian Gulf War finally put to rest the ghost of Vietnam, changed the nature of future wars, and opened up the military for female combatants. However, the debate over the effectiveness of high-tech air power in the Persian Gulf War continues. Some say that if "body counts" are used as the "bottom line" in measuring success or failure in war, the Persian Gulf War represented an unqualified success story. Air-power champions concluded that Desert Storm provided a lesson on "the value of air power" and taught the United States that it must maintain command of the skies to win quick and decisive wars. President Bush argued that during the Persian Gulf War, "our air strikes were the most effective, yet humane, in the history of warfare."[32]

Others continue to be skeptical and cautious of America's new reliance on air power in future wars. They note new reports on the problems with the Patriot missile and warn the nation not to be lulled into a false sense of security by its high-tech arsenal, especially when it comes to air power and quick victories. Some scholars and defense analysts argue that the success in the Gulf was a regional victory with limited application elsewhere. In the words of Joseph Nye, Jr., and Roger K. Smith, who studied the "lessons" from the Gulf War, "No one should be deluded into believing that the military capability that can easily defeat an army with 4,000 tanks in the desert is going to be the decisive factor in a jungle or urban guerrilla war." They conclude, "The key to avoiding such entanglements is for the United States to use its new strength to deter these conflicts rather than fight them."[33]

In its final report assessing the air-power campaign, the Department of Defense hailed the success of the new high-tech weaponry, but cautioned that conditions in the Persian Gulf conflict were "ideal." Atypical weather and the desert terrain helped lead to air-power success. DOD admitted that conditions may be much more difficult in the future and "opponents may possess more advanced weapons systems and be more skilled in using them."[34] The report also reminded Americans that inevitably, the UN coalition used ground troops to push the Iraqi army out of Kuwait.

Some politicians question the wisdom of the United States reshaping its military policy in part by shifting responsibility to NATO, while others embrace American technological superiority as the specific American contribution to keeping world order. Although Desert Storm was used as a model for the UN air attack in Kosovo (1999), military strategists are still arguing about whether that bombardment actually ended or prolonged the Yugoslav conflict. The future for women in the military is still under study by the U.S. government, but Desert Storm proved a positive testing ground. For many, the question remains—will technology be a constructive force for incorporating female combatants into key military positions and opening up previously closed doors? Restrictions placed on the media must be reconsidered in the next war, and a balance between the need for tight security and the democratic rights of a free press must be reached.

In the end, the Persian Gulf War created a cohesive spirit and a new confidence in America's future, and perhaps the nation finally broke away from the anguish of its past defeats. Journalist Stanley W. Cloud concluded, "Americans were haunted by Vietnam, but they also learned from it. For proof of that, there is no need to look any further than the meticulous way in which George Bush and his military and civilian team went about engineering their stunning quick triumph in the desert.... Hello Kuwait. Goodbye Vietnam."[35]

NOTES

1. Charles Krauthammer, "How the War Can Change America," *Time*, January 28, 1991, p. 100.

2. "What Happened to the Body Counts?" *Time*, January 28, 1991, p. 24.

3. Russell F. Weigley, *The American Way of War: A History of United States Military Strategy and Policy* (New York: Macmillan, 1977), p. 233.

4. "Desert Storm," *U.S. News and World Report*, January 28, 1991, p. 30.

5. Quoted in Nancy Gibbs, "Can the Pro-War Consensus Survive?" *Time*, February 18, 1991, p. 32.

6. Tom Wicker, "The Key to Unity," *New York Times*, January 30, 1991, p. A23.

7. Daily Congressional Record, vol. 137, *Proceedings and Debates of the 102nd Congress, 1st Session*, January 11, 1991 (Washington, DC: U.S. Government Printing Office, 1991), p. H353.

8. Quote from Major Kevin Smith, comp., *United States Army Aviation during Operations Desert Shield and Desert Storm*, Office of the Aviation Branch Historian, U.S. Army Aviation Center, Fort Rucker, Alabama, June 20, 1991, pp. 11, 5–6; Colonel Harry G. Summers, Jr., *On Strategy II: A Critical Analysis of the Gulf War* (New York: Dell, 1992), pp. 195–199.

9. Philip Elmer-Dewitt, "The Weapons: Inside the High-Tech Arsenal," *Time*, February 4, 1991, pp. 46–47.

10. Thomas L. Friedman, "The Air or the Ground: A Debate over Strategy," *New York Times*, January 23, 1991, p. A8.

11. Richard Perle, "A Ground War Is Foolish," *U.S. News & World Report*, February 18, 1991, p. 1.

12. Gregg Easterbrook, "Robowar," *New Republic*, February 11, 1991, p. 17.

13. "The Triumph of Desert Storm," *U.S. News & World Report*, March 11, 1991, p. 1.

14. Easterbrook, "Robowar," p. 18.

15. James Blackwell, "JSTARTS Could Save Thousands of Lives in a War with Iraq," *Army Times*, January 14, 1991, p. 330.

16. Friedman, "The Air or the Ground," p. A8.

17. Ibid.

18. "Desert Storm," *U.S. News & World Report*, January 28, 1991, p. 30.

19. Report to the Ranking Minority Member, Committee on Commerce, House of Representatives, *Operation Desert Storm: Evaluation of the Air Campaign* (Washington, DC: General Accounting Office, National Security and International Affairs Division, June 12, 1997), pp. 14–15, xviii.

20. Gary Hart, "The Military's New Myths," *New York Times*, January 30, 1991, p. A23.

21. Michael Wines, "CNN Reports Allied Bombs Killed 24 Civilians in Iraqi Neighborhood," *New York Times*, January 26, 1991, p. 5.

22. "Michael Wines, U.N. Report: Iraq Says Air Raids Have Killed 324 Civilians," *New York Times*, January 29, 1991, p. A12.

23. *Conduct of the Persian Gulf War: Final Report to Congress* (Washington, DC: Department of Defense, United States of America, April 1992), pp. 613, 612–17.

24. "Performance of the Patriot Missiles System," *Activities of the House Committee on Governmental Operations*, One Hundred Second Congress, First and Second Sessions, 1991–1992, Report 102-1086, p. 179. The Henry L. Stimson Center's *The Nuclear Roundtable*, Background Document.

25. Ibid., p. 188.

26. Joseph S. Nye, Jr., and Roger K. Smith, eds., *After the Storm: Lessons from the Gulf War* (Lanham, MD: Madison Books, 1992), p. 260.

27. James F. Dunnigan and Austin Bay, *From Shield to Storm: High-tech Weapons, Military Strategy, and Coalition Warfare in the Persian Gulf* (New York: William Morrow, 1992), p. 386.

28. *Conduct of the Persian Gulf War: Final Report to Congress*, April 1992, pp. 647–649.

29. *Human Events*, "The Persian Gulf War Proves Women's Inability to Serve in Combat," in *Women in the Military*, ed. Carol Wekesser and Matthew Polesetsky (San Diego, CA: Greenhaven Press, 1991), pp. 93–95.

30. Major General Jeanne Holm, *Women in the Military: An Unfinished Revolution*, revised edition (Novato, CA: Presidio Press, 1992), pp. 463–464.

31. *Conduct of the Persian Gulf War: Final Report to Congress*, April 1992, pp. 647–649.

32. Ibid., p. 89.

33. Nye and Smith, *After the Storm*, p. 262.

34. *Conduct of the Persian Gulf War: Final Report to Congress*, April 1992, p. xxiii.

35. Stanley W. Cloud, "Exorcising an Old Demon," *Time*, March 11, 1991, pp. 52–53.

DOCUMENTS

11.1.   **Congress Debates Whether to Declare War on Iraq**

On January 11, 1991, congressional leaders debated whether to support the Gephardt-Hamilton amendment (sponsored by Richard Gephardt, Democratic congressman from Missouri, and Lee Hamilton, Democratic congressman from Indiana), which called for a continuation of economic sanctions against Iraq, or the Michel-Solarz resolution (sponsored by Robert Michel, Republican congressman from Illinois, and Stephen Solarz, Democratic congressman from New York), authorizing force against Iraq. The Vietnam War became a key discussion of the debate as many congressmen warned against a protracted war in the Gulf.

Mr. FORD of Michigan. Mr. Speaker, I rise in support of the Gephardt-Hamilton amendment and oppose the declaration of war amendment.

War, and the inevitable death of thousands of Americans, must be a last resort and must be undertaken only for the gravest reasons, for the most important national interests. We have not exhausted our other options, and our national interest in removing Iraq from Kuwait is less significant than the President claims. I cannot at this time vote to authorize a declaration of war.

What is Kuwait? Why is its survival of the highest importance to the people of Michigan and the United States? Not because it is a democracy. Even South Vietnam for whom 58,000 Americans died, could make plausible claims that it was a democracy threatened by communism. But Kuwait is a monarchy. Its rulers suspended the country's parliament in 1986 in the face of a movement for democratic reforms. Not because Kuwait is a friend of the United States. Kuwait voted against us 9 out of 10 times in the United Nations over the last 10 years. We have no treaty obligation to defend Kuwait. . . .

I served in Congress during the Vietnam war and shared responsibility for the commitment of troops we made in 1965–67. When I turned against the war, it was because I realized we had been lied to about its purposes and chances for success. I learned that the decision to send American soldiers to war—and some to their death—is the heaviest responsibility of a Member of Congress, one that should never be made easily and without the total support of the American people. Nothing in this conflict with Iraq makes me willing to send young men and women to their deaths. . . .

Mr. BALLENGER. Mr. Speaker, I rise today to support the bipartisan Michel-Solarz resolution authorizing force to implement the U.N. Security Council resolutions concerning Iraq's unlawful invasion of Kuwait. I do not take this position easily or lightly. . . . I read with interest a recent article by a freelance writer, Marc Wilson, entitled "This Vietnam Protester Won't Be Quick to Oppose Gulf War." I would like to read a few passages from his article.

"The Persian Gulf is not Vietnam. We would be fighting to protect the lives of millions of noncombatants whom Hussein, without losing a wink of sleep, would self-righteously gas to death on a moment's notice.

We would be fighting to prevent the inevitability of nuclear weapons devolving into the hands of a man who would surely use them indiscriminately and without provocation."

MR. WILSON goes on to say that

"The moment we . . . of liberal inclination . . . hear "war," our knee jerks quicker than our mind scrutinizes. Before we mindlessly shout "Another Vietnam!" and get swept up in heady anti-war rhetoric, we need to ponder again, when the all-compelling quest for human harmony can be actualized only by waging battle against those forces that are maniacally bent on disrupting it. . . . Passage of this resolution may help prevent a war. It is a risk, but I believe it is a risk worth taking. Make no mistake about it, any military action should be quick and decisive. The American people will not stand for American casualties mounting month after month from a prolonged conflict. The reasons we are involved in the gulf region are justified, but we should accomplish our mission and bring our young men and women home."

Mr. FALEOMAVAEGA. Mr. Speaker, I am honored and always grateful for the opportunity to address my colleagues and the people of our great Nation. I have no doubt that no one in this chamber is without sons and daughters, relatives, friends and even constituents who are among the 400,000 Americans in military uniforms in Saudi Arabia—all anxiously awaiting what course of action our President and the Congress will take against Saddam Hussein and the people of Iraq.

Mr. Speaker, I have listened with keen interest to the speeches and remarks made by our colleagues about the horrors of war. We have built a monument as a testimony to history and to our Nation—some 50,000 American lives that were sacrificed in Vietnam and some untold hundreds of thousands more who were among the missing, wounded, and maimed and even today, many still wonder if the American people appreciated the services they rendered while in military uniforms in Vietnam.

Mr. Speaker, I have not visited our soldiers and sailors in Saudi Arabia, but I have been to Vietnam like some of our colleagues in this chamber. Throughout the entire year from April 1967 to May 1968, I never doubted for any moment the possibility that I might return either in a body bag or as a cripple for life. I've shed many tears for my buddies and relatives who lost their lives in that terrible conflict, but I'm not going to trouble my colleagues with my personal experiences in that troubled part of the world. . . .

[FROM THE *WASHINGTON POST*, JAN. 10, 1991]
WAR SHOULD BE A LAST RESORT (BY SENATOR SAM NUNN)
[ENTERED AS PART OF THE *CONGRESSIONAL RECORD*]

At the heart of the debate that begins today on the floor of the House and the Senate will be a deeply felt difference of opinion—not over the ends of U.S. policy in the crisis but over the means of attaining them. I continue to favor President Bush's original strategy—economic sanctions, a continued military threat and patience. . . .

If Congress authorizes the president to wage war or he initiates it on his own, what kind of war should be waged? I am afraid too many recall our most recent conflicts in bumper-sticker terms: "Vietnam: long, drawn out—bad;" "Grenada/Panama: quick, decisive—good. . . ." If war comes, Iraq's fondest hope is that the United States will commit substantial ground forces to frontal assaults, thus giving Iraq a chance to inflict heavy casualties. Saddam's military leaders are not fools. They realize that they will lose any war with the United States, but entertain the hope that high U.S. casualties would weaken our resolve.

Are there military lessons to be learned from Vietnam? Of course. We should hit military targets with awesome power at the beginning of any conflict, as well as knocking out power and communications, electrical, nuclear and chemical facilities. At the same time, we should not "overlearn" the Vietnam lesson. We in America like instant results. We want fast food and fast military victories. However, our nation places a higher value on human life, especially on the lives of our men and women in uniform. Depending upon developments after the first wave of air attacks, a short war may be possible and may save lives. But we must avoid "instant victory" demands and expectations that could cause a premature and high casualty assault on heavily fortified Kuwait by American ground forces. . . .

Mr. MANTON. . . . I rise tonight in support of the resolution offered by the majority leader, Mr. GEPHARDT, and the gentleman from Indiana (Mr. HAMILTON). . . .

The memories of Vietnam remain painfully clear in Woodside. Before my constituents are willing to sacrifice a new generation they must be convinced war is our only alternative. . . .

Mr. CUNNINGHAM. . . . I rise in support of our servicemen and women and for my draft-age son by supporting the Michel-Solarz for peace. No one in this room has my combat experience, and, in most cases, all of them put together. Gephardt-Hamilton means a war of attrition, our attrition.

It pains me . . . that Gephardt-Hamilton revisits a personal nightmare. In Vietnam our hands were tied, and over 55,000 Americans were killed. Double that number were lost of our allies. . . .

Let me tell Members a personal experience. I have flown the Mirage fighter in the Middle East. I know the Iraqi skills and their mindset. I flew 300 combat missions in Vietnam and was part of Operation Proud Deep.

President Johnson had stopped the action against the North Vietnamese. None of us wanted to be there. We wanted to get the job done and get home. From 1968 through 1972, the North Vietnamese were allowed to rebuild. We saw clearly the need for striking North Vietnam, but his forces and our politicians held us back. . . .

It is not that this Congress should shrink from its constitutional responsibilities of declaring war. Far from it, rather, we should clearly vest our President with the authority he needs in these crucial times so that our world can for now grasp a tenuous hold on peace.

Source: Daily Congressional Record, vol. 137, *Proceedings and Debates of the 102nd Congress, 1st Session*, January 11, 1991 (Washington, DC: Government Printing Office, 1991), pp. H272–H353.

11.2.   The *New York Times* Reports on Deaths of Iraqi Civilians, January 26, 1991

Despite the increased precision of the new high-tech weapons and the coalition's efforts to avoid the civilian population, civilian casualties did occur. This New York Times *article discusses one of the first reported cases of deaths of Iraqi civilians.*

WASHINGTON, Jan. 25—Peter Arnett, the last correspondent for an American news organization in Iraq, reported today that allied jets had bombed what appeared to be a residential neighborhood 100 miles north of Baghdad, killing 24 civilians. The Pentagon later said the area was home to several military installations.

Mr. Arnett, of the Cable News Network, said he had counted 23 destroyed houses in the town of Al Dour, 12 miles from the hometown of

President Saddam Hussein of Iraq. "They were flattened as though shaken by an earthquake," he said of the houses.

Mr. Arnett quoted residents as saying that the town had no military installations and no bomb shelters because it had not been considered a likely target. The residents said 24 civilians had been killed, he said.

CIVILIAN DEATHS ARE INEVITABLE

Mr. Arnett made clear in his report that he was led to the scene by the Iraqi authorities, and that his report was cleared by Iraqi censors. A videotape prepared by Iraqi officials that accompanied Mr. Arnett's report showed piles of debris along a broad street and the framed photograph of a child hung from a tree in front of one rubble-strewn lot.

The White House this week urged viewers to regard Mr. Arnett's reports skeptically. A CNN official said "it is in the interests of our viewers to maintain the only western journalist to watch and report from Baghdad."

While the Pentagon may have had reason to attack Al Dour, Mr. Arnett said today, there was "no way" that Iraq could have staged the bombing.

"Viewers will have to get used to reports of this nature," he said, adding that massive bombing campaigns inevitably produce civilian casualties.

"WHO DID WHAT TO WHO"

A Pentagon spokeswoman said this evening that she was waiting for a transcript of the broadcast before making a formal response. But Gen. Thomas Kelly, director of operations for the Joint Chiefs of Staff, said at an afternoon news conference that Iraqi military installations were located near Al Dour.

"In the vicinity of that town there was a military munitions depot, a chemical warfare production and storage facility, and a military communications site," he said. "I can't comment on what was on television. I have the same human feelings that you do, I'm certain.

"But they were Iraqi-controlled films and I don't know how they made them or who did what to who."

The Pentagon has previously said that allied forces seek to avoid civilian casualties and that pilots are instructed not to release their bombs or missiles until they have confirmed that they will reach their assigned targets.

Source: Michael Wines, "CNN Reports Allied Bombs Killed 24 Civilians in Iraqi Neighborhood," *New York Times*, January 26, 1991, p. 5.

11.3.   Former Senator Gary Hart Cautions Against "The Military's New Myths," January 30, 1991

Former Senator Gary Hart (Democrat of Colorado), who had been a member of the Senate Armed Services Committee from 1975 to 1987, cautioned against the nation's growing reliance on new, expensive high-tech weapons. In this New York Times *article, he argued that computer-driven weapons should not replace the thinking skills of military leaders or the less expensive, "reliable" weapons.*

In the first euphoric hours of the Persian Gulf war, statements were made that the military reformers of the 1980's—who argued for using technology to produce larger numbers of simpler weapons that could operate dependably and successfully in combat—had clearly been proved wrong. In war, the first casualty may be the truth, but the first creation is myth.

Two myths have already emerged from this war: One is that technology in itself is a battlefield determinant. The other is that "high quality" weapons have proved their superiority over "low quality" weapons. But only one new technological *fact* has been established: Expensive anti-missile missiles, the Patriots, can knock down most cheap, militarily ineffective missiles, the Scuds.

Overwhelming this fact, however, is a more important fact. The most sophisticated technological weapon system of the 1980's, the B-1 bomber, is not in the gulf. It grounded itself without an Iraqi shot being fired. It has proved to be either too ineffective at high levels, too vulnerable at low levels or too prone to self-destruction. At $25 billion for 100 planes, that is an expensive lesson to learn about the limitations of technology.

To date in the war, we have lost as many of our superior planes as we have shot down inferior Iraqi planes. "Smart" precision-guided bombs apparently have been more effective against infrastructure targets (at what "collateral damage" to civilians our military is not heard to say) than they have been against well-protected military targets.

A disproportionate number of air sorties are dedicated to destroying Scud mobile-missile launchers in order to achieve a political objective— keeping Israel out of the war—not any serious military objectives.

Virtually without exception, all electronic weapons technologies can be confused or defeated by a substantially cheaper countermeasure. Superiority is enjoyed only in the period between the deployment of the weapon and the discovery of an appropriate countermeasure. Steven Canby, a military reformer, has pointed out that sophisticated heat-seeking missiles can be confused by ordinary smoke pots.

Other than this, no other apparent conclusions can be drawn (let alone myths created) from the preliminary phase of an air war by a super-power against a quantitatively and qualitatively inferior regional power.

Indeed, the real combat—on land—has yet to begin. There we face a numerically equal, reasonably well-armed opponent defensively deployed. . . .

They will do great damage to allied armored columns and cause considerable inconvenience to supporting air and sea assets. For the sake of our nation's sons, we should pray that the relatively crude, old-technology B-52 carpet bombers now flying sorties over Kuwait do a more effective strategic job than they did in Vietnam. And we should also pray that the even cruder garden of cheap landmines that the Iraqis have laid do not destroy our best tank battalions.

When the land war begins, we will have a much better measure of the role of technology in the battlefield. Even though our forces are qualitatively superior overall, there is greater parity in land weaponry than air weaponry. Much has been made of the role of battlefield computers, but military reformers have warned for more than a decade against substituting technology for *thinking*.

If our strategy, tactics or doctrine are wrong, no amount of computers or sophisticated technology will fix them. In the friction of combat, a dramatic increase in the quantity of information does not guarantee that it is "good" or useful information. Compared to the vast capacity of the human mind for flexibility, creativity and imagination, the inflexibility of a computer makes it supremely vulnerable to the disaster that surprise can bring.

As it is much too early to evaluate the relative performances of vast categories of weapons, so it is much too early in a war that promises to last a considerable time to permit a new military mythology to be created.

Source: Gary Hart, "The Military's New Myths," *New York Times*, January 30, 1991, p. A23.

11.4.   A Journalist Evaluates the New High-Tech Arsenal, February 4, 1991

In February 1991, Philip Elmer-Dewitt of Time *magazine applauded the initial performance of the new high-tech weapons, but warned that it was too soon to measure their wartime success.*

For years, American military hardware has been the butt of bitter jokes, taxpayer complaints and congressional investigations. To judge by the cost overruns and testing mishaps, the U.S. arsenal seemed to consist of planes that spun out of control, tanks too cumbersome to maneuver and spare parts with Tiffany price tags. What a difference a war makes. Now that U.S. Patriots are chasing down Scuds and laser-guided bombs are nailing targets in Iraq, the once derided weaponry has become the star of the war. Suddenly, everybody is a weapon buff.

For military planners, the apparent success of their high-tech equipment in the early weeks of the battle is sweet vindication. Though Operation Desert Storm still relies in part on armaments of Vietnam War and even World War II vintage, the Pentagon has staked its reputation on its state-of-the-art showpieces. For 40 years, it has pursued a sometimes controversial doctrine that says the best way to counter a potential adversary's superior number is with superior technology. Now military experts are watching the payoff with excitement but also apprehension. The high-speed electronics and precision engineering that make the new weapons so effective also make them vulnerable.

The most visible symbol of the United States' technological edge—those pinpoint strikes on Iraqi targets—actually represents some fairly straightforward bombing. The key technology is a simple laser detector on the nose of a glide bomb that is electronically linked to adjustable fins in the bomb's tail. All the pilot has to do is point a pencil-thin laser beam at his target and push a button. A stabilizing computer keeps the beam locked in place, freeing the pilot to pitch and roll as necessary to evade enemy fire while the bomb rides along the beam's reflection, flying into the target like a moth to a flame.

The real technological marvels in the U.S. missile array are the sea-launched Tomahawk cruise missiles that smashed Iraqi air defense systems early in the war. Packed with advanced electronics and several different guidance systems, they are essentially flying computers capable of sailing through the goalposts on a football field from a range of several hundred miles. They can also perform dizzying acrobatics, as witnessed by U.S. reporters who before they were ousted from Iraq, watched with amazement as a Tomahawk streaked below their hotel windows and made a pair of swooping 90 [degree] turns to avoid the Al Rasheed in downtown Baghdad. . . .

The danger with any endeavor so dependent on advanced electronics and jewel-like engineering is that when such systems encounter unexpected trouble they usually do not just slow down; they crash. The Pentagon has not shown any TV pictures of "smart" bombs flying a perfect path into the side of a camel. But as the Scud hits have demonstrated, mistakes do happen. . . .

Another natural phenomenon that might cause trouble is electromagnetic radiation from the sun. Heightened solar-flare activity, expected over the next few months, could disrupt military communications and satellite traffic. Air Force officials have called this issue "too sensitive for comment."

It is still too early to say whether the Pentagon's grand doctrine of fighting superior numbers with superior technology will ultimately prevail. It may yet be possible to foil the world's most sophisticated—and expensive—weapons with countermeasures, some of which are literally dirt cheap. They include burning smoke pots to deflect heat-seeking missiles, draping targets with pictures of bomb craters to discourage further attack, and hunkering down in caves and sand dunes to wait out the blitz. In the end, no electronic marvel is going to liberate Kuwait. That is a job that will probably fall to the ultimate biological weapon; the G.I.

Source: Philip Elmer-Dewitt, "The Weapons: Inside the High-Tech Arsenal," *Time*, February 4, 1991, pp. 46–47.

11.5.   Eliot A. Cohen Argues against a Land War, February 11, 1991

Eliot A. Cohen, a professor of strategic studies at the School for Advanced International Studies, Johns Hopkins University, argued in the New Republic *that the air-power war should be given a chance to achieve victory before the UN coalition deployed ground troops.*

The opening stage of the Persian Gulf war has gone spectacularly well. It appears that the United States and its allies have grounded most of the Iraqi air force and wiped out those portions daring enough to rise and fight. Headquarters buildings in Baghdad and elsewhere have been smashed without damage to civilian dwellings. Iraqi forces in the field have been pummeled retail—by sharpshooting, precision-guided laser bombs—and wholesale, by B-52 carpet bombing. And most astonishing of all, this result has been achieved at minimal cost. . . .

This success has many explanations, including the technological superiority of Western military hardware, the probable cooperation of Iraq's erstwhile arms suppliers in providing information about its defenses, and the inexperience and relatively low priority of the Iraqi air defense system, which did not do much during the Iran-Iraq war either. Above all other explanations, however, stand the skill of our pilots and the competence of the complex organizations that support them. . . .

On Sunday, January 20, the theater commander, General Norman Schwarzkopf, hinted at the possibility of a war won from the air alone. But with this exception, press reports and the statements of senior officers indicated that a ground offensive is in the works. . . . *All wars must be decided on the ground; air power has never won a war.*

Assertions of this kind carry astonishing weight, particularly when delivered by serving or retired officers as elementary and unshakable military orthodoxy. Yet surely these are, in part, historical judgments, and on matters of military history civilians may reasonably differ with soldiers. And insofar as such dicta are intended to shape current policy, they must go beyond an appeal to authority and demonstrate their logic.

Now, it is quite true that air power alone has never won a war, although one can plausibly argue that it came remarkably close to just that in the Pacific war. By the spring of 1945 American army and naval aviators had demolished Japan's civilian and military industries, sunk most of the Japanese fleet, and established a virtual blockade of the Japanese islands (with the aid of American submarines). Ground and purely naval forces had served mainly to seize and hold forward bases for the projection of air power. In 1945, before it had become clear that the atom bomb would work, Chief of Staff George Marshall and Chief of Naval Operations Ernest King had argued about the need for an invasion of the Japanese homeland—Marshall favoring it, King thinking that a tight blockade and intense bombardment could do the trick. The dispute is memorable for two reasons: first, Marshall was probably wrong—even without the atom bomb the Japanese would have collapsed sooner or later without the horrendous casualties inherent in a strategy of invasion. The most revered American military figure of the twentieth century showed himself strategically fallible as he had on other occasions, and this in itself is no small lesson.

Moreover, the Marshall-King dispute shows that there is really no such thing as a single "expert" military judgment, for here was a case where two formidable experts in the art of war disagreed. In the present case, we may have lost the chance of hearing a military "second opinion" because the chief of staff of the Air Force, General Michael Dugan, lost his job in part for suggesting that a ground offensive might be unnecessary. . . .

It is not clear that a ground invasion of Kuwait or even a shallow envelopment through southern Iraq would be decisive. Assume, for the moment, that Kuwait would fall quickly; would the war necessarily come to an end? If Saddam continued to fight, would the United States have to drive on to Baghdad and occupy that city? Were we to dispatch a large force to occupy a major Arab capital, would our coalition tolerate it, and would the costs be bearable? Would a war that gave Iraqis the opportunity, or even the imperative, of fighting to defend their homes be a short one? And do we wish the responsibility of garrisoning a hostile nation, suppressing guerrilla enemies, and reconstructing the Iraqi government?

Winston Churchill once wrote: "the success of a commander does not arise from following rules or models. It consists in an absolutely new comprehension of the dominant facts of the situation . . . and all the forces at work. Cooks use recipes for dishes and doctors have prescriptions for diseases, but every great operation of war is unique." There may be specific reasons for preferring a ground attack to a prolonged air siege, but those have nothing to do with military proverbs, even those uttered by men with stars on their shoulders. . . .

Public declarations about "leaving the war to the military" notwithstanding, it appears that President Bush has, in fact, overruled his commanders at least once, by insisting on war in mid-January, rather than in mid-February as ground commanders in Saudi Arabia clearly preferred. An even greater task looms, for here he must intervene not only with respect to the "when" of an operation but the "how." He is surrounded by talented men, but they seem unlikely to favor an exclusively air campaign. . . . Military and civilian, these leaders are able and decent men, and they may, in the end, opt for an air campaign in order to hold casualties down, despite their deepest convictions about the nature of war. But they may not, and if so, it will be the ultimate test of George Bush as commander in chief to probe their arguments and their evidence to the utmost, yielding nothing to military conventional wisdom, and considering only the facts and logic of the case before him. The lives of thousands of young Americans, and the cause for which he has ordered them into battle, will hang on his choice.

Source: Eliot A. Cohen, "The Unsheltering Sky: The Case Against a Land War," *New Republic*, February 11, 1991, pp. 23–25.

11.6. The Department of Defense's Report to Congress on the Persian Gulf War, April 1992

In its Final Report to Congress, *the Department of Defense evaluated the success of the new "revolutionary" weapons in the Persian Gulf War. Although the new weaponry impressed DOD, it recognized the unusual conditions presented in Desert Storm, which may have also contributed to the success of the air-power campaign.*

[A] general lesson of the war is that high-technology systems vastly increased the effectiveness of our forces. This war demonstrated dramatically the new possibilities of what has been called the "military technological revolution in warfare." This technological revolution encompasses many areas, including stand-off precision weaponry, sophisticated sensors, stealth for surprise and survivability, night vision capabilities and tactical ballistic missile defenses. In large part this revolution tracks the development of new technologies such as the microprocessing of information that has become familiar in our daily lives. The exploitation of these and still-emerging technologies promises to change the nature of warfare significantly, as did the earlier advent of tanks, airplanes, and aircraft carriers.

The war tested an entire generation of new weapons and systems at the forefront of this revolution. In many cases these weapons and systems were being used in large-scale combat for the first time. In other cases, where the weapons had been used previously, the war represented their first use in large numbers. For example, precision guided munitions are not entirely new[;] they were used at the end of the Vietnam war in 1972 to destroy bridges in Hanoi that had withstood multiple air attacks earlier in the war but their use in large numbers represented a new stage in the history of warfare.

Technology greatly increased our battlefield effectiveness. Battlefield combat systems, like the M1A1 tank, AV-8B jet, and the Apache helicopter, and critical subsystems, like advanced fire control, the Global Positioning System, and thermal and night vision devices, gave the ground forces unprecedented maneuverability and reach. JSTARS offered a glimpse of new possibilities for battlefield intelligence. Our forces often found, targeted and destroyed the enemy's before the enemy could return fire effectively.

The Persian Gulf War saw the first use of a U.S. weapon system (the Patriot) in a tactical ballistic missile defense role. The war was not the first in which ballistic missiles were used, and there is no reason to think that it will be the last. Ballistic missiles offered Saddam Hussein some of his few, limited successes and were the only means by which he had a plausible opportunity (via the attacks on Israel) to achieve a strategic objective. While the Patriot helped to counter Saddam Hussein's use of conventionally-armed Scud missiles, we must anticipate that in the future more advanced types of ballistic missiles, some armed with nuclear, chemical or biological warheads, will likely exist in the inventories of a number of Third World nations. More advanced forms of ballistic missile defense, as well as more effective methods of locating and attacking mobile ballistic missile launchers, will be necessary to deal with that threat. . . . Indeed, the decisive character of our victory in the Gulf War is attributable in large measure to the extraordinary effectiveness of air power. . . .

On the other hand, air power alone could not have brought the war to so sharp and decisive a conclusion. Saddam not only underestimated the importance of the Coalition air forces, but he underestimated our will and ability to employ ground and maritime forces as well. The ground offensive option ensured that the Coalition would seize the initiative. A protracted air siege alone would not have had the impact that the combination of air, maritime and ground offensives was able to achieve. Without the credible threat of ground and amphibious attacks, the Iraqi defenders might have dispersed, dug in more deeply, concentrated in civilian areas, or otherwise adopted a strategy of outlasting the bombing from the air. . . .

As we assess the impressive performance of our weaponry, we must realize that, under other circumstances, the results might have been somewhat less favorable. Conditions under which the Persian Gulf conflict was fought were ideal with respect to some of the more advanced types of weapons. Even though the weather during the war was characterized by an atypically large percentage of cloud cover for the region, the desert terrain and climate in general favored the use of airpower. The desert also allowed the U.S. armored forces to engage enemy forces at very long range before our forces could be targeted, an advantage that might have counted for less in a more mountainous or built-up environment.

In addition, future opponents may possess more advanced weapons systems and be more skilled in using them. . . .

The war showed that we must work to maintain the tremendous advantages that accrue from being a generation ahead in weapons technology. Future adversaries may have ready access to advanced technologies and systems from the world arms market. A continued and substantial research and development effort, along with renewed efforts to prevent or at least constrain the spread of advanced technologies, will be required to maintain our advantage.

Source: *Conduct of the Persian Gulf War: Final Report to Congress* (Washington, DC: Department of Defense, United States of America, April 1992), pp. xx–xxiii.

ANNOTATED RESEARCH GUIDE

Books and Articles

Atkinson, Rick. *Crusade: The Untold Story of the Persian Gulf War.* Boston: Houghton Mifflin, 1993. A prize-winning journalist provides a detailed study of the American military forces in the Persian Gulf, including analysis of the air war.

Blackwell, James. *Thunder in the Desert: The Strategy and Tactics of the Persian Gulf War.* New York: Bantam Books, 1991. Military analyst provides an overview of the Gulf War, primarily focusing on strategy and tactics of the war.

Dunnigan, James F., and Austin Bay. *From Shield to Storm: High-tech Weapons,*

Military Strategy, and Coalition Warfare in the Persian Gulf. New York: William Morrow, 1992. Historians examine the diplomatic, political, and military aspects of the Persian Gulf crisis and provide details and analysis on the new revolutionary weapons and their effectiveness.

Freedman, Lawrence, and Efraim Karsh. *The Gulf Conflict, 1990–1991: Diplomacy and War in the New World Order*. Princeton, NJ: Princeton University Press, 1993. Historians examine the history of the Persian Gulf War. The book includes a chapter that details the strategic air campaign.

Gordon, Michael R., and Bernard E. Trainor. *The Generals' War: The Inside Story of the Conflict in the Gulf*. Boston: Little, Brown, 1995. Journalists examine the planning and implementation of the war in the Gulf and explore the friction that developed between Powell, Schwarzkopf, and other top military leaders. Includes a review of air-power planning and an analysis of the success of the air war.

Gunzinger, Mark A. "Toward a Flexible Theater Air Warfare Doctrine." *Air Power History* 43, no. 4 (1996): 50–57. A historian compares American air-power doctrine in World War II with its evaluation in the Persian Gulf and analyzes the outcome of the air campaign in Desert Storm.

Hallion, Richard P. *Storm over Iraq: Air Power and the Gulf War*. Washington, DC: Smithsonian Institution Press, 1992. A historian traces the evolution of air-power-strategy doctrine and evaluates the impact of air power on the Persian Gulf War.

Herring, George C. "Reflecting the Last War: The Persian Gulf and the 'Vietnam Syndrome.' " *Journal of Third World Studies* 10, no. 1 (1993): 37–51. A historian compares Desert Storm to the Vietnam War and analyzes the break from the failures of Vietnam.

Mazarr, Michael J., Don M. Snider, and James A. Blackwell, Jr. *Desert Storm: The Gulf War and What We Learned*. Boulder, CO: Westview Press, 1993. Provides an analysis of U.S. diplomacy, military strategy, and the air campaign.

Nye, Joseph S., Jr., and Roger K. Smith. *After the Storm: Lessons from the Gulf War*. Lanham, MD: Madison Books, 1992. Analyzes the diplomatic, economic, political, and strategic lessons of the war, including an evaluation of the air war.

Palmer, Michael A. "The Storm in the Air: One Plan, Two Air Wars." *Air Power History* 39, no. 4 (1992): 24–31. A historian examines the success of the air war and the military leaders who implemented the campaign.

Putney, Diane T. "From Instant Thunder to Desert Storm: Developing the Gulf War Air Campaign's Phases." *Air Power History* 41, no. 3 (1994): 38–50. A historian explores the various phases of the war and analyzes the necessity of a ground war.

Record, Jeffrey. *Hollow Victory: A Contrary View of the Gulf War*. Washington, DC: Brassey's, 1993. Offers observations on the political, military, and strategic questions left unanswered by the war, including an analysis of the air war.

Summers, Colonel Harry G., Jr. *On Strategy II: A Critical Analysis of the Gulf War*. New York: Dell, 1992. Military analyst provides a critical examination of

America's military strategy and tactics from the Vietnam "syndrome" through the successes of the Persian Gulf War.

Warden, John A., III. *The Air Campaign: Planning for Combat.* Revised Edition. New York: toExcel, 2000. Military analysis traces the Desert Storm air war from its inception to its execution.

Werrell, Kenneth P. "Air War Victorious: The Gulf War vs. Vietnam." *Parameters* 22, no. 2 (1992): 41–54. A historian compares the failure of the Vietnam air campaign with the success of the Persian Gulf air war.

Yetiv, Steve. *The Persian Gulf Crisis.* Westport, CT: Greenwood Press, 1997. A rich source of commentary, primary documents, ready-reference materials, and interviews with key players.

Web Sites

http://www.pbs.org. Public Broadcasting System's homepage. Search "Persian Gulf" for a multitude of interviews, primary sources, classroom activities, and debates.

http://www.pbs.org/wgbh/pages/frontline/gulf. PBS Web site offers *Frontline* oral histories with military and political leaders, stories from combat soldiers, maps, tapes, and transcripts, and a discussion of many Persian Gulf analysts.

Select Bibliography

Adams, David Wallace. *Education for Extinction: American Indians and the Boarding School Experience, 1875–1928*. Lawrence: University Press of Kansas, 1995.

Adams, Michael C.C. *The Best War Ever: America and World War II*. Baltimore, MD: Johns Hopkins University Press, 1994.

Allen, Thomas B., and Norman Polmar. "Code-Name Downfall." *American History* 30, no. 4 (1995): 50–61.

Alperovitz, Gar. *The Decision to Use the Atomic Bomb*. New York: Vintage Books, 1996.

Anderson, David L., ed. *Facing My Lai: Moving Beyond the Massacre*. Lawrence: University Press of Kansas, 1998.

Atkinson, Rick. *Crusade: The Untold Story of the Persian Gulf War*. Boston: Houghton Mifflin, 1993.

Babits, Lawrence E. *A Devil of a Whipping: The Battle of Cowpens*. Chapel Hill: University of North Carolina Press, 1998.

Bain, David Haward. *Sitting in Darkness: Americans in the Philippines*. Boston: Houghton Mifflin, 1984.

Bauer, Jack K., and Robert W. Johannsen. *The Mexican War, 1846–1848*. Lincoln: University of Nebraska Press, 1992.

Berlin, Ira, Joseph P. Reidy, and Leslie S. Rowland, eds. *Freedom's Soldiers: The Black Military Experience in the Civil War*. Cambridge: Cambridge University Press, 1998.

Bernstein, Barton J. "The Atomic Bombings Reconsidered." *Foreign Affairs* 74, no. 1 (January/February 1995): 135–152.

Bernstein, Iver. *The New York City Draft Riots: Their Significance for American Society and Politics in the Age of the Civil War*. New York: Oxford University Press, 1990.

Bilton, Michael, and Kevin Sim. *Four Hours in My Lai*. New York: Viking, 1992.

Bird, William L., Jr., and Harry R. Rubenstein. *Design for Victory: World War II Posters on the American Home Front*. New York: Princeton Architectural Press, 1998.

Blackwell, James. *Thunder in the Desert: The Strategy and Tactics of the Persian Gulf War*. New York: Bantam Books, 1991.

Blight, David W. *Race and Reunion: The Civil War in American Memory*. Cambridge, MA: Belknap Press of Harvard University Press, 2001.

Bowers, William T., William M. Hammond, and George MacGarrigle. *Black Soldiers, White Army: The 24th Infantry Regiment in Korea*. Washington, DC: U.S. Army Center of Military History, 1997.

Bristow, Nancy K. *Making Men Moral: Social Engineering during the Great War*. New York: New York University Press, 1996.

Buchanan, John. *The Road to Guilford Courthouse: The American Revolution in the Carolinas*. New York: John Wiley & Sons, 1997.

Burton, William L. *Melting Pot Soldiers: The Union's Ethnic Regiments*. Bronx, NY: Fordham University Press, 1998.

Chambers, John Whiteclay, II. *To Raise an Army: The Draft Comes to Modern America*. New York: Free Press, 1987.

Chambers, John Whiteclay, II, and David Culbert, eds. *World War II, Film, and History*. New York: Oxford University Press, 1996.

Chambers, John Whiteclay, II, and G. Kurt Piehler, eds. *Major Problems in American Military History*. Boston: Houghton Mifflin, 1999.

Clinton, Catherine, ed. *Southern Families at War: Loyalty and Conflict in the Civil War South*. New York: Oxford University Press, 2000.

Clinton, Catherine, and Nina Silber. *Divided Houses: Gender and the Civil War*. New York: Oxford University Press, 1992.

Coleman, Michael C. *American Indian Children at School, 1850–1930*. Jackson: University Press of Mississippi, 1993.

Cooper, Jerry M. *The Army and Civil Disorder: Federal Military Intervention in Labor Disputes, 1877–1900*. Westport, CT: Greenwood Press, 1980.

———. *The Rise of the National Guard: The Evolution of the American Militia, 1865–1920*. Lincoln: University of Nebraska Press, 1997.

Cottrell, Robert C. "Roger Nash Baldwin: The National Civil Liberties Bureau and Military Intelligence during World War I." *Historian* 60 (1997): 87–106.

Cress, Lawrence Delbert. *Citizens in Arms: The Army and the Militia in American Society to the War of 1812*. Chapel Hill: University of North Carolina Press, 1992.

Daniels, Roger; consulting editor, Eric Foner. *Prisoners without Trial: Japanese Americans in World War II*. New York: Hill and Wang, 1993.

Dower, John W. "The Bombed: Hiroshima and Nagasaki in Japanese Memory." *Diplomatic History* 19, no. 2 (1995): 275–295.

Drea, Edward J. "Previews of Hell." *MHQ: The Quarterly Journal of Military History* 7, no. 3 (1995): 74–81.

Dunnigan, James F., and Austin Bay. *From Shield to Storm: High-Tech Weapons, Military Strategy, and Coalition Warfare in the Persian Gulf*. New York: William Morrow, 1992.

Early, Frances H. "Feminism, Peace, and Civil Liberties: Women's Role in the

Origins of the World War I Civil Liberties Movement." *Women's Studies* 18, no. 2–3 (1990): 95–115.

Erenberg, Lewis A., and Susan E. Hirsch, eds. *The War in American Culture: Society and Consciousness during World War II*. Chicago: University of Chicago Press, 1996.

Faust, Drew Gilpin. *Mothers of Invention: Women of the Slaveholding South in the American Civil War*. New York: Vintage Books, 1997.

———. *Southern Stories: Slaveholders in Peace and War*. Columbia: University of Missouri Press, 1992.

Fautua, David T. "The 'Long Pull' Army: NSC 68, the Korean War, and the Creation of the Cold War U.S. Army." *Journal of Military History* 61, no. 1 (1997): 93–120.

Feaver, Peter D., and Richard H. Kohn, eds. *Soldiers and Civilians: The Civil-Military Gap and American National Security*. Cambridge, MA: MIT Press, 2001.

Fehrenbach, T.R. *This Kind of War: The Classic Korean War History*. Washington, DC: Brassey's, 1998.

Fellman, Michael. *Inside War: The Guerilla Conflict in Missouri during the American Civil War*. New York: Oxford University Press, 1989.

FitzGerald, Frances. *Fire in the Lake: The Vietnamese and the Americans in Vietnam*. New York, Vintage Books, 1973; revised July 1989.

Ford, Nancy Gentile. *"Americans All!": Foreign-born Soldiers in World War I*. College Station: Texas A&M University Press, 2001.

Franklin, H. Bruce. *War Stars: The Superweapon and the American Imagination*. New York: Oxford University Press, 1988.

Frazier, Donald S., ed. *The United States and Mexico at War: Nineteenth-Century Expansionism and Conflict*. New York: Simon and Schuster, 1998.

Fussell, Paul. *The Great War and Modern Memory*. New York: Oxford University Press, 2000.

Gallman, J. Matthew. *Mastering Wartime: A Social History of Philadelphia during the Civil War*. New York: Cambridge University Press, 1990.

Geary, James W. *We Need Men: The Union Draft in the Civil War*. De Kalb: Northern Illinois University Press, 1991.

George, Linda S. *World War I*. New York: Benchmark Books, 2001.

Glatthaar, Joseph T. *Forged in Battle: The Civil War Alliance of Black Soldiers and White Officers*. Baton Rouge: Louisiana State University Press, 2000.

Gluck, Sherna Berger. *Rosie the Riveter Revisited: Women, the War, and Social Change*. New York: Penguin Books, 1988.

Goldberg, Stanley. "Racing to the Finish: The Decision to Bomb Hiroshima and Nagasaki." *Journal of American-East Asian Relations* 4, no. 2 (1995): 117–128.

Goodwin, Doris Kearns. *No Ordinary Time: Franklin and Eleanor Roosevelt: The Home Front in World War II*. New York: Simon and Schuster, 1994.

Goossen, Rachel Waltner. *Women against the Good War: Conscientious Objection and Gender on the American Home Front, 1941–1947*. Chapel Hill: University of North Carolina Press, 1997.

Gordon, Michael R., and Bernard E. Trainor. *The Generals' War: The Inside Story of the Conflict in the Gulf*. Boston: Little, Brown, 1995.

Hallion, Richard P. *Storm over Iraq: Air Power and the Gulf War*. Washington, DC: Smithsonian Institution Press, 1992.

Hammond, William M. *Reporting Vietnam: Media and Military at War*. Lawrence, KS: University Press of Kansas, 1998.

Hassler, Warren W., Jr. *With Shield and Sword: American Military Affairs, Colonial Times to the Present*. Ames: Iowa State University Press, 1982.

Hawley, Ellis W. *The Great War and the Search for a Modern Order: A History of the American People and Their Institutions, 1917–1933*. New York: St. Martin's Press, 1979; reprinted by Waveland Press, 1997.

Hendrickson, David C. *Reforming Defense: The State of American Civil-Military Relations*. Baltimore, MD: Johns Hopkins University Press, 1988.

Herring, George C. *America's Longest War: The United States and Vietnam, 1950–1975*. New York: McGraw-Hill, 1996.

Hickey, Donald R. *The War of 1812: A Forgotten Conflict*. Urbana: University of Illinois Press, 1990.

Higginbotham, Don. *George Washington and George Marshall: Some Reflections on the American Military Tradition*. Colorado Springs, CO: U.S. Air Force Academy, 1984.

———. *War and Society in Revolutionary America: The Wider Dimension of Conflict*. Columbia: University of South Carolina Press, 1988.

———. *The War of American Independence: Military Attitudes, Policies, and Practice, 1763–1789*. New York: Macmillan, 1971.

Higham, John. *Strangers in the Land: Patterns of American Nativism 1860–1925*. New York: Atheneum, 1970.

Hoganson, Kristin L. *Fighting for American Manhood: How Gender Politics Provoked the Spanish-American and Philippine-American Wars*. New Haven, CT: Yale University Press, 1998.

Ignatieff, Michael. *Virtual War: Kosovo and Beyond*. New York: Henry Holt, 2000.

Jeffreys-Jones, Rhodri. *Peace Now!: American Society and the Ending of the Vietnam War*. New Haven, CT: Yale University Press, 1999.

Johannsen, Robert W. "America's Forgotten War." *Wilson Quarterly* 20 (1996): 96–107.

Johannsen, Robert Walter, John M. Belohlavek, Thomas R. Hietala, Sam W. Hayes, and Christopher Morris, eds. *Manifest Destiny and Empire: American Antebellum Expansionism*. College Station: Texas A&M University Press, 1997.

Jones, D. Clayton. *Refighting the Last War: Command and Crisis in Korea, 1950–1953*. New York: Free Press, 1993.

Josephy, Alvin M., Jr. *The Nez Perce Indians and the Opening of the Northwest*. Boston: Houghton Mifflin, 1997.

Just, Ward. *To What End: Report from Vietnam*. New York: Public Affairs, 2000.

Kaiser, David E. *American Tragedy: Kennedy, Johnson, and the Origins of the Vietnam War*. Cambridge, MA: Belknap Press of Harvard University Press, 2000.

Karnow, Stanley. *In Our Image: America's Empire in the Philippines*. New York: Ballantine Books, 1990.

———. *Vietnam, A History*. New York: Penguin Books, 1997.

Karsten, Peter, ed. *Civil-Military Relations*. New York: Garland Publications, 1998.

————. *The Military in America: From the Colonial Era to the Present*. New York: Free Press, 1980.

Kaufman, Burton I. *The Korean War: Challenges in Crisis, Credibility, and Command*. Philadelphia: Temple University Press, 1986.

Keene, Jennifer D. *Doughboys, the Great War, and the Remaking of America*. Baltimore, MD: Johns Hopkins University Press, 2001.

————. *The United States and the First World War*. New York: Longman, 2000.

Keim, Albert N., and Stolzfus, Grant M. *The Politics of Conscience: The Historic Peace Churches and America at War, 1917–1955*. Scottdale, PA: Herald Press, 1988.

Kennedy, David M. *Over Here: The First World War and American Society*. New York: Oxford University Press, 1990.

Kenner, Charles L. *Buffalo Soldiers and Officers of the Ninth Cavalry, 1867–1898: Black & White Together*. Norman: University of Oklahoma Press, 1999.

Kessler-Harris, Alice. "Rosie the Riveter": Who Was She? *Labor History* 24, no. 2 (1983): 249–253.

Kohn, Richard H. *Eagle and Sword: The Federalists and the Creation of the Military Establishment in America, 1783–1802*. New York: Free Press, 1975.

————, ed. *The United States Military under the Constitution of the United States, 1789–1989*. New York: New York University Press, 1991.

Koistinen, Paul A.C. *The Military-Industrial Complex: A Historical Perspective*. New York: Praeger, 1980.

————. *Mobilizing for Modern War: The Political Economy of American Warfare, 1865–1919*. Lawrence: University Press of Kansas, 1997.

Langellier, J. Phillip. *Uncle Sam's Little Wars: The Spanish-American War, Philippine Insurrection, and the Boxer Rebellion, 1898–1902*. London: Greenhill Books, 1999.

Leslie, Stuart W. *The Cold War and American Science: The Military-Industrial-Academic Complex at MIT and Stanford*. New York: Columbia University Press, 1993.

Linn, Brian McAllister. *The Philippine War, 1899–1902*. Lawrence: University Press of Kansas, 2000.

Litoff, Judy Barrett, and David C. Smith, eds. *Since You Went Away: World War II Letters from American Women on the Home Front*. Lawrence: University Press of Kansas, 1991.

Luebke, Frederick C. *Bonds of Loyalty: German Americans and World War I*. De Kalb: Northern Illinois University Press, 1974.

Maddox, Robert James. "The Biggest Decision: Why We Had to Drop the Atomic Bomb." In *Taking Sides: Clashing Views on Controversial Issues in American History since 1945*, ed. Larry Madaras. Guilford, CT: McGraw-Hill/Dushkin, 2001. pp. 4–12.

McCaffrey, James M. *Army of Manifest Destiny: The American Soldier in the Mexican War, 1846–1848*. New York: New York University Press, 1992.

McPherson, James M. *Battle Cry of Freedom: The Civil War Era*. New York: Oxford University Press, 1988.

————. *For Cause and Comrades: Why Men Fought in the Civil War*. New York: Oxford University Press, 1997.

————. *The Negro's Civil War: How American Blacks Felt and Acted During the War for the Union*. New York: Ballantine Books, 1991.

————. *Ordeal by Fire: The Civil War and Reconstruction*. Boston: McGraw-Hill, 2001.

————. *What They Fought For, 1861–1865*. New York: Doubleday, 1995.

Miller, Edward A., Jr. *The Black Civil War Soldiers of Illinois: The Story of the Twenty-ninth U.S. Colored Infantry*. Columbia: University of South Carolina Press, 1998.

Miller, Randall M., Harry S. Stout, and Charles Reagan Wilson, eds. *Religion and the American Civil War*. New York: Oxford University Press, 1998.

Miller, Stuart Creighton. *"Benevolent Assimilation": The American Conquest of the Philippines, 1899–1903*. New Haven, CT: Yale University Press, 1982.

Millett, Allan R., and Peter Maslowski. *For the Common Defense: A Military History of the United States of America*. Revised and expanded. New York: Free Press; Toronto: Maxwell Macmillan Canada; New York: Maxwell Macmillan International, 1994.

Mitchell, Reid. *The Vacant Chair: The Northern Soldier Leaves Home*. New York: Oxford University Press, 1993.

Mlyn, Eric. *The State, Society, and Limited Nuclear War*. Albany: State University of New York Press, 1995.

Morrison, Michael A. *Slavery and the American West: The Eclipse of Manifest Destiny and the Coming of the Civil War*. Chapel Hill: University of North Carolina Press, 1997.

Muller, Eric L. *Free to Die for Their Country: The Story of the Japanese American Draft Resisters in World War II*. Chicago: University of Chicago Press, 2001.

Neely, Mark E., Jr. *Confederate Bastille: Jefferson Davis and Civil Liberties*. Milwaukee, WI: Marquette University Press, 1993.

————. *The Fate of Liberty: Abraham Lincoln and Civil Liberties*. New York: Oxford University Press, 1991.

Neimeyer, Charles Patrick. *America Goes to War: A Social History of the Continental Army*. New York: New York University Press, 1996.

Nye, Joseph S., Jr., and Roger K. Smith, eds. *After the Storm: Lessons from the Gulf War*. Lanham, MD: Madison Books, 1992.

O'Brien, Kenneth Paul, and Lynn Hudson Parsons, eds. *The Home-Front War: World War II and American Society*. Westport, CT: Greenwood Press, 1995.

Olson, James S., and Randy Roberts. *My Lai: A Brief History with Documents*. Boston: Bedford Books of St. Martin's Press, 1998.

Otis, D.S. *The Dawes Act and the Allotment of Indian Lands*. Norman: University of Oklahoma Press, 1973.

Palladino, Grace. *Another Civil War: Labor, Capital, and the State in the Anthracite Regions of Pennsylvania, 1840–68*. Urbana: University of Illinois Press, 1990.

Palmer, Laura. *Shrapnel in the Heart: Letters and Remembrances from the Vietnam Veterans Memorial*. New York: Vintage Books, 1988.

Paludan, Phillip Shaw. *A People's Contest: The Union and Civil War, 1861–1865*. Lawrence: University Press of Kansas, 1996.

————. *War and Home: The Civil War Encounter*. Milwaukee, WI: Marquette University Press, 1998.

Pearlman, Michael D. *Warmaking and American Democracy: The Struggle over Mil-

itary Strategy, 1700 to the Present. Lawrence: University Press of Kansas, 1999.

Perret, Geoffrey. *Old Solders Never Die: The Life of Douglas MacArthur*. New York: Random House, 1996.

Piehler, G. Kurt. *Remembering War the American Way*. Washington, DC: Smithsonian Institution Press, 1995.

Powaski, Ronald. *March to Armageddon: The United States and the Nuclear Arms Race, 1939 to the Present*. New York: Oxford University Press, 1987.

Redkey, Edwin S, ed. *A Grand Army of Black Men: Letters from African-American Soldiers in the Union Army, 1861–1865*. New York: Cambridge University Press, 1992.

Rehnquist, William H. *All the Laws But One: Civil Liberties in Wartime*. New York: Vintage Books, 2000.

Royster, Charles. *A Revolutionary People at War: The Continental Army and American Character, 1775–1783*. New York: W.W. Norton, 1981; reprinted by University of North Carolina Press, 1996.

Schaffer, Ronald. *America in the Great War: The Rise of the War Welfare State*. New York: Oxford University Press, 1991.

Scott, Edward Van Zile. *The Unwept: Black American Soldiers and the Spanish-American War*. Montgomery, AL: Black Belt Press, 1996.

Shindler, Colin. *Hollywood Goes to War: Films and American Society, 1939–1952*. London: Routledge and Kegan Paul, 1979.

Shy, John. *A People Numerous and Armed: Reflections on the Military Struggle for American Independence*. Ann Arbor: University of Michigan Press, 1990.

Singletary, Otis A. *The Mexican War*. Chicago: University of Chicago Press, 1962.

Skeen, C. Edward. *Citizen Soldiers in the War of 1812*. Lexington: University Press of Kentucky, 1999.

Stagg, J.C.A. *Mr. Madison's War: Politics, Diplomacy, and Warfare in the Early American Republic, 1783–1830*. Princeton, NJ: Princeton University Press, 1983.

Stuart, Reginald C. *War and American Thought: From the Revolution to the Monroe Doctrine*. Kent, OH: Kent State University Press, 1982.

Summers, Colonel Harry G., Jr. *On Strategy II: A Critical Analysis of the Gulf War*. New York: Dell, 1992.

Sutherland, Daniel E., ed. *Guerrillas, Unionists and Violence on the Confederate Home Front*. Fayetteville: University of Arkansas Press, 1999.

———. *Seasons of War: The Ordeal of a Confederate Community, 1861–1865*. Baton Rouge: Louisiana State University Press, 1998.

Sweet, Timothy. *Traces of War: Poetry, Photography, and the Crisis of the Union*. Baltimore, MD: Johns Hopkins University Press, 1990.

Toland, John. *In Mortal Combat: Korea, 1950–1953*. New York: William Morrow, 1991.

Trudeau, Noah Andre. *Like Men of War: Black Troops in the Civil War, 1862–1865*. Boston: Little, Brown, 1998.

Waddell, Brian. *The War against the New Deal: World War II and American Democracy*. De Kalb: Northern Illinois University Press, 2001.

Wainstock, Dennis. *The Decision to Drop the Atomic Bomb*. Westport, CT: Praeger, 1996.

Walker, Keith. *A Piece of My Heart: The Stories of 26 American Women Who Served in Vietnam*. Novato, CA: Presidio Press, 1986.

Walker, Samuel. *In Defense of American Liberties: A History of the ACLU*. New York: Oxford University Press, 1990.

Ward, Harry M. *The War for Independence and the Transformation of American Society*. London: UCL Press, 1999.

Weigley, Russell F. *The American Way of War: A History of United States Military Strategy and Policy*. New York: Macmillan, 1977.

———. *A Great Civil War: A Military and Political History, 1861–1865*. Bloomington: Indiana University Press, 2000.

———. *History of the United States Army*. New York: Macmillan, 1967.

———. "The Soldier, the Statesman, and the Military Historian." *Journal of Military History* 63, no. 4 (1999): 807–822.

Weintraub, Stanley. *The Last Great Victory: The End of World War II, July/August, 1945*. New York: Dutton, 1995.

———. *MacArthur's War: Korea and the Undoing of an American Hero*. New York: Free Press, 2000.

Westheider, James E. *Fighting on Two Fronts: African Americans and the Vietnam War*. New York: New York University Press, 1997.

Wiley, Bell Irvin. *The Life of Billy Yank: The Common Soldier of the Union*. Garden City, NY: Doubleday, 1971 [c1952].

———. *The Life of Johnny Reb: The Common Soldier of the Confederacy*. Reprint ed., Baton Rouge: Louisiana State University Press, 1978.

Winders, Richard Bruce. *Mr. Polk's Army: The American Military Experience in the Mexican War*. College Station: Texas A&M University Press, 1997.

Winkler, Allan M. *Home Front U.S.A.: America during World War II*. Wheeling, IL: Harlan Davidson, 2000.

———. *Life under a Cloud: American Anxiety about the Atom*. New York: Oxford University Press, 1993.

Young, Elizabeth. *Disarming the Nation: Women's Writing and the American Civil War*. Chicago: University of Chicago Press, 1999.

WEB SITES

http://www.army.mil/cmh-pg/   United States Army Center of Military History.

http://www.fordham.edu/halsall/mod/modsbook.html   Fordham University.

http://www.jefferson.village.virginia.edu/vshadow/vshadow.html   Edward L. Ayer's The Valley of the Shadows Project.

http://www.law.cornell.edu   Cornell Law School.

http://www.law.ou.edu/hist/   The University of Oklahoma, College of Law.

http://www.law.umkc.edu/faculty/projects   University of Missouri-Kansas, School of Law.

http://www.loc.gov/homepage/lchp.html   The Library of Congress.

http://www.mtholyoke.edu/acad/intrel/feros-pg.htm   Mount Holyoke College.

http://www.nuclearfiles.org   Nuclear Age Peace Foundation.

http://www.nyhistory.org/index.html   The New-York Historical Society.

http://www.pbs.org/   Public Broadcasting System.

http://www.trumanlibrary.org or *http://www.whistlestop.org/index.html*   Truman Library.

http://www.yale.edu/lawweb/avalon/diplomacy/br1814m.htm   Yale University School of Law.

Index

Abolition, 108–9, 118. *See also* Slavery
ACLU (American Civil Liberties Union), 11
Adams, Charles Francis, 159
Adams, David Wallace, 124
Adams, John, 4, 50
Adams, Samuel, 4
Addams, Jane, 9, 159, 179, 186
AFL (American Federation of Labor), 181
African Americans: Civil War roles of, 109–10; and New York draft riot, 107–8, 114; and nineteenth-century racism, 156–57. *See also* Slavery
Aguinaldo, Emilio, 162–63
Air war doctrine, 11–12, 287–98, 305–12
Alien and Sedition Acts (1798), 4, 50–51
Allaire, Lt. Anthony, 28, 36–38
Ambrose, Stephen E., 267, 269
American Civil Liberties Union (ACLU), 11
American Federation of Labor (AFL), 181

American Indians. *See* Native Americans
Americanization of Indians, 8, 123–24, 128–31, 149–51
American Protection League, 184
American Revolution: anti-Loyalist position, 34–36, 38–40, 42–43; anti-Patriot position, 36–38, 43–44; on fair treatment of Loyalists, 40–42; issues in Battle of King's Mountain, 19–32; summary, 2–4; Washington's views on militia, 32–34
American Union against Militarism (AUAM), 177, 185, 191–94
Anglo-Saxonism, 9, 82, 156–57
Antifederalists, 60–62. *See also* Federalists vs. Democratic-Republicans
Anti-imperialism vs. imperialism, 9–10, 155–63, 165–73
Army, American. *See* Military, American
Army Air Service, establishment of, 11
Army War College, 10
Arnett, Peter, 294

Index

About the Author

NANCY GENTILE FORD is Professor of History at Bloomsburg University in Pennsylvania. She is the author of *Americans All!: Foreign-Born Soldiers in World War I*, as well as a number of articles on war and ethnicity, gender, and citizenship.